Luminos is the Open Access monograph publishing program
from UC Press. Luminos provides a framework for preserving and
reinvigorating monograph publishing for the future and increases
the reach and visibility of important scholarly work. Titles published
in the UC Press Luminos model are published with the same high
standards for selection, peer review, production, and marketing as
those in our traditional program. www.luminosoa.org

A

Philip E. Lilienthal

B O O K

The Philip E. Lilienthal imprint
honors special books
in commemoration of a man whose work
at University of California Press from 1954 to 1979
was marked by dedication to young authors
and to high standards in the field of Asian Studies.
Friends, family, authors, and foundations have together
endowed the Lilienthal Fund, which enables UC Press
to publish under this imprint selected books
in a way that reflects the taste and judgment
of a great and beloved editor.

What Is a Family?

The publisher and the University of California Press Foundation gratefully acknowledge the generous support of the Philip E. Lilienthal Imprint in Asian Studies, established by a major gift from Sally Lilienthal.

This title is freely available in an Open Access edition with generous support from The Library of the University of California, Berkeley.

What Is a Family?

Answers from Early Modern Japan

———

Edited by

Mary Elizabeth Berry and
Marcia Yonemoto

UNIVERSITY OF CALIFORNIA PRESS

University of California Press, one of the most distinguished university presses in the United States, enriches lives around the world by advancing scholarship in the humanities, social sciences, and natural sciences. Its activities are supported by the UC Press Foundation and by philanthropic contributions from individuals and institutions. For more information, visit www.ucpress.edu.

University of California Press
Oakland, California

Suggested citation: Berry, M. E. and Yonemoto, M. (eds). *What Is a Family? Answers from Early Modern Japan*. Oakland: University of California Press, 2019. DOI: https://doi.org/10.1525/luminos.77

Library of Congress Cataloging-in-Publication Data

Names: Berry, Mary Elizabeth, 1947- editor. | Yonemoto, Marcia, 1964- editor.
Title: What is a family? : answers from early modern Japan / edited by Mary Elizabeth Berry and Marcia Yonemoto.
Description: Oakland, California : University of California Press, [2019] | Includes bibliographical references and index. | This work is licensed under a Creative Commons CC BY-NC-ND license. To view a copy of the license, visit http://creativecommons.org/licenses.
Identifiers: LCCN 2019008998 (print) | LCCN 2019016499 (ebook) | ISBN 9780520974135 (ebook) | ISBN 9780520316089 (pbk. : alk. paper)
Subjects: LCSH: Families—Japan—History—Edo period, 1600-1868. | Japan—Social life and customs—1600-1868. | Japan—History—Tokugawa period, 1600-1868.
Classification: LCC HQ681 (ebook) | LCC HQ681 .W43 2019 (print) | DDC 306.850952—dc23
LC record available at https://lccn.loc.gov/2019008998

28 27 26 25 24 23 22 21 20 19
10 9 8 7 6 5 4 3 2 1

CONTENTS

ILLUSTRATIONS AND TABLES

ILLUSTRATIONS

vii

TABLES

A NOTE TO READERS

This volume emerged from a small conference held at the University of California, Berkeley, in the fall of 2014. For support of the conference, the editors wish to thank The Japan Foundation, New York; the Association for Asian Studies Northeast Asia Council; the UC Berkeley Center for Japanese Studies; and the donors to the Class of 1944 Chair. For support of this publication, we gratefully acknowledge generous subventions by the Library of the University of California, Berkeley, and the University of California Press. The Class of 1944 Chair funded several smaller production costs.

With particular pleasure, we thank Ayomi Yoshida and the Art Institute of Chicago for permission to use as the cover image *One More Scene—Storehouses, Tomo* a photoetching and color woodblock print created in 1988 by the great Yoshida Hodaka. It represents now–aged and weathered storehouses of the sort that once protected—with their tile roofs and plaster walls—the family and administrative documents central to most of our essays. Reliance on such buildings connected otherwise dissimilar families of the early modern era. It also connects them to us.

We are grateful, as well, to important interlocutors at the 2014 conference— Daniel Botsman, Sungyun Lim, and Kären Wigen—who did not contribute essays but significantly shaped our work with their comments. Kären magnified her contribution as an invaluable peer reviewer of the manuscript for the Press. An anonymous reviewer also provided wise counsel.

Like the subject of this book, which is too immense for anything approaching comprehensive treatment, the community of potential contributors was large and formidable. The group we gathered is a serendipitous company of our closer colleagues who were game for a nascent project and able to devote considerable time to realizing it. Suggested by our bibliographies is the great range of scholars, throughout the world, making major contributions to the histories of Japanese families on manifold topics.

We note that each essay includes its own bibliography of works cited. The appendix, which is not a collective bibliography but a list of suggestions for further reading, is weighted toward English-language publications and intended mainly for readers outside the circle of Tokugawa-period specialists. While a representative sample of the seminal work by Japanese scholars is cited there, the sheer magnitude of their publications precludes bibliographic control. We also note that Japanese individuals mentioned in the text are identified according to Japanese convention: family names precede personal names.

Finally, for readers unfamiliar with Japanese, we note that the frequently invoked term for family—*ie*—is pronounced EE-eh, two syllables combining the long vowel sound e (as in see) with the short vowel sound e (as in yes).

Introduction

Mary Elizabeth Berry and Marcia Yonemoto

Over the past two decades, new studies on demography, the status order, law, literacy, and gender have significantly changed our understanding of early modern Japanese society. Yet, oddly, no recent study in English has focused on what is arguably the key social institution of the time—the family.[1] The essays assembled here help to right the balance by exploring a variety of family histories, each of them discrete, from early modern Japan. They range across a large space, from the northeast to the southwest of the archipelago, and over a long stretch of time, from the sixteenth to the mid-nineteenth century. They focus variously on the military elite, agrarian villagers, urban merchants, communities of outcastes, and the circles surrounding priests, artists, and scholars. They draw on diverse sources—from population registers and legal documents to personal letters and diaries, from genealogies and household records to temple death registers and memorial tablets, from official compendia of exemplary conduct to popular fiction and drama. And they combine high vantages on collective practices (the adoption of heirs and the veneration of ancestors, for example) with intimate portraits of individual actors (such as a runaway daughter and a murderous wife).[2]

Together the essays challenge the dominant postwar narratives, epitomized in the social-scientific scholarship of the 1970s and 1980s, which tend to see the family in structuralist and nationalist terms as the foundation for Japanese insularity, social and political stability, and economic success.[3] This collection, in contrast, envisions the family less as a fixed institution or ideological construct than a process—one responsive to individual circumstances, subject to contestation, and marked by diversity across time and space. Although our sample of subjects is inevitably limited, the following chapters intimate the variety and disparity of experience among families that—while they certainly share certain key characteristics and were shaped alike by the pressures of a common polity—remain too unalike to authorize much generalization. In short, we disagree with Tolstoy's artful proposition that "happy families are all alike; every unhappy family is unhappy in its own way." Up close, every family looks different. Felicity takes as many forms as suffering; the divide between happiness and unhappiness is rarely stark; shared experiences do not guarantee shared sentiments.

ORIENTATIONS ON THE HISTORICAL CONTEXT

The circumstances and choices that made one family unlike another were framed, then as now, by the prevailing laws, norms, and controls on resources that shaped all lives. The merit of exploring families in a particular place and time lies in the prospect of understanding the diversity of individual family histories within the structural pressures of a distinctive regime. In the case of early modern Japan, the challenge is bracing. The unique features of the early modern polity generated equally unique patterns of family practice, unknown elsewhere in a similar configuration. For readers unfamiliar with the general contours of early modern Japanese history, we offer here a brief overview.[4]

Japan was governed from 1603 to 1868 by hereditary heads of the Tokugawa family, headquartered in Edo (now Tokyo), who used the title of shogun. The title was bestowed by successive heads of the imperial family, headquartered in Kyoto, who had reigned for over a millennium but had long ceded practical power to surrogates. The Tokugawa proved the strongest and most durable of them. Victors of civil wars that had raged for a century and more, they forged a peace that would last fifteen generations. Their polity was founded on a federal form of alliance that accorded substantial authority over local territorial domains to some two hundred daimyo lords, many of them former rivals. It was secured by remarkable policies of pacification. The Tokugawa regime stripped the landscape of the petty fortifications critical to continuing combat, allowing each daimyo a single major castle, and purged villages and monasteries of weapons. After several decades of relatively open international relations, the regime addressed the menace from abroad by combining long-standing bans against Christian proselytism and conversion with radical curtailment of contact. Foreign traders were limited by nationality and confined to a single port; travel overseas by Japanese was prohibited. And, most ambitiously, the regime enforced the policy, initiated by Toyotomi Hideyoshi, that required the relocation of an immense population of samurai warriors from villages (where they had enjoyed a dangerous independence) to the castle headquarters of their daimyo lords (where they would live as urban consumers on typically modest stipends).

These policies all but eliminated the violence of war (as well as its opportunities) and any routine encounter with the outside world (including licit migration).[5] Weightier as a factor of daily life was the social stratification effected by an evolving status system. The law and customary practice of the Tokugawa regime accorded great privilege to the samurai—constituting, with their families, about 7 percent of the population—who monopolized public office and presided over the commoner community of primary producers, craftspeople, and merchants. Privilege was complicated by paradox, nonetheless. Lacking much martial purpose as peace took hold, the samurai remained too numerous to employ gainfully, even in the bloated bureaucracies of the shogun and the daimyo. While some fashioned new lives as scholars, physicians, or writers, and others simply dropped off samurai rolls, the unemployed or underemployed majority became a costly burden to the regime—and not a comfortable one. Fixed but inflation-ridden stipends failed to cover the expenses of a presumptive elite often in debt and sometimes reduced to meager livelihoods.

Crucial here was a changing economy. The relocation of samurai from villages to castle towns set in motion a process of urbanization unparalleled in scale and speed elsewhere in the early modern world. By 1700 the once-small population of Japanese city dwellers surpassed 15 percent, distributed across the archipelago. The Tokugawa capital of Edo, then the largest city in the world, numbered over 1 million; the luxury craft center of Kyoto and the wholesale commodity market of Osaka approached 400,000 each; and dozens of castle towns exceeded 30,000.[6] This transformative growth of cities required the no less transformative development of a nationally integrated market that could supply city people—both the samurai and the ever-larger waves of commoner migrants they attracted—with the materials of daily life. The ensuing penetration of a monetized commercial economy generated new wealth for successful commodity producers, transporters and wholesalers, and a range of enterprising manufacturers and financiers. It also transferred substantial wealth from the martial elite to commoner entrepreneurs.

Contradictions in values followed, for while the polity was founded on social hierarchy, samurai privilege, and the primacy of honor, the economy thrived on expanding competition, improving performance, and the primacy of profit. The regime chose to live with the contradictions. Without either demobilizing the samurai or attempting a thorough reform of their roles, the shogun and daimyo combined wavering forms of fiscal amelioration (from low-interest loans and supplementary job stipends to price-fixing and currency manipulation) with unwavering affirmations of a samurai-first morality: they were cast as public men whose virtue underpinned a functionally differentiated but interdependent society of benevolent superiors and deferential inferiors. At the same time, the shogun and daimyo maintained an arresting flexibility in their relations with commoners.

They left all economic activity—including mining, minting, finance, and international trade—in merchant hands. They entrusted most local rule—including tax collection and policing—to self-governing associations in rural villages and urban neighborhoods. And, despite chronic fiscal distress, they relied on loans and deficit financing instead of aggressively raising agrarian taxes or instituting much more than token levies on commerce. In effect, they paid the price of sustaining an anachronistic status system by relinquishing economic power.

What impact did these political and social structures have on the formation of families? At a very general level, the division of society into function-based status groups inspired the principle that families would pass down hereditary occupations to fulfill social and political as well as filial obligations. Stratification by status inspired the further principle that marriages would unite social peers to preserve hierarchical boundaries. Mobility in employment certainly occurred, particularly among noninheriting sons. Intermarriage among commoners of different callings became unremarkable; unions between commoners and low-ranking samurai were not unknown. Still, continuity in family calling and (general) status parity among spouses remained pronounced in early modern Japan. Insularity and prolonged peace abetted this stability, to be sure, since neither foreign encounter nor deracinating violence disturbed customary practice with the shock of external example or internal breakdown.

Family history in the Tokugawa period was most profoundly defined, however, by the widespread adoption of the *ie* or stem model of succession. It is the *ie* or stem family that is the subject of almost all essays in this volume, together with those practices (notably, the routine adoption of heirs) helping to ensure its survival. We should emphasize, however, that stem family formation became a majority, though by no means universal, practice in early modern Japan. A fully representative collection would engage the alternative formations (nuclear and compound, with any variety of permutations) elected by many houses.[7] While awaiting the research that will enable greater representation, we focus on the stem family not only because it spread across social sectors but also because it remains remarkable as a dominant choice in the early modern world. The choice clearly addressed the political and social exigencies of the time, if in multifarious ways that we must reckon with.

THE *IE*: DEFINITIONS AND MARTIAL ORIGINS

A protean term, *ie* referred, most simply, to both a physical domestic space (the home) and the kin residing there (the family).[8] It extended in meaning to include any nonkin who shared the residence, whether through contractual understanding or informal consent (the household), as well as participants in the family enterprise, whether lodged together or not (the staff). Thus, for example, the *ie* of a substantial merchant included his apprentices and clerks; the *ie* of a large-scale farmer included his laborers. In its most circumscribed form, moreover, the term described a descent group that linked current members to generations of both deceased ancestors and unborn descendants to come (the lineage). And this linkage was secured, optimally across the ages, by the practice of succession to a unitary inheritance.

The characteristics of the *ie* are, for the most part, congruent with those of the stem family; in this volume we acknowledge but set aside ongoing debates over strict definitions and nomenclature to use the terms *stem family* and *ie* more or less interchangeably.[9] In its ideal form, the model *ie* had two defining features. First, the headship and major assets of a house passed to a single heir, which occurred with increasing frequency upon the retirement rather than the death of the incumbent (to ensure a smooth transition). Although a family with means might provide dowries for daughters and start-up resources for noninheriting sons, the bulk of the estate—beginning with the primary residence and any hereditary titles—devolved on the new head. So, too, the responsibilities for sustaining the *ie*—from honoring the ancestors and providing an heir to protecting resources and perpetuating the enterprise—devolved on that head as well. Second, the adult siblings of the heir departed the family, typically upon the heir's marriage. Daughters moved in with their husbands (unless circumstances required or favored the adoption as heir of a son-in-law, who joined the household and assumed his wife's family name). Noninheriting sons were variously set up as heads of branch lines, dispatched to paid labor, or adopted into families in need of heirs. Any siblings who continued to reside in the household remained single. The model *ie* thus consisted, in mature form, of three co-resident generations: the retired head and his wife, the incumbent successor and his wife, and the heir-in-waiting. It continued with the marriage of the heir-in-waiting (accompanied by the departure of siblings) and the transfer of headship from the now-retiring incumbent to the now-succeeding heir (once a new heir-in-waiting was established).

Stem family formation was new to the Tokugawa period as a dominant practice cutting across status groups; by the end of the seventeenth century most Japanese would spend at least part of their lives in a stem family.[10] Among the samurai elite, however, the roots of the *ie* were old and deep. They lay in the early medieval period, when warrior houses sought to concentrate their resources, and protect them for the future, amid rising military competition.[11] Daughters felt the pain of the change first. Over the course of the twelfth and thirteenth centuries, they gradually but decisively lost entitlements to land rights and other wealth, growing steadily more dependent on kinsmen or husbands for economic support and social standing. During the thirteenth and fourteenth centuries, surplus sons were excluded as well, as unitary inheritance became the norm in substantial warrior families: the headship and assets of the *ie* passed to a single male successor, not necessarily a first-born or even a biological son.[12] The need for superior leadership, if found in a younger child or adoptee, surpassed the privilege of primogeniture. Surplus sons might head branch families, though in inferior positions of wealth and authority; increasingly, they were sent out through adoption to head other households.

Yet this streamlining of inheritance and succession did not signal a contraction or degradation of the *ie*. In another seminal development, martial houses expanded their capacity by embracing mounting numbers of nonkin as *ie* members. Particularly during the era of Warring States (c. 1467–1590), the great contenders for power sought loyalty and selfless service by casting their soldiers as filial near kin who shared not just the victories but the reputation, the ethos, and the future of a collectively imagined house. The notion of the *ie* as enterprise—as a union of the stem lineage and those enabling it to prosper—was catalyzed in wartime, when group purpose, fortified by an ideology of mutual reliance, became a daily urgency.

Despite the changed circumstances of peacetime, the *ie* gained even greater traction among martial houses during the Tokugawa period. On the one hand, the ruling community of shogun, daimyo, and their chief officers cultivated an ever more elaborate cult of hereditary honor to replace the lost legitimacy of performance on the battlefield. Resourceful constructions of *ie* genealogies and histories, escalating rites of passage and commemoration—these were the devices that ennobled contemporary authority with the weight of the past. Even as they justified their ascendancy with claims to just and benevolent custody of the public good, these rulers continued to invoke the integrity of the lineage as the foundation of rightful rule. On the other hand, the samurai in service to the shogun and daimyo, from major deputies to the humblest retainers, founded their own *ie* as an essential form of security. Once mobile fighters with landed bases in villages and voluntary bonds to lords, they became, under Tokugawa rule, castle town consumers who depended on the highly variable stipends (from princely to paltry) that corresponded with their highly stratified ranks. Their capital, now a matter of rank and stipend, was heritable—but only by a single male successor. Effectively enforced, then, was the penetration of the stem family from the highest to the lowest reaches of the samurai population. Although still identified with the collectively imagined *ie* of his lord, the individual samurai needed his own clear line of succession to transmit the rank and stipend signifying elite status. Hence, like his lord, that samurai transferred the headship and the critical assets of his family to a designated heir, sending daughters and surplus sons elsewhere. Also like his lord, that samurai turned to adoption when biology failed or disappointed.

Indeed, the adoption of heirs, a practice of great martial families from the medieval period onward, occurred with such startling frequency in the early modern period as to become a near-defining feature of the *ie* system. Between 25 and 40 percent of the successors to samurai houses in mid- to late Tokugawa Japan were adoptees.[13] Insofar as roughly half of them were sons-in-law wedded to natal daughters, continuity in the bloodlines of adopting houses was often maintained.

Even so, the high incidence of nonkin successors—who sometimes replaced natal sons—indicates that the persistence of the *ie*, rather than the integrity of a biological line of descent, came first. Why this commitment to persistence above or beyond the claims of blood? The motives for adoption, when they are at all clear in individual cases, were diverse. An adoptee could bring talent to a house in decline, useful or prestigious connections to a house on the ascendant, or escape from discord in a house divided. An adoptee could also perpetuate the name and honor, and venerate the ancestors, of a house lacking heirs. Other purposes and other notions of security, compounded over time by the inertia of social expectation, drove a practice that put not just the *ie* but the persistence of the *ie* at the core of martial family values.

THE SPREAD OF THE *IE*

Stem family formation gradually extended from the samurai to all other status groups in Tokugawa Japan, becoming a majority practice around the turn of the eighteenth century. Some groups, such as outcaste beggars, came to stem succession in the same fashion as the lower echelons of the samurai: they were vested by shogunal or daimyo officials with assets (such as exclusive begging turfs) that could be passed to a single heir alone.[14] For most rural and urban commoners, however, *ie* formation was a more elective process pursued without strict official controls on resources.

The regime did, to be sure, make the family—as an elemental group of co-resident kin and nonkin dependents—foundational to political order. It was the basic unit of taxation and of surveillance as well: neighboring families, in villages and cities alike, were charged in groups of five to police one another and enforce corporate responsibility for conduct. Notably, moreover, shogunal policy made the family the unit of registration in surveys of land and population and, in doing so, effectively reinforced its primacy as a sociopolitical actor.[15] Among the most important records premised on the family unit were those of sectarian affiliation (*shūmon aratame-chō*), which documented on an annual basis the affiliations of commoners with Buddhist temples of their choice. Presumptive proof that registrants were non-Christian, this mandatory documentation generated the demographic data that, remarkable for its quantity and quality in the early modern world, allow historians to trace the spread of stem family formation throughout the commoner population.[16]

The movement toward the *ie* is clear in the data. The majority of commoner households chose, by around 1700, the practices characteristic of martial households: the transmission of the headship and most assets to a single successor; the adoption of heirs when necessary or desirable; and the inclusion of nonkin in service to the family as household members. Many embraced the perpetuation of the *ie* as the core value and affirmed its gravity by transferring personal names across generations, composing edifying genealogies and family histories, and maintaining reverent witness to the dead. But if this movement among commoners toward *ie* formation is clear, the reasons are not.

Before we explore the motives for the widespread adoption of the *ie*, three points deserve emphasis. First, *the institutions of state in early modern Japan were engaged selectively and remotely in family formation.* Both shogun and daimyo did issue regulations concerning adoption practices in samurai houses and retained the right to approve the selection of samurai spouses. Adultery became a focus of criminal law for all classes.[17] And prohibitions against the taking of life, notably associated with the shogun Tokugawa Tsunayoshi in the late seventeenth century, came to include widespread denunciations of infanticide in the late eighteenth century.[18] Moreover, as Fabian Drixler points out, official anxiety over the population explosion around 1680 provoked both scattered regulations concerning commoner marriage (pertaining to the ages, residential origins, and property qualifications of spouses) and more pervasive regulations forbidding partible inheritance.[19] Still, such regulations, never universal in the first place, were neither clearly enforced nor systematically sustained, especially as population growth slowed. While acknowledging their importance, we note that any formal registration of critical family decisions—including marriage, divorce, remarriage, adoption, succession, and the transfer of resources—occurred at the village or neighborhood level. And if disputes over family relations were hardly uncommon, adjudication was typically undertaken by the commoner elders who governed village and neighborhood associations.[20]

Second, and unlike the church in western Europe, for example, *religious establishments were removed from the active supervision of family formation in early modern Japan.* The temples enlisted to confirm the Buddhist (and, hence, non-Christian) affiliation of commoners did seize opportunity by exacting donations from their expanding congregations and normalizing the funerary rituals that were vital to a spreading cult of ancestor worship.[21] A likely source of solace for mourners and a sure source of solvency for clergy, the rituals fully implicated temples in the passage of death. Other passages—marriage and remarriage, childbearing and birth, childhood initiations, divorce—went largely unregulated by Buddhist law and unmarked by Buddhist services.

The priests and priestesses of Shinto shrines may have blessed the newborns and young children of the military elite during the Tokugawa period, though popular ceremonies of initiation emerged only in the late nineteenth century. As a general matter, the various Shinto cults of the time projected a family-centered ethos, given their association with fertility rituals and, in the case of the Ise cult, the rites of imperial succession. But it was the Confucian tradition alone that offered formal principles for ordering family conduct. At the loftiest levels, the study of disparate streams of Confucian philosophy took place in academies and coteries across Japan, many of them patronized by the shogun and daimyo, who undergirded their authority with Confucian ideas and encouraged their samurai to cultivate Confucian learning. For most of the population, a simple catechism of Confucian virtue was conveyed in the didactically rich edicts issued by the regime, the basic Chinese texts used for elementary schooling, and the immense advice literature generated by commercial publishers.[22] Filial piety toward family elders came first in all cases. Loyalty and obedience to superiors, fidelity to duty, and respect for ancestors were complementary seconds. This catechism, resonant throughout the sources of the period, undoubtedly helped sustain the *ie*. Consider, though, that it prescribed no ideal family structure. Nor was it backed by anything like a Confucian establishment that made family law or authorized family decisions.

Third, and as a consequence of limited oversight by state or religious institutions, *commoners formed their families with a fair latitude for choice*. Their turn to the *ie* could not have been strictly voluntary, of course, for no social practice is free of the force of communal, no less than individual, interests. It is precisely here that we find the lure of family history in early modern Japan. Because institutional dictates alone cannot explain the spread of the *ie* across status boundaries, we must look to those communal and individual interests as critical drivers of change. The relationship between family form and changing social pressures is often oblique when state and church decree the norms, more direct when norms are shaped substantially by the actors. The challenge for historians lies in connecting the newly ascendant form of the stem family or *ie* to the specific social and political pressures that encouraged the shift.

WHY THE *IE*?

At the heart of the challenge is the recalcitrance of our sources about motivation: they are as emphatic about the importance of the *ie* as they are elusive about the reasons for forming and maintaining it. In a kind of tautology, the sources invoke the perpetuation of the family as the prime value of a stem succession system designed to achieve exactly that. We doubt that residents of early modern Japan ever announced themselves as members of ancestor-venerating stem families or bothered to explain why they were; *ie* membership came to be simply understood as normal and right. But for us, just why perpetuation of the stem family became more necessary or desirable than alternative values looms as a key question. After all, the costs of *ie* formation were not minor: the choice entailed the disinheritance and separation from the household of offspring other than the succeeding head, and it yoked that head to punishing responsibilities for the lineage's prosperity, reputation, survival, and ancestral devotions. The imposition on his wife of corresponding responsibilities, the abrasion of sibling and parental sentiment, the subordination of the self to the collective—many such concerns unfolded from the stem choice. Insofar as the goal of persistence prevailed over the claims of blood, moreover, natal kin stood to be replaced—in commoner as well as samurai houses—by adoptees favored to ensure it. Yet whatever the costs, the texts of the time take the *ie* as so self-evident a good, so essential a frame for human association, that justification appears superfluous. Thus, for example, the copious regulations of the Mitsui financial house exhort obedience based solely on the authority of the founder and the need to sustain his *ie* "eternally, throughout the generations of children and grandchildren."[23]

To be sure, any practice that gains wide acceptance must inspire conformity for many reasons, some of them complementary, others not. And, indeed, when we press our sources for the recurrent concerns that inform us about the goals of stem family formation, the disclosures lead in disparate directions, some of them parallel, others not. One concern found in the documents of commoner notables, urban and rural alike, centers on reputation, a notion that combines the honor of a name with its successful transmission from one bearer to the next.[24] The samurai model of prestige was certainly influential here, perhaps especially for wealthy merchants and craftspeople who had close ancestors, or close patrons, in the military ranks. But commoners could also look to pre-Tokugawa houses in the arts, for example, and, increasingly, to one another. Formerly elite practices of lineal promotion spread among social climbers who projected the past sources of contemporary dignity in genealogies and household histories. They commissioned portraits of founders and mortuary monuments for successive heads; they insisted on fastidious maintenance of their legacies in codes of conduct for descendants. Even across the humbler spectrum, commoners embraced the simple customs that marked generational continuity. They began to transfer to heirs both personal names and the equivalent of surnames; they fashioned ceremonies to welcome brides and mourn the dead. Alive in all such practices was a conflation of reputable standing with continuity over time.

Diverse texts and artifacts—temple death registers, ledgers of memorial donations, ancestral tablets, tombstones—attest to another, specifically religious concern motivating stem family formation. Distributed in different regions across Japan, the evidence suggests the penetration, from the late seventeenth century, of the rites of ancestral veneration associated with funerary Buddhism. The development depended in part on mercenary marketing by temples, which registered commoners as (non-Christian) adherents in exchange for the donations that came to feature services for the dead. It depended, too, on a promise: that those services would convert the threatening spirit of a deceased antecedent into an ancestral deity.[25] The conditions? The rites had to be sponsored by the descendants of the deceased, under the supervision of Buddhist priests, for as long as thirty-three years. While binding the living to the dead, belief in such ritual efficacy also bound the living to unborn successors (who would execute the rites on their own behalf). Belief all but demanded, in consequence, the formation of stem families that, unlike nuclear or compound families, might enforce the transgenerational discipline required for effectively limitless ritual regimes.[26] Once great-grandparents and then grandparents achieved transcendence, parents (and then their successors) would await devotions. The motive here for stem formation extended, when biology disappointed, to ready reliance on adoption as well. If imperiled by either infertility or lack of confidence in offspring, the ritual fidelity owed first to the distant dead and, ultimately, to the incumbent head required the selection of a competent adoptee. Insofar as ancestral veneration loomed large for the *ie,* the purity of the bloodline mattered less than reliable religious service by the heir.

If samurai and commoner alike saw opportunities in stem succession to consolidate spiritual and symbolic assets, the consolidation of material capital was fundamental. Germane here is the coincidence between majority conversion to the *ie* model and increasing economic challenge. On the agrarian front, the aggressive expansion of farmland during the seventeenth century slowed significantly in many areas during the eighteenth, as Japan approached a ceiling on the reclamation possible without modern technology. Ever more intensive agriculture, focused on small households, replaced the once-extensive growth in arable that could support multiple offspring. Demographic adjustment followed: Japan's population had grown by a third or more during the seventeenth century but leveled off in the eighteenth as agrarian households variously matched size to resources and privileged well-being over numbers.[27] The concentration of family assets in a single heir through stem succession appears to have been a coordinated response to the threat of asset depletion—one perhaps influenced by the laws against partible inheritance issued by officials alarmed by the population swell but more convincingly mandated by the empirical reality of limited arable land.[28]

On the urban front, the competition for labor in a time of demographic leveling was compounded by the unpredictability of the regime. A fiscally troubled shogunate rattled the market by turning to forced and then canceled loans, price-fixing, currency devaluations and revaluations, fees imposed on expanding numbers of trade associations, and the multiplying sumptuary laws battering high-end businesses. Major traders reacted to this volatility with household precepts that insist, in general, on a bunker mentality and, in particular, on the fortification of the *ie* as the surest guardian of wealth. Their documents address, zealously, the need to conserve capital, avoid risk, hew to proven paths, enforce frugality, educate heirs, improve management, defer to authorities, and, always and everywhere, avoid distractions. Although the voices of lesser traders are harder to detect, their conduct conforms to a pattern of consolidation in a time of financial trial.

Another matter germane to the financial motives for stem family formation concerns the absence of legal guarantees in early modern Japan for property, contracts, credit, and judicial access.[29] Even as the commercial economy moved substantial assets to commoner entrepreneurs in villages as well as cities, neither the shogun nor the daimyo ensured protection of those assets or the complex transactions a viable market requires. In this vacuum of legal security, commoners devised among themselves an arsenal of self-defense. Written agreements accompanied most business operations—including employment, indenture, property sales and rentals, credit, loans, and partnerships. And those agreements concluded with the ever more elaborate verification conveyed by oaths, seals, witnesses, and guarantors. Still, the best-attested agreement is perilous without judicial recourse for injury, which no commoner was assured. A critical form of insurance under such circumstances was the backing, and the stability, of the *ie*. Insofar as the ascendants and descendants of a continuing lineage were implicit cosignatories when an incumbent head put the family seal on a document, the house became the instrument of commercial trust. This development reminds us with particular clarity that the *ie* was an enterprise.

The centrality of enterprise to the spread of the *ie* is especially stark in houses whose members assumed custody—variously as performers, craftspeople, and teachers—over numerous artistic disciplines (broadly defined). Represented in this volume by the Hirata family of scholars, the Raku family of potters, and the Sen family of tea masters,[30] these houses figured in the thousands at elite levels (and in geometrically larger numbers at lower levels) in fields as diverse as fencing, football, painting, poetry, music, carpentry, gardening, printing, stone carving, and cookery. Their staffs were rarely large. But their income from clients and students depended on both the expertise and the consistency in transmission promised by the name of a reputable *ie* and embodied in the incumbent head. Some of these houses had old roots. All drew on the association between superior knowledge and esoteric initiation long ascendant in domains such as poetry, drama, and calligraphy. They arose in remarkable numbers, however, to exploit the consumer marketplace of Tokugawa cities. Such *ie* pushed fidelity in practice and replication of product as the guarantors of value. Here, again, the *ie* became an instrument of commercial trust. But here, too, the *ie* remained so fused with enterprise that its institutional character—and the primacy of capable leadership—had to prevail over the immediate interests, and succession, of kin.[31]

In agrarian villages, too, the family as enterprise figured significantly in social definition and management. The basic unit of taxation throughout village society, it was also the unit of communal membership, administration, and ceremonial participation. So tightly was it knitted into activities ranging from water control to harvest festivals that village elders urgently sought successors to the headship of declining houses rather than accept extinction as a matter of course. Indeed, they kept failed *ie* on their books in the hope of filling vacant headships with volunteers from inside or outside the community. The personal considerations here were peripheral. The *ie* was the instrument of village rule.

Finally, we must take account of what we might call the *ie* consciousness (as distinct from *ie* practice) that spread through print culture. One conduit was an immense body of didactic literature, from primers to household encyclopedias, that warned readers against the many hazards to family well-being even as it depicted the successful *ie* as the essential source of felicity (*saiwai, shiawase, kokoro yasuku*).[32] Another conduit was contemporary drama and fiction, which typically centered on those hazards to identify the family as the locus of pain and conflict. Happy endings occurred on occasion. We also find comedic riffs on personal failing (avarice, vanity, fecklessness) that cheerfully blame the pain on protagonists who deserve it. Nonetheless, the unhappiness featured in popular scripts and stories belonged not to some natural order but to a world gone wrong, usually an *ie* gone wrong. Dramatists, for example, based some of their most sensational plays on the quarrels over succession that violently splintered daimyo houses. They based some of their most wrenching plays on the murder-suicides of lovers unable to reconcile desire with family obligations. For insatiable consumers of prose fiction, writers produced equally melodramatic tales about houses ruined by dissolute heads, wayward heirs, estranged couples, and the angry ghosts of wronged spouses. The point was that the *ie* was imperiled on many fronts. Yet the moral was that peril needed to be faced and wrong needed to be righted. Failure ensured tragedy. Resourceful intercession promised the contentment achievable through familial integrity. Intercession sometimes involved the shocking sacrifice of elders and parents and children who, bound as much by affection as virtue, risked (and lost) their lives to save relatives in times of hardship (poverty, debt, illness, famine, disaster, crime, and the like). The limit cases appeared in stories of revenge, which dominated the fiction market for a time, as rival authors portrayed children avenging murdered parents (in ever more fantastic circumstances) to recover the honor and security of the house. All in all, commercial drama and fiction insisted, family life was hard life. But like the pedagogical literature, contemporary drama and fiction enforced a common message: the *ie* deserved sacrifice because fulfillment was unachievable outside it.[33]

OUR ESSAYS

The foregoing discussion of what the early modern Japanese *ie* was, why it was formed, and how it spread situates the essays that follow. We divide the chapters into two parts, mindful that distinctions are imperfect and readers will navigate the collection independently. The essays in part 1, "Norms: Stem Structures and Practices," plot—from generally high vantages—the paths taken by early modern families to constitute and perpetuate themselves as *ie*. David Spafford explores the medieval origins of stem succession in warrior houses, emphasizing not just the emergence of unigeniture but the fusion in the *ie* of kin with nonkin, membership with service, kindred filiality with nonkindred loyalty, and conjugal with natal ties of belonging. Marcia Yonemoto looks at succession practices within an early modern warrior elite that, much more so than its ruling-class counterparts in East Asia, used various forms of adoption to perpetuate and extend family-based control over resources and power.[34] Fabian Drixler charts the emergence of the stem family as the dominant form of social organization among commoners in the late seventeenth century and posits the rise of ancestor veneration as the main impetus for stem family perpetuation. Morgan Pitelka shows how leading martial houses, as well as elite merchant and artisanal houses such as the Sen and the Raku, used the collection of valuable material objects to maintain and expand family legacies. And Maren Ehlers focuses on how outcaste groups (*hinin*) in urban and rural areas organized themselves into *ie* to transmit hereditary rights to begging turfs and other official duties and privileges, even while such self-identification made them targets for exclusion and discrimination. It bears emphasis that these essays do not propose a typology or ideal structure for the *ie*; rather, they offer different visions of the choices families made in different contexts to consolidate capital and influence.

If the essays in part 1 tell stories of integration and consolidation—offering broad-based examples of opting *into* the *ie*—the essays in part 2, "Case Studies: Stem Adaptations and Threats," narrow the focus to closer studies of individual family histories. Each involves trouble; each also involves resourceful coping with trouble to sustain the *ie*.[35] Three of the chapters focus on the internal dynamics of domestic life disclosed vividly (if always through the lens of self-interest) in intensely personal documents. Luke Roberts investigates the ambiguous circumstances surrounding the murder of the lover of a samurai wife. Amy Stanley focuses on the escape of a rebellious temple daughter to a new life in Edo. And Anne Walthall examines the unconventional family of the esteemed nativist scholar Hirata Atsutane. All of these *ie* are complex: each maintained its integrity by accommodating human commotion and unpredictable circumstances. Intense feeling runs rife throughout the cases as impulsive individuals, acting on desire, sow confusion in their households. Some misbehavior is as lurid as anything on the stage; most belongs to quieter rebellion and self-indulgence. It occasions, nonetheless, the jealousy, divided loyalties, shame, and alienation that compound the routine trials of guaranteeing succession and protecting resources. Stress bends all families into varied shapes, of course. The *ie* was no exception. What we find in these three instances is bending in the service of the *ie*'s reputation, survival, and internal coherence. Dissolution was not an option. The preservation of familial integrity consumed the prime players in each case.[36]

The final essays by Mary Elizabeth Berry and David Atherton integrate fictional portrayals of the family (in Berry's case a popular stage play; in Atherton's, mass-market novels) with contemporaneous documentation of particular family experiences. Berry relates the stage play to the archive of the megamerchant house of Mitsui; Atherton connects the popular novels to a shogunal compilation of exemplary biographies of family-saving heroes. Again, trouble dominates both the documentary and the fictional sources. The former direct successors to paths of prevention and escape accessed by familial vigilance and virtue; the latter depict the family's disintegration in excruciating extremity, and its reconstitution as the restoration of a natural order.

By way of conclusion, we alert readers to several key themes in the essays that follow.

(1) The families we survey were resilient and flexible: they display a striking tolerance for trouble, belying both the moralism of the pedagogues and the melodrama of the storytellers. Their households managed to provide for runaway daughters, absorb concubines and other outsiders, and survive scandal. And in such persistence they remind us that families are, finally, voluntary and variable alliances of people who, even within rule-ridden systems, accord some freedom to one another.

(2) But these families also required systemic safety nets. Uniquely under threat because of the imperative of survival and the challenge of succession, the *ie* was protected most obviously by the widespread acceptance of (and reliance on) adoption. The evidence for licensed prostitution and concubinage in early modern Japan suggests, too, an acceptance of extramarital pleasure for men in a social order of arranged marriage focused on the family enterprise and reputation.[37] The ease of divorce and remarriage, however, amplifies the picture to suggest some latitude for women as well. Accord in marital unions (routinely emphasized in family codes) was too important to preclude escape and new choices when accord dissolved. The expectation of satisfaction for couples who led their *ie*—and the possibility of pleasure in each other—appears indispensable to the logic of divorce.

(3) A corollary, emphasized in many of our essays, is that women mattered, in and outside the family: they exercised considerable influence as daughters, wives, and mothers but also as workers, record keepers, mediators, and temporary or de facto heads of household. Focusing on the family as a primary unit of social organization reveals how gender roles that have often been seen as prescribed or static could also be dynamic and self-fashioned.[38]

(4) Families and households varied across space, time, and social status. In the spatial register, some of our essays focus on urban centers (Berry, Pitelka); most bridge the distance between province and city (Atherton, Ehlers, Spafford, Stanley, Walthall, Yonemoto); several focus on localities far afield from urban centers (Drixler, Roberts).

In the temporal register, some essays engage the longue durée (Drixler, Ehlers, Yonemoto); most engage narrower periods (for Spafford the late medieval period, for Pitelka the seventeenth century, for Berry the turn of the eighteenth century, for Atherton the turn of the nineteenth century, for Walthall, Roberts, and Stanley the nineteenth century).

In the status register, some essays deal mainly with the martial elite (Roberts, Spafford, Yonemoto); one essay deals with outcastes (Ehlers); another with the agrarian population (Drixler); another with merchants (Berry); another with the household of a Buddhist priest (Stanley); and another with a scholarly house of samurai status (Walthall). Pitelka addresses both the martial elite and prestigious urban traders in goods and services. Atherton addresses humble players across the status spectrum.

Such juxtapositions across spatial, temporal, and status frames of analysis reveal variations in family structure even as they expose those processes of *ie* maintenance—notably concerning succession—that became common, if not uniform, among households otherwise quite disparate.

Our deeply different stories are linked by the structural constraints that, always modulated by human and systemic allowances for deviation, make the early modern *ie* in Japan a site for collective inquiry.

NOTES

1. In the interests of readability, the endnotes for this introduction cite only selectively the voluminous literature in English and Japanese that, line by line, guides our thinking. To facilitate further bibliographic exploration, see the appendix, which contains suggestions for further reading.

2. As the endnotes to the following chapters attest, each author's research relies on the exceptional record keeping of both the governing regime and the many individual households that prodigiously cached everything from letters to ledgers to testaments in family storehouses.

3. The essays in this collection focus on the Japanese stem family or *ie*. We discuss the debates over terminology, structure, and development of the stem family or *ie* later in this introduction.

4. Those well acquainted with the historical narrative may choose to skip ahead to the next section.

5. Revisionist views of Tokugawa foreign relations, emphasizing regulation of foreign relations over isolation, have dominated the historiography since the 1970s. For overviews in English, see Tashiro and Videen 1982, Toby 1984, and Hellyer 2010; on Tokugawa–Chosŏn Korea relations, see Kang 1997 and J. Lewis 2003; on Tokugawa-Dutch relations, see Clulow 2013; on Tokugawa expansion into northeastern (Ezo) and southwestern (Ryūkyū) borderlands, see, respectively, Walker 2006 and Smits 1999.

6. See McClain, Merriman, and Ugawa 1994; McClain and Wakita, 1999; Fiévé and Waley, 2003.

7. A number of the essays in this volume, particularly those by Amy Stanley and Anne Walthall, introduce a variety of actors (servants and temporary household residents, for example) who do not fit into the *ie* model. And few of the subjects of David Atherton's essay are identified specifically as members of stem households.

8. For further reading on the definition and structure of the *ie*, see the appendix.

9. For further reading on the stem family and the *ie*, and on comparative frameworks for understanding stem families versus *ie*, see the appendix.

10. See the essay by Fabian Drixler in this volume.

11. See the essay by David Spafford in this volume.

12. Mass 1989; Tonomura 1990.

13. Percentages of adoptees varied significantly by time period, region, and status; see the essays by Marcia Yonemoto and Anne Walthall in this volume.

14. See the essay by Maren Ehlers in this volume.

15. Herman Ooms (1996) sees the penetration of shogunal rule at the local level in starker terms, as a "colonial" regime focused on conquest, and emphasizes the conflict inherent in the "juridical sphere" of the Tokugawa village.

16. See Cornell and Hayami 1986.

17. Extramarital liaisons by wives threatened lineal continuity and thus were policed strictly by community members and officials alike. See the essay by Luke Roberts in this volume.

18. See Bodart-Bailey 1985 and 2006; Drixler 2013 and 2015.

19. See Drixler 2013, pp. 61–62, 305n5, 305n7.

20. Never a universal polity with direct relationships to the governed, the regime of shogun and daimyo depended on "nested containers" of subordinates who were administered by immediate

(typically local) superiors; for a more fully developed spatiotemporal analysis of the household as one such "container," albeit in the quite different context of early China, see M. Lewis 2006.

21. See the essay by Fabian Drixler in this volume; see also Hur 2007.

22. On this literature, see Berry 2006; Kornicki 2000; and Rubinger 2007.

23. See the essay by Mary Elizabeth Berry in this volume.

24. See essays by Morgan Pitelka, David Spafford, Amy Stanley, and Anne Walthall in this volume. For a recent study of the influence of Confucian thought in Japan, see Paramore 2016.

25. See Hur 2007.

26. See the essay by Fabian Drixler in this volume.

27. The locus classicus for the preceding arguments, in English, may be found in Smith 1959 and 1977.

28. Fabian Drixler argues that increased opportunity for wage work without long periods of indenture was a major factor in falling fertility (and resulting population stability) around 1700; see Drixler 2013, pp. 83–84. On declining indentures, see also Ramseyer 1995.

29. See the essay by Berry in this volume for discussion of these matters in the merchant context. For surveys of Tokugawa law, see Hiramatsu 1981 and Hirai 1992.

30. See the essays by Morgan Pitelka and Anne Walthall in this volume.

31. We find another example of *ie* penetration in the leadership of Buddhist temples, which administered large, often wealthy establishments from generation to generation. See the essay by Amy Stanley in this volume.

32. Although largely bypassed in the scholarship, what we might call happiness figured throughout the illustrations, sample letters, and vocabulary lists of published instructional texts, especially for women.

33. See the essay by David Atherton in this volume.

34. Also note, in the essay by Anne Walthall, the important role of temporary adoption.

35. Our emphasis on the precarity of stem families echoes an important theme in Pratt 1999.

36. Two studies in English that also discuss inclusion and exclusion from early modern families are Gary Leupp's study of urban lower-class tenement dwellers (Leupp 1992) and Joyce Lebra's article on the contested familial legacy of a woman head of a saké-brewing concern (Lebra 1991).

37. See Lindsey 2007 and Stanley 2012.

38. On women's roles as discursive ideals as well as lived experiences, see Yonemoto 2016.

REFERENCES

Berry 2006
    Berry, Mary Elizabeth. *Japan in Print: Information and Nation in the Early Modern Period.* Berkeley: University of California Press, 2006.
Bodart-Bailey 1985
    Bodart-Bailey, Beatrice. "The Laws of Compassion." *Monumenta Nipponica* 40:2 (1985): 163–89.
Bodart-Bailey 2006
    Bodart-Bailey, Beatrice M. *The Dog Shogun: The Personality and Policies of Tokugawa Tsunayoshi.* Honolulu: University of Hawai'i Press, 2006.
Clulow 2013
    Clulow, Adam. *The Company and the Shogun: The Dutch Encounter with Tokugawa Japan.* New York: Columbia University Press, 2013.
Cornell and Hayami 1986
    Cornell, Laurel L., and Akira Hayami. "The Shūmon Aratame Chō: Japan's Population Registers." *Journal of Family History* 11:4 (1986): 311–28.

Drixler 2013
> Drixler, Fabian. *Mabiki: Infanticide and Population Growth in Eastern Japan, 1660–1950.* Berkeley: University of California Press, 2013.

Drixler 2015
> Drixler, Fabian. "Conjuring the Ghosts of Missing Children." *Demography* 52:2 (2015): 667–703.

Fiévé and Waley 2003
> Fiévé, Nicolas, and Paul Waley, eds. *Japanese Capitals in Historical Perspective: Place, Power, and Memory in Kyoto, Edo, and Tokyo.* London: New York: RoutledgeCurzon, 2003.

Fuess 2001
> Fuess, Harald. *Divorce in Japan.* Stanford, CA: Stanford University Press, 2001.

Hellyer 2010
> Hellyer, Robert I. *Defining Engagement: Japan in Global Contexts, 1640–1868.* Cambridge, MA: Harvard University Asia Center, 2010.

Hirai 1992
> Hirai, Atsuko. "The Legitimacy of Tokugawa Rule as Reflected in its Family Laws." *Hōgaku kenkyū: Journal of Law, Politics, and Sociology* 65:11 (1992): 136–92.

Hiramatsu 1981
> Hiramatsu Yoshirō, "Tokugawa Law." Translated by Dan Fenno Henderson. *Law in Japan* 14 (1981): 1–48.

Hur 2007
> Hur, Nam-lin. *Death and Social Order in Tokugawa Japan: Buddhism, Anti-Christianity, and the Danka System.* Cambridge, MA: Harvard University Asia Center, 2007.

Jannetta 1987
> Jannetta, Ann Bowman. *Epidemics and Mortality in Early Modern Japan.* Princeton: Princeton University Press, 1987.

Kang 1997
> Kang, Etsuko Hae-Jin. *Diplomacy and Ideology in Japanese-Korean Relations: From the Fifteenth to the Eighteenth Century.* New York: St. Martin's Press, 1997.

Kornicki 2000
> Kornicki, Peter. *The Book in Japan: A Cultural History from the Beginnings to the Nineteenth Century.* Honolulu: University of Hawai'i Press, 2000.

Lebra 1991
> Lebra, Joyce Chapman. "Women in an All-Male Industry: The Case of Sake Brewer Tatsu'uma Kiyo." In *Recreating Japanese Women, 1600–1945,* edited by Gail Lee Bernstein, 131–48. Berkeley: University of California Press, 1991.

Leupp 1992
> Leupp, Gary. *Servants, Shophands, and Laborers in the Cities of Tokugawa Japan.* Princeton: Princeton University Press, 1992.

Lewis 2003
> Lewis, James B. *Frontier Contact between Chosŏn Korea and Tokugawa Japan.* New York: RoutledgeCurzon, 2003.

Lewis 2006
> Lewis, Mark Edward. *The Construction of Space in Early China.* Albany: State University of New York Press, 2006.

Lindsey 2007

Lindsey, William. *Fertility and Pleasure: Ritual and Sexual Values in Tokugawa Japan.* Honolulu: University of Hawai'i Press, 2007.

Mass 1989

Mass, Jeffrey P. *Lordship and Inheritance in Early Medieval Japan: A Study of the Kamakura Soryō System.* Stanford, CA: Stanford University Press, 1989.

McClain, Merriman, and Ugawa 1994

McClain, James L., John M. Merriman, and Ugawa Kaoru, eds. *Edo and Paris: Urban Life and the State in the Early Modern Era.* Ithaca, NY: Cornell University Press, 1994.

McClain and Wakita 1999

McClain, James L., and Wakita Osamu, eds. *Osaka: The Merchants' Capital of Early Modern Japan.* Ithaca, NY: Cornell University Press, 1999.

Ooms 1996

Ooms, Herman. *Tokugawa Village Practice: Class, Status, Power, Law.* Berkeley: University of California Press, 1996.

Paramore 2016

Paramore, Kiri. *Japanese Confucianism: A Cultural History.* Cambridge: Cambridge University Press, 2016.

Pratt 1999

Pratt, Edward E. *Japan's Protoindustrial Elite: The Foundations of the Gōnō.* Cambridge, MA: Harvard University Asia Center, 1999.

Ramseyer 1995

Ramseyer, J. Mark. "The Market for Children: Evidence from Early Modern Japan." *Journal of Law, Economics, and Organization* 11:1 (1995): 127–49.

Rubinger 2007

Rubinger, Richard. *Popular Literacy in Early Modern Japan.* Honolulu: University of Hawai'i Press, 2007.

Smith 1959

Smith, Thomas C. *The Agrarian Origins of Modern Japan.* Stanford, CA: Stanford University Press, 1959.

Smith 1977

Smith, Thomas C. *Nakahara: Family Farming and Population in a Japanese Village, 1717–1830.* Stanford, CA: Stanford University Press, 1977.

Smits 1999

Smits, Gregory. *Vision of Ryukyu: Identity and Ideology in Early Modern Thought and Politics.* Honolulu: University of Hawai'i Press, 1999.

Spafford 2015

Spafford, David. "What's in a Name? House Revival, Adoption, and the Bounds of Family in Late Medieval Japan." *Harvard Journal of Asiatic Studies* 74:2 (2015): 281–329.

Stanley 2012

Stanley, Amy. *Selling Women: Prostitution, Markets, and the Household in Early Modern Japan.* Berkeley: University of California Press, 2012.

Tashiro and Videen 1982

Tashiro Kazui and Susan Downing Videen. "Foreign Relations during the Edo Period: Sakoku Reexamined." *Journal of Japanese Studies* 8:2 (1982): 283–306.

Toby 1984

Toby, Ronald P. *State and Diplomacy in Early Modern Japan: Asia in the Development of the Tokugawa Bakufu.* Princeton: Princeton University Press, 1984.

Tonomura 1990

Tonomura, Hitomi. "Women and Inheritance in Japan's Early Warrior Society." *Comparative Studies in Society and History* 32:3 (1990): 592–623.

Wakita and Phillips 1993

Wakita Haruko and David P. Phillips. "Women and the Creation of the *Ie* in Japan: An Overview from the Medieval Period to the Present." *U.S.-Japan Women's Journal: English Supplement*, No. 4 (1993): 83–105.

Walker 2006

Walker, Brett. *The Conquest of Ainu Lands: Ecology and Culture in Japanese Expansion, 1590–1800.* Berkeley: University of California Press, 2006.

Yōnemoto 2016

Yonemoto, Marcia. *The Problem of Women in Early Modern Japan.* Berkeley: University of California Press, 2016.

PART ONE

Norms

Stem Structures and Practices

1

The Language and Contours of Familial Obligation in Fifteenth- and Sixteenth-Century Japan

David Spafford

Forgetting the repeated grace of your lord and father is a lapse in loyalty and filial piety

—*IMAGAWA PRECEPTS* (EARLY FIFTEENTH CENTURY)

By the fourteenth century, the house (*ie*) had emerged throughout Japan as the fundamental unit of kinship among warrior elites; in its mature form it would endure, without major structural evolution, until the abolition of the warrior class in the late nineteenth century. Rather than surveying the entire arc of the warrior house's existence, I focus here on the fifteenth and sixteenth centuries, when the survival of individual houses was threatened most acutely by ongoing country-wide strife and when daily concern with violence inspired a raft of documents on the values that might hold members together. Over nearly 150 years, in law codes and collections of moral precepts but also in private missives and political nego-tiations, warriors again and again reflect upon family relations, both in idealized abstractions and the contingent cases of their own houses.

In the following pages, I explore these documents and the ways they frame a preoccupation with what I call the contours of familial obligation. I expose, in particular, how a native vocabulary of service is overlaid with a Chinese vocabu-lary of loyalty and filial piety, the demands of which served to bind increasingly distant and potentially estranged relatives as well as increasingly long serving non-kin affiliates (housemen). Crucial to this integration, I argue, is the dominance of the language of loyalty (theoretically directed at nonkin) over the language of piety (directed at kin) and the recurrent fusion of kin and nonkin under the rubric of loyalty. The blurring of distinctions enhanced the cohesiveness of a group in which membership was potentially elective by taking advantage of the essential homology, in the ethical framework borrowed from the continent, between the lord-subject and father-son relations.

THE CORPORATE HOUSE'S AFFILIATES

As an institution, the warrior house was several things at once, but its core function was managing property rights and the access of members to offices. To a one-time observer, a house would look like a stem family composed of three generations: a house head and his wife, the couple's (sometimes adopted) son and successor, and the head's parents. Yet to those within it, invested in the perpetuation of ancestral status and wealth, the house was always conceived in terms of its history, as a lineage stretching back in time to its founder. Over the generations, membership expanded and contracted and grew ambiguous along the edges.

A house encompassed both dependent kin and variously affiliated nonkin. Noninheriting relatives—primarily the current head's unmarried daughters and nonsucceeding sons, and secondarily his siblings, aunts and uncles, and their off-spring—sometimes remained part of the house and often played significant roles despite their exclusion from the main line of succession. But brothers' sons were cousins; cousins' sons were second cousins; and so on. How distant must a relative become before he was no longer viewed as a member of the house? When needed, the proliferation of dependent kin was controlled by allowing noninheriting males to found their own separate houses. These were patrimonially independent but closely allied to the founders' natal houses (at least before time loosened the ties of kinship). More distant relations often remained, in fact if not in theory, members of the house. These included the descendants of nonsucceeding sons of previous heads as well as the maternal relatives of current or past heads, many of whom left their natal houses and threw in their lot with in-laws.

The marginalization of daughters and nonsucceeding sons marked the house as much as the (loose) inclusion of more distant kin, underscoring how the institution took shape in response to twin warrior concerns: on the one hand, with the fragmentation of wealth and prestige over time; on the other hand, with the maximization of military resources (and personnel) in times of turmoil. Sons and daughters, who in the twelfth and thirteenth centuries had been entitled to a share of their parents' assets, saw their claims sacrificed to the imperative of house survival, as the development of the role of designated successor (not necessarily the firstborn) led to the eclipse of partible inheritance.[1] Indeed, the designated son's monopoly on resources completed not only the house's patriarchal transformation but also, in a sense, its reification as an institution. As it emerged by the fourteenth century, the house transcended contingent configurations by linking the family name with a body of "ancestral" holdings that, handed down from generation to generation, signified its identity and continuity.[2]

The house had not always been the prevalent model of familial organization. Before the appearance of warriors as political actors in the twelfth century, extended kinship groups known as *uji* (sometimes translated as "clans") had dominated the political scene at the imperial court in Kyoto. Members of *uji* practiced uxorilocal marriage and selected as heads those members who held the highest ranks and offices at court, thus relying neither on primogeniture nor on lineal succession. Warriors did not, for the most part, start out as members of the tightly knit Kyoto aristocracy, nor were they as invested in the shared system of honors and rewards that defined it. As their involvement in political struggles grew, they did begin to compete for the prestige (and in some cases the authority) conferred by courtly titles. But this competition did not take place within the extended kinship group of the clan, as it did for courtiers, or give shape to its succession crises. Rather, much like land and followers, ranks and offices became assets to be transmitted lineally, from generation to generation. Because eligibility for public office was a resource assigned through the framework of the house, membership became the primary determinant of a man's standing in local society. The house, then, did more than structure kinship; in an increasingly fragmented and unsettled society, it also organized political life. Indeed, in its fullest definition, the house should be understood as functioning as a *corporate* rather than simply a kinship group.

This corporate group included nonkin as constituent, necessary members. Men (and, indirectly, women) who shared neither a surname nor an ancestor with the house head or his successor played vital roles in managing a house's assets and fighting its battles. More even than distant relatives, these nonkin affiliates expose the porousness of the boundary between the familial and the political. The subordinate affiliation of these nonkin followers was voluntary, subject to negotiation and renegotiation as circumstances and opportunities dictated. Yet, at their most successful, these ties of patronage and service could be long lasting, spanning multiple generations. Unlike the ties that bound kin, which weakened inexorably over time, the bonds of service between lords (heads of a house) and housemen were believed to grow stronger with every new generation. And while such beliefs often clashed with realities, long track records of unflagging and distinguished support did allow nonkin to rise to positions of leadership within a house. Some secured for themselves and their descendants titles such as *elder* or *majordomo* that gave them an important say in matters of policy and succession. Men like Asakura Takakage (1428–81) and Nagao Tamekage (1489?–1543) are now notorious for betraying their lords and taking their places, but both began their careers (and had the chance to mount their rebellions) because of the influence they wielded within the houses they served.

So, what was a houseman? The term is an ambiguous one that translates equally ambiguous Japanese terms (such as *kashin* or *kerai*), which denote anyone in the service of a house. And, in practice, *housemen* refers to a great range of subordinates. Some were petty warriors who resided near or with the house they served and enjoyed very little autonomy. Others had greater landed wealth and followings of their own and might oscillate, as political and military circumstances dictated, between unequal alliances and fully fledged submission. The more autonomous among them could and would negotiate the terms of their service, though appointment to offices within the house's administrative apparatus was as sure a sign as any that bonds were long lasting and commitment to the house was strong.

Still, being or not being part of a house could be a matter of perspective. Turning neighboring warriors into housemen (Japanese scholars refer to the process as *vassalization*) was a long-term proposition and even the greatest families often struggled to forge reliable ties with would-be followers.[3] Beginning in the latter half of the fourteenth century, those who held offices in the central regime's provincial administration, such as military governors, appointed trustworthy followers as deputies, using official posts to bolster private alliances. Governors also exploited their powers of requisition to commandeer revenues (and, eventually, actual plots of land) from local estates, which they then distributed among their worthier followers. These acts carried the validation of public authority. At the same time, such rewards exposed the authority of the state as contiguous to, and barely more awesome than, that of the house. They bought the services of local warrior houses but highlighted the negotiable character of allegiance. In the end, for many great houses that held official appointments in the provinces, the failure to make local warriors into fully fledged housemen—the failure to transform a jurisdiction into a house—would spell doom.

In practice, the very distinction between what was state sanctioned and public and what was house based and private seems to have been largely rhetorical. The conflation, in the service of the house, of public resources with private ends was not occasional or accidental; the ambiguous boundaries between these spheres were essential to the house's function as the center of warrior networks of sociability and power. Indeed, as a model for relations based on service, the corporate house was so versatile that it operated in much the same fashion at all levels of warrior society. Despite differences of scale, houses that controlled entire provinces and thousands of warriors negotiated relations with kin and nonkin affiliates in ways perfectly intelligible to houses with few holdings and mere dozens of members. However rickety in times of crisis, the pyramidal structure of houses, which made the heads of lesser houses into the housemen of more powerful houses (the "great names," or daimyo, of the age), coincided with the country's political hierarchy: the house of the shogun, who rested his authority to rule on a mandate from the imperial court, stood at the pinnacle of warrior society as the "Buke," *the* Warrior House.

The corporate character of the house, then, was at once its critical attribute and its critical operational challenge. Given the centrality of the house to warrior society, its elastic and composite character, and the ambiguity of resulting relations, it is no surprise that the *ie* became the object of pervasive rhetorical scrutiny in times of civil unrest.

THE CALCULUS OF SERVICE AND REWARD

By the fifteenth century, we find countless missives, composed on the eve of campaigns or in the wake of battles, dotted with references to loyalty and loyal service. Most often authored by great lords in times of need, these letters reflected neither academic philosophy nor ruminative indulgences; they combine congratulations for service rendered with exhortations to future deeds. And they tend, throughout, toward formulaic turns of phrase. In 1473, for example, the shogunal deputy Hosokawa Katsumoto urged a local warrior to "serve loyally" in exchange for confirmation of rights to various parcels of land.[4] Ashikaga Shigeuji, a relative and rival of the shogun, praised two of his partisans, sixteen years apart (in 1451 and 1471), in nearly identical language: their loyalty was "[truly] incomparable, the height of service."[5] In 1506, Shigeuji's son and heir lauded a follower's "unique loyalty."[6] Local lords were no less grandiose in their effusions: Utsunomiya Shigetsuna praised a follower's "incomparable loyalty" in 1495, adding that "he rejoiced at [the man's] repeated [demonstrations of] loyalty."[7]

Two observations arise from this handful of examples. First, *service* was the fundamental currency of political and military transaction. It governed all acts of political affiliation and partisanship. The actions of a houseman fighting on behalf of his lord's house and those of a local warrior answering the muster of a shogunal official deserved the same sort of praise because they were not conceptually (or morally) distinct. And regardless of actual sentiment, both were carried out for reward and then cloaked in the guise of personal fidelity.

Second, these documents are not only formulaic but hyperbolic. Lavish effusions were evidently as expected as familiar turns of phrase and were possibly more necessary. The effusions compel us to recognize that the ties binding nonretainers to a house, however crucial to advancement, were both theoretically and practically voluntary.[8] The very real possibility that service might not be performed in moments of need, or that rewards might not be forthcoming afterward, is implicit in the trove of synonyms that developed to describe lords' and followers' respective obligations and to extol their proper fulfillment. Indeed, the rote formulas privileged in this sort of document may well have served to reassure parties that the terms of the contract would be fulfilled without deviating from stipulations. All meaningful action was service, and all service was negotiated.

Yet the mechanics of the transactions were not laid bare. A subordinate's search for the most advantageous deal stood in perpetual tension with a lord's need for reliable supporters. Hence, the marketplace logic of negotiable service had to be downplayed in lords' pronouncements: service was always and emphatically loyal service. The most striking assertion of this association is in a letter to a follower

written in 1489 by Uesugi Sadamasa: "Loyalty is service."[9] In offering what amounts
to a definition of loyalty, Sadamasa's statement alerts us to the way in which such
an ideal suffuses the rich and ubiquitous vocabulary of service. If, indeed, loyalty
is service, we must consider service as both a form of social and political affiliation and an expression of morally virtuous conduct. References to service become
references to loyalty.

The tension between loyalty and contract, willfully suppressed in brief letters of
congratulation, is evident in more extensive documents where rote but flamboyant
praise gives way to greater nuance. In *Hobby Horse Notes* (*Chikubashō*), a collection of precepts composed in 1383 by shogunal deputy Shiba Yoshimasa, a criticism
is leveled at fellow warriors: "As for serving one's lord, everyone believes he must
receive favor before offering loyalty and service."[10] Yoshimasa, one of the most
powerful figures of his day, wrote at a time of relatively strong central authority
when the balance of power between lords and followers tipped decidedly toward
the former. Yet even he was forced to recognize how seldom so-called loyalty and
service were offered without up-front payment. The burden of initiative, he seems
to tell us, was on would-be recipients of service.

A mid-sixteenth-century author accustomed to decades of civil war and volatile alliances was less critical, if no less explicit, about the negotiated character
of loyalty and service. In the *Recorded Sayings of Asakura Sōteki,* a collection of
reflections on rulership and political strategy, the phrase "serving loyally" recurs
over and over as if all service must be a matter of loyalty. Yet the contractual nature
of the ties that bound lords and followers is also explicit: "Since [various petty
warriors] have been granted [fiefs] so widely, all feel grateful and serve loyally,
and consequently until now our province has long been ever more prosperous."[11]
Here, Sōteki echoes Yoshimasa in suggesting that rewards for service were, in fact,
advance payments. Perhaps because Sōteki was not the head of the Asakura house
but an advisor to its leadership, he is also attentive to the daimyo's obligations to
his followers: "In particular, it goes without saying for those who have served for
a long time, but even for those who have newly joined our side, that after a life
of loyal service if they have young children, you must act considerately and treat
them with the greatest care, so that they grow up [and prosper]."[12] In this formula-
tion, the moral power of "loyal service" constrains lords and followers alike.

In declaring that "loyalty is service," Uesugi Sadamasa seems to have been
intent on giving a practical dimension to a crucial virtue. Yet if loyalty was in
need of definition, service itself did not seem to require much explanation at all,
at least if we judge from extant statements. In the *Recorded Sayings of Asakura
Sōteki* we find references to simply "being personally in attendance" and "being
of great use."[13] In other fifteenth- and sixteenth-century texts, warriors write of
"being in attendance" or of "serving their lord."[14] Somewhat less opaquely, they
boast of many years of "military service," using a term (*gun'yaku*) that equates service with an actual levy of sorts.[15] To be sure, both in articles of law and in moral

injunctions the Japanese expressions are more varied than the English translations. My monotonous use of the rubric of service may lend to the actions in question greater semantic homogeneity (and conceptual consistency) than they had; it
likely also makes them out to be more abstract than they were conceived. In their
variety, the original utterances suggest an understanding of service that was not
driven by a formal and unitary set of rules but, rather, assembled through custom
out of an array of discrete actions and interactions. Even in normative statements
like Sadamasa's, service and loyalty were loose categories of conduct that emerged
organically and dialectically from the process of warrior society formation.

And here lies the key: what was invoked most urgently was not the ideal ("loyalty") but the actual conduct and duty that embodied it ("loyal service"). And as
something one *did,* serving loyally could be quantified and verified and—when
successful warlords began to regulate their authority in writing—legislated. In
practice, loyal service meant providing troops when requested. Records of mobilizations from the fifteenth and early sixteenth centuries, relatively scarce and
laconic, do not lend themselves to quantitative assessments of the quid pro quo
that enabled ongoing relationships. We must deduce patterns from the rare references to individual negotiations during campaigns (such as one that took place
in the early 1470s between the Iwamatsu and the Uesugi).[16] But by the mid-six-
teenth century, daimyo did begin systematizing their demands, exacting set troop
mobilizations from subordinates on the basis of the value of the lands granted to
them.[17] Another measure of loyal service, particularly when warriors with little
leverage answered the summons of provincial authorities, was distinction on the
battlefield, which authorized claims to rewards. In 1473 Shogun Ashikaga Yoshimasa sent nearly identical letters of commendation to various lords fighting in
his army: "Several among your vassals either perished or suffered wounds; this is
most splendid. . . . I am most moved by your loyal success."[18] Killing enemies or
sustaining casualties represented convenient metrics for performance. That both
inflicting and sustaining damage could be considered as measures of merit points
yet again to the moral dimension of service. Loyalty measured effort and sacrifice.

The legal codes issued by daimyo, which appear rather suddenly from the 1520s,
offer no systematic reassessment of the compacts between houses and their affiliates, but they do help us gauge the concrete ramifications of the vague invocation
of "loyal service."[19] Article 10 in the 1553 supplement to the Imagawa house code,
for instance, is entirely devoted to how the manifestations of the daimyo's favor
(the lands bestowed as rewards for meritorious conduct) may be handed down
to descendants.[20] Because service generated rewards that were then bequeathed
to sons and grandsons, the transferred lands were visible and quantifiable bonds.
They created expectations of continuing relationships between lineages. In this
regard, a daimyo's "favor" tethered his house to his followers' houses as surely as
it cast the relationship in unmistakably hierarchical terms. But those terms were
also conditional. The choice of euphemism matters: implicit in the choice of the

word *favor* (rather than the more explicit *land*) is the sense that continued tenure depended on continued goodwill.

Another sixteenth-century code, issued by the Chōsogabe house in 1596, is more explicit in casting service and favor as foundations for bonds expected to last generations—relationships between houses rather than individuals. Article 84 states: "In the matter of succession to a loyal family: When the heir's service has been lacking and a punishment is in order, if his failings have been light the penalty should not attach to the family name; if they have been serious, the penalty must attach to the family name."[21] Here, the authority of the lord's house extends not only to individual nonkin affiliates but considers followers' entire households as nested within the lordly house and regulates their succession—that most crucial and perilous of processes—in accordance with service rendered. Not individuals but families were the performers of loyal service; serious lapses by individual members were met with penalties that affected an entire family's name.

The ostentatious appeals to morality, then, served to ennoble a relationship that was contractual; they established a protocol of sorts that made more palatable the conditional nature of both service and favor to lords and followers alike. The moral nature of the compact, in turn, allowed lords to remind followers, and those followers' descendants, of their ongoing obligations by offering them the opportunity to renew the original virtuous commitment. But such reminders signal the effort through which lords cultivated other houses' ongoing affiliation and submission—an inherently unstable relationship made all the more unstable by the dangers and opportunities of civil war. If loyalty could be used to cloak the contractual nature of such relationships, further articulation of the concept was necessary to ensure their stability.

LOYALTY AND PIETY IN THE MAKING OF THE VIRTUOUS HOUSE

One crucial way of stabilizing relations between houses and their supporters was to recast provisional, negotiated alliances as exchanges of virtue—to obscure, in effect, the quasi-egalitarian and contingent dimensions of contractual agreements by representing them as moral agreements in accord with unchanging ideals of conduct. Daimyo did not have to search far for a useful moral vocabulary. The Confucian moral order, with its emphasis on archetypical social relations, each governed by appropriate behavior, had been known in Japan for centuries. Most apposite among the virtues advocated by Confucianism was loyalty, which was not simply the obedience a follower owed to his master (since a good subject was expected, for example, to remonstrate with a master who strayed) but an ideal of moral conduct that could elevate "loyal service" to a form of exemplary human fulfillment (not least because the words for "loyalty" and "loyal service" were cognates).

Would-be moralizers in Japan used the Chinese template in a variety of ways, often simultaneously. They drew on the connotations of the continental virtue when they claimed, implicitly or explicitly, that loyalty and service were one and the same. They also leaned on Chinese textual authority to lend force to their own maxims (a practice used as early as the seventh century in Prince Shōtoku's "Seventeen-Article Constitution"). Thus, for example, each of the injunctions in the code of Takeda Nobushige (1525–61) backs up advice with quotes from canonical or semicanonical continental texts: "Never forget loyal vassals. *Three Strategies* says, 'If good and evil are treated as the same, skilled vassals will be at a loss.'"[22] Only a few decades later, Tokugawa Ieyasu would use a similar combination of pragmatic instructions and (sometimes ill-fitting) continental references in his 1615 code for daimyo, the "Laws Governing the Military Houses" (*Buke shohatto*).

Yet examples like Nobushige's, I would submit, illuminate a more crucial valence of the borrowing process: references to Confucian loyalty immerse statements about a follower's obligations to a house in a broader discourse about a society's foundational relationships. Invoking one relationship, with the behavior appropriate to it, meant invoking the Confucian system as a whole. Extolling the loyal subject, for instance, inevitably implied embracing other, "parallel" paragons of virtue, such as the pious son. Uesugi Sadamasa (quoted above) uses textual authorities to criticize his son and heir for his lack of virtue: "Even if he should read the *Analects* and the *Classic of Filial Piety*, we would see he has no filial piety and righteousness at all."[23] A mid-sixteenth-century chronicle comments on the conduct of a Japanese warlord by quoting the *Analects*: "In that other country [China] it is said that if, in mourning a parent, one does not stray from one's father's path for three years, then one is filial."[24]

Indeed, the influence of continental texts is meaningful less in the direct borrowing of vocabulary or the citing of authorities than in the underscoring of associations between different categories of conduct. Stepping beyond filial piety's nominally familial ambit, Sadamasa's letter invokes the same virtue as a *political* necessity—for a son to become an heir and thus the next head of a house. The slippage between virtues of a son and those of a subject was not unique to Japan. In China, piety and loyalty had long been understood as essentially homologous: the ideal of lord-vassal relations, which called for loyalty to one's master and benevolence toward one's follower, was viewed as the public extension of the private ideal of father-son relations, and vice versa. But it was the father-son relationship, demanding piety of the son just as the lord-vassal relationship demanded loyalty of the vassal, that was held to be foundational in writing about social relations. The *Classic of Filial Piety*, a quasi-canonical treatise thought to have been compiled around the turn of the fourth century BCE and widely circulated in Japan, states: "[Piety] commences with the service of parents; it proceeds to the service of the ruler; it is completed by the establishment of the character."[25] Elaborating further on the relationship between piety and other virtues, the text claims: "As they serve their fathers, so they serve their mothers, and love them equally. As they serve their fathers, so they serve their rulers, and reverence them equally. Hence love is what is chiefly rendered to the mother, and reverence is what is chiefly rendered to the ruler, while both of these things are given to the father."[26]

In Japan, the homology of loyalty and filial piety figured early on in warrior discourse; it was well established by the time it appeared in the famous chapter of the fourteenth-century epic *The Tale of the Heike,* in which the virtuous son of a wayward political leader reprimands his father as a loyal subject would. Ubiquitous mention of loyalty and filial piety in medieval Japanese texts attests to the wide currency of continental ideas. But was the normative character of precepts about families analytically alive, malleable, or was it no more than an inert touchstone? In other words, were filial piety and loyalty (and other such ideals) drawn upon self-consciously and with specific goals in mind, or had they long since become little more than a set of ingrained moral reflexes, to be used not as starting points for speculation but as reliable support for the reiteration of urgently felt (if not freshly interrogated) needs? In China, the concepts of *zhong* and *xiao* acquired somewhat stable connotations of loyalty and filial piety in the second half of the first millennium BCE.[27] In Japan, numerous commentaries on the *Classic of Filial Piety* were authored or copied between the late fifteenth and the late sixteenth centuries, yet judging from the similarity between statements found in the *Classic of Filial Piety* and in daimyo's writings, medieval Japanese had not come very far in developing the originals' premises.[28] No doubt, cultural and linguistic translation contributed to simplification, though it is difficult to avoid the sense that statements such as those collected in the *Classic of Filial Piety* drew whatever power they had from their simplicity and seeming self-evidence. Repeated over and over, formulaically, they had become axiomatic.

Still, even formulas could be used as more than rhetorical flourishes. If daimyo did not create the homology, they nonetheless made aggressive use of it: in the service of their houses' prosperity, they conflated the loyalty demanded of nonkin followers and the filial piety expected of offspring. They did so most consequentially in the law codes they started issuing in the sixteenth century. These codes typically combined laws governing the daimyo's house and housemen (which drew at least in part from the long tradition of writing moral injunctions for heirs and followers) with laws governing the domain (which derived from the regulations issued in previous centuries by centrally appointed military governors).[29] Self-consciously or not, the moral authority claimed by injunctions was borrowed in the definition of mandatory (rather than purely desirable) behaviors and punishable (rather than simply reprehensible) offenses. Such borrowing suggests that the link between loyalty and filial piety mattered beyond the confines of rhetoric. In their laws, daimyo underscored the link in two ways: through the textual proximity of those who must be loyal and those who must be filial, and—less often but more significant— through shared rules for the two groups.

The legal space shared by kin and nonkin in law after law is striking.[30] In a joint oath sworn by Shimazu Tomohisa and four others in 1480, "those who have ties" to "this honorable house" are listed with "longtime friends" in more than one article: "Whether it is someone with ties to this honored house, or someone who has long been its friend, turning one's back on the governor's directives should come to cause disturbances throughout the country." The oath also invokes "someone in the family who is at odds with Takehisa, whether he is a father or a son or a brother or a close friend."[31] A similar grouping is found in the Imagawa house code: "One must not go so far as to report on the good and bad of a generous lord, of a teacher or superior, of a father and mother."[32] In the comprehensive code of laws issued by the Takeda house of Kai in 1547, an article addresses together the private oaths of "relatives, retainers, and others," claiming that what keeps kin and nonkin followers loyal is serving side by side, not oaths.[33]

Some codes go further, with regulations imposed at once on kin and nonkin. In the rules that Kuroda Josui laid down upon taking possession of Bizen province in 1587, not only are kin and nonkin subject to the same strictures, but the language of vassal duty is applied to kin: "Those who turn their backs upon the head of the house or upon their parents shall be punished."[34] Although it may be an overstatement to claim that "turning one's back" specifically describes those who are disloyal (rather than those who are unfilial), there is no doubt that kin, here, are equated with nonkin as objects of legislation and penalty. Nor were the Takeda and Kuroda rules novel. In an oath recorded by Kikkawa Mototsune and eight other local warriors in 1512, the conduct and punishment of kin and nonkin are indistinguishable: "When kin or retainers or others in our warrior band flee, whether because they despise their lord or because they have received a punishment, there must be no leniency."[35] Examples abound.[36]

More than the occasional grouping together of kin and nonkin, this conflation suggests that, as categories of membership in the house, the same rules applied to relatives and vassals. To be sure, outside the immediate household of the daimyo even relatives were often tied to the main house as retainers. Yet this association often went so far as to include sons. The link between filial piety and loyalty operated even in legal definitions and, indeed, these codes share the presumption that kin and nonkin were liable to behave (and misbehave) similarly. The shogunal deputy Hosokawa Masamoto may have put it most clearly in 1501, when he decreed: "In the case of a family without assets/titles, if someone must be put to death, as in other matters, do not speak of the distinctions between lieutenants, relatives, retainers, followers, even if there are some sorts of gradations; first [the situation] must be relayed [to the authorities] by means of a messenger and a verdict must be issued [on the basis] of the Great Law."[37] Another document, a 1526 oath by a far less eminent warrior (one Nakajō Fujisuke), is similarly opposed to making distinctions between kin and nonkin before the law: "Whether for a lieutenant or a relative, if things come to a judgment, we must not go as far as to back them, but entrust [the matter] to a directive from the provincial [governor's] office."[38]

That a "feudal" vocabulary of service and favor-benefice developed indigenously means that the overlay of the vocabulary of Chinese virtue was not only unnecessary but also a leap. It was made, with intention, to reconfigure the transactional nature of relations as moral. No doubt, the Chinese-Confucian template did not exhaust ways of expressing the idea of loyal service; the late sixteenth and early seventeenth centuries were a time of almost unprecedented searching for new, more advantageous articulations of the fundamental exchange at the heart of the ties that bound daimyo (and then hegemons) to their followers. The simple availability of Confucian morality, then, does not alone explain its centrality to discourse on "the family" in Japan. Although Confucian ideas provide a full range of familial relations, the authors of many of our texts did not feel the need to systematically address each of them. Rather, these hoary continental ideals of lord-vassal and father-son relations were harped upon over and over because—together—they did an excellent job of capturing the structure of the *ie* and its most vital preoccupations. The parallel between loyalty and filial piety serves well in a context in which relations with kin and nonkin could advantageously be treated as homologous.

Making the house head into both a father and a lord, the daimyo codes regularized the conduct of inheriting and noninheriting offspring by subjecting them to laws. They also elevated the investment of nonkin by intimating (truthfully or not) that they would be held in the same emotional regard as kin. At the same time, daimyo took advantage of the widespread familiarity and systematic character of Confucian moral norms to suggest that the ideals of conduct for offspring and affiliates could be applied to both more or less interchangeably. The resonances between filialness and loyalty amplified the normative power of each. In many respects, an undifferentiated house membership is an objective running through the entire body of daimyo legislation. If achieved, though, it could create as many practical problems for a house as it resolved.

THE BOUNDARIES WITHIN AND BETWEEN HOUSES

My survey of texts that intimate, if not continuity, at least contiguity between a house's blood-kin core and its variously affiliated followers, raises two interrelated considerations. The first is that the categories of kin and nonkin are broad simplifications. There are sons and parents, but also relatives and those "of the same name"; there are retainers and housemen and followers, as well as those who have been clients and lieutenants. And not all codes or oaths juxtapose the same group of kin with the same group of nonkin. Pairing relatives and followers or, say, sons and retainers, no doubt blurred different lines. Treating the various laws cited above as expressive of similar premises runs the risk of overshadowing the specific relations and the specific points each text was intent on making. Yet the admittedly imprecise equation of a broad variety of kin with an even broader variety of non-kin allows us to establish what we might think of as the conceptual and rhetorical contours, the outer limits, of the house as the organizational hub of warriors' social and political life.

The second consideration derives from the first. That the two broad groups are itemized in articles of law and oaths is undeniable evidence that the two groups were indeed distinct, and that the distinction was worth underlining even in documents mandating one rule for all. The rhetoric of analogy served to underscore the members' shared investment in the house in the face of ever-present evidence that hierarchical distinctions were also differences of belonging (and, more dangerously, of investment). Yet the rhetoric was not only rhetoric, and the repeated grouping of kin and nonkin forces us to think more subtly about the problem of a house's internal hierarchies and differences; the line dividing kin and nonkin, while ever visible (and often problematic), was far from straight (or sharp). For example, Mōri Motonari, who otherwise was wont to exploit the flexible boundaries of kinship to his advantage, wrote to his son about how he must not trust housemen but only relatives by blood and marriage.[39] At first glance, Motonari's comment seems to run against the grain of prevailing statements of equal or at least comparable membership for kin and nonkin, intimating that such statements did not always translate into equal treatment or trust. But it is worth drawing attention to his unusual classificatory scheme: in-laws are kin, a characterization that in ignoring the contingent and arbitrary character of kinship by marriage yet again complicates clear-cut distinctions between kin and nonkin, turning a binary into a gradient in which different factors could determine one's position.

Systemically, the line setting apart kin and nonkin within the hierarchy of the house was tangled by marriage ties between lords and followers. But the vagaries of individual personalities and skills also conspired to complicate clear-cut distinctions. Nonkin chief retainers often wielded more influence than distant cousins who happened to share a surname with their lords. We see this in countless succession crises, when factions emerged to support vying pretenders; when marriage alliances and ties of patronage became essential to success; and when senior housemen played outsized roles in the eventual selection, forging compromises that averted dangerous rifts among the house's affiliates. A notable example is that of Ise Sōzui (1456–1519, better known as Hōjō Sōun), an important retainer of the Imagawa house whose sister became the wife of its head, Yoshitada. When Yoshitada died on the battlefield, it was Sōzui—both Yoshitada's houseman and brother-in-law—who protected the infant heir against a rival claimant and brokered his succession. In the end, Sōzui emerged triumphant as the uncle of the new lord.[40]

Historical examples of the complex relations and multilayered roles played by house members are easy enough to come by. Far rarer are documents that plumb such relations with anything more than pious generalities or legal prescriptions.

One such document, a memorandum for a young bride-to-be, was produced by a member of the Hōjō house of Odawara, a warrior known to us as Gen'an. A younger son of the same Sōzui mentioned above, he was born around 1505 and believed to have lived into the 1580s. (Gen'an was, thus, a witness to both the early expansion of the Hōjō under his father and to their rise to regional hegemony under his brother, nephew, and great-nephew. He may have lived long enough to see the house's demise in 1590.)[41]

Gen'an was one of the more senior members of the Hōjō by 1562, when, it is believed, he composed his *Memorandum* (known as *Hōjō Sōtetsu oboegaki*) for a daughter of the third Hōjō head, Ujiyasu.[42] The young woman, whom the text addresses without naming, was about to become the wife of the heir to the Kira, an old and prestigious but by then powerless house. Such marriage alliances were central to the expansion of Hōjō power, preparing and consolidating battlefield successes. The house head's daughters could expect to be married off to the heads of other houses;[43] his noninheriting sons might be adopted by other houses as prospective heirs.[44] In this case, the young Hōjō woman was reinforcing an existing alliance, for the father of her groom-to-be was married to one of Ujiyasu's many sisters.[45]

The *Memorandum* is an unusual document in that it is addressed to a young woman rather than a son or an heir. (One scholar has argued that the bride was actually Gen'an's daughter, adopted by Ujiyasu to marry her off.)[46] The *Memorandum* is also unusually revelatory, for its instructions on interactions with retainers, with hereditary vassals, with elders, and with the lord's attendants remind us that the language seen elsewhere uniting kin and nonkin overlays a recognition that fine shades of status existed in the face of a rhetoric of unity. Reaching for different ways of signifying difference, the *Memorandum* ends up privileging status relative to house affiliation.

The text's twenty-four articles—some concise, some extensive—are not meant to cover all of the young woman's future duties or even most of them. Gen'an says nothing about a wife's role in managing the household or raising the next generation of Kira. Instead, he focuses on the etiquette of the lady's interactions with members of her natal and marital houses as well as with lords and retainers of different status.[47] Typical of his concerns is the proper reception of elders from hereditary vassal houses (article 9); of elders from the future husband's natal house (article 10); of Kira house elders (article 11); and of close attendants of the Kira lord (article 12).[48] In forging a marriage alliance with the Kira, a house with a reputation for expertise in matters of ceremony, the Hōjō leadership no doubt wished to draw on their in-laws' knowledge. At the same time, it is hard to escape the sense that such expertise put pressure on Gen'an to prove himself (and the bride-to-be) ceremonially competent.

Gen'an's *Memorandum* was intended as a primer for a bride, not a treatise on alliances and politics. Still, set against the backdrop of other sources, it reveals a tendency to refashion the sharp boundaries between houses into vague distinctions within a house. In the Hōjō-dominated Kantō region, the renewal of the alliance with the Kira reaffirmed a distinctly unequal partnership, one that exalted the Kira even as it threatened to extinguish the independence of the house. But not entirely: the Kira are absent from a 1559 register of all Hōjō kin and vassals,[49] which indicates that the Hōjō had not established formal lord-follower relations with them and had not integrated them into their new military recruitment mechanism. No loyal service was expected from the Kira.

We do know that other alliances the Hōjō forged through marriage were meant to blur, if not erase, the boundaries between themselves and other houses, and, in this case too, Gen'an seems to presume considerable integration between in-laws.[50] Several articles deal with the proper way of maintaining contacts with Gen'an's son Ujinobu and a nephew.[51] Ujinobu would soon take over from Gen'an as the castellan in nearby Kozukue, and Gen'an repeatedly mentions him and other warriors associated with that stronghold.[52] The young bride-to-be, the *Memorandum* implies, could expect to have plenty of dealings with Ujinobu in the future. For example, article 20 advises: "As for sending greetings to Ujinobu, in spring you must do so often. You should inquire with [your mother-in-law]."[53] The bride would remain in close contact with her Hōjō relatives, while seeking—and obtaining, it is assumed—permission and guidance from members of her new family.

If marriage alliances symbolically united two houses, the *Memorandum* construes the union as literal: to Gen'an and other Hōjō, the Kira were now family. We see this when Gen'an instructs his great-niece on the differences and similarities to be observed in treating members of her birth family and in-laws. Article 1, on how to address the Kira lord, also dwells on how to address the Hōjō lords. The same title is used for both; a place-name is all that clarifies which lordship is which.[54] Article 4, almost banal in offering instruction on the proper etiquette for interactions with Lord Kira before and after the wedding (use a go-between before the wedding but not afterward), reflects the shortening distance between the two houses if not their transformation into a single house.[55]

To be sure, in a primer on etiquette, distinctions remain all important. Yet the operative variable throughout is not kinship or membership in one house or the other. In sorting out the young bride's future interactions, Gen'an reveals to us one way past the ever-present tension between the ideal of inclusiveness and the reality of differences: what must organize interactions between house members was not the degree of kinship but rather each member's status. In article 16, Gen'an explains that the treatment of messengers should reflect the differences of status between the men who sent them: "[Reception of] a messenger conveying greetings from any among your relatives, such as Lord Ujiteru or Ujinobu, and of a messenger from [Lord Kira] should be slightly different. You should consult with [your mother-in-law] and make preparations."[56] How they should differ is not specified; messengers from relatives were presumably to be treated with a little less ceremony than a messenger sent by Lord Kira. Yet significant here is that junior kin like

Ujinobu and Ujiteru are set side by side with the head of the Kira house, separated primarily (and only slightly) by degrees of deference. Indeed, status rather than kinship is the determining factor, as shown in article 15: "You will be receiving greetings from the two [Hōjō] lords of Odawara [Ujiyasu and his heir, Ujimasa]. You must convey them [to Lord Kira], giving their messenger the reception you would an elder. Even if the messenger is [only] a close attendant, if he is a messenger from the lords, the reception must be the same. This is because the Lord [of Odawara] is currently [Kantō] Deputy. As for his messenger, failure to make every effort will not do."[57]

That both the Hōjō and the Kira were to be counted as family is no doubt a function of the *Memorandum*'s first order of business: to help a young woman move from one house to another and negotiate relations with both. But repeated discussion of nonkin housemen complicates matters. Whose housemen? we must ask in such a situation. Were they Kira housemen or Hōjō housemen or neither— retainers attached to the bride-to-be? If status-based treatment of members of the Kira and Hōjō overshadows individual house loyalties (thereby affirming a new, higher loyalty to the hegemonic power, the Hōjō), the ambiguity surrounding the roles and affiliations of nonkin housemen underscores the difficulty of maintaining the view of houses as coherent and exclusive organizations. For these "housemen without a house," no less than for their social betters, the status they derived by proximity to the bride mattered more than affiliation with one or the other side of the marriage alliance. Men who had once been Hōjō affiliates were now expected to render service to the new bride; she, in turn, should treat those Hōjō followers who called on her as the new lady of the Kira house as if they were elder retainers, following their counsel on how to navigate relationships in her new household. (articles 18 and 19).[58]

These recommendations make clear that the ambiguous position was not women's alone. Three of the warriors mentioned in articles 18 and 19—Shimizu, Kasahara, and Takahashi—were members of the Izu band (one of the units of the Hōjō military machine used to mobilize supporters), which was under Gen'an's command. Kasahara, in particular, is listed first among its members in the 1559 register of Hōjō vassals. That Gen'an should single out him and Shimizu and mark them for special deference is not surprising.[59] But Takahashi Gōzaemon's circumstances may have been different. An old Hōjō vassal (and a grandson of Sōzui on his mother's side), he was well versed in matters of etiquette and continued to serve the bride as she settled down in the Kira house. According to historian Tabata Yasuko, brides who left their natal families were typically accompanied by retainers of their own. As a result, high-level marriages had a direct impact on lower-level warrior families, for whom negotiating new, complex loyalties became a form of service toward the bride's father.[60] Takahashi and a fourth warrior, Mizushi (the latter repeatedly cited as a messenger), seem to have served the bride-to-be in such a capacity, and recurring references to them underscore the text's expectation of assiduous interaction between the bride-to-be and members of her natal family.

The precepts' attention to the fine and not-so-fine shades of status and function helps make sense of the internal organization of a house. The text's mixing of Kira and Hōjō even while fastidiously minding status differences within both is suggestive of where the real distinctions were meant to be. Any *ie* was by necessity a composite of many kinship groups, and one's position within it, the *Memorandum* says, depended on one's role in the organization and one's status. Status was often determined by office and title in the country at large, metrics that may appear to transcend the confines of the house, but Gen'an shows us that its value (as well as its attainment) was of primary importance *within* the house. If his *Memorandum* highlights distinctions between different sorts of members and followers, it also shares with other texts we have encountered a basic understanding of the house's composition: the *ie* was not about family—or perhaps, depending on our how we feel about "family," family wasn't solely about kin. Truly, if self-referentially, the *ie* was about the organization. The demands on men like Takahashi and Mizushi— on a permanent tour of duty in the retinue of a woman forever caught between two lineages—suggest the degree to which "loyal service" came to be rendered less and less as part of a contractual relationship and more and more as part of a commitment to an expansive (and expanding) conception of the house. In the name of the conflation between kin and nonkin, the investment expected of kin had come to be expected of housemen as well.

IN CONCLUSION

In the Tokugawa period, the demands of loyalty became more absolute. In the didactic texts authored by righteous warriors, as in the commercial publications meant less somberly for a wider public, the emphasis on duty and self-sacrifice became paramount, all but obscuring the contractual nature of service. This may have been due, in part and increasingly as the decades went by, to the nostalgia of warriors alienated from their calling by their new condition as underemployed urban administrators. Inactivity no doubt made for a certain idealization of the warring past, while peace lowered the stakes of loyalty and disloyalty considerably.

But nostalgia's link to the transformation of loyalty is not causal. Rather, both were manifested as by-products of the development and dissemination, in the late sixteenth century, of ideas of public authority and assertions of the Toyotomi and Tokugawa regimes' exclusive right to judicial authority and the violence concomitant with its enforcement. The stripping by daimyo of their followers' right to self-redress, which was heightened at the end of the civil war by the removal of warriors from the countryside, also undermined much of the conceptual justification for negotiating loyalty and service. Little rhetorical space was left for any devotion short of absolute. One need only think of Yamamoto Tsunetomo's *Hagakure*, a text strident in its advocacy of the Nabeshima house's excellence and lapidary (and hyperbolic) in its declaration that the meaning of the Way of the Warrior was to be found in death—the ultimate, and definitive, act of loyal service.[61]

At the same time, the subjugation of daimyo to the shogunal regime in Edo created new problems: the house, for over a century the sole object of loyalty, now had to be understood as subsumed under a higher source of authority, for all daimyo houses were now themselves vassals of the Tokugawa house. Warlords were fitted into the Japan-wide framework of Tokugawa rule, so, even at the highest level, their houses could not stand alone as self-referential foci of service and attachment. In light of the realities of early modern rule, Yamamoto's scornful dismissal of other houses' martial traditions, as inferior and ultimately unnecessary to any Nabeshima warrior, rings hollow. Perhaps unsurprisingly, Yamamoto does not take a critical look at the real struggle behind the creation of the imperative of loyalty, for the uncompromising ideal he embraces and extols was the product of policies enacted by daimyo *upon* their followers. These policies were driven by, and beneficial to, the house as a politically autonomous unit and were rendered both widespread and less urgent by the new peace.

Although in pacifying the country the Tokugawa hegemons opted not to push for complete centralization, thus stepping back from the absolutist ideals of authority self-aggrandizingly promoted by daimyo during the civil war, pacification brought about a sort of upward transposition of claims to authority. The sphere of the public—and thus the legitimate—came to be preeminently associated with the rulers in Edo, leaving daimyo under suspicion of "private-ness."[62] The newly problematic character of marriage alliances illustrates the limits imposed on warrior houses' claim to paramount positions. In the first of many versions of the "Laws Governing the Military Houses," the shogunate was blunt: "Marriage must not be contracted in private" (article 8).[63] The encroachment on the familial (*ie*) sphere that was at the heart of the regime's monopolization of public and legitimate action helps us make sense of the paradoxical character of calls for absolute loyalty to one particular daimyo house—as seen in Yamamoto Tsunetomo's eighteenth-century rumination on the way of the warrior, *Hagakure*, but also, more flamboyantly, in the celebrated plays about the forty-seven *rōnin*'s vendetta. Based on real events, the plays dramatized one of the central dilemmas of the age: the tension between, on the one hand, the shogunate's need to suppress feuding and uphold its monopoly on violence and, on the other, warriors' urge to display their prowess and rectitude through acts of absolute, even self-destructive abnegation.[64]

Yet the relocation to the dubious sphere of the private of nonsanctioned interactions between daimyo houses does not overshadow the fundamental continuities in the assumptions of both rulers and ruled. The new ideas of public, suprafamilial authority that undergirded both the Tokugawa's awesome accumulation of power and the daimyo's erosion of their followers' autonomy did not do away with the house as an institution. Marriages remained political affairs. Gen'an's lesson remained valid and potentially threatening. As his primer reminds us, if the warrior house was indeed a corporate group, a new marriage could be as good an occasion as any other to renegotiate its membership. If alliances were political affairs, so too were the contours of family.

NOTES

Epigraph: The *Imagawa Precepts* (*Imagawa kabegaki*; also known as the *Imagawa Letter* [*Imagawa jō*]) is a letter of admonition said to have been written by the warrior Imagawa Ryōshun (1326–1420) to his brother and heir around the turn of the fifteenth century. Reprinted in Arima and Akiyama 2012, 46.

1. Tonomura 1990; Takahashi 1991; Takahashi 2004, 32–51.
2. Spafford 2013, 123–68.
3. Sakai 1999; Matsumoto 2001; Itō 2003.
4. *Gunma-ken shi*, vol. 7, p. 247, doc. 1748.
5. *Tochigi-ken shi*, vol. 2, p. 129, doc. 49, and p. 107, doc. 71; the only difference between the two is the term "truly" (*makoto ni*), which appears only in the latter document.
6. *Gunma-ken shi*, vol. 7, p. 311, doc. 1864.
7. *Tochigi-ken shi*, vol. 3, p. 119, doc. 4. Other examples can be found, for instance, in long letters written by Ōta Dōkan in 1480 (*Saitama-ken shi*, vol. 5, p. 636, doc. 1003): "rendering loyal service together"; and by Uesugi Sadamasa in 1489 (in *Saitama-ken shi*, vol. 5, p. 656, doc. 1019): "striving in our loyal successes for the main house."
8. It could be argued that, to a certain extent, the ties that bound kin to a house were also negotiable, as younger sons could and did leave to establish new houses and take new surnames. While blood and kinship themselves were not easily denied, economically junior houses were distinct; absent shared entitlement to offices or landholding portfolios, political alignment could be precarious.
9. *Saitama-ken shi*, vol. 5, p. 657, doc. 1019.
10. *Chikubashō*, in *Buke kakun*, 67.
11. *Asakura Sōteki waki*, 4.
12. *Asakura Sōteki waki*, 2.
13. *Asakura Sōteki waki*, 1. The phrase recurs. See ibid., 2–3: "When it is important, they will be of great use." Also ibid., 3: "[If a lord is not beloved by his housemen], when it is important, it will be difficult [for them] to be of use by laying down their lives for him."
14. *Saitama-ken shi*, vol. 5, p. 635, doc. 1003 ("being in attendance"); *Takeda Nobushige kakun*, 124 ("serving their lord").
15. *Hōjō Ujitsuna kakioki*, in *Buke kakun*, 120.
16. I discuss this episode at length in Spafford 2013.
17. See *Odawara-shū shoryō yakuchō*.
18. Letter to Nagao Kagenobu, in *Gunma-ken shi*, vol. 7, p. 242, doc. 1730. For several other examples by Yoshimasa during the same campaign, see *Tochigi-ken shi*, vol. 4, pp. 315–26, docs. 15, 36, 37, 50, and 53–56.
19. Whether these laws simply record and regularize customary practices or expand daimyo prerogatives—and, if so, how and how much—is an important question that must be left for another study.
20. *Imagawa kana mokuroku*, 126–27.

21. *Chōsogabe-shi okitegaki*, in *Chūsei hōsei shiryō shū*, vol. 3, p. 299.

22. *Takeda Nobushige kakun*, 126. *Three Strategies* (Ch. *San lue*) is a book of military strategy thought to have been produced at the end of the first century BCE. A virtually identical sentiment is expressed, without explicit reference to Chinese textual authority, in *Ōtomo Yoshiaki okibumi* (p. 204): "There must be no forgetfulness about the depth of one's service or the closeness of one's loyalty."

23. *Saitama-ken shi*, vol. 5, p. 655, doc. 1019.

24. *Kawagoe ki*, 595; the passage is from *Lunyu* I.11.

25. Legge 1966, 466–67.

26. Legge 1966, 470.

27. Knapp 1995; Knapp 2005, 8–9, 13–26; Brown 2007, 65–84; Goldin 2011, 31–38.

28. *Kokusho sōmokuroku* (vol. 3, pp. 211–15) lists six extant titles dating back to the Warring States period, one of them, by Kiyohara Nobukata, in multiple copies bearing different dates; others must have been lost.

29. Katsumata 1976.

30. In some cases, space was shared in a literal sense, on the page: in the 1617 *Kikkawa-shi hatto*, lord-vassal and father-son relations are treated in consecutive articles (nos. 50–51 in *Chūsei hōsei shiryō shū*, vol. 3, pp. 317–18); in *Ōtomo Yoshiaki okibumi*, rules of service and rules for family sit next to each other (nos. 9–10, p. 204).

31. *Chūsei hōsei shiryō shū*, vol. 4, p. 151, doc. 199.

32. *Imagawa kana mokuroku*, 134. This is the last article of the "*Sadame*," which appears after the *tsuikahō* in the Kurokawa-bon version of the code.

33. *Kōshū hatto no shidai*, in *Chūsei hōsei shiryō shū*, vol. 3, p. 204.

34. *Kuroda Josui kyōkun*, in *Buke kakun*, 188.

35. *Chūsei hōsei shiryō shū*, vol. 4, p. 177, doc. 255.

36. See, for instance, one other entry in *Ōtomo Yoshiaki okibumi*, 204: "As for a crime by members of the same surname or relatives or lieutenants: if there is a judgment of the lawfulness or not, there must be no collaboration of members of the same surname or members of different surnames."

37. *Hosokawa Masamoto sadamegaki*, in *Chūsei hōsei shiryō shū*, vol. 4, p. 164, doc. 226.

38. *Nakajō Fujisuke kishōmon*, in *Chūsei hōsei shiryō shū*, vol. 4, pp. 197–98, doc. 298.

39. Quoted in Tabata 1998, 253.

40. Horton 2002, 31. See also the *Imagawa kafu*, 154.

41. Kuroda Motoki estimates that Gen'an was born around 1505 (about a decade later than generally stated); the last document he authored was dated 1582 (Kuroda 1989, 30–33).

42. Fujioka Tsuguhei's proposed date of composition remains accepted, as does his conclusion that the Hōjō woman about to marry the head of the Kira was one of Ujiyasu's daughters (Fujioka 1901, 1497–1506, 1521). See also Ogino 1975, 91–94.

43. Apart from the alliance with the Kira, several others among Ujiyasu's sisters and daughters found husbands among the great lords of the time: a sister married Ashikaga Haruuji of Koga; daughters married, among others, Haruuji's son, Yoshiuji, Imagawa Ujizane, and Takeda Katsuyori (see the figure in Kuroda 2012, 8).

44. Spafford 2014, 315–23.

45. Kuroda 1997, 292–93. As for the groom-to-be, his situation was even more complicated. He was born into the Horikoshi house of Tōtōmi and his biological mother was yet
another of Hōjō Ujiyasu's sisters (Shimoyama 1975, 293).

46. Kuroda 1997, 297.

47. Although two articles (21, briefly; and 24, at great length) discuss the protocol of
interactions with merchants and guild leaders, the majority of the primer focuses on kinsmen, in-laws, and different sorts of nonkin followers.

48. *Hōjō Sōtetsu oboegaki*, 302.

49. See *Odawara-shū shoryō yakuchō*. See also Ogino 1975, 66–78.

50. Spafford 2014.

51. For the sake of clarity in the translations that follow, I use the names Ujinobu and
Ujiteru even when the original refers to Shinzaburō and Genzō.

52. Article 17 mentions several retainers of varying rank, from middling (Mizushi Mukunosuke, Konogi Zusho) to lower rank (Ōya, Nakata); *Hōjō Sōtetsu oboegaki*, 303. Of these,
only Nakata is listed in *Odawara-shū shoryō yakuchō* (p. 204), as a member of the Kozukue
band, though Mizushi is mentioned repeatedly as a messenger, which may imply that he,
and possibly the others as well, were warriors from southern Musashi Province, assigned to
serve the bride-to-be in the nearby Kira residence.

53. *Hōjō Sōtetsu oboegaki*, 304.

54. *Hōjō Sōtetsu oboegaki*, 301. The subtle variations are impossible to render faithfully
in English: "You must refer to Lord Kira (*Kira-dono*) as 'On'yakata' [his lordship]. As for our
[Hōjō] lord, it is good to refer to him as 'Odawara on'yakata.' Otherwise, you should refer to
him either as 'Odawara-dono' or '[Odawara]-sama.'"

55. *Hōjō Sōtetsu oboegaki*, 301. "When you are to go to Lord Kira, someone of high status
must act as a go-between. Conversely, after [you have been married], too much distance
could be a bad thing as well."

56. *Hōjō Sōtetsu oboegaki*, 303.

57. *Hōjō Sōtetsu oboegaki*, 303–4.

58. *Hōjō Sōtetsu oboegaki*, 303–4. Art. 18: "When Shimizu [Yasuhide] and Kasahara
[Mimasaka no kami] come to offer greetings, you should treat them as elders." Art. 19:
"When the next day, employing Mizushi Mukunosuke as a messenger, you call for the elders
who have come to welcome you, it is good to deliver word with great care. When wonder-
ing how to treat someone of great status, you should consult with [Takahashi] Gōzaemon.
On whether you also give [a gift] to the messenger even after being offered greetings, you
should trust the matter to Gōzaemon's opinion."

59. According to a contemporary chronicle, *Odawara kyūki*, Kasahara was among the so-
called five elders (*gokarōshū*) and the castellan of Shimoda (quoted in *Odawara-shū shoryō
yakuchō*, p. 239, n. 122). Both Kasahara and Shimizu, like most members of the Izu band,
mainly held lands in that province (*Odawara-shū shoryō yakuchō*, 122, 124, respectively),
though Kasahara is also listed as having three holdings in Sagami, the Hōjō home province.

60. Tabata 1994, 80–82.

61. *Hagakure*, 220.

62. See Toby 2001.

63. *Buke shohatto*, 454.

64. For an extended discussion of literature on the theme of revenge, see David Atherton's article in this volume.

LIST OF REFERENCES

Arima and Akiyama 2012
Arima Sukemasa and Akiyama Goan, eds. *Bushidō kakunshū*. 1906. Reprinted, Tokyo: Hakubunkan Shinsha, 2012.

Asakura Sōteki waki
Asakura Sōteki waki. In *Zoku zoku gunsho ruijū*, 4th ed., edited by Kokusho Kankōkai, vol. 10, pp. 1–12. Tokyo: Zoku Gunsho Ruijū Kanseikai, 1984.

Brown 2007
Brown, Miranda. *The Politics of Mourning in Early China*. Albany: State University of New York Press, 2007.

Buke kakun
Ozawa Tomio, ed. *Buke kakun, ikun shūsei*. Revised and expanded. Tokyo: Perikansha, 2003.

Buke shohatto
Buke shohatto. In *Kinsei buke shisō*, edited by Ishii Shirō. Vol. 27 of *Nihon shisō taikei*, edited by Ienaga Saburō et al., 454–62. Tokyo: Iwanami Shoten, 1974.

Chūsei hōsei shiryō shū, vol. 3
Satō Shin'ichi, Ikeuchi Yoshisuke, and Momose Kesao, eds. *Chūsei hōsei shiryō shū*, vol. 3. Tokyo: Iwanami Shoten, 1965.

Chūsei hōsei shiryō shū, vol. 4
Satō Shin'ichi and Momose Kesao, eds. *Chūsei hōsei shiryō shū*, vol. 4. Tokyo: Iwanami Shoten, 1998.

Fujioka 1901
Fujioka Tsuguhei. "Hōjō Gen'an oboegaki no kō." *Shigaku zasshi* 12:12 (1901): 1490–1522.

Goldin 2011
Goldin, Paul R. *Confucianism*. Berkeley: University of California Press, 2011.

Gunma-ken shi
Gunma-ken Shi Shiryō Hensan Iinkai, ed. *Gunma-ken shi shiryōhen*. 27 vols. Maebashi-shi: Gunma-ken, 1977–88.

Hagakure
Yamamoto Tsunetomo. *Hagakure*. Annotated by Saiki Kazuma and Okayama Taishi. In *Nihon shisō taikei*, vol. 26, *Mikawa monogatari, Hagakure*, edited by Saiki Kazuma, Okayama Taishi, and Sagara Tōru, 213–579. Tokyo: Iwanami Shoten, 1974.

Hōjō Sōtetsu oboegaki
Hōjō Sōtetsu oboegaki. In *Sengoku ibun: Gohōjō-shi hen*, edited by Sugiyama Hiroshi and Shimoyama Haruhisa, vol. 4, pp. 301–5. Tokyo: Tōkyōdō Shuppan, 1992.

Horton 2002
Horton, H. Mack. *Song in an Age of Discord: The Journal of Sōchō and Poetic Life in Late Medieval Japan*. Stanford, CA: Stanford University Press, 2002.

Imagawa kafu
Imagawa kafu. In *Zoku gunsho ruijū*, edited by Hanawa Hokinoichi, vol. 21, part 1, pp. 141–60. Tokyo: Zoku Gunsho Ruijū Kanseikai, 1958.

Imagawa kana mokuroku
Imagawa kana mokuroku. In *Chūsei hōsei shiryō shū*, vol. 3, edited by Satō Shin'ichi, Ikeuchi Yoshisuke, and Momose Kesao, 115–34. Tokyo: Iwanami Shoten, 1965.

Itō 2003
Itō Toshikazu. "Chūsei kōki shōenseiron no seika to kadai." *Kokuritsu Rekishi Minzoku Hakubutsukan kenkyū hōkoku* 104 (March 2003): 5–15.

Katsumata 1976
Katsumata Shizuo. "Sengoku-hō," in *Iwanami Kōza Nihon rekishi,* edited by Asao Naohiro et al., vol. 8, pp. 175–210. Tokyo: Iwanami Shoten, 1976.

Kawagoe ki
Kawagoe ki. In *Shinkō gunsho ruijū,* edited by Kawamata Keiichi, vol. 16, pp. 595–99. Tokyo: Naigai Shoseki, 1928–38.

Knapp 1995
Knapp, Keith N. "The *Ru* Reinterpretation of *Xiao.*" *Early China* 20 (1995): 195–222.

Knapp 2005
Knapp, Keith N. *Selfless Offspring: Filial Children and Social Order in Medieval China.* Honolulu: University of Hawai'i Press, 2005.

Kokusho sōmokuroku
Kokusho sōmokuroku. Revised and expanded. 8 vols. Tokyo: Iwanami Shoten, 1989–91.

Kuroda 1989
Kuroda Motoki. "Kuno Hōjō ni kansuru ichi kōsatsu: Hōjō (Gen'an) Sōtetsu to sono zokuen kankei o chūshin to shite." *Miura kobunka* 45 (June 1989): 30–46.

Kuroda 1997
Kuroda Motoki. *Sengoku daimyō ryōgoku no shihai kōzō.* Tokyo: Iwata Shoin, 1997.

Kuroda 2012
Kuroda Motoki. *Koga kubō to Hōjō-shi.* Tokyo: Iwata Shoin, 2012.

Legge 1966
Legge, James, trans. *The Sacred Books of China: The Texts of Confucianism.* Vol. 1, *The Shū King: The Religious Portions of the Shih King, the Hsiāo King.* Oxford: Clarendon Press, 1879. Reprinted, New Delhi: Motilal Banarsidass, 1966.

Matsumoto 2001
Matsumoto Kazuo. *Tōgoku shugo no rekishiteki tokushitsu.* Tokyo: Iwata Shoin, 2001.

Odawara-shū shoryō yakuchō
Sugiyama Hiroshi, ed. *Odawara-shū shoryō yakuchō.* Tokyo: Kondō Shuppansha, 1969.

Ogino 1975
Ogino Minahiko. "Musashi no Kira-shi ni tsuite no kenkyū: Gohōjō-shi no kōbō ni kanren shite." In *Kira-shi no kenkyū,* edited by Ogino Minahiko, 11–114. Tokyo: Meicho Shuppan, 1975.

Ōtomo Yoshiaki okibumi
Ōtomo Yoshiaki okibumi. In *Chūsei hōsei shiryō shū,* vol. 4, edited by Satō Shin'ichi and Momose Kesao, pp. 203–5, doc. 307. Tokyo: Iwanami Shoten, 1998.

Saitama-ken shi
Saitama-ken, ed. *Shinpen Saitama-ken shi shiryōhen.* 26 vols. Urawa: Saitama-ken, 1979–90.

Sakai 1999
Sakai Kimi. "Ōnin no ran to zaichi shakai." In *Kōza Nihon shōenshi,* edited by Amino Yoshihiko, Ishii Susumu, Inagaki Yasuhiko, and Nagahara Keiji, vol. 4, *Shōen no kaitai,* 105–50. Tokyo: Yoshikawa Kōbunkan, 1999.

Satō 1989
    Satō Hironobu. *Koga kubō Ashikaga-shi no kenkyū.* Tokyo: Azekura Shobō, 1989.
Shimoyama 1975
    Shimoyama Haruhisa. "Kira-shi kenkyū no seika to kadai." In *Kira-shi no kenkyū,* edited by Ogino Minahiko, 275–322. Tokyo: Meicho Shuppan, 1975.
Spafford 2013
    Spafford, David. *A Sense of Place: The Political Landscape in Late Medieval Japan.* Cambridge, MA: Harvard University Asia Center, 2013.
Spafford 2014
    Spafford, David. "What's in a Name? House Revival, Adoption, and the Bounds of Family in Late Medieval Japan. *Harvard Journal of Asiatic Studies* 47:2 (December 2014): 281–331.
Tabata 1994
    Tabata Yasuko. *Nihon chūsei joseishi ron.* Tokyo: Kashiwa Shobō, 1994.
Tabata 1998
    Tabata Yasuko. *Nihon chūsei no shakai to josei.* Tokyo: Yoshikawa Kōbunkan, 1998.
Takahashi 1991
    Takahashi Hideki. "Chūseiteki 'ie' no seiritsu to chakushi." *Shigaku zasshi* 100:9 (September 1991): 62–82.
Takahashi 2004
    Takahashi Hideki. *Chūsei no ie to sei.* Tokyo: Yamakawa Shuppansha, 2004.
Takeda Nobushige kakun
    Takeda Nobushige kakun. In *Buke kakun, ikun shūsei,* edited by Ozawa Tomio. Revised and expanded, 124–45. Tokyo: Perikansha, 2003.
Tochigi-ken shi
    Tochigi-ken Shi Hensan Iinkai, ed. *Tochigi-ken shi shiryōhen.* 25 vols. Utsunomiya: Tochigi-ken, 1973–80.
Toby 2001
    Toby, Ronald P. "Rescuing the Nation from History: The State of the State in Early Modern Japan." *Monumenta Nipponica* 56:2 (Summer 2001): 197–237.
Tonomura 1990
    Tonomura, Hitomi. "Women and Inheritance in Japan's Early Warrior Society." *Comparative Studies in Society and History* 32:3 (July 1990): 592–623.

2

Adoption and the Maintenance of the Early Modern Elite

Japan in the East Asian Context

Marcia Yonemoto

More than anywhere else in the early modern world, adoption in late imperial China, Chosŏn Korea, and Tokugawa Japan was a way of life. Legally codified and socially sanctioned, the practice of adopting to acquire an heir was not simply a strategy to optimize family success; given the demographic realities pertaining at the time, it was absolutely necessary for perpetuating the family system itself, in political, economic, and spiritual terms.

The reliance on adoption stemmed from a problem common across early modern East Asia: in contrast to the demographic pattern typical in preindustrial societies, in which rates of fertility and mortality tended to be high and population growth substantial, the Chinese, Korean, and Japanese populations overall between the sixteenth and late nineteenth centuries experienced relatively low fertility, moderate mortality, and low to moderate population growth.[1] At the same time, due to shared Confucian ideals, families felt compelled to practice male primogeniture in matters of succession and inheritance. These two essentially incompatible factors—strict succession rules on the one hand, and a limited pool of potential heirs on the other—made an alternative solution necessary if the family system were to survive. Adoption was that solution.

However, adoption took quite different forms across East Asia, in great part because kinship, marriage, and succession practices—indeed the structure of family systems themselves—developed along distinct trajectories in each place over time. This chapter begins by briefly summarizing recent research in the historical demography of late imperial China and Chosŏn Korea with regard to adoption, and then uses those findings as the broader context in which to discuss the results of my own and other scholars' research on adoption and succession in Tokugawa Japan. While the bulk of the research discussed here pertains to the elite classes—the Chinese imperial bureaucracy, the Chosŏn aristocracy, and the early modern Japanese shogunal and daimyo houses—I also include additional information on adoption practices among rural commoners in early modern Japan, information made possible by the maintenance and preservation of local demographic records dating from the early seventeenth through the late nineteenth centuries, and decades of historical research drawing on those records. Ultimately, I argue that even in the East Asian context, in which adoption of heirs was common and accepted, early modern Japanese warrior and commoner families stand out in terms of the frequency and flexibility with which they implemented adoption. To a greater degree than their contemporaries in China and Korea, early modern Japanese families adopted adults and children, men and women, kin and nonkin in an exceptionally free and unregulated manner. Although the form, practice, and ideology of adoption in Japan shifted significantly after the late nineteenth century, the importance of adoption—in particular the adoption of adults and, within that category, of sons-in-law—in maintaining the Japanese family system in ways that, notably, benefited both men (directly) and women (indirectly) has few parallels in world history.[2]

HOW COMMON WAS ADOPTION AMONG THE RULING ELITE IN EARLY MODERN EAST ASIA?

We may begin by comparing rates of adoption within the early modern East Asian elite, specifically, the Ming (1368–1644) and Qing (1644–1911) imperial lines, the Qing nobility, the Korean royal house (Yi or Chosŏn dynasty, 1392–1910), the upper ranks of the Korean aristocracy in the Chosŏn period, the Tokugawa shogunal house (1603–1868), and a sampling of early modern Japanese warrior houses. There are several reasons for beginning an assessment of adoption with the ruling classes. First, across the region the importance of lineage as a determinant of power compelled political regimes to compile detailed genealogical records for the elite. While not without their biases and inaccuracies, these records contain an extraordinary amount of information about births, deaths, marriage, and succession in elite families—and by extension the ruling regimes themselves—that is invaluable for examining how they sustained and perpetuated themselves over time. Only in Japan does a comparable volume of demographic information for commoners survive. Second, across the region the educated upper classes bore responsibility for embodying Confucian values and practices, and as a result one would think that the dictates of male primogeniture—specifically, succession by the eldest biological son of the principal wife—would be most strictly observed among the elite. Third, Confucian prescriptions regarding adopted heirs—namely, that adoption should be resorted to only in the absence of biological male heirs, and that adoptees should be chosen from among the ranks of close male agnatic kin—would presumably be followed more closely by elite families. The latter two reasons suggest that adoption among elites would reflect a relatively greater degree of attention to orthodoxy and exercise of restraint, making it a "limit case" exemplifying the lowest level of tolerance for heir adoption.

If we make this assumption—that adoption among the elite would for ideological reasons be limited and restrained—it is not surprising to see that there were no adoptions for succession in the Ming or Qing imperial lines, and only one case of adoption out of twenty-five cases of succession in the Chosŏn, or Yi, royal lineage (see table 2.1). By contrast, four out of the fourteen men who succeeded to the office of shogun in the Tokugawa period were adopted by their predecessors (28 percent of all shogunal successions). And, further, if we look to adoption within the broader elite classes, the frequency of adoption for heirship increased substantially overall across the region, with Japanese elites again adopting heirs at significantly higher rates than their East Asian neighbors: 6.5 percent of surveyed succession cases among the Qing nobility involved adopted heirs, whereas the figure is 19 percent among the Chosŏn high aristocracy, and between 17 percent (in the seventeenth century) and 27 percent (in the eighteenth century) among early modern Japanese warrior houses of all ranks.[3] In all three countries, elite families adopted most frequently because they lacked sons, and the most ideologically appropriate solution was to adopt a single male kinsman to serve as heir.[4] Further, when adopting for heirship, Chinese, Korean, and Japanese families generally preferred to adopt an older child or adult in part to avoid the perils of infant and early childhood mortality, but also to discern whether or not the adoptee would make a suitable heir and house head. Across the region, rates of adoption by elite families increased steadily from the late seventeenth through the early nineteenth centuries.

But in each country there were also extenuating circumstances that influenced the decision to adopt and that shaped the particular and distinct forms that adoption took. These differences require some explanation. In Korea in the early Chosŏn period (c. fifteenth to sixteenth centuries) elite families engaged in a variety of adoption and inheritance practices, including adopting daughters, adopting couples, adopting the husbands of biological or adopted daughters as heirs, and allowing heirship to pass to younger sons.[5] By the seventeenth century, however, Confucian ideals had taken firm hold among the Korean aristocracy, and convention dictated inheritance only by eldest sons; evidence of assumption of heirship by younger sons all but disappears from the genealogical records, and the subsequent ritual and demographic pressures compelled more frequent adoption of sons to serve as heirs.[6] A similar trend toward more frequent adoption can be seen among the Qing nobility in the seventeenth through nineteenth centuries, but in this case the pressures were less ideological than demographic; as Wang Feng and James Lee show, there was a direct correlation between the decrease in the number

TABLE 2.1. Succession by adoption within the early modern East Asian ruling elite

	Chinese imperial line (Ming)[1]	Chinese imperial line (Qing)[2]	Qing nobility (1640–1900)[3]	Korean royal house (Yi)[4]	Korean aristocracy (Yi)[5]	Tokugawa shogunal house[6]	Japanese warrior houses, 17th cent.[7]	Japanese warrior houses, 18th cent.
Adopted heirs, as percentage of all (or all sampled) succession cases	0	0	6.5	4	19	28	17	27
Adopted sons-in-law allowed?	No	No	No	No	No	Yes	Yes	Yes
Adopted sons-in-law, as percentage of all (or all sampled) adopted heirs	N/a	N/a	N/a	N/a	N/a	0	41	30

[1] Percentages derived by the author from information on Ming imperial succession in Rawski 2015, 148, table 4.1.

[2] Percentages derived by the author from information on Qing imperial succession in Mote 1999, 822; and Rawski 1998

[3] See Wang and Lee 1998, 411–27.

[4] Percentages derived by the author from information on Joseon royal succession in Rawski 2015, 167, table 4.5.

[5] See Kim and Park 2010, 443–52.

[6] Percentages derived by the author from information on Tokugawa shogunal succession in Rawski 2010, 161, table 4.4, and in *Kokushi daijiten*, vol. 10, pp. 287–89.

[7] Percentages derived by the author from data collected by Tsubouchi Reiko on 10,665 cases of succession in the Hagi Mōri, Saga Nabeshima, Morioka Nanbu, Akita Satake, Aizu, and Kaga Maeda domains in the seventeenth and eighteenth centuries; see Tsubouchi 1992, 63–74; Tsubouchi 2000; and Tsubouchi 2001, 29–59, 81–94, 98–113, 121–32, 137–49.

of sons born to elite families and the increase in the number of adoptions for heirship in those same families.[7]

Small family size and the absence of biological heirs also compelled Japanese warrior families to adopt heirs; but we must also consider other factors in accounting for their significantly higher rates of adoption. One contributing factor was the relative importance of blood ties as a determinant of membership in a given house or family. As compared to the Qing nobility and the Chosŏn aristocracy, the need to maintain close blood ties between generations—that is, between house or lineage heads and their successors—was comparatively weak in early modern Japan.[8] Unlike the Tokugawa, the Qing was an ethnic-minority conquest dynasty that sought throughout its reign to actively promote Manchu ethnicity and identity within its ruling elite by strategically intermarrying with Han and Mongol elites, and by compelling officeholders to demonstrate proficiency in Manchu language as well as in martial arts, administration, and scholarship.[9] Direct blood ties, especially to the founding dynasts, Nurgaci and Hongtaiji, remained the main conduit of ethnicity and the main determinant of kinship.[10] From the seventeenth century onward, the Chosŏn aristocracy, for its part, pursued the adoption of male agnatic kin in the absence of biological male heirs in order to maintain blood ties through the patriline over time. It did so in order to observe Confucian principles, but also to counteract the power traditionally held (during the Koryŏ [918–1392] and early Chosŏn periods) by the ruler's affinal kin, whose interests, when asserted, had caused numerous violent succession struggles in the royal house.[11] Limiting heirs to agnatic kin thus constrained the number of potential heirs and was intended to contain conflict as well, although this strategy did not prove entirely successful.[12]

The Tokugawa warrior elite, by contrast, lacked the ethnic difference of the Manchu dynasts and the recent history of severe competition between agnates and affines in matters of succession that troubled the Chosŏn dynasty. The Japanese warrior elite thus had greater latitude to determine kinship in ways that served particular family and lineage needs, and its members were relatively freer to choose heirs from a wider range of possible successors: affines, agnates, and distantly related and unrelated individuals were all possible adoptees. Even cross-generational adoption (adopting one's younger brother as one's son, for example), which directly violated Confucian ritual principles of succession, was allowed and frequently practiced in Tokugawa Japan.[13] Still, at the highest levels of the warrior class, adoption practices conformed at least nominally to Confucian norms: within the shogunal house, the four adoptees who assumed the title of shogun were all agnatic kin, drawn from the ranks of the collateral houses of the Tokugawa.

But among daimyo and warrior houses outside the Tokugawa shogunal line, adoption practices varied more widely. Table 2.1 aggregates and broadly summarizes Tsubouchi Reiko's research on succession during the seventeenth and eighteenth centuries in more than ten thousand warrior houses in six large domains scattered throughout Japan: Nanbu in the far northeast, Akita and Aizu in inland eastern Honshu, Kaga on the Japan Sea coast, Hagi on the southwestern tip of Honshu, and Nabeshima in northern Kyushu. In all these domains in the seventeenth century, in a significant majority of succession cases heirship went to the oldest son. In the eighteenth century, however, the frequency of oldest-son succession decreased, in some cases quite dramatically, and the frequency of adoption for heirship rose at a correspondingly significant rate. The decrease in oldest-son succession and the increase in succession by adoptees was greatest in Nabeshima domain, where oldest-son succession decreased from 71 to 47 percent from the seventeenth to the eighteenth century, and adoptee succession rose from 12 to 22 percent during the same time period. Similar, if slightly smaller, ratios of decline and increase could be seen in Hagi, Aizu, and Akita domains.[14] Overall, in every one of the six domains surveyed, the general trend over time was for family headship to go less often to oldest sons and more often to adoptees, both single adoptees and adopted sons-in-law. Furthermore, among single adoptees, in three of the six domains it is possible to discern whether adopted heirs were kin (*dōsei yōshi*) or nonkin (*isei yōshi*), and in all three cases nonkin significantly outnumbered kin adoptees.[15]

What explains these trends? The primary cause was the absence of biological male offspring. This was due to in part to higher mortality, exacerbated in certain areas, such as the northeast, by economic hardship in the eighteenth century. But warrior families also lacked heirs because they strategically sent their sons out for adoption to other houses. For younger sons, who would not expect to inherit house headship in their natal families, adoption into another family in order to become its heir was not only preferable but desirable. One example is the Sakaki-bara of Takada domain in Echigo Province, a wealthy high-ranking daimyo house of 150,000 *koku*. In the early Tokugawa period, the Sakakibara were financially able to establish younger sons in branch houses, and there are no recorded adoptions of males out of the family until the late eighteenth century. But from the 1770s on, as domain finances deteriorated, nearly all noninheriting sons were adopted out to other houses; the ninth-generation heir Masanaga (1735–1808) adopted out six of his sons. The trend continued with his heir Masaatsu (1755–1819), who adopted out two sons, and also with the subsequent eleventh-generation heir Masanori (1776–1861), who adopted out four sons in spite of the fact that domain finances had revived somewhat by his time.[16] The majority of these sons went to lower-ranking daimyo or direct shogunal retainer (*hatamoto*) families, but since they were adopted as heirs, their future prospects for independence, if not for advancement, were brighter than they would have been had they stayed at home.[17] However, this strategy sometimes backfired, for a family that had adopted out its "surplus" sons itself found that it had no heir if the remaining male offspring died young or became incapacitated, making adoption of an heir necessary.

Such cases bring us to a second reason that might account for the relative frequency of heir adoptions among the early modern Japanese warrior elite: the widespread practice of adopting a daughter's husband as heir. Such adopted sons-in-law, most commonly referred to as *muko yōshi* or *iri muko*, constituted an average of 40 percent of all adoptions for succession and an average of 10 percent of all succession cases in the six warrior houses surveyed by Tsubouchi from the seventeenth and eighteenth centuries. Adopted sons-in-law were and remain a distinctly Japanese phenomenon. Elite families in late imperial China rarely adopted sons-in-law, and never for heirship; while son-in-law adoption was tolerated in early Chosŏn Korea, within the aristocracy the practice all but ceased by the seventeenth century.[18] For early modern Chinese and Korean elites, nominal patrilineality was not enough: to adopt a son-in-law was to achieve lineage continuity through daughters rather than sons, and this was fundamentally unacceptable. But the early modern Japanese warrior elite, as discussed above, were much less bound by principles of patrilineality and blood ties. As a result adopted sons-in-law, many of whom were distant kin or nonkin, played a crucial role in shoring up an otherwise fragile stem-family system. Wakita Osamu argues that house heads in the Fukōzu Matsudaira, a Tokugawa collateral house, adopted sons-in-law so frequently that they effectively continued their line of descent through their daughters as much as they did through their sons (biological or adopted).[19] Among fourteen other Matsudaira lineages in the same period, a third of household successions went to adoptees, and a third of those adoptees were sons-in-law, the majority of whom were nonkin.[20] Because the Matsudaira were high-ranking collaterals, they could be expected to be somewhat more conservative in their approach to adoption, and they could also be expected to want to keep descent within the kin group; however, their adoption practices suggest that neither was the case.

Indeed, for such warrior families, adopting a daughter's husband as heir could be an optimal succession strategy. In terms of kinship ties, the adoptee's offspring would still be direct descendants of the house head, albeit through the matriline rather than the patriline. For warrior houses of lower status, the economic benefits of adoption were also compelling. Adopting sons-in-law counteracted the threat of resource dispersion, for the possibility that family assets would be scattered more broadly, and potentially subject to the control of "outsiders," was held in check by matrilineal continuity through daughters.

Even more critically, due to the practice of providing dowries for adopted sons-in-law when they married into their wives' families, adoption could be economically beneficial to a receiving family.[21] For while the Tokugawa period was an era of significant economic growth and change, that growth, as we know, was largely confined to the commoner class. By the eighteenth century, access to rank and office had become hereditary, and social mobility among samurai declined. Perpetuation of the family became practically more difficult, and additional financial resources had to be sought outside the regular channels of stipend or borrowing. Warrior families therefore had to find ways to maximize limited opportunities for achievement for both male and female offspring. Adoption of sons-in-law not only enabled the family to achieve stability because it could secure an heir, but also ensured that the adopting family's daughter would at least maintain the status of her own family, for she never left it. Finally, adopted sons-in-law often came from families of higher rank than those into which they married and were adopted. The receiving family could then benefit from the status and wealth of their heir's natal family.

Furthermore, adoption of sons-in-law, who were often adolescents or adults at the time of adoption, proved beneficial because, to put it bluntly, adoption of an heir could be more expedient than birthing and raising one. Adoption of a son-in-law was more efficient with regard to succession because the adoptee was brought into the family in late childhood or early adulthood, when his physical survival was more likely, his potential as house head could be more accurately gauged, and the not inconsiderable costs of his early upbringing and education had already been covered by his natal family. The sending family, for its part, benefited as well. While they had to render the dowry, which was a financial burden for them, by adopting out a noninheriting son, the family was able (again, putting it bluntly) to shed a dependent who would otherwise contribute relatively little to the family's fortunes and, indeed, could possibly become a drain on them. Curiously, adoption could also make intrafamily relationships more harmonious. As Tsubouchi shows, in Hagi domain in the seventeenth and eighteenth centuries, even if there were one or more sons in the household at the time of succession, an adopted son-in-law might be preferable as heir: of warrior houses with only one son, about half chose to send the biological son out for adoption to another house and to adopt a son-in-law as heir in his stead.[22] This was perhaps because, especially in houses of higher rank, if sons were not born to the principal wife, or were born of a successor wife and were substantially younger than siblings, they were more likely to cause conflict over succession, and this might compel a house head to adopt out his biological sons and designate a son-in-law as heir to ensure smoother transition of heirship.[23]

The economic as well as social benefits of adopting a son-in-law are well documented in the literature. Clearly, poorer samurai families benefited considerably from the dowries that adopted sons and sons-in-law could bring, but even wealthy and powerful houses adopted strategically, with an eye to the extra income an adoptee could bring.[24] Tahara Noboru has shown, through analysis of lineage records as well as "inside" sources documenting negotiations over adoption, that by the late eighteenth century, even the powerful and wealthy daimyo that controlled entire provinces (the so-called kunimochi daimyo) began to look outside their kin group to adopt sons and sons-in-law as heirs who had proved themselves capable, or whose families of origin were politically well connected.[25] These cases show how adopted sons-in-law could be a practical solution to the perpetual problem of maintaining or increasing status and wealth through a distinctly early modern version of an old pattern in which elite families gained power through marriage politics.[26] Using adoption strategically in this way was a tactic used most extensively by early modern Japanese warrior families. In part it grew out of a long tradition—informal and extralegal though it had become by the early modern period—of reckoning kinship bilaterally (that is, on the maternal as well as paternal sides) in Japanese elite families. But it was also a response to the growing economic pressures on the warrior elite in the mid- to late Tokugawa period. Barred from commerce and agriculture and therefore unable to benefit from the economic growth that fueled commoner prosperity, the samurai's only assets were his name, his office, and his stipend. And since transmission of those assets had become almost entirely hereditary by the eighteenth century, an elite family's fortunes depended entirely on how well it managed and preserved the integrity of its lineage. With the stakes so high, it is no wonder that even high-status families dispensed with niceties and made sure their heirs and, through them, their families' futures were bought and paid for.

THE EFFECTS OF HEIR ADOPTION

While assessing the social and economic context of heir adoption might well give us some insight into the reasons families chose that option, we also need to attend to the effects that the practice had on families themselves. The long-term consequences of adoption on individual families and on the family structure were many, but I address here what I believe are two of the more significant effects. One was that frequent adoption of heirs significantly lessened the pressure on women to bear sons. With the biological imperative made less pressing due to the safety net provided by heir adoption, husbands and families could look beyond reproductive function to value wives and daughters for other qualities; they could also spare time and resources, when available, to foster their other skills and talents. No less than Kaibara Ekiken, in the section of his popular work *Teachings on Nurturing Life* (*Yōjōkun*, 1713), devoted to "methods for educating girls," emphasizes this very point in his seldom-read commentary on female infertility, which was one of the oft-cited "seven reasons" a man could divorce his wife. He writes that even if she cannot bear children, "if the wife has a gentle heart, if her actions are good, if she is not envious, does not deviate from the proper path of womanhood, and satisfies her husband and father-in-law, a man might consider adopting a child from one of his siblings or other relatives and continuing the family line [in this manner], without divorcing his wife. Or, if a mistress or concubine has a child, even if the [legitimate] wife doesn't produce an heir, she need not be divorced."[27] In other words, for Ekiken, a woman's innate virtues and talents and her compatibility as a spouse were of greater value than her fertility. A family heir could be acquired by other means, through adoption or by a concubine. Indeed, beyond Ekiken's opinions, fecundity itself was not much valued in prescriptive writings for women. While instructional manuals often lay out for their readers clear guidelines for ensuring the conception and birth of physically and morally healthy offspring, they do not uncritically advocate the position that more children is better.[28]

Such values also might also serve to explain why samurai house heads would choose to adopt heirs instead of taking in concubines to produce more offspring and increase the pool of potential biological heirs. Like Chinese and Korean elite males of high status, samurai men regularly kept concubines. In fact, concubines were key to the perpetuation of ruling regimes across the region, for despite professed adherence to the principal of succession by eldest sons of principal wives, substantial numbers of heirs to the Ming and Qing imperial throne, the Yi royal house, and the Tokugawa shogunate were the offspring of secondary consorts; in two of the four cases, the Qing emperors and the Tokugawa shoguns, the majority of heirs were born to secondary consorts.[29] In early modern Japan, sons born of concubines of samurai house heads could succeed their fathers on the same terms and with the same privileges as sons born to the principal wife. But for many lower-ranking Tokugawa samurai looking to perpetuate their lineages, maintaining concubines was not easy, for acquiring and supporting them and their children were costly, a privilege only wealthier families could afford. For those lower on the status hierarchy, adoption may have been a more accessible option than concubinage for procuring an heir.

Another reason adoption may have been preferable to taking concubines had to do with intrafamilial personal relationships: concubines and mistresses often caused disharmony within families, no matter what their status. The prescriptive literature for women is full of admonitions to wives not to succumb to jealousy or envy of their husband's concubines. A good wife, the texts repeat, should tolerate her husband's other women and should welcome his children by them into her family and raise them as her own. One suspects, however, that for many women, such equanimity was difficult to achieve in practice, and if an heir could be acquired by other means that endangered family harmony less, that would have been preferable. Furthermore, especially in families of high rank, principal wives often were themselves daughters of houses of wealth and status, and affinal ties could be important for advancing and maintaining a family's status. Designating a son of a concubine as heir—even if the heir were accepted and raised by the principal wife—might endanger politically and economically important relationships with a wife's kin. All of the above factors combined helped make it possible for an elite society predicated on patrilineal descent and deeply influenced by a pro-natalist philosophy to perpetuate a family system that accommodated women who bore few or no sons.

ADOPTION AMONG COMMONER FAMILIES

If we pursue this logic further, it stands to reason that adoption would be even more prevalent within the commoner class, whose members had fewer resources to support large families and keep concubines, and in which the pressure to maintain blood ties within a lineage across time was perhaps felt less intensely, even though family continuity remained extremely important.[30] Japanese historical demographers have turned their attention to adoption and family survival strategies among rural commoners in the Tokugawa period. Kurosu Satomi analyzed changes over time in two villages in northeastern Honshu, Shimomoriya and Nihonmatsu, for which population data are relatively complete for most of the Tokugawa period. Along with Ochiai Emiko, Kurosu also examined a detailed population register compiled in 1870 by the Meiji government for villages in South Tama, located just west of Tokyo, and Hayami Akira studied village population registers in Nishijō, in the Nobi Plain in central western Honshu.[31] In these four communities, the scholars were able to discern overall rates of adoption for heirship and, in two cases, rates of adoption of sons-in-law as heirs. Their findings are summarized in table 2.2.[32] It is immediately apparent that while elites (defined here as the Tokugawa shogunal house and the warrior houses discussed above) adopted heirs at slightly higher rates, commoners in these four rural areas chose to adopt sons-in-law considerably more often than their samurai contemporaries. For commoner families, the economic benefits of son-in-law adoption (dowry), as well as its relatively greater efficiency and security as a succession strategy (no worry about finding a bride for an adopted son; keeping a daughter at home), made it the succession strategy of choice for a considerable majority of the commoner families surveyed.[33]

One notable aspect of son-in-law adoption worth emphasizing further was that the practice allowed families to keep a daughter who otherwise would have married and moved to her husband's residence, in the natal home. The prevalence of adoption of sons-in-law arguably increased the importance of female offspring, for daughters became more valuable to families because they could attract in-marrying husbands who, like their samurai contemporaries, tended to be non-inheriting younger sons who would benefit from becoming heirs to their wives' families. The results of this increased valuation of daughters can be seen in part in demographic records. Whereas the biological imperatives of consanguineal family systems such as China's contributed to the well-documented prevalence of female infanticide and skewed sex ratios, the Tokugawa archives show no evidence of consistent and widespread measures taken to suppress the number of female offspring in favor of males.[34] To be sure, infanticide was common, especially among farm families, but it tended not to be consistently sex-selective in favor of males. Rather, when possible, parents seem to have preferred to vary the sexes of their children to achieve a balance of female and male offspring, showing a marked preference for sons only when the ideal number of children had been reached.[35] For their part, instructional manuals for women devote considerable attention to childbearing and child-rearing, but they do not show pervasive gender bias in favor of males. In other words, even though the threat of lineage extinction due

TABLE 2.2. Adoption and succession in four rural communities, 1720–1870

	Shimomoriya, NE Japan, 1757–1829[1]	South Tama peasant household registers, 1870[2]	Nihonmatsu, NE Japan, 1720–1870[3]	Nishijō, Nobi Plain, 1773–1869[4]	Average for sampled commoners	Average for sampled elites
Adopted heirs, as percentage of all sampled succession cases	29	20	24	12	21	27
Adopted sons-in-law, as percentage of all adopted heirs	70	53	N/a	N/a	66	30

[1] Data from Kurosu 1998.
[2] Data from Kurosu and Ochiai 1995.
[3] Data from Kurosu 1998.
[4] Data from Hayami 1992.

to the absence of male heirs loomed large, Japanese families appear not to have maneuvered to have sons at the cost of daughters. It can be argued that the prevalence of adoption for succession in general, and of adopted sons-in-law in particular, was one of the main reasons Japanese women avoided the fate that befell their Chinese contemporaries.

Furthermore, adopting a son-in-law enabled a family to continue to benefit from a daughter's labor and natural authority within the family, and allowed her to remain in familiar surroundings rather than suffering the fate of most women in conventional marriages, who found themselves in their husbands' homes under the watchful eye of his relatives and, if his parents were still living, under the thumb of his mother-in-law, the outgoing (at least in theory) household manager. Like in-marrying wives, adopted sons-in-law were not in an enviable position. The demands placed upon them were pressing, and their responsibilities were many, for the fate of the lineage depended on their fulfilling the role for which they were brought into their wives' families. At the same time, they lacked the day-to-day support that might have been provided by their natal families. Wakita Osamu has shown that divorce in adopted son-in-law alliances among the warrior class was relatively frequent, and that women sometimes took successive married-in heirs-husbands serially. He contends that the divorce of adoptive heirs and remarriage of daughters to subsequent adopted sons suggests that families used not only marriage but remarriage(s) of their daughters as a strategy for securing the most suitable heir, even if it meant trying out and rejecting one or more sons-in-law in the process.[36] Ōtō Osamu, by contrast, shows that in peasant communities, divorcing an adopted son-in-law was a complicated process because of the cooperative and interdependent nature of rural farm life and village structure; a family's decision to send away an adopted son-in-law had repercussions for the village at large, and families therefore had to obtain the consent of village officials in order to finalize a divorce.[37] Still, the aphorism "An only daughter can choose among eight potential husbands" suggests that despite the challenges and the possibilities for failure, men seeking adoption as sons-in-law were not few.[38]

Finally, the practice of adopting sons-in-law may well have contributed to the relatively high degree of "conjugal power" possessed by Japanese commoner women. G. William Skinner, in his study of peasant communities in the Nobi Plain during the Tokugawa period, found that power relations in marriage and in the family were much less skewed in favor of men and husbands than in patrilineal joint families in late imperial China. In Japanese peasant families, Skinner observed, women and men had essentially complementary roles in the family in terms of their labor and their spheres of authority. Skinner calls the early modern Japanese family system one in which patriarchy was notably "attenuated."[39] I have argued elsewhere that this attenuation—but by no means erasure or negation—of patriarchy also characterized gender relations in the warrior class, although it took different forms of expression.[40]

In sum, adoption, especially of sons-in-law, allowed early modern Japanese families to achieve what should have been impossible: a pattern of descent that was both patrilineal and often consanguineal, but that did not require a couple to bear a son. Flexible and frequent adoption made it possible to bypass the constraints of biology and continue the *ie* indefinitely. It also enabled the full utilization of the energies of every member of a household, especially its women. Son-in-law adoption in particular encouraged a greater degree of gender role complementarity than was commonly seen in Chinese or Korean elite families in the early modern period, because it freed women from the biological imperative to birth a son and also from the social pressures that role entailed. Overall, the history of adoption reveals, perhaps better than any other social or legal practice, the durable nature, the critical importance, and the extraordinary flexibility of the *ie* in Japan. Focusing on adoption also reveals how the *ie* differs significantly in structure and function from the family systems prevalent in other parts of East Asia, most notably in its responsiveness to change, circumstance, and even, occasionally, individual desires and aspirations.

NOTES

1. The findings of scholars of historical demography indicate that population dynamics in China, Korea, and Japan in the early modern period were roughly similar in general trajectory, yet strikingly asynchronous: each country saw initial periods of sustained, moderate to high levels of population growth, followed by a period of stasis; but in China the stasis period lasted from the eleventh through the sixteenth century, in Korea from the late eighteenth through the mid-nineteenth century, and in Japan from the early eighteenth through the late nineteenth century. This static phase was followed by dramatic population growth in the mid- to late nineteenth century (in the case of China, growth was significant but steady in the seventeenth and eighteenth centuries and exploded in the early twentieth century; in Japan and Korea, growth began to accelerate in the late nineteenth century). More significant are findings regarding fertility: early modern China, Japan, and Korea were characterized by relatively low fertility as compared to European countries; see comparative statistics in Wang, Lee, and Campbell 1995, p. 385; see also Lee and Wang 2001. On Japan's demographic profile, see Hayami 2009 and 2015; see also Drixler 2013.

2. While the differences in the nature and frequency of adoption practices in early modern Japan as compared to the rest of East Asia is noticeable, the contrast between Japan and western Europe in the early modern period is striking. Adoption for heirship was widely practiced in the Roman Empire and in classical Greece, much in the way it was and continues to be practiced in East Asia; but with the advent of Christianity such practices disappeared, to the extent that the demographic historian Antoinette Fauve-Chamoux describes the history of adoption in Europe as "a history of non-adoption." See Fauve-Chamoux 1996, 1–14; see also Fauve-Chamoux 1998. Recent studies have modified this picture, if selectively, and rarely with regard to elites. Eighteenth-century Finnish farm families, for example,

seem to have adopted sons-in-law in the absence of biological male heirs, and adoption of children, even by single women, appears to have occurred quite often among the middling commoner classes in urban France during the sixteenth century, occasionally for the purpose of continuing the family into the next generation. On the Finns, see Moring 2009, 173–202; on forms of adoption in sixteenth-century urban France, see Gager 1996. While elite families did begin to engineer strategies for economic and social success in early modern England, adoption does not appear to have been among those strategies; see, for example, Stone 1979. One example I have found of adoption among European elites is some evidence of strategic adoption of heirs and godparenting of politically powerful younger male kin by a few kings of sixth-century Gaul; see Jussen 2000. For a summary discussion in English of Japan's distinctive adoption culture, see MacFarlane 2003, 360–66.

3. The figure of 17 percent (seventeenth century) to 27 percent (eighteenth century) for adopted heirs in early modern warrior houses is likely on the low side. Takeuchi Toshimi surveyed daimyo genealogies in the early-nineteenth-century *Kansei chōshū shokafu* compiled by the Tokugawa shogunate and found that in the early seventeenth century (Kan'ei through Keian eras, 1614–51), approximately 8.2 percent of all men born into daimyo houses were adopted; this figure rose dramatically to 31.3 percent by the late eighteenth century (Kanpō 11 to Kansei 6, 1741–94) and continued to rise into the nineteenth century. Taniguchi Nobuo found that approximately 30 percent of heirs were adopted in the eighteenth-century Okayama domain, and Hattori Hiroshi found approximately 50 percent of heirs were adopted in the late-eighteenth- and early-nineteenth-century Kanazawa domain. The data are summarized in Kamata 1988, 62–63. As Anne Walthall observes in her article in this volume, these figures lead Kamata to state that "around 40 percent of all cases of succession [in warrior houses] were the result of adoption" (Kamata 1988, 62–63). However, because Kamata does not give comprehensive evidence to substantiate this rough estimate, I have chosen here to draw on Tsubouchi Reiko's more extensive data (see Tsubouchi 1992, 2000, and 2001). One should note further that these figures refer only to officially documented adoptions for heirship; they do not take into consideration the various forms of informal adoption, including the types of temporary adoption described by Anne Walthall in this volume, nor do they include adoption of daughters, siblings, or others who were not heirs.

4. On the absence of sons and agnatic kin adoption in the Qing nobility, see Wang and Lee 1998, 418; on the absence of sons and agnatic kin adoption in the Chosŏn aristocracy, see Kim and Park 2010, 447; data show that in the vast majority of both the Chinese and the Korean adoption cases, the adopting family did not have biological sons.

5. See Kim and Park 2010, 444. While the Chosŏn dynasty began in the late fourteenth century, scholarly consensus holds that not until the sixteenth century were Neo-Confucian norms widely assimilated into Korean society, and not until the seventeenth century did social structures change to the degree that they had a significant and widespread impact on individuals and families. See Ko, Haboush, and Piggott 1994, 11.

6. Kim and Park 2010, 448; Peterson 1996, 164.

7. Whether the decline in sons born is due to decreased fertility or increased mortality is not clear; see Wang and Lee 1998, 448–49.

8. As David Spafford's article in this volume shows, for samurai, active and loyal service to the lord was valued more than kinship in forming a strong and unified house.

9. Rawski 1998, 60–61.

10. Rawski 1998, 60–61.

11. As Mark Peterson argues, "the Korean society we often refer to as traditional, or Confucian, developed in the relatively recent past. . . . Women in the early Yi [Chosŏn] dynasty could succeed to their own family lines, provide successors to their husbands' lines through either sons or daughters, and even have successors in their own right. With the complete Confucianization of society, a woman in the late Yi dynasty retained only the right of providing a successor to her husband's line, and that right was forfeited if she did not bear a son." Peterson 1983, 42–43. On succession struggles in the Chosŏn royal house, see Rawski 2015, 166–84; see also Haboush 1996.

12. In both the late imperial Chinese and Chosŏn Korean cases, one should be careful to avoid suggesting that adoption of nonkin never occurred in any circumstances; as in Japan, unofficial and off-record adoptions almost certainly took place, but there is no reliable way to quantify them.

13. Peterson 1996, 195; see also McMullen 1975.

14. In Kaga Maeda domain the decline in oldest-son succession over time was negligible (57 percent to 53 percent), but the increase in succession by adoptees was more substantial (19 percent to 29 percent); see Tsubouchi 2001, 121–35.

15. The ratios of nonkin adoptees to kin adoptees was 2:1 in Kaga Maeda domain, 5:1 in Akita Satake domain, and 6:1 in Morioka Nanbu domain; see data in Tsubouchi 2001, 29–59, 81–94, 98–113, 121–32, 137–49. This finding reinforces the point made in David Spafford's article in this volume that kinship was not the only, or even the most important, type of relationship binding members of warrior houses.

16. Matsuo 2002, 242–46.

17. Ray Moore argued that within the samurai class, adoption did not positively influence the social or political mobility of the adoptee; Moore 1970. By contrast, among the Chosŏn nobility, adopted sons were more likely to succeed to higher office or gain status than were biological sons; Kim and Park 2010, 450.

18. Nonkin and son-in-law adoptees may well have been adopted informally, however.

19. Even high-ranking families such as the Matsudaira seem to have used adoption not as a last-ditch tactic but as one strategy employed among many to secure the most appropriate male heir and thus better safeguard the family's future. See Wakita 1982, 28.

20. Ōguchi 2001, 5–25. Nonkin adoptees seem to have been preferable in cases of son-in-law adoption, even though in premodern Japan there was remarkably little stigma against close-kin marriage.

21. The term for the dowries brought by adopted sons-in-law was *jisankin*, the same word used for the dowry a bride took to her husband's house in a typical virilocal marriage.

22. Tsubouchi 2000, 124, table 15.

23. Tsubouchi 2000, 124. On intrafamilial conflict over succession, see also Luke Roberts's chapter in this volume.

24. For poorer samurai families, an adopted son-in-law's dowry could be the key to economic survival. See the case of Itō Kaname (d. 1864), his wife, Maki, and their adopted and biological children in Mega 2011, 48–51. Wealthier warrior families also engaged in

strategic adoption; see the case of vigorous bargaining over an adopted son-in-law and his dowry pursued by Aoki Kazuyoshi, a daimyo in Settsū Province, and by a branch of the Date family in the early eighteenth century, in Ōmori 2002. See also Yonemoto 2016, 164–92.

25. Tahara 1998, 135.

26. I refer here to the situation among the court nobility in the Heian period (794–1185), in which powerful male courtiers sought to marry their daughters into the imperial line. Because elite marriages were often matrilocal, if and when their daughters or sisters married well, fathers, brothers, and other male affinal kin could wield significant power in court politics at the highest level. See Nickerson 1993; McCullough 1967.

27. Kaibara 1961, 270–71.

28. For example, Namura Jōhaku opens his discussion of pregnancy and childbirth in the *Onna chōhōki* (a text originally aimed at the lower ranks of the samurai class) by pointing out that whereas in ancient China a couple was advised to delay childbearing until both had achieved physical maturity themselves, in Japan men and women have typically married young and commenced childbearing immediately, with deleterious effects; Namura 1993.

29. The figures for succession by consorts' offspring are as follows: 62 percent of Ming emperors succeeded their biological fathers, and of these, 40 percent were sons of consorts, not of principal wives; among Qing emperors, the respective figures are 80 percent and 60 percent; among Yi dynasty sovereigns, 44 percent and 30 percent; among Tokugawa shoguns, 57 percent and 79 percent.

30. Fabian Drixler's article in this volume explores in some detail the prevalence of adoption among commoners in various regions of Japan, most notably northeastern Honshu.

31. See Kurosu 1998; Kurosu and Ochiai 1995; Hayami 1992.

32. Fabian Drixler's article in this volume posits increasing rates of adoption among commoner families in northeastern Japan between the mid-seventeenth and early nineteenth century. His data from population registers for the northeastern provinces show that by the early nineteenth century "nearly 27 percent of married men whose father or father-in-law served as household head were not the head's biological son," but he notes that this estimate is likely on the low side.

33. The recent work of Toishi Nanami adds an important new perspective on adoption in early modern villages. Toishi argues that adoption was much less an individual familial decision than a corporate village-level decision, and that adoption was a key strategy for village leaders to maintain the number of households—and with it the community's economic and political viability—in an era marked in many regions by declining or static population. See Toishi 2017.

34. On infanticide in China, see Mungello 2008.

35. See, e.g., Drixler 2013, esp. ch. 6.

36. Wakita 1982, 26.

37. Ōtō 1995.

38. Yamakawa 1992, 103.

39. Skinner 1993.

40. Yonemoto 2016, 13–14.

REFERENCES

Deuchler 1983
Deuchler, Martina, Laurel Kendall, and Mark Peterson, eds. *Korean Women: View from the Inner Room*. Cushing, ME: East Rock Press, 1983.

Drixler 2013
Drixler, Fabian. *Mabiki: Infanticide and Population Growth in Eastern Japan, 1660–1950*. Berkeley: University of California Press, 2013.

Fauve-Chamoux 1996
Fauve-Chamoux, Antoinette. "Beyond Adoption: Orphans and Family Strategies." *History of the Family* 1:1 (1996): 1–13.

Fauve-Chamoux 1998
Fauve-Chamoux, Antoinette. "Introduction: Adoption, Affiliation, and Family Recomposition—Inventing Family Continuity." *History of the Family* 3:4 (1998): 385–92.

Gager 1996
Gager, Kristin Elizabeth. *Blood Ties and Fictive Ties: Adoption and Family Life in Early Modern France*. Princeton: Princeton University Press, 1996.

Haboush 1996
Haboush, JaHyun Kim, ed. and trans. *The Memoirs of Lady Hyegyŏng: The Autobiographical Writings of a Crown Princess of Eighteenth-Century Korea*. Berkeley: University of California Press, 1996.

Harafuji 1983
Harafuji Hiroshi. *Bakuhan taisei kokka no hō to kenryoku*, vol. 5: *Sōzoku no tokushitsu*. Tokyo: Sōbunsha, 1983.

Hayami 1992
Hayami Akira. *Kinsei Nobi chihō no jinkō, keizai, shakai*. Tokyo: Sōbunsha, 1992.

Hayami 2009
Hayami Akira. *Population, Family, and Society in Pre-modern Japan*. Folkestone, UK: Global Oriental, 2009.

Hayami 2015
Hayami Akira. *Japan's Industrious Revolution: Economic and Social Transformations in the Early Modern Period*. Tokyo: Springer, 2015.

Jussen 2000
Jussen, Bernhard. *Spiritual Kinship as Social Practice: Godparenthood and Adoption in the Early Middle Ages*. Newark: University of Delaware Press, 2000.

Kaibara 1961
Kaibara Ekiken. "Wazoku Dōjikun." In *Yōjōkun/Wazoku Dōjikun*, edited by Ishikawa Ken, 194–280. Tokyo: Iwanami Shoten, 1961.

Kamata 1988
Kamata Hiroshi. "Bushi shakai no yōshi—bakuhan hikaku yōshi hō." In *Giseisareta oyako: yōshi*, edited by Ōtake Hideo et al., 61–90. Tokyo: Sanseidō, 1988.

Kim and Park 2010
Kim, Kuentae, and Hyunjoon Park. "Family Succession through Adoption in the Chosun Dynasty." *Reproduction in East Asian Historical Demography* 15:4 (October 29, 2010): 443–52.

Ko, Haboush, and Piggott 1994
Ko, Dorothy, JaHyun Kim Haboush, and Joan R. Piggott, eds. *Women and Confucian Cultures in Premodern China, Korea, and Japan*. Berkeley: University of California Press, 2003.

Kokushi daijiten
Kokushi Daijiten Henshū Iinkai, ed. *Kokushi daijiten*, 15 vols. Tokyo: Yoshikawa Kōbunkan, 1979–97.

Kurosu 1998
Kurosu Satomi. "Long Way to Headship, Short Way to Retirement: Adopted Sons in a Northeastern Village in Pre-industrial Japan." *History of the Family* 3:4 (January 1, 1998): 393–410.

Kurosu and Ochiai 1995
Kurosu, Satomi, and Emiko Ochiai. "Adoption as an Heirship Strategy under Demographic Constrains: A Case from Nineteenth-Century Japan." *Journal of Family History* 20:3 (1995): 261–88.

Lee and Wang 2001
Lee, James Z., and Wang Feng. *One Quarter of Humanity: Malthusian Mythology and Chinese Realities, 1700–2000*. Cambridge, MA: Harvard University Press, 2001.

Macfarlane 2003
Macfarlane, Alan. *The Savage Wars of Peace: England, Japan, and the Malthusian Trap*. Oxford: Blackwell, 1997.

Matsuo 2002
Matsuo Mieko. "Kinsei buke no kon'in, yōshi to jisankin: Daimyō Sakakibara-shi no jirei." In *Kon'in to kazoku, shinzoku*, edited by Yoshie Akiko, 235–69. Nihon kazoku ronshū 8. Tokyo: Yoshikawa Kōbunkan, 2002.

Moring 2009
Moring, Beatrice. "Land, Inheritance, and the Finnish Stem Family." In *The Stem Family in Eurasian Perspective*, edited by A. Fauve-Chamoux and E. Ochiai, 173–97. Bern, Switzerland: Peter Lang, 2009.

McCullough 1967
McCullough, William H. "Japanese Marriage Institutions in the Heian Period." *Harvard Journal of Asiatic Studies* 27 (1967): 103–67.

McMullen 1975
McMullen, I. J. "Non-agnatic Adoption: A Confucian Controversy in Seventeenth- and Eighteenth-Century Japan." *Harvard Journal of Asiatic Studies* 35 (1975): 133–89.

Mega 2011
Mega Atsuko. *Buke ni totsuida josei no tegami: Binbō hatamoto no Edo kurashi*. Tokyo: Yoshikawa Kōbunkan, 2011.

Moore 1970
Moore, Ray A. "Adoption and Samurai Mobility in Tokugawa Japan." *Journal of Asian Studies* 29:3 (1970): 617–32.

Moriguchi 2010
Moriguchi, Chiaki. "Child Adoption in Japan, 1948–2008: A Comparative Historical Analysis." *Keizai kenkyū* 61:4 (2010): 342–57.

Mote 1999
Mote, Frederick W. *Imperial China, 900–1800*. Cambridge, MA: Harvard University Press, 1999.

Mungello 2008
Mungello, D. E. *Drowning Girls in China*. Lanham, MD: Rowman and Littlefield, 2008.

Namura 1993
Namura Jōhaku. "Onna Chōhōki." In *Onna chōhōki, Otoko chōhōki*, edited by Nagatomo Chiyoji, 10–196. Tokyo: Shakai Shisōsha, 1993.

Nickerson 1993
Nickerson, Peter. "The Meaning of Matrilocality: Kinship, Property, and Politics in Mid-Heian." *Monumenta Nipponica* 48:4 (1993): 429–67.

Ōguchi 2001
Ōguchi Yūjirō. "Kinsei buke sozoku ni okeru isei yōshi." In *Onna no shakai shi: 17–20 seiki—'ie' to jendaa wo kangaeru*. Tokyo: Yamakawa Shuppansha, 2001.

Ōmori 2002
Ōmori Eiko. "Daimyo ni okeru yōshi kettei katei: Uwajima-han Date-ke shiryō no bunseki kara." In *Nihon kinsei kokka no shosō*. Vol. 2. Tokyo: Tōkyōdō Shuppan, 2002.

Ōtō 1995
Ōtō Osamu. "Fufu kenka, rikon to sonraku shakai: Suruga no kuni higashi-gun Yamanojiri-mura no meishu ke no nikki kara." In *Kinsei Nihon no seikatsu bunka to chiiki shakai*, 177–206. Tokyo: Kawade Shobō, 1995.

Peterson 1983
Peterson, Mark A. "Women without Sons: A Measure of Social Change in Yi Korea." In *Korean Women: View from the Inner Room*, edited by Martina Deuchler, Laurel Kendall, and Mark Peterson, 33–44. Cushing, ME: East Rock Press, 1983.

Peterson 1996
Peterson, Mark A. *Korean Adoption and Inheritance: Case Studies in the Creation of a Classic Confucian Society*. Cornell East Asia Series, 80. Ithaca, NY: East Asia Program, Cornell University, 1996.

Rawski 1998
Rawski, Evelyn Sakakida. *The Last Emperors: A Social History of Qing Imperial Institutions*. Berkeley: University of California Press, 1998.

Rawski 2015
Rawski, Evelyn Sakakida. *Early Modern China and Northeast Asia: Cross-Border Perspectives*. Cambridge: Cambridge University Press, 2015.

Skinner 1993
Skinner, G. William. "Conjugal Power in Tokugawa Japanese Families." In *Sex and Gender Hierarchies*, edited by Barbara Diane Miller, 236–70. Cambridge: Cambridge University Press, 1993.

Stone 1979
Stone, Lawrence. *The Family, Sex, and Marriage in England, 1500–1800*. New York: Harper and Row, 1979.

Tahara 1998
Tahara Noboru. "Kinsei daimyo ni okeru yōshi sōzoku to bakuhansei shakai: 'Ta-ke' yōshi wo chūshin toshite." *Shigaku* 67:2 (1998): 123–48.

Toishi 2017
Toishi Nanami. *Mura to ie wo mamotta Edo jidai no hitobito: jinkō genshō chiiki no yōshi seido to hyakushō kabushiki*. Tokyo: Nōsan Gyoson Bunka Kyōkai, 2017.

Tsubouchi 1992
    Tsubouchi Reiko. *Nihon no kazoku, ie no renzoku to furenzoku.* Kyoto: Akademia Shuppankai, 1992.
Tsubouchi 2000
    Tsubouchi Reiko. "Hagi-han hanshi ni okeru kakei no danshō to jinkōgakuteki yōin." *Nihon kenkyū* 22 (2000): 111–29.
Tsubouchi 2001
    Tsubouchi Reiko. *Danshō no jinkō shakaigaku.* Tokyo: Mineruboa Shobō, 2001.
Wakita 1982
    Wakita Osamu. "Bakuhan taisei to josei." In *Nihon joseishi,* edited by Joseishi Sōgō Kenkyūkai, vol. 3, pp. 1–30. Tokyo: Tokyo Daigaku Shuppankai, 1982.
Wang and Lee 1998
    Wang Feng and James Lee. "Adoption among the Qing Nobility and Its Implications for Chinese Demographic Behavior." *History of the Family* 3:3 (1998): 411–28.
Wang, Lee, and Campbell 1995
    Wang Feng, James Lee, and Cameron Campbell. "Marital Fertility Control among the Qing Nobility: Implications for Two Types of Preventive Check." *Population Studies* 49 (1995): 383–400.
Yamakawa 1992
    Yamakawa, Kikue. *Women of the Mito Domain: Recollections of Samurai Family Life.* Tokyo: University of Tokyo Press, 1992.
Yonemoto 2016
    Yonemoto, Marcia. *The Problem of Women in Early Modern Japan.* Berkeley: University of California Press, 2016.

3

Imagined Communities of the Living and the Dead

The Spread of the Ancestor-Venerating Stem Family in Tokugawa Japan

Fabian Drixler

In 1901 the living presence of dead ancestors could seem as quintessentially Japanese as shrine gates and cherry blossoms. Lafcadio Hearn, that conjurer of old Japan for an Anglophone readership, made it the theme of one of his short stories that year, "The Case of O-Dai":

> O-Dai pushed aside the lamplet and the incense-cup and the water vessel on the Buddha shelf, and opened the little shrine before which they had been placed. Within were the ihai, the mortuary tablets of her people . . . [and a] scroll, inscribed with the spirit-names of many ancestors. Before that shrine, from her infancy, O-Dai had been wont to pray. The tablets and the scroll signified more to her faith in former time—very much more—than remembrance of a father's affection and a mother's caress; . . . those objects signified the actual viewless presence of the lost. . . . All this O-Dai ought to have known and remembered. Maybe she did; for she wept as she took the tablets and the scroll out of the shrine, and dropped them from a window into the river below.[1]

The young woman discarded the totems of ancestor worship at the instigation of two English missionaries. Up to this moment, her neighbors had humored her new religion. Now Hearn ventriloquized their "universal feelings" as follows:

> Human society, in this most eastern East, has been held together from immemorial time by virtue of that cult which exacts the gratitude of the present to the past, the reverence of the living for the dead, the affection of the descendant for the ancestor. . . .

To the spirit of the father who begot her, to the spirit of the mother who bore her, O-Dai has refused the shadow of a roof, and the vapor of food, and the offering of water. Even so to her shall be denied the shelter of a roof, and the gift of food, and the cup of refreshment. And even as she cast out the dead, the living shall cast her out.[2]

Although Hearn added and subtracted some details, he based the outline of O-Dai's story on his understanding of actual events that transpired in Matsue sometime in the 1880s.[3] He may also have been broadly correct that, in the mid-Meiji period, the social consensus expected descendants to care for their ancestors' spirits as a matter of course.[4] Yet Hearn was mistaken in one respect: the household imagined as a community of the living and their dead ancestors was not a timeless feature of Japanese society, nor even a particularly ancient one.

The only household form that is potentially immortal, and can thus grow into a tight-knit transgenerational community of the kind that O-Dai violated, is the stem family. In stem families, the heir marries and remains with his or her parents; all other children move out upon reaching adulthood. As parents retire or die and children take their places, the household never has more than one married couple per generation. No other household form can continue indefinitely.[5] Nuclear families dissolve once the children move out to light hearths of their own. Joint families, in which several married children stay with their parents, eventually grow into lineages, too large to function as households.

Stem families have existed in many times and places.[6] Their ability to replicate themselves continuously made them ideal for protecting material assets and social capital. Presumably for this reason, the stem family was the default for elite samurai by the fourteenth century.[7] For non-elite groups in Japan, the chronology is altogether different. Among Japanese commoners, the stem family became the culturally dominant household form only after 1600. It also took on a highly specific form that one of its foremost students, Ōtō Osamu, has defined as "an institutional mechanism that has its own name (kamei), occupation (kagyō), and property (kazai), oriented toward perpetuating itself indefinitely across generations with ancestor veneration as its spiritual pillar."[8]

The diffusion of the stem family to commoner society must rank among the great transformations of the Tokugawa period. Here, I begin to document the timing and sequence of this transformation, as well as something of its geography. I am unable to narrow all uncertainties. My evidence is extensive for eastern Honshu but very limited in some other regions; even when sources are abundant, they often permit a range of interpretations. We can nonetheless trace the gradual strengthening of the ancestor-venerating stem family in a variety of media: in patterns of co-residence as recorded in the registers of religious surveillance; in the practices of Funerary Buddhism; and in expressions of a wish for continuity, such as names passed from father to son and heirs adopted to lead the family into a new generation.

Despite its limitations, the evidence presented here is consistent with my three main arguments, each of which is fleshed out in its own section. First, in the late seventeenth century, the stem family became the setting in which most commoners in some Japanese regions spent at least a part of their lives (section 1, "The Living"). Second, by the mid-Tokugawa period, the stem family was at once a unit of production and consumption and an imagined community of the living and the dead (section 2, "The Dead"). These two aspects of the stem family may have reinforced each other, but proving causal links lies beyond the purview of this chapter. What can be said with confidence is that stem families were structurally amenable to the services Funerary Buddhism had to offer. In time, the very attraction of those services may have moved increasing numbers of families to form stem lines. Third, the importance of the stem family grew continually in the course of the Tokugawa period (section 3, "The *Ie* Perpetuated and Unified"). The growth was in one sense faster in the late seventeenth century than in the early nineteenth, when many indicators had reached saturation levels. However, as family altars became crowded with dead yet present ancestors, the weight of obligation on the living probably continued to grow in the late Tokugawa period. So did devotion to this precious social organism that promised a kind of immortality to its members. This would at least explain why a variety of indicators for identification with the stem family and a concern for its perpetuation point upward throughout the late Tokugawa period.

THE LIVING
Unknowns of the Sixteenth Century

From the lost tapestry of commoner family structures in the sixteenth century, only a few motes of lint have come down to us. In these small samples from the Kansai (Tanba, Izumi, and Ōmi) and central Japan (Kai), we observe a transition to using family surnames (*myōji*) instead of lineage names (*ujina*), suggesting a move away from earlier arrangements in which nuclear households formed and dissolved within larger lineage communities.[9] Wives, who had once kept their separate property and original family names, now typically shared both with their husband.[10] There are also indications of a concern with maintaining the household as a goal in itself; for example, when the household of a condemned criminal was held in trust until his heir was old enough to head it. William Wayne Farris concludes from such evidence that "in essence, the general outline of the Tokugawa-period stem household seems to have been in existence among the peasantry by 1500 in the Kinai and perhaps by the mid-1500s in central and western Japan."[11] The wording is admirably judicious, because the phrase "in existence" makes no commitment as to whether this was the cultural mainstream or the practice of a few exceptional pioneers. The use of surnames and a concern with household continuity cannot tell us whether people actually lived in stem households, let alone how they might have imagined their dead ancestors. In addition, a few settlements cannot stand in for large swaths of Japan, especially when we consider that the sample may be biased: communities more concerned with household continuity may have been more likely to create and preserve sources that speak to household arrangements of any kind.

Caution must therefore temper any conclusion about the penetration of the stem system before the Tokugawa period. We know that other household models remained common enough to provoke Toyotomi Hideyoshi, in 1594, to forbid farming families with separate incomes to live under the same roof.[12] And we know that terminology is slippery: in the earliest population registers, from the 1600s to the 1630s in Kyushu, the term *ie* sometimes signifies "building" rather than "family."[13] Finally, our small samples from the Kansai and Kai cannot be assumed to represent the whole archipelago. The regional diversity in household forms during later centuries warns against projecting uniform conditions earlier.

Roofs and Umbrellas: The Household of the Registers

By the mid-seventeenth century, a new type of source captures something of the patterns of co-residence in commoner society: population registers, variously entitled "register of religious inspection" (*shūmon aratamechō* and similar names) and "register of population inspection" (with titles such as *ninbetsu aratamechō* and *ninzū aratamechō*). Every village was ordered to compile such lists, and even from this early period, they survive in some numbers—usually in the fair copy the headman kept after he submitted the original to the authorities. Such documents group individual villagers into households and usually also state their ages and roles within the household—head, wife, mother, cousin, and so on. As such, they are a fabulous, and abundant, source for reconstructing the residential patterns of the population. Yet the relationship between record and reality is inevitably less straightforward than first meets the eye.

In particular, the registers invite questions as to what the household units recorded there actually represent. A 1670s directive on enforcing population registration specified that commoners should be recorded "building by building," suggesting that individuals were herded into households according to the house they occupied—and also that other alternatives could be imagined.[14] Although the close linguistic association between house and household in Japanese may reconcile us to this privileging of the roof as the basic unit of society,[15] the organization of resources and social obligations—land rights, labor burdens, tax and service duties, the sharing of food and other goods—did not necessarily respect the walls of individual buildings.[16] Perhaps for this reason, some people gave different answers about how far their household extended, depending on who was asking.

Cadastral surveys, which assigned landholdings and tax obligations, do not always agree with population registers in their reporting of household units.[17] Disagreements also sometimes surface in finer-grained social surveys. In 1808, a village south of Nara tried to make its request for lower taxes more persuasive by adding a detailed record of the income and expenses of each household. The precision is impressive, with notations like "food for three and a half people." In the economic ties the document describes, the membership of the households often differs from that stated in the population register for the same village.[18] One way to understand this discrepancy is to consider that the population registers were designed to attach individuals to a household legally, not to define who ate where. Law and economics may have coincided in many cases, but not in all.

Population registers were instruments of control, not of nuanced description. As such, they were never designed to render a full account of the many-layered bonds of kinship, interdependence, and solidarity that are among the most meaningful aspects of household life. Nonetheless, even the greatly simplified versions of reality we see in their pages sometimes define households in ways that challenge taxonomists.

Take, for example, a compound in the village of Honma in Shinano, recorded in 1663.[19] It consisted of a main house, a formal tatami residence, a storehouse, and two smaller dwellings. The headman of Honma resided in the big house with his wife and children. In one of the humbler *soeya* (side building, also the term for a dependent), his brother's widow dwelt with hers. In the second *soeya*, there lived a fifty-five-year-old man and his nuclear family, whose kinship ties with the headman remain unstated. Seven other individuals are listed as servants. That three of them were recorded as belonging to the widowed sister-in-law suggests that she managed her affairs with a degree of independence.[20] The landholdings, meanwhile, were stated for the compound as a whole. All this suggests that the three residential groups did not share all consumption and production, but nonetheless retained a degree of interdependence. Should we then classify them as three nuclear families, one joint family, or—if we exclude the residential group without clear kinship ties to the other two—as one joint and one nuclear family?

Hanging the distinction on the bonds among kin has problems of its own, since population registers do not always record them across subhouseholds. In the same document from Honma, the compound of one Magouemon appears with four separate houses, occupied by four nuclear families. Three of these buildings are designated as *soeya*, subsidiary buildings. From the register alone, one might conclude that the three *soeya* families were all servants of Magouemon. But other documents in the village reveal them to be two cousins and a younger brother.[21] Should we therefore classify the compound as one sprawling joint family?

It seems a better solution to respect the categories of our sources by creating a separate term for compounds with clearly delineated subunits: an umbrella household (see table 3.1). Honma's register is somewhat unusual in its attention to architectural detail. Far more commonly, a simple layout distinction, such as

TABLE 3.1. The taxonomy of households used in this chapter

Nuclear family: one and only one married couple or combination of a parent and his or her children. No married lateral kin (brothers, sisters, uncles, aunts, cousins).

Stem family: one and only one married couple or parent per generation, with at least two such generations present. No married lateral kin.

Joint family: at least two married couples or parents in the same generation.

Solitary: one-person household.

Other: a residual category, which includes nonkin households (for example, in temples) and frerêches (unmarried siblings sharing a household).

Each of these five household types can either be independent or part of an umbrella household.

---

an indentation, signals that we are dealing with an umbrella household.[22] At one extreme, such compounds may have functioned as joint families; at the other, as clusters of families that acted as little more than neighbors. In between lie infinite gradations, but all had enough of a separate corporate identity to prompt the headman to try to acknowledge it in the layout of his listing.[23]

Structure versus Process

With the caveats just spelled out, the registers tell us what the structure of households was at the moment the headman put brush to paper. Useful as this is, they do not tell us how the members understood the rules of that household and what aspirations they nurtured for its future. This is a problem, because the stem *ie* discussed in this chapter is a process and a narrative rather than a thing.[24] It is a son's decision to bring a wife to live with him and his parents, and the younger couple's long-term plan to keep one and only one married child living under their roof. Unfortunately, my data set can capture such decisions only in the form of past events that are implied in present structures.[25] A snapshot of a household operating by stem rules is not always obvious as such: if the head's father died before his son married, the stem family looks like a nuclear family. This nuclear phase is in fact quite common for stem families. Even in a snapshot of a society in which every household followed stem family rules, we would expect to see a sizable fraction of households in a nuclear configuration.

Studying Tokugawa-period households through population registers, then, is like reviewing a color movie through a series of black-and-white stills. As long as we are aware of their limitations and idiosyncrasies, they are an immensely valuable source on the types of households in which the commoner population of Tokugawa Japan lived.

The Rise of Stem Co-residence in Eastern Honshu

With these qualifications acknowledged, it is high time to turn to the data. This subsection analyzes about 3,300 registers from some 1,000 villages in

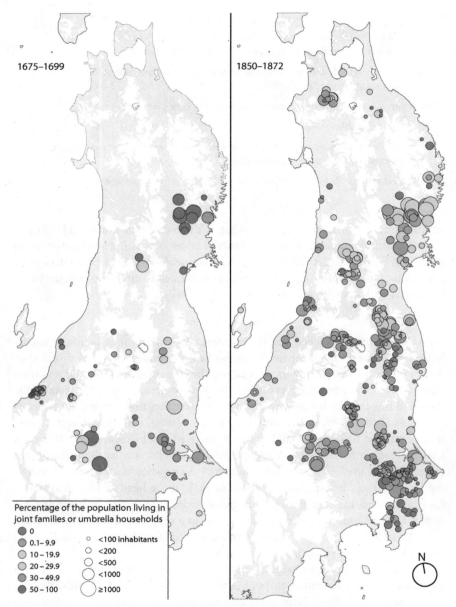

1675–1699

1850–1872

Percentage of the population living in
joint families or umbrella households

- 0
- 0.1–9.9
- 10–19.9
- 20–29.9
- 30–49.9
- 50–100

- ○ <100 inhabitants
- ○ <200
- ○ <500
- ○ <1000
- ○ ≥1000

N

FIGURE 3.1. Joint families and umbrella households in the villages of eastern Honshu,
1675–1699 and 1850–1872

SOURCES AND METHOD: Villages with multiple registers in a quarter century have been averaged and appear only once
on each map. For a list of the villages, see Drixler 2013, 261–75.

the eastern third of Honshu. Written between 1650 and 1872, their pages list about 780,000 individuals in about 150,000 households. From this library, two major observations emerge: one, eastern Honshu was diverse in its household culture; and two, within that enduring diversity, joint families and umbrella households receded in the seventeenth and eighteenth centuries as stem families advanced.

I once thought of demographic differences between neighboring villages as statistical noise, to be fused into the emergent melodies of ever-larger samples. But increasingly I have come to see that diversity itself as an important finding. Neighboring villages might disagree about the wisdom and virtue of infanticide;[26] over whether one family could support multiple temples;[27] and over whether retired household heads should move to a separate dwelling.[28] In famine, a few hour's walk could lead from a village in which half the population died to one that showed no anomalous spike in deaths that year.[29] So, too, with joint families and umbrella households (figure 3.1). To be sure, a trend toward greater homogeneity within and between regions unfolded from the seventeenth to the nineteenth century. But it bears further thought that even in the last years of the shogunate, close to half the people of some villages still lived in joint families while in others, a short walk away, not one such family existed.

Figure 3.1 tells a second story: that joint families and umbrella households became much rarer over time. To visualize this trend in the context of all household types, it is useful to narrow the dataset to one region at a time. Figure 3.2 plots the changing proportions of different household types in Sendai. In this most populous domain of eastern Honshu, both joint families and umbrella households were particularly numerous in the seventeenth century and held out longer than elsewhere.[30]

When we conduct the analysis at the level of regions (figure 3.3), a spatial and temporal narrative emerges that is not as easily visible in the village-level maps. The retreat of joint families and umbrella households occurred throughout eastern Honshu, but was staggered across space.[31] At the southern end of the area—in Hitachi and the Bōsō provinces—less than a quarter of the population lived in such contexts even in the earliest registers, while in Sendai and Echigo, that proportion exceeded four-fifths. The staggered retreat meant that eastern Honshu had a pronounced gradient from the southeast to the north and west in the seventeenth century, before it converged on a much narrower range in the last quarter of the eighteenth century.

As joint families and umbrella households retreated, stem families advanced in an approximate mirror image (figure 3.4). It was only in the early nineteenth century that the majority of people in all parts of eastern Honshu lived in stem families at any given moment (apart from the far north, perhaps, for which my sample is too small to permit confident conclusions). Since the snapshots classify some fraction of families operating by stem rules as nuclear, the point at which

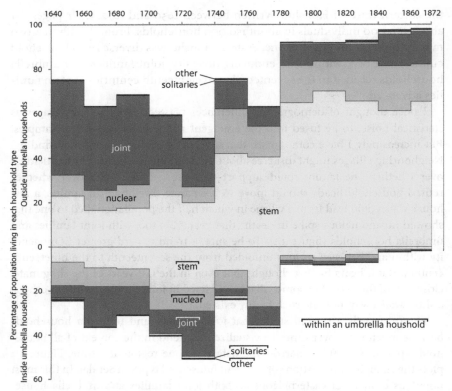

FIGURE 3.2. The changing balance of household types in Sendai domain, based on their structure in the year of observation

SOURCES AND METHOD: A sample of population registers from 118 villages containing c. 123,000 observations of individuals. Villages with multiple registers in a twenty-year period have been averaged and counted only once in that timespan. Sendai's branch domain of Ichinoseki is included in this data. For a list of the villages, see Drixler 2013, 262–64.

every region of eastern Honshu had a stem majority may have been reached a few decades earlier.[32] Considering that scholars routinely treat stem families as the very definition of the Tokugawa-period Japanese *ie*, this is a surprising finding, which forces us to see the Tokugawa centuries as an age not of cultural stability in household patterns, but of continual evolution. As we shall see at the end of this chapter, this cannot easily be dismissed as the peculiarity of a backward eastern periphery; in 1880, the year of the first comprehensive statistics, it was eastern Honshu where stem families were more numerous than in any other Japanese macroregion of the same size. (See Figure 3.12, below.)

Eagle-eyed readers may already have noticed a complication to this otherwise neat narrative. In the last decades of the Tokugawa period, joint families (though

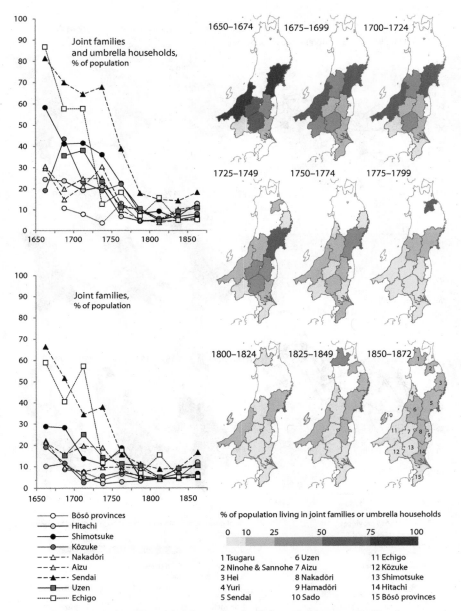

FIGURE 3.3. The decline of joint families and umbrella households in eastern Honshu

SOURCES AND METHOD: A sample of population registers from 1,040 villages. Villages with multiple registers in a quarter century have been averaged and counted only once. For a list of the villages, see Drixler 2013, 261–75.

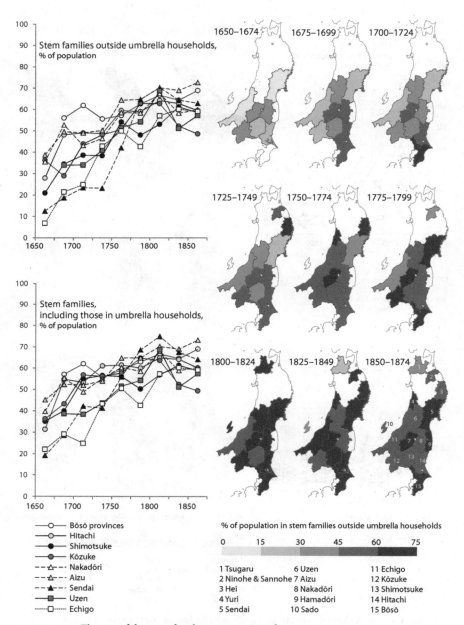

FIGURE 3.4. The rise of the stem family in eastern Honshu

SOURCES AND METHOD: A sample of population registers from 1,040 villages. Villages with multiple registers in a quarter century have been averaged and counted only once for each such period. For a list of the villages, see Drixler 2013, 261–75.

not umbrella households) experienced a small renaissance at the expense of stem families in some eastern regions. This was in part the result of parents raising more children than before. Since for households with a single surviving adult son or daughter, the temptation to form joint families would have been small, the larger sibset sizes created more situations in which joint families were a serious option. Yet this may not be the whole story. As I have argued elsewhere, new discourses and policies emerged around 1800 in the Kantō and the Northeast that envisioned the household as an entity that could grow branches.[33] The ideal of this vision was not necessarily a joint family, but rather that noninheriting children should found their own branch households. Still, it is possible that this ideal created the conditions in which joint families became waiting rooms for branch households, where nonheirs and their spouses bided their time while saving up the necessary funds to strike out on their own.[34]

While we therefore cannot read the small rebound in joint family residence as a sign that more people hoped to ultimately live in this arrangement, we also cannot assume that the stem family ever became the universal ambition of rural commoners in eastern Honshu. It is not clear whether in local societies dominated by stem families, the minority who lived in joint families did so by preference or by necessity. It is possible that such families held different values and resisted what was now a dominant culture of stem households. However, such low levels are also consistent with a society that considered the stem family as normative but at times allowed other concerns—helping a married sibling or obtaining labor of the right age and gender for the household—to override that preference.

What can be said with certainty is that even in the 1850s, there were some local societies in which the joint family was more than a compromise solution for specific circumstances. The village of Mizuki stood on the Tsugaru Plain, at the time Japan's northernmost expanse of rice paddies and an area where, as we have just seen, joint families remained numerous till the end of the Tokugawa period. In 1850, Mizuki had 484 inhabitants, including a tofu maker, a carpenter, a cooper, a thatcher, an acupuncturist, and shops for saké, salted fish, sundries, and fish oil.[35] Some other villagers worked as servants as far afield as Matsumae and Akita. With more than 2 koku of arable land per capita, Mizuki appears to have been a well-off place, though any sense of prosperity may have been tempered by the memories of deadly famines that had swept Tsugaru as recently as the 1830s and left the landscape dotted with stone memorials to the victims. The famines may also have been a reason that twenty-one houses stood empty in Mizuki.

The fish oil seller Heisaku owned nearly 40 koku of land, more than the largest landholders in most Tokugawa villages. If there were material constraints on the formation of his household, they would have been other than the threat of abject poverty. At thirty-nine, Heisaku oversaw a family of thirteen, who all lived under the same roof: his wife, two daughters, a son-in-law, and two sisters, one of whom had brought a husband into the household and given birth to no fewer than five boys. Perhaps the brother-in-law took care of the rice paddies while Heisaku devoted himself to the fish oil business? The owner of the sundries store, Jūjirō, had even more land, nearly 56 *koku*. At age forty, he gathered under his roof a mother, a wife, a daughter, two sons, a sister with husband and children, and a brother with wife and children. When the headman updated the population register six years later, four children had been born, Jūjirō's younger sister had married, and a nephew had taken a bride. Instead of founding households of their own, both new couples remained with Jūjirō. Such sprawling joint families were not the preserve of shop owners with big farms. Even in the household of the headman, we see a logic at work that allowed any member of the family to stay on after marriage. The household head's two sons, an adopted daughter, and two granddaughters had all brought spouses into the family. In Mizuki at least, the joint family was holding its own even during the last generation of the Tokugawa period.

Examples like those from Mizuki notwithstanding, a great quantity of evidence suggests that while we must acknowledge the continued importance of other living arrangements, the stem family was the culturally privileged household form of Japan by the end of the Edo period. This status was not just a matter of the economic advantages of several generations pooling their labor and resources under the same roof: as the following section shows, the living had come to imagine the stem family as a condominium with their dead.

THE DEAD
An Age of Dread and Distance

In medieval Japan, fear of the dead generally prevented the living from including them in any sense of synchronous community. I know of no evidence that their spirits were regarded as a benign presence among the living. There is, on the other hand, ample evidence that the living looked upon the bodies of the dead with horror and only very gradually came to erect grave markers that suggest a desire for communion with their souls.

Between the seventh and the seventeenth century, elaborate funerary rituals of any kind were rare in Japan. Huge ancient tomb mounds still loomed in the landscape, but no one now emulated such monuments. In the Heian period, non-elites commonly disposed of their dead without burial at all.[36] Such "wind funerals" (*fūsō*) minimized contact with the corpse and protected the living from the pollution emanating from death; by supplying more disturbing sights and smells than cremation or interment, they may also have perpetuated fear and revulsion of the dead. Even among court nobles and warriors, funerals were often furtive affairs, conducted at night and often without the presence of the bereaved;[37] even the location of graves was often quickly forgotten.[38] Communal non-elite cemeteries appeared from around 1150, but even within their precincts, dead bodies were often left to decompose on the surface.[39] When a body was interred, it was usually placed in a communal grave or a shallow pit, to be reused in rapid succession.[40]

Over a large swath of Japan, the death pollution taboo remained so strong that those who raised memorial stones typically used them as cenotaphs separate from the actual places of burial.[41]

While grave markers and cenotaphs were rare before the sixteenth century, their morphology indicates a changing balance between a fear of dead souls and a concern for their well-being.[42] The imperial court, adapting a continental Buddhist practice, began building stupas as a means of acquiring merit in the tenth century.[43] By 972, the head of the Tendai sect advised monks to prepare stupas for their own burials and enshrine mantras within them. By the twelfth century, laymen had sufficiently embraced the custom to make stupas common sights in cemeteries around Kyoto.[44] Yet even as these structures channeled merit to the deceased, most were inscribed with dharani spells, intended to protect the living from the spirits of the dead.[45]

The balance between fear and loving concern continued to shift with the growing popularity of Pure Land Buddhism, which promised that the salvific power of buddhas and bodhisattvas, rather than individual merit, could transport departed souls to a paradise that effectively removed them from the cycle of reincarnation.[46] By the fourteenth century, the majority of tombstones adopted designs that connected the dead with the intercession of Amida or Dainichi Nyorai. In the sixteenth century, wealthy commoners in the Kinai appropriated such elite customs and began to erect funerary stupas and stelae in large numbers. Indeed, the Pure Land sect came to treat the management of the dead as the critical link between Buddhist clergy and the faithful. Tamamuro Fumio argues that Pure Land initiatives inspired sect after sect to treat funerary rites as the key to increasing the number of adherents and to securing stable revenues.[47] For Sōtō Zen, death rituals became, in the words of Duncan Ryūken Williams, "the central practice" for parish priests.[48] By the time the Tokugawa shogunate resolved to uproot Christianity through religious registration in the 1630s, the basic culture and institutions of what Tamamuro calls Funerary Buddhism had taken shape.

How Funerary Buddhism Bridged the Chasm of Death

Foundations in place, Funerary Buddhism gradually reconfigured the relationship of the living with the dead. It did so through a ritual technology that promised to transform potentially threatening dead spirits (*shiryō*) into ancestral deities (*sorei*), released into a serene existence beyond the cycle of rebirth and suffering. Crucially, however, a soul otherwise destined for judgment, atonement, and reincarnation could become an ancestral deity only through the correct rites, arranged by its descendants with the aid of Buddhist priests. During the forty-nine-day period following death, seven precisely timed rituals would help the spirit on its journey through the courts of hell. In a second stage, six more required rituals would complete the transformation on the thirty-third anniversary of death.[49]

In effect, Funerary Buddhism introduced a new theme into the relationship of the living with the dead: the possibility of an alliance promising priceless benefits to ancestors and descendants alike. In exchange for ritual observance, the living could enjoy the protection of their deified antecedents. And when death came, each individual would in turn join the collectivity of his or her dead ancestors, as long as the next generation continued to do its duty.

An example of ancestor veneration in this mode can already be found in the records of a late-fourteenth-century Kyoto courtier.[50] Some necrologies, lists of death dates used for scheduling the requisite rites, stretch back deep into the Middle Ages.[51] However, the great flowering of Funerary Buddhism occurred only after the 1630s, when the Tokugawa shogunate ordered all subjects to register with a Buddhist temple and thereby demonstrate their rejection of Christianity, even in regions where the Catholic missionaries had made no inroads. Many people now entered a formal and exclusive relationship with a temple for the first time. Some Buddhist priests may have felt pressured to make themselves useful to the swollen ranks of their parishioners. For all its attractions, however, the promise of ancestral deification does not seem to have captivated all laypeople overnight. Even in 1655, veneration of stem family ancestors was sufficiently unfamiliar to commoners to motivate didactic writings on its benefits. That year, Suzuki Shōsan, a Zen priest and one of the more influential advisors to Tokugawa Ieyasu, authored *Inga monogatari,* a collection of tales about the karmic law of cause and effect. In several tales, the vengeful spirits of neglected ancestors are at length pacified when their descendants assume their ritual obligations.[52] As we shall see in a moment, that was still very much a minority practice in 1655.

Funerary Buddhism brought with it a distinctive material culture: necrologies (*kakochō*) for scheduling memorial services, ledgers of funerary donations (*ekōchō*), ancestral tablets (*ihai*), and tombstones. These objects survive in vast numbers today, the losses kept small by their great ritual importance. For social historians, necrologies and tombstones in particular are a gift. Relatively easy to count at scale, they enable us to track the spread of a new way of understanding the afterlife. In preparing this chapter, I analyzed a collection of *kakochō* necrologies from 961 parishes with a total of 1.9 million deaths in the Tokugawa period. I omit the chart, sources, and methodological explanations here because of space constraints. What can be said in summary is that in necrologies that go back to the early seventeenth century, deaths at first typically appear at intervals of several months or even years. From about 1630, the numbers increase, generally well in excess of population growth but also sufficiently slowly to continue their upward trend throughout the Tokugawa period.[53] One likely explanation for such growth across several centuries is that the adoption of *kakochō* expanded gradually to new sects, new temples, new families, and, within families, new categories of the recently deceased. In the earliest entries, former heads of elite households may have been greatly overrepresented. At the other end of the intrafamily status hierarchy, stillborn children were rarely memorialized in a necrology before the nineteenth century. In between those two extremes, it remains a question for future research by what decade core members of stable households could generally expect to be inscribed into a necrology upon their death. In the Northeast at

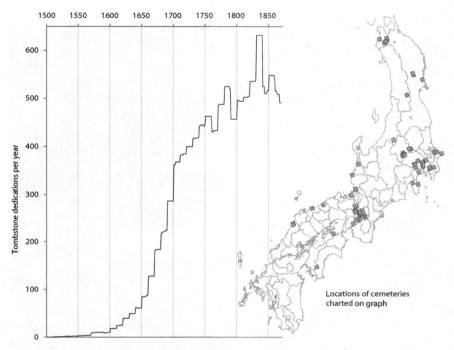

FIGURE 3.5. Japan-wide trends in tombstone dedications for commoners, 1500–1869

SOURCES AND METHOD: This chart presents a synthesis of 92,400 tombstone dedications in about 540 cemeteries from the following published studies: Akiike 1989, 60–65; Fussa shishi jōkan, 772, 777; Hattori 2003, 80–81; Hattori 2006, 60; Hattori 2010, 54, 60, 80–81; Hirose 2008, 102; Ichikawa 2002, 7; Ikegami 2003, 42; Itō Shishi Hensan Iinkai 2005, 238; Jishōin Iseki Chōsadan 1987, 160; Kutsuki 2003, 3; Kutsuki 2004, 80–81; Masaoka 1999, 394; Matsuda 2001, 123; Miyoshi 1986, 31–40; Nagasawa 1978, 64–67; Nishimoto 2015, 171; Saitō 1981; Nakayama Hokekyōji-shi Hensan Iinkai 1981, 338; Sekiguchi 2000, 61; Sekiguchi 2004, 482; Sekine 2018, 82, 118, 124, 130; Sekine and Shibuya 2007, 33–34; Shintani 1991, 139; Shiroishi, Kutsuki, and Senda 2004, 16, 24, 29, 33; Shiroishi, Kutsuki, Muraki et al. 2004, 57, 102–3; Tanigawa 1989, 5, 9; Yoshizawa 2004, 177. Cemeteries known to contain numerous samurai graves are excluded from the sample.

The studies typically report the number of tombstones by either reign period or decade. Within each time series, I have distributed them evenly across years and then added them up. The result is that mortality crises are less visible (but note the peaks in the 1780s and 1830s) and that the overall curve has uneven steps. These are simply artifacts of the information loss during the publication process of the studies that underlie this chart. The chart counts tombstones, not names inscribed on them. In many locations, the curves for the two are very similar before the widespread adoption of family tombs in the modern period, but already in the Tokugawa period, the two measures diverge widely in some cemeteries. See, for example, Sekine 2018, 198–99.

least, this point had likely been reached by 1750; by this time, dead children appear in the *kakochō* in numbers that are consistent with other sources, as do famine victims—often including those who died far from home or without descendants.

In the same decades that priests began to routinely record their parishioners' posthumous names, more and more tombstones were rising in the cemeteries of Japan—each of them a mineral metaphor of the new vertical bond between the living and the dead.[54] Figure 3.5 combines the published efforts of several dozen Japanese scholars who have studied hundreds of graveyards. In this Japan-wide

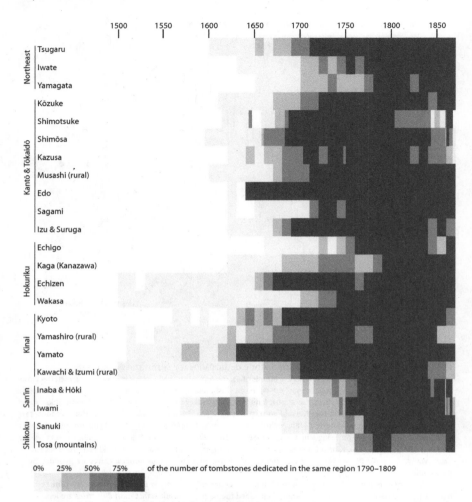

FIGURE 3.6. Regional trends in tombstone dedications, 1500–1869
SOURCES AND METHOD: This chart groups the 540 or so cemeteries of figure 3.5 into twenty-three different regions. These are listed in their approximate sequence from northeast to southwest. To keep the focus on commoner practice, cemeteries known to contain numerous samurai graves are excluded. For every year, the chart compares the number of new tombstones to the average for 1790–1809, by which time the diffusion process was complete in many areas. For the precise location of the cemeteries in each region, see figure 3.5.

sample, the number of tombstones followed a logistic growth curve, characteristic of diffusion processes. The second half of the seventeenth century coincided rather neatly with the period of fastest diffusion, with growth continuing at a gentler pace into the mid-nineteenth century.[55]

Tombstones appeared particularly early in the Kinai and adjacent areas on the Japan Sea coast; by the late sixteenth century, stones also began to mark graves in a few other locations. However, in most of Japan, the early adopters embraced this new custom only in the first half of the seventeenth century, to be followed in the second half by a rapidly growing and ultimately universal share of their neighbors. In the areas that lagged behind this trend—in this sample, cemeteries in Shikoku and on the Japan Sea side between Yamagata and Shimane—apparent saturation levels were nonetheless reached in the late eighteenth century (figure 3.6). Even after that point, however, Tokugawa Japan may never have had a fully unified funerary culture. True Pure Land Buddhism, one of Japan's most powerful denominations, long had doctrinal reservations against erecting grave markers,[56] and modern students of folklore found that in some specific locales they examined in the twentieth century, people threw away the ashes of their dead without fashioning a proper gravesite.[57] Such counterexamples notwithstanding, there can be little doubt that by the late eighteenth century, most Japanese who could afford to do so buried their dead under a carefully worked stone.

Beyond the raw count, the morphology of tombstones has long been recognized as a rich source for the mentalité of those who raised them. Throughout the seventeenth century, the medieval forms like stupas and prow-shaped stones with Buddhist carvings remained in style. But from about 1700, simple rectangular poles that could be inscribed with posthumous names and family crests began to dominate cemeteries. By the late eighteenth century, some of these came to mark household rather than individual graves, as if to suggest that the individual would dissolve into the transgenerational community of his or her household. These *senzo daidai no haka* remained exceptional in the Tokugawa period and became a mainstay of Japanese funerary practice only in the twentieth century.[58] In this, they anticipate the theme of this chapter's final section (albeit for a century not explored further here): that even after the immortal stem family was fully established, it continued to strengthen its hold on the imagination of its living members over time.

THE *IE* PERPETUATED AND UNIFIED

The ascendancy of the stem family did not end with its spread as a residential arrangement and as an imagined community of the living and the dead. The indicators discussed in this final section suggest that people's commitment to the perpetuation and unity of the *ie* intensified throughout the Tokugawa period.

The Unification of Temple Affiliations

When, in the 1630s, commoners were first ordered to register with temples to prove that they were not Christians, they did so on an individual rather than a household basis. In some areas, this practice led to the phenomenon of *handanka*, or multiple temple affiliations within a single household.[59] Initially, moreover, temple affiliations were portable. When women and men married into new

households, they took their established relationships with them. While this custom of personal portable affiliations (*mochikomi handanka*) became rare after
1700, split affiliations did not disappear. Hereditary household-based relationships with several temples (*ietsuki handanka*) took their place and remained common throughout the eighteenth century. In this system, new members, whether
they entered by birth or adoption or marriage, were assigned one of these affiliations to secure a personal tie to each temple ministering to the soul of a deceased
household member.[60]

Families that practiced hereditary *handanka* used three different modes to
determine the parish affiliations of brides, adoptees, and children: balancing numbers, assignation by sex, and generational alternation.[61] Each mode implies that the
individual bonds of brides and adoptees to blood relatives were now subordinated
to the interests and identity of their new household. Instead of venerating blood
ancestors by maintaining their original temple affiliations, brides and grooms were
to serve the marital and adoptive ancestors whom they would join when their own
lives had run their course.[62]

Or so a pleasingly straightforward interpretation of the evidence would
suggest. There are complications. In his monograph on *handanka*, Morimoto
Kazuhiko counsels caution in reading religious ideas and social attitudes into
patterns of registration. Citing rapid oscillations between 1638 and 1669 in the
village of Niremata in Mino, Morimoto argues that any ordering of temple
affiliation by sex in early registers reflects government policy rather than individual choice.[63]

It is also possible, however, to read early oscillations between affiliation patterns as evidence of a society new to temple registration and not yet much concerned with ancestor veneration. The system of religious affiliation was, after all,
an imposition by the authorities, and people may have taken time to internalize
it as a meaningful part of their spiritual lives. Even decades later, the registers
were no straightforward reflection of individual ideas about the household, but
a negotiated outcome between rulers, temples, and the populace. It is nonetheless telling that multiple affiliations did decline as households gradually unified
their temple memberships over the course of the eighteenth century. In Morimoto's impressively large Japan-wide dataset, 41 percent of population registers
before 1700 include households with multiple temple affiliations. The figure falls
steadily to 14 percent in the early nineteenth century.[64] Although official policy
played some role, the decline was gradual enough, even within villages, to suggest
that individual parishioners had at least as much say in the matter as rulers and
priests (figure 3.7).[65]

We may surmise that families that maintained split temple affiliations saw
their ancestors as individuals, while those that unified their affiliations emphasized the collectivity of the ancestral spirits, residing in the same altar, cared
for by the same temple, and gradually dissolving their individuality. Split affili-

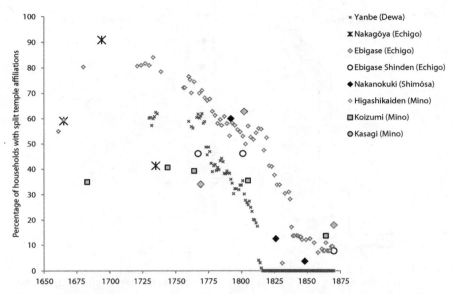

FIGURE 3.7. The decline of split temple affiliations in eight villages in which they were especially common

SOURCES AND METHOD: Adapted from graphs, tables, and discussions in Morimoto 2006, 96–97, 166–70, 196–97, and his appendix, 11–23. To create a legible chart from the hundreds of villages in Morimoto's study, I selected villages that met the following conditions: information on at least three separate years, at least one of which had to precede 1800; and more than 40 percent *handanka* in at least one year.

ations may have been abandoned for a number of reasons, including prosaic administrative concerns. Yet the process also suggests the ascendancy of a vision of the family as a single, unified, and aspirationally immortal home for its permanent members.

Name Inheritance

The same subsumption of individual lives into the family is evident in the custom of name inheritance (*shūmei*). Elite warriors had long emphasized lineal continuity by reusing one character in their personal names (*imina*) across generations. Thus, for example, all but three of the sixteen Hōjō regents of the Kamakura shogunate used the character *toki*, and even the three exceptions repeated other characters from their predecessors' names. Tokugawa-period commoners took the practice one step further. By the late seventeenth century, some household heads bequeathed their whole names to successors.[66] When the head of the Raku workshop of potters retired in 1691, he handed the name Kichizaemon to his adopted son.[67] Other transgenerational brands were born in 1704 and 1709, when Ichikawa Danjūrō II and Sakata Tōjūrō II succeeded the famed kabuki actors who had borne those names before them.[68] Around the same time, name inheritance was being

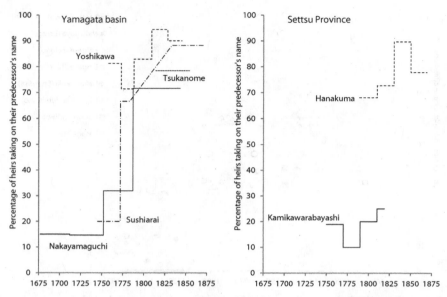

FIGURE 3.8. Name inheritance in four villages in the Yamagata basin (Northeastern Japan) and two in Settsu Province (Kansai)

SOURCES AND METHOD: Yamagata basin: Ōtō 1996, 217–20. Settsu Province: my own calculations from Kawaguchi Hiroshi's DANJURO Database. Reflecting the different age of available population registers, Ōtō uses different periodizations for the four villages. There is also a difference in method. For the villages of Yoshikawa, Sushiarai, and Tsukanome, the figure shows the percentage of successions in each time period that involved the heir taking on his predecessor's name. For Nakayamaguchi, Ōtō compared households at the beginning and the end of each period and counted which of them had a head with a new age but the same name as his predecessor. For Kamikawarabayashi, I defined name inheritance as the male heir taking on his male predecessor's name up to two years before or after assuming the headship of the household. In Hanakuma, all cases of name inheritance occurred in the same year as the actual succession.

practiced by about one-sixth of the commoners in Nakayamaguchi, a village in the Yamagata basin analyzed by Ōtō Osamu.[69]

For the eighteenth century, Ōtō was able to expand his study to a total of four villages (figure 3.8). Within each, the frequency of name inheritance rose rapidly enough in the second half of the eighteenth century that, by the early nineteenth, household heads who did not take their father's name were the exception.[70] Similarly, in her study of a village in the Northeastern domain of Nihonmatsu, Mary Louise Nagata concludes that lineal continuity in names was unimportant before 1760 but common after 1800.[71] In faraway Settsu Province, just north of Osaka, the evidence from two villages either highlights local diversity or points to a longer transition period. In one settlement, name inheritance occurred in only a quarter of succession cases even in the 1810s, when its run of population registers ends. In the other, more than two-thirds of male heirs took on their male predecessor's name already in the late eighteenth century (figure 3.8).

By itself, name inheritance does not tell us whether the custom was a matter of outward identity or deeply felt bonds with ancestors and future descendants.[72] At times, other materials help us narrow the possibilities. For example, in his study of the Raku workshop, Morgan Pitelka highlights that the first case of name inheritance occurred just three years after the family created a new genealogy for internal consumption.[73] Even where no other documentation aids our interpretation of the role of transgenerational identities in prompting name inheritance, we may reflect on the effects that name inheritance, irrespective of its original motivation, had on individual identity. As every lifelong male member of the stem household could anticipate a period in which he would assume the name that his ancestors had borne before him, and that his descendants would bear after him, name inheritance may have done its part to reinforce the sense that the living and their dead ancestors formed one insoluble community.

Adoption

As that community became more intensely felt, efforts for its future preservation grew in urgency. Adoption—typically of a man between his late teens and early thirties—could serve that end when no suitable male blood descendant could lead the family into a new generation. Adopting a capable young man was a means of securing the future of the family and of inviting a worthy new member to ultimately join the collectivity of the ancestors. Frequently, he was married to a daughter of the house, blurring the line between adoption and uxorilocal marriage.[74]

In my sample of village population registers from what I like to call Japan's Deep East (the area between Edo and the northern borders of Sendai domain), adoptions became more and more frequent over the decades, as we might expect if there was indeed a growing concern with household continuity. The following figures consider only households with married heirs, and therefore exclude nuclear families by definition. For the 1660s, we find about one married adopted son (including sons-in-law) for every nine married sons. Thereafter, the proportion of adoptees rose gently for a few decades and then surged between the 1710s and the 1820s (figure 3.9).[75] By then, nearly 27 percent of married men whose father or father-in-law served as household head were not the head's biological son. Since the language of some registers fails to distinguish between blood relations and adoptions, the actual rates must have been somewhat higher still.

If we conduct the same calculations for Echigo (figure 3.9), Tokugawa Japan's irrepressible regional diversity once again rears its head. In Echigo—an area in which fewer people resided in stem families and the adoption of Funerary Buddhism lagged behind the Deep East—the smaller sample of registers shows no trend sustained across more than a century.

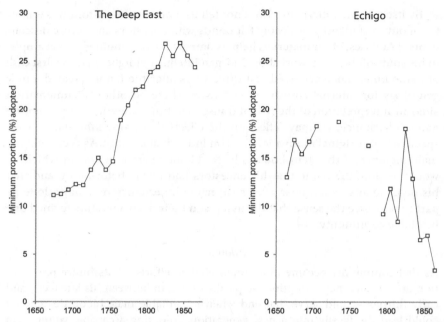

FIGURE 3.9. Married adopted sons in two parts of eastern Honshu, 1660–1869, as a proportion of all married men recorded as a son or adopted son of the household head

SOURCES AND METHOD: For the purposes of this chart, adopted sons include uxorilocal sons-in-law (*muko*). The population sample consists of 783 villages in Japan's Deep East (that is, the north and east Kantō and the southern two-thirds of the Northeast) and 169 in Echigo. For the names of the villages, see Drixler 2013, 261–75. Villages with multiple population registers in a decade are averaged and counted only once per decade. Only decades with at least 150 married sons (adopted or biological) are shown.

Sacrificed Babies

In a particularly stark expression of the concern with household continuity, a discourse in some regions treated excessive numbers of children as a threat. Its early signs include the appearance of *mabiki*, originally an agricultural term for thinning out young plants or pruning trees, as a metaphor for infanticide in the 1690s.[76] The term *mabiki* worked at multiple levels, but in a society that often used plant metaphors to describe the nature of the household, it implied that killing children could serve the health and longevity of the stem line.[77] In their analyses of the motives of infanticide, observers noted that people feared "the lush growth of the branches and leaves of their descendants" or "weakening the root house (*honke*) by pouring their resources into the tips of the twigs (*suezue*)."[78] Moral suasion against infanticide sometimes used an inversion of the same metaphor, warning for example that "if a great tree sheds its leaves and twigs, even the stem withers."[79] This sentence could do its didactic work only if the intended audience felt invested in the vigor of that trunk. The same pamphlet also explicitly describes this mindset; it cites an inscription at a temple which warned that "to kill a child

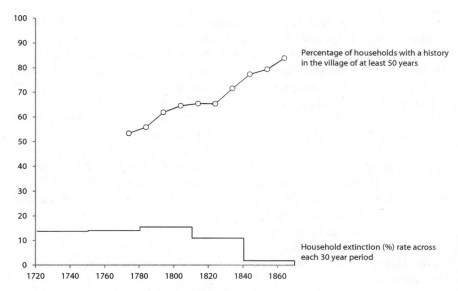

FIGURE 3.10. Household continuity in the village of Niita in Nihonmatsu, 1720–1870
SOURCE: Hirai 2008, 67–69.

thinking that this will make one's family flourish is similar to eating the flesh of one's child and chewing on its bones."[80]

Beginning in the 1790s, *shison hanjō,* or "the prosperity of descendants," became one of the most prominent phrases in exhortatory writings against infanticide. This suggests that their authors believed that the future well-being of the household was already an important goal for infanticidal parents. As implicitly defined by the men who crafted such texts, the task was not to persuade the audience to change its aspirations, which placed the interests of the household collective over that of small souls attempting to join it, but to abandon the apparently common opinion that killing some children was an effective and legitimate means to perpetuate a family line.[81]

Successful Successions

It may be that the apparently growing concern with continuing the stem family translated into greater success at actually doing so. To date, the most detailed study of this issue has been conducted by Hirai Shōko in the village of Niita in the Northeastern domain of Nihonmatsu. There, only 11 percent of households survived throughout the 151 years for which we have evidence.[82] Over time, however, the Niita households became better at perpetuating themselves. In the 1770s, only 53 percent of households had continued for fifty years or more. That proportion increased steadily, even during the Tenmei famine of the 1780s, until, by the 1860s, 84 percent of households in Niita could look back on fifty or more years of endurance (figure 3.10).[83] In this village with a long-declining population, the extinction rate was stable at around 14 percent between 1721 and 1810 but then plunged to under 2 percent in the mid-nineteenth century.[84]

Another study, conducted by Yamamoto Jun on the village of Kazeya in Yamato Province, focuses on the fraction of retirements or deaths of household heads that were followed by succession as opposed to the extinction of the household. Between 1738 and 1785, 82 percent of such transitions were successful. Between 1786 and 1858, fully 98 percent were. One other statistic may suggest a growing concern with household continuity: between the two periods, the proportion of successions occasioned by the death of the head declined from 69 percent to 33 percent, while the average age of the successor decreased slightly. Perhaps new attitudes toward the joys of retirement played a role. It is also possible that the villagers of Kazeya believed that managed transitions increased the odds of household continuation, a goal that became invested with ever-greater meaning as the generations passed.[85]

Two village studies barely suffice to establish a hypothesis. It is plausible that a growing concern for household continuity increasingly produced the desired outcome. However, it is too early to tell whether this was in fact the case throughout late Tokugawa Japan.

CONCLUSION

For all their uncertainties and limitations, the different strands of evidence reviewed here show that across more than two centuries, the influence of a stem family ideal on the way Japanese villagers lived and died strengthened gradually (figure 3.11). Some measures—residence in stem families, commemoration with tombstones, and locally also the use of necrologies—reached saturation levels by the mid-eighteenth century. But other indicators suggest that the commitment to enduring households continued to grow thereafter. In our small sample, name inheritance expanded rapidly in the late eighteenth century. The curves for the unification of temple affiliations within households, adoption rates, and (in two out of two villages) actual success at perpetuating the household all point upward even during the nineteenth century.[86]

The penetration of the stem family system did not occur in the absence of government policy. As we have seen, already Toyotomi Hideyoshi issued laws that effectively favored stem households over other living arrangements. In the 1680s and 1690s, moreover, authorities throughout Japan banned partible inheritance and constrained the marriages of younger sons.[87] While primarily a response to fears of excessive population growth and the fragmentation of farms, the combination of laws consolidating inheritance and curtailing marriage meant, if they were followed, that all families would become stem households.

In a pattern familiar to Tokugawa Japan, such rules were often honored in the breach.[88] That said, at least in the early eighteenth century, when overpopulation fears still ran high, we find attempts at enforcement. In 1713, for example,

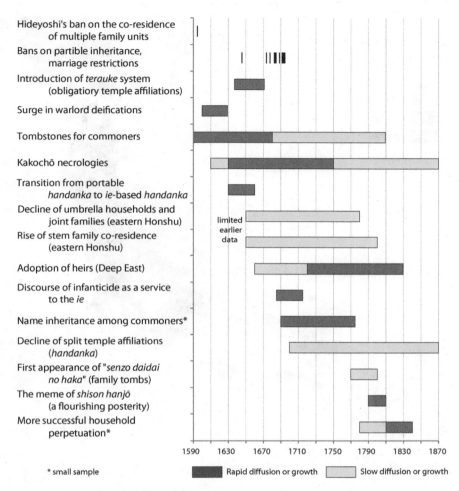

FIGURE 3.11. Timeline of the diffusion of various indicators of devotion to the stem household

the shogunate rebuked "lazy officials" who condoned the illegal establishment of branch households: their negligence caused the "number of people and houses to increase to a level unsuitable for the village."[89] Still, the temporal congruence between official advocacy and demonstrable adoption of the stem household model remains very loose. Similar decrees affected most regions of Japan at roughly the same time. But commoners adopted the full suite of stem family practices only gradually, in disparate regional and chronological waves.

Why did a family consciousness centered on the stem line arise jaggedly over decades and across the country? Why do the diverse indicators for devotion to the

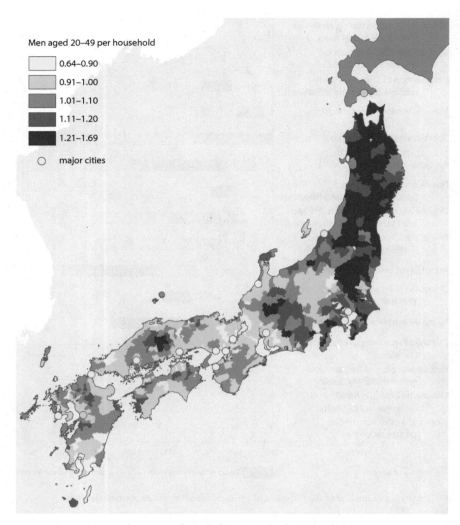

FIGURE 3.12. Men aged 20–49 per household in 1880, by district and city
SOURCE AND METHOD: Naimushō Sōmukyoku Kosekika 1881. No age brackets are reported for the Izu Islands, which therefore remain blank on the map. Since Hokkaido was thinly settled in 1880, I have aggregated the numbers for this northern territory rather than displaying them by district. This district-level map is inspired by a prefecture-level analysis of married couples per household in Hayami and Ochiai 2001, 410.

stem household fail to reach mature intensity at roughly the same time? A partial answer may be that momentum mattered. When Funerary Buddhism was young, the living venerated a few dead ancestors of whom they likely had personal memories. Over time, as commemorative tablets accumulated on family altars, those who knelt before them no longer knew the faces or voices once attached to the names inscribed there. At that point, visions of a collectivity subsuming individual members may have begun to make intuitive sense. At the same time, with each passing generation, the responsibility resting on the shoulders of the living became heavier. It was one thing to fritter away a legacy in 1640. By 1850, another ten generations of spirits sat in judgment. The sheer venerability of the more durable households made them irreplaceably precious. And as more and more ancestors relied on the living to preserve the line intact, the investment in continuity justified ever-greater personal sacrifices.

Even as we acknowledge the hold the stem family had on many imaginations, we must also remember that there were always sizable numbers of Japanese for whom it held at best a diminished meaning. Noninheriting children had to leave the welfare of their ancestors in the care of a sibling. Many became permanent members of other long-established households through marriage or adoption. But for the rest, life would have been shaped by a different narrative. Some may have aspired to becoming venerated ancestors themselves, but others must have realized that for people in their position, an unbroken line of heirs was not a particularly likely outcome. In the commoner sections of the major cities, such people with neither the security nor the burdens of immortal households were likely in the majority.

Surprisingly, the same may have been true for some areas of the countryside. Statistics from the early Meiji period create the impression that in many parts of western Japan, the nuclear family remained a viable alternative to the stem household; in many rural districts between Aichi and Kagoshima, as well as in most of the major cities, the average number of adult men per household is too low for a society dominated by stem families (figure 3.12).

About what the stem family meant for heirs and their spouses, too, this chapter raises more questions than it answers. Did a man who assumed his father's name become, in some sense, his father? Were people who lived their lives in stem households less afraid of death than contemporaries who had to make do with less stable arrangements? How did they cope with the enormous expectations weighing on them? Did those expectations in turn give meaning and direction to their lives? Lafcadio Hearn elided history when, in 1901, he spoke of the obligations of the living to the dead as a timeless institution. But when he described the devotion of the descendant to her ancestors as the very substance of human society in Japan, he may have only moderately exaggerated a mindset that the late Tokugawa period bequeathed to the next generation.

NOTES

1. Hearn 1901, 243–45.
2. Hearn 1901, 247–49.
3. Letter from Hearn to Basil Hall Chamberlain, February 4, 1893, in Hearn 1922, 368–70. The letter makes no mention of mortuary tablets, however, and explains the young woman's

ostracism with her work as a preacher. Hearn already gave the "beautiful and touching worship of ancestors" a prominent place in the preface to his first book on Japan, *Glimpses of Unfamiliar Japan* (1894).

4. While the model for O-Dai came from a former samurai family, and presumably lived in a former samurai neighborhood of Matsue, Hearn's phrase "human society, in this most eastern East" implies that this expectation prevailed irrespective of the household's position in the recently abolished status order.

5. This has led some scholars to define the stem family not (or not merely) by its "residential rule that only one married child remains with the parents" (as I do here) but as "a domestic unit of production and reproduction that persists over generations, handing down the patrimony through non-egalitarian inheritance." Fauve-Chamoux and Ochiai 2009, 3.

6. See, for example, Fauve-Chamoux and Ochiai 2009.

7. See David Spafford's contribution in this volume; note, however, that Spafford uses the term *ie* rather than *stem family*.

8. Ōtō 1989, 177.

9. Farris 2006, 87, citing Sakata Satoshi's studies of the early fourteenth century in two communities in Tanba and Ōmi.

10. Sakata 1989, cited in Glassman 2007, 381.

11. Farris 2006, 154, 248–49, 251–52, 254. This view is broadly in line with that of other medievalists; however, as Sakata Satoshi (2016) points out, students of medieval and early modern Japan use different definitions of the *ie* and thus date its origins and spread to different centuries.

12. Furushima 1991, 482.

13. That *ie* could mean "building" is clear from the ratio of *ie* to people in these early population reports, implying that the *ie* count included stables and granaries and the huts of unmarried servants. For example, the 1622 *Kokura-han Genna jinchiku aratamechō* apportioned the 38,818 rural inhabitants of four districts in Buzen to no fewer than 17,057 *ie*.

14. "Shūmon aratame no gi ni tsuki on-daikan e tatsu," *Tokugawa kinrei-kō*, decree number 1614 of Kanbun 10.10.30 (1670), cited in Ōishi 1976, 319. It is unclear whether, in relation to enumerating people house by house, the 1670 order restated an earlier practice or attempted a national unification of different recording principles.

15. Already in the Edo period, *ie* could mean both "house" and "household," and may derive from a term for "hearth." See Hur 2007, 199.

16. Nor did those assembled under one roof necessarily act as one household. A 1650 register from Shinano reports a house that was subdivided into two sections (*aiya*), one occupied by a man of thirty-seven and his wife, two sons, and mother, the other inhabited by a younger brother and his wife and daughter. The register listed the horse ahead of the younger brother, implying that it was the exclusive property of the elder sibling. Another house in the village contained two nuclear families with no stated kinship tie. If the house was separated into two sections, the register makes no mention of it, and instead reports that the two families divided a parcel of landholdings between them (*aiji*). A bovine is listed at the end of the first nuclear family, a horse at the end of the second. *Nagano kenshi Kinsei shiryōhen* 5, 341.

17. Nakamura 1959. The disagreement between the two types of documents may also reflect the incentives for misrepresenting land use and ownership in cadastral surveys, with

their connection to taxes and laws regulating maximum individual holdings. In this sense, the population registers may be a better guide. On the negotiated process of land surveying, see Brown 1993.

18. Kinoshita 2017, 73–74.

19. "Shinano-no-kuni Saku-gun Honma-mura ninbetsuchō" (1663), in Hasegawa et al. 1991, 68–72.

20. I am here restating the analysis of Hasegawa et al. 1991, 72.

21. "Shinano-no-kuni Saku-gun Honma-mura ninbetsuchō," (1663), in Hasegawa et al. 1991, 69–70.

22. I have also designated servants with families as subunits.

23. For a classic discussion of the evolving relationship of hereditary servants, dependent subhouseholds, and their masters in seventeenth century Japan, see Smith 1959, 13–49, 124–56.

24. Already in 1959, Koyama Takashi called for a move away from a household typology based on structure in a single moment and to replace it with a focus on the life cycle of households (Koyama 1959, 69). See also Lee and Gjerde 1986.

25. With longitudinal data it would be possible to classify a family through the decisions it made regarding its membership. For example, the arrival of a second daughter-in-law would prove that at that moment, the household was operating under joint family rules. To my knowledge, this type of analysis has not been fully implemented, though Takahashi Miyuki's exemplary study of Kōriyama Kamimachi takes an important step in that direction by tabulating the transitions between different household types (2005, 284–95). Even studies of longitudinally linked population registers—long the mainstream of Japanese historical demography—have generally calculated changing fractions in a structural taxonomy (see, e.g., Takahashi 2005, 296–98; Kinoshita 2015, 73–82; and Hirai 2016, 103). Perhaps this is the better part of wisdom, because a classification of household types by event would largely consist of probabilistic ranges. In a typical year, a household would be suspended between two states, like Schrödinger's cat in its box. For example, a household with a husband, a wife, and an eighteen-year-old son would at once be possibly nuclear and possibly stem, until the arrival of a daughter-in-law or the departure of the son settle the question.

26. Drixler 2013, 37–38, 60, 183–85.

27. Morimoto 2006, esp. 90.

28. Nagashima and Tomoeda 1984, 180.

29. Unpublished work for my book project on Tokugawa Japan's volcanic winters.

30. In reviewing this figure, it is important to note that each twenty-year period contains a different set of villages. We may hope that the sample is nonetheless large enough to be representative of the overall trends among Sendai's rural commoners, but this is more likely to be true for the broad outlines of the trend than the precise fractions in every twenty-year period.

31. Joint families and umbrella households also retreated in other parts of Japan. See Smith 1959, 124–56.

32. The snapshot approach also classifies some families operating by joint rules as stem. However, this is unlikely to cancel the stem-as-nuclear shift. For one, the share of joint-as-stem in the population was smaller. For another, while any stem family is at risk for passing through a nuclear phase—all it takes is the late marriage of the heir combined with

an untimely death in the older generation—many joint families contained more than two married couples per generation, requiring extraordinary circumstances in the cycle of arrivals and departures to induce a stem phase.

33. Drixler 2013, 130–37.

34. Whether this was indeed the case lies beyond the scope of this chapter and is best examined in well-documented and longitudinal case studies.

35. "Masudate-gumi Mizuki-mura tō kosū ninbetsu zōgen aiaratamechō" (1850), in *Tokiwa sonshi shiryōhen* 2, 133–201.

36. Katsuda 2003, 40–46, 252–64.

37. Tanaka 1978, 183–204; Gerhart 2009, 41.

38. Glassman 2007, 389–90; Gerhart 2009, 107.

39. One such burial ground is depicted in a late-twelfth-century illustrated scroll, the *Gaki sōshi*. The *Gaki sōshi* shows hungry ghosts in various settings; since it may have been designed to titillate and shock, it has to be treated with due caution as a descriptive source. Yet its image of a cemetery littered with bones and decaying bodies in open coffins has been confirmed by archaeological finds of coffin nails on the perimeter of medieval burial mounds in Ichinotani (Shizuoka). Yamamura 1997, 320; Shintani and Sekizawa 2005, 170.

40. Tanaka 1978; Bitō 1991, 384; Katsuda 2003; Hur 2007, 21–22.

41. Shintani 1991.

42. Shintani 1991, 216–24.

43. Tanaka 1978, 123–43; Shintani 1991, 216.

44. Cemeteries with stupas appear in the *Gaki sōshi* (late twelfth century) and *Ippen shōnin eden* (1299, scroll 5), in which the holy man visits his grandfather's grave—a simple, if stately, mound overgrown with grass. See Iwata 2006, 131–33.

45. Shintani 1991, 219.

46. Shintani 1991, 224.

47. Tamamuro 1964. See also Matsuo 2011.

48. Williams 2005, 38.

49. For a much subtler and fuller discussion of this process than is possible here, as well as of the connections between Funerary Buddhism and *ie* society, see Hur 2007, 141–215, and Williams 2005, 45–50. Different temples differed in the timing of their rituals.

50. Shintani 1991, 222–24; Gerhart 2009, 18–49.

51. Farris 2006, 187–88.

52. Williams 2005, 25.

53. These statements apply to regional summaries of the Northeast, the Kantō and Tōkaidō regions, and the snowy areas on the Japan Sea coast between Iwami and Echigo, including the inland province of Hida. In other areas, my collection contains too few *kakochō* to permit even these cautious generalizations.

54. In the first half of the Tokugawa period, tombstones and necrologies did not always come as a package. Depending on the locale, stone could precede paper, or vice versa. For the case study of one family, see Sekiguchi 2004, esp. 479–80.

55. In assessing the extent to which the number of tombstones is a telling gauge of people's views of death and household continuity, the effects of mundane material factors must be considered—the number, skill, and wages of stonecutters, the availability of suitable stone, and the economic means of potential patrons. Kutsuki uses case studies of three

localities of the Kinai to examine these issues (2004, 70–138). It is also possible that the body of published studies as a whole suffers from selection bias; if researchers were drawn to cemeteries with older tombstones, figure 3.11 overestimates the speed of diffusion.

56. Hur 2007, 417, n. 216.

57. Gamaike 1993, 226–31.

58. Ichikawa 2002; Sekine 2018, 128–34. For an elegant English summary of the changing shapes of gravestones, see Hur 2007, 198–99.

59. The densest clusters that have so far been identified are in Yamagata, Niigata, Chiba, and Gifu prefectures. For a map and a discussion of methodological issues, see Morimoto 2006, 88–104.

60. Morimoto 2006, esp. 261–65, 276.

61. Morimoto 2006, 71–76.

62. Morimoto 2006, 286.

63. Morimoto 2006, esp. 274–86. By emphasizing the haphazard nature of early registration, Morimoto contradicts Fukuta Ajio's 2004 thesis that sex-specific succession expressed the supposed bilinearity of kinship in Japan; Morimoto is similarly skeptical of Ōkuwa Hitoshi's 1979 interpretation of mixed registration as a transitional phenomenon specific to the period between the dissolution of the medieval patriarchal joint family and the rise of the early modern stem family.

64. Morimoto 2006, 91. In Morimoto's Japan-wide sample of population registers, the percentage that contains *handanka* households declines from 40.7 pre-1700, to 37.3 in 1701–50, 32.8 in 1751–1800, and 13.8 in 1801–50.

65. With this view, I depart from Morimoto Kazuhiko, who cites the official decrees on the unification of *danka* affiliations to question whether the decline of *handanka* is really evidence for the absorption of the stem family ideal. Morimoto 2006, 275, drawing on the arguments of Hōzawa 2001.

66. Takagi 1981.

67. Pitelka 2005, 81–82.

68. Name inheritance among actors may have been more than a matter of personal identity or outward branding. Satoko Shimazaki argues that it made their bodies "archives of popular memory that could be passed down from one generation to the next" (2016, 82–84). Yet her account of Ichikawa Danjūrō II also suggests that memorializing his father (after he was murdered on stage) was a key motivation. That audiences embraced this move may be significant in understanding popular attitudes toward name inheritance and the worldviews that underpinned it.

69. Ōtō 1996, 218. Household lineality also found expression in the repetition of characters in posthumous Buddhist names.

70. Ōtō 1996, 217–20. In Nakayamaguchi, landowners led the trend by several decades, but their landless neighbors eventually reached similar levels. In the other three villages, there is no statistically significant difference in the rate of name inheritance between the two groups.

71. Nagata 2009, 361–77, esp. 371–75.

72. On the view that *shūmei* expressed a subjective consciousness as a member of an *ie* as a transgenerational perpetual unit, see Ōtake (1962) 1982, 187. In an analysis of three villages Mary Louise Nagata argues that heirs used name inheritance to strengthen relatively weak claims to their position (2006, 329, 334).

73. Pitelka 2005, 70–82.

74. On the logic and practice of adoption in Tokugawa Japan, among both samurai and commoners, see Marcia Yonemoto's chapter in this volume. My argument in this section, which takes adoption rates as an indicator for a family's commitment to its continuity, is complicated by Nanami Toishi's observation that adoption rates could also be driven by the concerns of the village community, as is suggested by the fact that some adoptions were in fact resurrections of extinct or abandoned household lines (Toishi 2017).

75. The samurai of four domains reviewed by Marcia Yonemoto similarly all showed an upward trend in the proportion of adopted heirs between the seventeenth and the eighteenth century (2016, 171–75). Among daimyo houses, too, adoptions became more frequent in the course of the Tokugawa period, nearly quadrupling between the early seventeenth and the late eighteenth century, with further increases in the nineteenth (see Marcia Yonemoto's chapter in this volume, p. 61, n. 3 citing figures compiled by Takeuchi Toshimi).

76. The first appearances of *mabiki* as a term for infanticide are in a poem, a medical almanac, and a manual of magic, all in the 1690s. See Drixler 2013, 307, n. 31.

77. While botanical metaphors for the family evidently came easy to the people of Tokugawa Japan, no close analogue of the modern English term *stem family* existed, unless one wants to render *honke* as such (whose first character is a tree with its roots or trunk emphasized).

78. Tani (1719) 1997; Nagakubo (1773) 1971, 521. Stem or root house—*honke*—is also the typical term for the main household of a descent group as opposed to the branch household, or *bunke* (literally, "split household"); the "tips of the twigs" is here a literal rendition of *suezue*, which can also mean "descendants," "kin," or "siblings."

79. Nakahachi (n.d. [probably early nineteenth century]) 1978.

80. Nakahachi (n.d.) 1978.

81. For more on this, and in particular the related role of filial piety in motivating infanticide, see Drixler 2013, 61–68, 130–37; and Drixler 2016, 161–62.

82. 1720–1870. Hirai 2008, 65.

83. Hirai 2008, 67.

84. Hirai 2008, 69. The case is complicated by the fact that Hirai's study village of Niita participated in Eastern Japan's culture of infanticide—and depopulation—in the eighteenth century, and that the number of children whom couples in Niita raised increased during the nineteenth century.

85. Yamamoto 1999, 213. As Yamamoto notes, Kazeya was an unusual village in that its farmers owed no rice tribute and that after 1786 they were all raised to the status of *gōshi* (rural samurai). However, the rise in succession by retirement also occurred elsewhere. In Yachi in Kōzuke, such handovers increased from 11 percent between 1764 and 1802 to 54 percent between 1802 and 1857 (Furusawa 1999, 131, 136–37). In Shimoyuda in Sendai domain, the same proportion rose from 27 percent circa 1750 to 81 percent circa 1790 (Ritsumeikan Daigaku Takagi Zemi 1985, 161).

86. The figure includes two phenomena analyzed in a longer draft of this essay but omitted here for the sake of keeping this chapter at a readable length. The sources for the necrologies are too numerous to list here. Warrior deifications are based on Takano 2003 and 2005.

87. Restrictions on partible inheritance were introduced by Wakayama (1645), Okayama (1656), the shogunate (1673), Sendai (1677), Akita (proposed in 1682), Tsu (1683), Amagasaki (1684), Utsunomiya (by 1689), Tosa (1691), Kaga (1693), and Aizu (by 1695). Other domains that mentioned such restrictions in the prefaces of their *goningumichō* include Ashikaga, Hitotsubashi, Kasama, Sakura, and Takaoka in the Kantō; Shōnai, Fukushima, and Tanagura in the Northeast; Nagaoka and Itoigawa in Echigo; Ueda, Koromo, Takatō, and Nishio in central Japan; and Tsuyama in western Japan. This list derives from information in Harafuji 1957, 32; Kodama 1953, 374; Mori 1952; Ōtake (1962) 1982, 153–58; a document in *Nangō sonshi* 2, 618–22; and the 1689 population register of Wakatabi, in *Tochigi kenshi shiryōhen Kinsei 3*, 241.

88. On the continuing practice of partible inheritance and the establishment of branch households in various village studies, see Smith 1977, 134; Hayami 1983; Ritsumeikan Daigaku Takagi Zemi 1985, 168–76; Narimatsu 1992, 170–88; Furusawa 1999, 137–43; Narimatsu 2004, 190; Takahashi 2005, 286; Okada 2006, 213–32.

89. Ōtake (1962) 1982, 156.

REFERENCES

Akiike 1989
Akiike Takeshi. "Kinsei Kindai Ushibuse sagan no riyō ni tsuite: Ushibuse sagan-sei bohyō." *Tōgoku shiron* 4 (1989): 57–77.

Bitō 1991
Bitō Masahide. "Thought and Religion, 1550–1700." In *The Cambridge History of Japan*, vol. 4, edited by John Whitney Hall, 373–424. Cambridge: Cambridge University Press, 1991.

Brown 1993
Brown, Philip C. *Central Authority and Local Autonomy in the Formation of Early Modern Japan*. Stanford: Stanford University Press, 1993.

Drixler 2013
Drixler, Fabian. *Mabiki: Infanticide and Population Growth in Eastern Japan, 1660–1950*. Berkeley: University of California Press, 2013.

Drixler 2016
Drixler, Fabian. "The Discourse of the Louse: Regional Pride and Conflicting Cultures of Parenthood in Mid-Tokugawa Japan." In *Kindheit in der japanischen Geschichte: Erfahrungen und Vorstellungen*, edited by Michael Kinski, Eike Großmann, and Harald Salomon, 159–90. Wiesbaden, Germany: Harrassowitz Verlag, 2016.

Farris 2006
Farris, William Wayne. *Japan's Medieval Population: Famine, Fertility, and Warfare in a Transformative Age*. Honolulu: University of Hawai'i Press, 2006.

Fauve-Chamoux and Ochiai 2009
Fauve-Chamoux, Antoinette, and Ochiai Emiko, eds. *The Stem Family in Eurasian Perspective: Revisiting House Societies, 17th–20th Centuries*. Bern: Peter Lang, 2009.

Fukuta 2004
Fukuta Ajio. *Tera, haka, senzo no minzokugaku*. Tokyo: Taiga Shobō, 2004.

Furusawa 1999
  Furusawa Katsuyuki. "Kinsei chū, kōki no jinkō to sōzoku ni tsuite: Tone-gun Yachi-kumi no shūmon ninbetsuchō bunseki wo tōshite." *Gunma Kenritsu Hakubutsukan kiyō* 20 (1999): 127–44.
Furushima 1991
  Furushima Toshio. "The Village and Agriculture during the Edo Period." In *The Cambridge History of Japan*, vol. 4, edited by John Whitney Hall, 478–518. Cambridge: Cambridge University Press, 1991.
Fussa shishi jōkan
  Fussa Shishi Hensan Iinkai, ed. *Fussa shishi jōkan.* Fussa: Fussa-shi, 1993.
Gamaike 1993
  Gamaike Seishi. "'Mubosei' to Shinshū no bosei." *Kokuritsu Rekishi Minzoku Hakubutsukan kenkyū hōkoku* 49 (1993): 209–36.
Gerhart 2009
  Gerhart, Karen M. *The Material Culture of Death in Medieval Japan.* Honolulu: University of Hawai'i Press, 2009.
Glassman 2007
  Glassman, Hank. "Chinese Buddhist Death Ritual and the Transformation of Japanese Kinship." In *The Buddhist Dead,* edited by Bryan J. Cuevas and Jacqueline I. Stone, 378–404. Honolulu: University of Hawai'i Press, 2007.
Harafuji 1957
  Harafuji Hiroshi. "Kaga-han hyakushō sōzokuhō (1)." *Kanagawa hōgaku* 3:1 (1957): 1–78.
Hasegawa et al. 1991
  Hasegawa Zenkei, Takauchi Takao, Fujii Masaru, and Nozaki Toshirō. *Nihon shakai no kisō kōzō: Ie, dōzoku, sonraku no kenkyū.* Kyoto: Hōritsu Bunkasha, 1991.
Hattori 2003
  Hattori Keishi. *Kinsei bohyō no chōsa I. Tōkyō Kasei Gakuin Seikatsu Hakubutsukan nenpō* 13 (2003): 77–83.
Hattori 2006
  Hattori Keishi. "Kinsei bohyō no chōsa II." *Tōkyō Kasei Gakuin Seikatsu Hakubutsukan nenpō* 16 (2006): 57–65.
Hattori 2010
  Hattori Keishi. "Kinsei bohyō no chōsa III." *Tōkyō Kasei Gakuin Seikatsu Hakubutsukan nenpō* 20 (2010): 51–60.
Hayami 1983
  Hayami Akira. "The Myth of Primogeniture and Impartible Inheritance in Tokugawa Japan." *Journal of Family History* 8:1 (1983): 3–29.
Hayami and Ochiai 2001
  Hayami Akira and Ochiai Emiko. "Household Structure and Demographic Factors in Pre-industrial Japan." In *Asian Population History,* edited by Ts'ui-jung Liu, James Lee, David Sven Reher, Osamu Saito, and Wang Feng, 395–415. Oxford: Oxford University Press, 2001.
Hearn 1894
  Hearn, Lafcadio. *Glimpses of Unfamiliar Japan.* London: Osgood, McIlvaine, 1894.

Hearn 1901
Hearn, Lafcadio. "The Case of O-Dai" (1901). In *A Japanese Miscellany*, 243–52. Boston: Little, Brown, and Company, 1901.

Hearn 1922
Hearn, Lafcadio. *The Writings of Lafcadio Hearn*, vol. 15: *Life and Letters*, edited by Elizabeth Bisland. Boston: Houghton, 1922.

Hirai 2008
Hirai Shōko. *Nihon no kazoku to raifukōsu*. Kyoto: Mineruva Shobō, 2008.

Hirai 2016
Hirai Shōko. "Kinsei kōki ni okeru ie no kakuritsu." In *Ie to kyōdōsei*, edited by Katō Akihiko, Toishi Nanami, and Hayashi Kenzō, 93–113. Tokyo: Nihon Keizai Hyōronsha, 2016.

Hirose 2008
Hirose Ryōkō. "Kinsei Minami-Kantō ni okeru hakaishi zōryū no keishiki to sono hensen: Musashi-no-kuni Tachibana-gun Egasaki-mura Jutokuji bochi wo jirei toshite." *Komazawa shigaku* 70 (2008): 99–109.

Hōzawa 2001
Hōzawa Naohide. "Bakuhan kenryoku to jidan kankei." *Shigaku zasshi* 110:4 (2001): 523–62.

Hur 2007
Hur, Nam-lin. *Death and Social Order in Tokugawa Japan: Buddhism, Anti-Christianity, and the Danka System*. Cambridge, MA: Harvard University Asia Center, 2007.

Ichikawa 2002
Ichikawa Hideyuki. "Senzo daidai no haka no seiritsu." *Nihon minzokugaku* 230 (2002): 1–26.

Ikegami 2003
Ikegami Satoru. "Kinsei boseki no shosō." *Risshō Daigaku Jinbun Kagaku Kenkyūjo nenpō* 40 (2003): 15–45.

Itō Shishi Hensan Iinkai 2005
Itō Shishi Hensan Iinkai, eds. *Itō-shi no sekizō bunkazai*. Itō: Itō-shi Kyōiku Iinkai, 2005.

Iwata 2006
Iwata Shigenori. *"Ohaka" no tanjō: Shisha saishi no minzokushi*. Tokyo: Iwanami Shoten, 2006.

Jishōin Iseki Chōsadan 1987
Jishōin Iseki Chōsadan. *Jishōin iseki: Shinjuku Kuritsu Tomihisa Shōgakkō kaichiku ni tomonau kinkyū hakkutsu chōsa hōkokusho*. Tokyo: Tōkyō-to Shinjuku-ku Kyōiku Iinkai, 1987.

Kadokawa Nihon chimei daijiten
Kadokawa Nihon Chimei Daijiten Hensan Iinkai, ed. *Kadokawa Nihon chimei daijiten*. Tokyo: Kadokawa Shoten, 1978–1990.

Katsuda 2003
Katsuda Itaru. *Shisha-tachi no Chūsei*. Tokyo: Yoshikawa Kōbunkan, 2003.

Kinoshita 2015
Kinoshita Futoshi. "Dewa-no-kuni Murayama-gun Yanbe-mura ni okeru setai no hensen." In *Tokugawa Nihon no kazoku to chiikisei: rekishi jinkōgaku to no taiwa*, edited by Ochiai Emiko, 63–90. Kyoto: Mineruva Shobō, 2015.

Kinoshita 2017
    Kinoshita Mitsuo. *Hinkon to jiko sekinin no Kinsei Nihonshi.* Kyoto: Jinbun Shoin, 2017.
Kodama 1953
    Kodama Kōta. *Kinsei nōson shakai no kenkyū.* Tokyo: Yoshikawa Kōbunkan, 1953.
Koyama 1959
    Koyama Takashi. "Kazoku keitai no shūkiteki henka." In *Ie: Sono kōzō bunseki,* edited by Kitano Seiichi and Okada Yuzuru, 67–83. Tokyo: Sōbunsha, 1959.
Kutsuki 2003
    Kutsuki Ryō. "Kinsei bohyō no kōkogakuteki bunseki kara mita Edo kinkō no jiin: Hiratsuka-shi Ōkami Shinpōji bochi no jirei kara." *Edo Iseki Kenkyūkai kaihō* 90 (2003): 451–63.
Kutsuki 2004
    Kutsuki Ryō. *Bohyō no minzokugaku, kōkogaku.* Tokyo: Keiō Gijuku Daigaku Shuppankai, 2004.
Kyōto Kokuritsu Hakubutsukan 2006
    Kyōto Kokuritsu Hakubutsukan, ed. *Ōemaki ten.* Tokyo: Yomiuri Shinbunsha, 2006.
Lee and Gjerde 1986
    Lee, James, and Jon Gjerde. "Comparative Household Morphology of Stem, Joint, and Nuclear Household Systems." *Continuity and Change* 1:1 (1986): 89–111.
Masaoka 1999
    Masaoka Nobuhiro. "Nara bonchi ni okeru hakagō to bosei: Yamatokōriyama-shi Denpō haka no jirei kara." *Ōryō shigaku* 25 (1999): 369–400.
Matsuda 2001
    Matsuda Tomoyoshi. "Bohyō kara mita haka kannen no rekishiteki tenkai: Ōkawa-gun ni shozai suru jūyon bochi no Kinsei kara iebaka seiritsu-ki ni okeru yōso." *Kagawa kōko* 8 (2001): 114–46.
Matsuo 2011
    Matsuo Kenji. *Sōshiki bukkyō no tanjō: Chūsei no bukkyō kakumei.* Tokyo: Heibonsha, 2011.
Miyoshi 1986
    Miyoshi Yoshizō. "Kinsei bohyō no keitai to minshū no seishin no henka ni tsuite." *Risshō Daigaku Daigakuin nenpō* 3 (1986): 31–40.
Mori 1952
    Mori Kahei. "Kinsei nōgyō keiei no tekiseika taisaku." *Iwate Daigaku Gakugei Gakubu kenkyū nenpō* 4 (1952): 17–33.
Morimoto 2006
    Morimoto Kazuhiko. *Senzo saishi to ie no kakuritsu: 'Handanka' kara ikka ichiji e.* Kyoto: Minerva Shobō, 2006.
Nagakubo 1773) 1971
    Nagakubo Sekisui. *Sūjōdan.* Mito, 1773. In *Ibaraki-ken shiryō Kinsei shakai keizai hen,* edited by Ibaraki Kenshi Hensan Kinseishi Dai-2-Bukai, 519–25. Mito-shi: Ibaraki-ken, 1971.
Nagano kenshi Kinsei shiryōhen 5
    Nagano-ken. *Nagano kenshi Kinsei shiryōhen 5.* Nagano: Nagano Kenshi Kankōkai, 1973.

Nagasawa 1978
Nagasawa Toshiaki. "Kinsei sekizō botō no rekishiteki henka." *Nihon minzokugaku* 116 (1978): 64–76.

Nagashima and Tomoeda 1984
Nagashima, Nobuhiro and Hiroyasu Tomoeda, eds. "Regional Differences in Japanese Culture: Results of a Questionnaire." *Senri Ethnological Studies* 14 (1984): 1–220.

Nagata 2006
Nagata, Mary Louise. "Kamei ni miru ie no senryaku to kojin no sentaku: Nōbi to Tōhoku to no hikaku." In *Tokugawa Nihon no raifukōsu: rekishi jinkōgaku to no taiwa*, edited by Ochiai Emiko, 305–38. Kyoto: Minerva Shobō, 2006.

Nagata 2009
Nagata, Mary Louise. "Name Changing and the Stem Family in Early Modern Japan: Shimomoriya." In *The Stem Family in Eurasian Perspective: Revisiting House Societies, 17th–20th Centuries*, edited by Antoinette Fauve-Chamoux and Emiko Ochiai, 361–78. Bern, Switzerland: Peter Lang, 2009.

Naimushō Sōmukyoku Kosekika
Naimushō Sōmukyoku Kosekika, ed. *Nihon zenkoku minseki kokōhyō, Meiji 13-nen shirabe*. Tokyo: Naimushō Sōmukyoku Kosekika, 1881.

Nakahachi (n.d.) 1978
Nakahachi Haruchika. *Yōikukun*. Kusakisawa Ōsasa, n.d. (probably before 1840). In *Hanayama sonshi*, 237–38. Hanayama-mura, 1978.

Nakamura 1959
Nakamura Kichiji. "Kenchichō no ie." In *Ie: Sono kōzō bunseki*, edited by Kitano Seiichi and Okada Yuzuru, 164–87. Tokyo: Sōbunsha, 1959.

Nakayama Hokekyōji-shi Hensan Iinkai 1981
Nakayama Hokekyōji-shi Hensan Iinkai, ed. *Nakayama Hokekyōji-shi*. Ichikawa: Hokekyōji, 1981.

Nangō sonshi 2
Nangō Sonshi Hensan Iinkai, ed. *Nangō sonshi 2 shizen, kōko, Chūsei, Kinsei shiryō*. Nangō-mura (Fukushima-ken): Nangō-mura, 1985.

Narimatsu 1992
Narimatsu Saeko. *Edo jidai no Tōhoku nōson: Nihonmatsu-han Niita-mura*. Tokyo: Dōbunkan, 1992.

Narimatsu 2004
Narimatsu Saeko. *Nanushi monjo ni miru Edo jidai no nōson no kurashi*. Tokyo: Yūzankaku, 2004.

Nihon rekishi chimei taikei
Heibonsha Chihō Shiryō Sentā, ed. *Nihon rekishi chimei taikei*. Tokyo: Heibonsha, 1979–2004.

Nishimoto 2015
Nishimoto Kazuya. "Kinseibo kara mita Tōhoku san-daikikin: Miyagi-ken Motoyoshi-gun Minamisanriku-chō Shizugawa no Kinsei bohyō no chōsa kara." *Miyagi kōkogaku* 17 (2015): 169–80.

Ōishi 1976
  Ōishi Shinzaburō. *Kinsei sonraku no kōzō to ie seido*. Tokyo: Ochanomizu Shobō, 1976.
Okada 2006
  Okada Aoi. *Kinsei sonraku shakai no ie to setai keishō: Kazoku ruikei no hendō to kaiki*. Tokyo: Chisen Shokan, 2006.
Ōkuwa 1979
  Ōkuwa Hitoshi. *Jidan no shisō*. Higashimurayama: Kyōikusha, 1979.
Ōtake (1962) 1982
  Ōtake Hideo. *Hōken shakai no nōmin kazoku: Edo-ki nōmin kazoku no reksihiteki ichizuke*. 1962. Revised ed., Tokyo: Sōbunsha, 1982.
Ōtō 1989
  Ōtō Osamu. "Nōmin no ie to mura shakai." In *Nihon kazokushi*, edited by Sekiguchi Hiroko et al., 163–90. Matsudo: Azusa Shuppansha, 1989.
Ōtō 1996
  Ōtō Osamu. *Kinsei nōmin to ie, mura, kokka: Seikatsushi, shakaishi no shiza kara*. Tokyo: Yoshikawa Kōbunkan, 1996.
Pitelka 2005
  Pitelka, Morgan. *Handmade Culture: Raku Potters, Patrons, and Tea Practitioners in Japan*. Honolulu: University of Hawai'i Press, 2005.
Ritsumeikan Daigaku Takagi Zemi 1985
  Ritsumeikan Daigaku Takagi Zemi, ed. *Kinsei nōmin kazoku no rekishi jinkōgakuteki kenkyū: Ōshū Iwai chihō no ninzū aratamechō bunseki*. Kyoto: Sangyō Shakai Gakubu Takagi Kenkyūshitsu, 1985.
Saitō 1981
  Saitō Tadashi and Sen'yōji Botō-gun Chōsadan. *Sen'yōji botō-gun*. Ōsuka: Ōsuka-machi Kyōiku Iinkai, 1981.
Sakata 1989
  Sakata Satoshi. "Chūsei goki hyakushō no myōji, ie, ie ketsugō." In *Kazoku to josei no rekishi*, edited by Zenkindai Joseishi Kenkyūkai, 228–50. Tokyo: Yoshikawa Kōbundō, 1989.
Sakata 2016
  Sakata Satoshi. "Sengoku-ki Kinai Kingoku no hyakushō no ie." In *Ie to kyōdōsei*, edited by Katō Akihiko, Toishi Nanami, and Hayashi Kenzō, 21–44. Tokyo: Nihon Keizai Hyōronsha, 2016.
Sekiguchi 2000
  Sekiguchi Norihisa. "Gofunai ni okeru Kinsei bohyō no ichi yōsō: Tōkyō-to Ushigome Kagurazaka shūhen jiin-gun no bohyō chōsa kara." *Risshō kōko* 38, 39 (double issue) (2000): 51–84.
Sekiguchi 2004
  Sekiguchi Norihisa. "Kinsei Tōhoku no 'ie' to haka: Iwate-ken Maesawa-chō Ōmuro Suzuki-ke no bohyō to kakochō." *Kokuritsu Rekishi Minzoku Hakubutsukan kenkyū hōkoku* 112 (2004): 465–85.
Sekine 2018
  Sekine Tatsuhito. *Hakaishi ga kataru Edo jidai: Daimyō, shomin no haka jijō*. Tokyo: Yoshikawa Kōbubunkan, 2018.

Sekine and Shibuya 2007
    Sekine Tatsuhito and Shibuya Yūko. "Bohyō kara mita Edo jidai no jinkō hendō." *Nihon kōkogaku* 24 (2007): 21–39.
Shimazaki 2016
    Shimazaki, Satoko. *Edo Kabuki in Transition: From the Worlds of the Samurai to the Vengeful Female Ghost*. New York: Columbia University Press, 2016.
Shintani 1991
    Shintani Takanori. *Ryōbosei to takaikan*. Tokyo: Yoshikawa Kōbunkan, 1991.
Shintani and Sekizawa 2005
    Shintani Takanori and Sekizawa Mayumi, ed. *Minzoku shōjiten: shi to sōsō*. Tokyo: Yoshikawa Kōbunkan, 2005.
Shiroishi, Kutsuki, and Senda 2004
    Shiroishi Taiichirō, Kutsuki Ryō, and Senda Yoshihiro. "Uda, Tsuge chiiki ni okeru Chū, Kinsei bochi no chōsa (Yamato ni okeru Chū, Kinsei bochi no chōsa)." *Kokuritsu Rekishi Minzoku Hakubutsukan kenkyū hōkokusho* 111 (2004): 1–35, 429–76, 527–43.
Shiroishi, Kutsuki, Muraki, et al. 2004
    Shiroishi Taiichirō, Kutsuki Ryō, Muraki Jirō, et al. "Nara bonchi ni okeru gōbo no chōsa (Yamato ni okeru Chū, Kinsei bochi no chōsa)." *Kokuritsu Rekishi Minzoku Hakubutsukan kenkyū hōkokusho* 111 (2004): 37–121, 477–526, 544–62.
Smith 1959
    Smith, Thomas C. *The Agrarian Origins of Modern Japan*. Stanford, CA: Stanford University Press, 1959.
Smith 1977
    Smith, Thomas C. *Nakahara: Family Farming and Population in a Japanese Village, 1771–1830*. Stanford, CA: Stanford University Press, 1977.
Takagi 1981
    Takagi Tadashi. "Meiji Minpō shikō mae ni okeru shūmei." *Kantō Tanki Daigaku kiyō* 2 (1981): 27–42.
Takahashi 2005
    Takahashi Miyuki. *Zaigōmachi no rekishi jinkōgaku: Kinsei ni okeru chiiki to chihō toshi no hatten*. Kyoto: Mineruva Shobō, 2005.
Takano 2003
    Takano Nobuharu. "Bushi shinkakuka ichiran, kō (jō, Higashi-Nihon-hen)." *Kyūshū Bunkashi Kenkyūjo kiyō* 47 (2003): 1–105.
Takano 2005
    Takano Nobuharu. "Bushi shinkakuka ichiran, kō (ge, Nishi-Nihon-hen)." *Kyūshū Bunkashi Kenkyūjo kiyō* 48 (2005): 1–165.
Tamamuro 1964
    Tamamuro Taijō. *Sōshiki bukkyō*. Tokyo: Daihō Rinkaku, 1964.
Tanaka 1978
    Tanaka Hisao. *Sosen saishi no kenkyū*. Tokyo: Kōbundō, 1978.
Tani (1719) 1997
    Tani Shigetō. *Zokusetsu zeiben zokuhen*. Kyoto: Ibaraki Tasaemon, 1719. In Ōta Motoko. "Tosa hanryōnai no mabiki kankō kankei shiryō: hōrei, denshō, hōdō." In *Kinsei Nihon mabiki kankō shiryō shūsei*, edited by Ōta Motoko, 605–6. Tokyo: Tōsui Shobō, 1997.

Tanigawa 1989
   Tanigawa Akio. "Kinsei bohyō no hensen to ie ishiki: Chiba-ken Ichihara-shi Takataki, Yōrō chiku no Kinsei bohyō no saikentō." *Shikan* 121 (1989): 2–16.
Tochigi kenshi shiryōhen Kinsei 3
   Tochigi Kenshi Hensan Iinkai, ed. *Tochigi kenshi shiryōhen Kinsei 3*. Utsunomiya: Tochigi-ken, 1975.
Toishi 2017
   Toishi Nanami. *Mura to ie wo mamotta Edo jidai no hitobito: Jinkō genshō chiiki no yōshi seido to hyakushō kabushiki*. Tokyo: Nōsan Gyoson Bunka Kyōkai, 2017.
Tokiwa sonshi shiryōhen 2
   Tokiwa Sonshi Hensan Iinkai, ed. *Tokiwa sonshi shiryōhen 2*. Tokiwa: Tokiwa-mura, 2003.
Williams 2005
   Williams, Duncan Ryūken. *The Other Side of Zen: A Social History of Sōtō Zen Buddhism in Tokugawa Japan*. Princeton: Princeton University Press, 2005.
Yamamoto 1999
   Yamamoto Jun. "Mibun no henka to kazoku kōzō, jinkō kōzō no hendō: Nara-ken Yoshino-gun Totsukawa-mura Kazeya, 1738–1859." *Nihon kenkyū: Kokusai Nihon Bunka Kenkyū Sentā kiyō* 19 (1999): 203–19.
Yamamura 1997
   Yamamura Hiroshi. "Ichinotani seki nit suite." In *Chūsei toshi to Ichinotani Chūsei funbogun,* edited by Amino Yoshihiko, Ishii Susumu, Hirano Kazuo, and Minegishi Sumio, 303–23. Tokyo: Meicho Shuppan, 1997.
Yonemoto 2016
   Yonemoto, Marcia. *The Problem of Women in Early Modern Japan*. Berkeley: University of California Press, 2016.
Yoshizawa 2004
   Yoshizawa Satoru. "Nara bonchi to sono shūhen ni okeru Kinsei sekitō no zōryū keikō ni tsuite." *Kokuritsu Rekishi Minzoku Hakubutsukan kenkyū hōkoku* 111 (2004): 161–79.

4

Name and Fame

Material Objects as Authority, Security, and Legacy

Morgan Pitelka

In 1603 the reigning emperor elevated Tokugawa Ieyasu to the office of shogun, confirming his decisive military victory over opponents in 1600 and his subsequent, and far-reaching, assumption of governing prerogatives (from assigning landholdings to minting coins). Preceded by a fulsome courtship of imperial favor with gifts and ritual deference, the appointment led to both the amplified administrative initiatives and ceremonial performances that might secure a fragile peace. Ieyasu tacked back and forth between the imperial capital of Kyoto and his shogunal headquarters in Edo, working all political channels to build support for his regime. Backing mattered, particularly because the teenage heir of his former lord—Toyotomi Hideyoshi, who first brought union to the warring states—remained with his mother at Osaka castle as a rallying point for doubters and the disaffected. A potential division in fealty compounded the dangers of a nascent rule. Ieyasu took the precaution, consequently, of resigning the office of shogun in 1605. Surprising for a hungry ruler still establishing his mandate, the decision was prudent for a would-be dynast.

Succession tormented the houses of the warring states (1467–1603). Indeed, it was contests over the headship of three leading families that had provoked the opening hostilities of the Ōnin war in Kyoto and then tangled all provinces in violence. And, again and again, throughout the ordeals upending the Ashikaga shogunate and the very premises of medieval rule, problems over heirs shaped the course of conflict. Not least in Ieyasu's immediate memory. The ascendancy of the Oda house, abetted by Nobunaga's manipulation of yet another claimant to Ashikaga headship, came to a close when a turncoat eliminated both Nobunaga and his designated successor in 1582. The ascendancy of the Toyotomi house, abetted by Hideyoshi's manipulation of the infant he instated as Oda head, stalled when the unifier's death in 1598 left an only son, age five, in the care of Ieyasu and fellow guardians.

In the years immediately thereafter, Ieyasu's seizure of power announced a presumption of leadership even as his finesse in diplomacy appeared to quiet, or at least to defer, competition with the child. His appointment as shogun forced no reckoning, since the Toyotomi relied on courtly rather than military titles to legitimate authority, nor did his resignation of that office alter the relationship overtly. It nonetheless enabled a crucial transition with a resonant message. In the near term, Ieyasu's retirement cleared the way to establish an adult successor, tried by experience, as the new Tokugawa head and, thus, to stage a compelling transfer of household authority. In the longer term, it intimated a default solution to the Toyotomi problem: the sheer momentum of a Tokugawa regime, managed adroitly across generations, might erase pretenders.

With characteristic pageantry, Ieyasu prepared to relinquish his post during the fourth month of 1605 by receiving the heir Hidetada, accompanied by an awesome entourage of some 100,000 soldiers, at Fushimi castle. The two visited the court and, in a series of fancy gatherings, received the leaders of military, aristocratic, and religious society. Ieyasu then formally submitted his resignation; Hidetada immediately received shogunal appointment from the emperor. As a sort of surety of concord, Ieyasu lingered in Kyoto for another five months.

But the work of guaranteeing future successions was hardly complete. Three strategic relocations signaled a multipronged approach to household survival. In 1607 Ieyasu moved his ninth son from Kofu castle in Kai Province to Kiyosu castle in Owari Province, a key point along the Tōkaidō highway.[1] In 1609 he moved his tenth son from Mito to a domain double the size in Suruga and Tōtōmi, with a headquarters in Sunpu. At the same time, he moved his eleventh son from Shimotsuma to Mito.[2] Major construction accompanied the moves, particularly in Owari. There, Ieyasu dismantled Kiyosu castle in order to launch, in 1610, the building of a huge new fortress in Nagoya that required tens of thousands of laborers recruited by daimyo across the country.[3] The ninth son became lord of Nagoya.

Created through these flamboyant and enriching allocations were three cadet branches of the Tokugawa house that could provide shogunal successors in the event the main line in Edo failed to produce an heir (as would occur several times). The three—the Owari branch, the Mito branch, and the Kii branch (as it was known after the tenth son received a further transfer)—remained the wealthiest, most prestigious, most advantageously situated, and most influential of all the collateral branches established over time by the Tokugawa. Their role in succession politics, moreover, was compound. If they guaranteed a pool of heirs, they simultaneously expanded the pool of intimate allies with a stake in Tokugawa survival. A complementary consideration, especially during the shogunate's formative years, was the deflection of tension: placing young sons in powerful but scattered domains suppressed sibling conflict, a solution to what Conrad Totman called the problem of "how to appease or disempower those offspring not destined to succeed to one's own position."[4]

In the end, Ieyasu's dual approach to succession—transferring title to his heir and building a deep bench around him—did not erase the Toyotomi problem. Provoked alike by Toyotomi intransigence and Tokugawa impatience, a military showdown occurred in 1614–15. Notably, however, it came late and adventitiously. It brought no single daimyo to a Toyotomi side supported solely by the dispossessed "men of the waves" whose lords had been lost in the battles of 1600. And it resulted in a humiliating defeat of the Toyotomi partisans and the suicide of their head, Hideyoshi's now-twenty-two-year-old son, who left no heir of his own. In effect, if Ieyasu's succession provisions could not preclude threats, they so strongly positioned supporters of a coherent leadership against atavistic challengers without household organization that the disposition of hereditary power became all the clearer as one imperative of survival.

And the work continued. The politics of lineage extended for Ieyasu beyond succession itself to the protection and management of resources—not just landed revenue but the polymorphous arsenal of prestige that could be deployed to signify rightful authority and secure reputation. It included the generation of distinguished (if artful) genealogies, the construction of grand mortuary monuments, and the observation of ritual calendars centered on family anniversaries and passages. It also, and critically, included the assembly of material objects that were imbued with meaning, employed ceremonially, and passed on as visible depositories of honor to the heads of successive generations.

These practices and the variously tangible and intangible resources they animated form the subject of this chapter. They loomed large for Ieyasu in his tireless campaign to seal the Tokugawa purchase on the future. More than this, they proved precious to ambitious houses across the social spectrum, thus inviting a comparative vantage on the shared strategies that helped sustain the *ie* in early modern Japan. I begin with martial lineages, for which the transfer of property to maintain the family line is well established; and I continue with commercial lineages to demonstrate that these practices extended into the world of elite commoners and played a major role in steadying family succession over multiple generations while also shaping the materials that historians and art historians use to study the past.

WARRIOR THINGS: MATERIAL INHERITANCE IN THE TOKUGAWA AND HOSOKAWA HOUSES

From the beginning of warrior rule in Japan, great martial houses linked property with authority. The legitimacy of rule was predicated on the management of resources: not just the income from landholdings and the labor of subordinates but the heirlooms conveying righteousness. Consider the early medieval narrative of the Soga brothers, which equates patrimony with symbolically potent swords. Only when the swords are recovered from imposters by their proper inheritors is legitimate succession possible.[5] Examples proliferate of material witness to rightful authority—from banquets with luxury foodstuffs (testifying to faithful stewardship of nature's harvests) to ancestral mansions and ornaments (testifying to power made manifest through hereditary wealth).[6]

In the age of warring states, material mattered more, since the currency of rank and title that once underlay authority decayed with the institutions that granted them. Fortresses and conquered lands, arms and armor became the core claims on position—together, and increasingly, with more intimate symbols of household trust.[7] When Oda Nobunaga identified his eldest son as heir in 1575, he vested him with authority over Mino and Owari Provinces and installed him in Gifu castle. He also bestowed on the young man "the great sword Hishikiri" and most of "the priceless implements he had collected" (holding back "only his tea ceremony implements for himself").[8] Then, having tested the heir's suitability to rule over the course of two years,[9] Nobunaga finally relinquished his finest tea utensils in 1577, a perhaps ultimate symbol of confidence.[10] The treasure did not avert treachery (by an Oda vassal who steered an army of 13,000 into Kyoto to attack both Nobunaga and his heir in 1582).[11] Nor did it become dispensable as a medium of social influence, cultural capital, and political standing to other aspiring warlords.

Toyotomi Hideyoshi transferred to his child heir not only the largest and best-defended castle in Japan but also an opulent collection of Chinese art, Japanese tea utensils, heirloom arms and armor, and European objects of many varieties.[12] If they, too, were inadequate insurance against a martial reckoning between the Toyotomi and the Tokugawa in 1615, they nevertheless remained powerful lures to Ieyasu. Following the destruction by fire of the Toyotomi fortress at Osaka, Ieyasu sent deputies into the ashes to rescue key items from the Toyotomi collection, notably swords and Chinese ceramics. He then ordered master craftsmen to repair these pieces and added them to the already significant Tokugawa collection that he intended to bequeath to his descendants.[13] The authenticity of rule was coupled with the custody of fabled objects connecting both generations and regimes.

Although we do not know exactly how Ieyasu divided his material goods, evidence indicates that he wanted specific objects and amounts of cash to pass to the main Tokugawa house in Edo,[14] as well as to each of the three branch houses. It is likely, too, that he assigned items to his intended mortuary site on Mt. Kunō. The critical document concerning the transfer is preserved by the Owari branch of the Tokugawa: *The Record of Utensils Inherited from Sunpu Castle* (*Sunpu owakemono odōgu chō*).[15] Compiled between 1616 and 1618 at Sunpu in accord with Ieyasu's instructions, the record lists objects in eleven registers, including swords, sword-handle ornaments, clothing, medicine, and horse fittings.

Subsequent documents concerning the objects illuminate a remarkable pattern of circulation as their holders used them to reaffirm connections with the

Tokugawa founder. The main and cadet braches of the family repeatedly donated inherited items to the proliferating sanctuaries where Ieyasu's deified spirit was honored, the Tōshōgū (especially the principal shrine at Nikkō and the shrines in the branch domains of Owari, Kii, and Mito). Such donations occasioned a kind of reunion between the ancestral spirit and his treasure even as they transformed the objects into ritual goods with new social lives. Thus, for example, when Ieyasu's tenth son established a Tōshōgū during 1621 in Wakayama, home to the Kii branch of the family, he materialized the sacred presence with gifts—effectively, with relics—passed down by his father. To take just one category of object, military items still held by the shrine today, the donation included four long swords, a set of European armor with a helmet, a set of "body round" armor, lacquered saddles and stirrups, and several conch shells that had been blown in battle.[16] Similar offerings were made by almost every subsequent head of the Kii Tokugawa. Long swords, particularly popular, came to the shrine from the third-, fifth-, sixth-, seventh-, eighth-, ninth-, tenth-, eleventh-, twelfth-, and fourteenth-generation heads. This continuing circulation of Ieyasu's heirlooms through ceremony-rich endowments consecrated the lineage and renewed the links of donors to the founder and to one another.

Many warrior houses catalogued the treasures they bequeathed across generations, creating in the process documents of passage that served as family histories. Prominent among them is the Hosokawa house, which occupied high office in the Ashikaga shogunate, prospered under Toyotomi Hideyoshi, and became one of the wealthiest daimyo houses of the Tokugawa regime as castellans of Kumamoto in Kyushu. Their best-known heads in the early modern period—Hosokawa Fujitaka (1534–1610, also known as Yūsai) and his son Hosokawa Tadaoki (1563–1646, also known as Sansai)—were celebrated both as warriors and as men of culture, the father as a poet, the son as a tea connoisseur.

The Summary of the Famous Objects of this Honorable House is a ledger of the family heirlooms, compiled in its extant form in the eighteenth century, which offers revealing insights into the types of objects that families endeavored to preserve and their motives for doing so.[17] The catalog opens with swords, defining from the outset the house's martial status. Listed first are swords received by Hosokawa Tadaoki from the Tokugawa: one from Ieyasu; two from the second shogun, Hidetada; a fourth from the third shogun, Iemitsu. They testify to the meritorious service of Tadaoki to the Tokugawa founder and his ongoing intimacy with the successors (uncommon for a daimyo outside the circle of immediate Tokugawa allies). Listed next are swords variously acquired by Tadaoki and his father, including one received from the Toyotomi at the time of the Siege of Odawara Castle in 1590. Acknowledged here is the family's lustrous pre-Tokugawa pedigree as well as the father's role in its ascent. In effect, the ledger constructs a genealogy of authority and legitimacy not through objects themselves but through their provenance. How they were deployed remains obscure in the Hosokawa case, although voluminous evidence attests to the display of swords, armor, and other heirlooms at most warrior rituals of the period.

After the list of swords, the Hosokawa ledger continues with the martial trappings essential to such rituals—spears, saddles, arrows, battle surcoats (*ojinbaori*)—and then proceeds to hanging scrolls. Like the catalog of blades, the catalog of paintings includes references to the political notables who bestowed them on the house (chiefly the shoguns Hidetada and Iemitsu) as well as the cultural luminaries critical to the family history. Noted prominently is the tea master Sen no Rikyū, Tadaoki's teacher, who not only gave paintings by others to his disciple but sometimes brushed them personally. The same story of prestigious connection unfolds in the ledger's subsequent and heroic lists of additional items, most of them related to the practice of tea: tea caddies, tea bowls, tea scoops, kettles, water containers, wastewater containers, lid rests, tea whisk rests, incense containers, flower containers, tea jars, poetry manuals, folding screens, incense burners, lacquer dishes, water basins, and braziers. Rikyū and the Sen circle remain conspicuous in the attributions, together with a group of daimyo tea masters, as authenticators of the legitimate practice and authoritative knowledge they passed to the Hosokawa house. Thus we find, for example, a kettle once owned by Rikyū and a water container used by Hosokawa Tadaoki when he was invited to participate in Hideyoshi's Great Kitano Tea Gathering. Most telling, we find entries for objects lost to fire, confirmation that the ledger is no simple catalog of holdings but a chronicle of political and cultural power.

It is, however, an arrestingly focused chronicle. Although it was compiled well into the early modern period, Hosokawa Tadaoki remains the defining collector in a ledger that all but effaces the activity of his successors. Like Tokugawa Ieyasu, he becomes the prime ancestor—securer of the family fortunes in the wars of unification, witness to the legendary tea events that established the tradition—and a metonym for the house itself. Memory surpasses the labor of generations of heads as the font of legitimacy. The phenomenon would not be limited to warriors, and in fact appears across status groups as one stream in a larger shift to family-based identity.

COMMERCE AND THE FAMILY: MATERIAL LEGACY IN THE RAKU AND THE SEN HOUSES

As the market and cultural networks of Kyoto grew rapidly during the early modern period, the imperial capital became a center of "the arts of play" (*yūgei*) and the primary locus of such ritualized cultural activity as *noh,* tea, and related refinements. The family businesses at the core of the arts industry needed to manage their reputations every bit as avidly as the great martial houses, but their resources were different. Lacking the swords and armor of bygone glory, most lacked large, multigenerational collections of heirlooms as well. They nonetheless developed equivalent arsenals of prestige that variously recall and depart from martial models.

The two families I examine here worked in tea culture, an expensive and rarified world with a particularly strong presence in what is now Kamigyō ward, the area to the west of the imperial palace that was home to many elite artisans, merchants, and teachers. The kiln and workshop of the Raku family was here. The masters of the Sen tea school lived and worked nearby, as did Hon'ami Kōetsu, the fabled sword polisher, calligrapher, and amateur Raku potter. Networks both social and economic developed among such houses as they collaborated in projects and supported one another's businesses. Because their reputations were entwined, they frequently acted in mutually fortifying ways.

Their neighborhood boomed in the late sixteenth century, when Toyotomi Hideyoshi undertook reconstruction of the courtly complexes and erected for himself a palatial castle—Jurakudai, completed in 1587—to signify his authority in the capital.[18] Indeed, frenetic building across the city announced Kyoto's reemergence as Japan's cultural and political center after decades of turmoil. New enterprises, such as the Raku kiln, which may have been started by a Chinese ceramist well known for his sculptural roof tiles and three-color wares, found a foothold in the expanding marketplace. And the kiln thrived in the salon culture of the early seventeenth century by serving the resurgent Sen family, collaborating with the polymath Hon'ami Kōetsu, and selling tea bowls to an increasingly wide consumer base of urban warriors as well as the savvy merchants who pursued tea practice to advance their business interests.

By the latter half of the seventeenth century, however, the Kyoto market was too competitive for comfort. Gazetteers such as the *Kyoto Youth* (*Kyō warabe*,1658), the *Kyoto Sparrow* (*Kyō suzume*, 1665), and the *Kyoto Silk* (*Kyō habutae*,1685) guided readers through myriad shops, entertainment quarters, and studios of every sort (not to mention the countless famous places that linked the commercial present to the historical past).[19] New kilns emerged in and around Kyoto; ceramic traditions proliferated throughout Japan (including two with direct connections to the Raku workshop). If tea practitioners were mounting steadily in number, their options when considering a purchase were multiplying faster. They could buy utensils from a range of specialty retailers or from the kilns themselves. They could choose among wares produced locally or brought in from the provinces. They could find imports from Korea and, if they were affluent, the particularly prized antiques from China. Hence patrons of the small Raku workshop, which now produced ceramics exclusively for the tea ceremony, had to go there for good reason—perhaps a personal connection, a strong aesthetic preference, even a desire for something produced in the neighborhood.

The Raku responded to the challenge by promoting a single, direct line of house heads and obscuring the collaborative nature of their work. They embraced new naming practices and exalted a founder. They made replication of legacy objects a business model. Appearing to mimic some of the strategies of warrior houses for cementing authority, the response may also reflect, as the legal historian Mizubayashi Takeshi argued, a shift in social identity during the latter half of the seventeenth century. Once founded on individual accomplishment, identity increasingly derived from household membership.[20]

In 1688, seemingly for the first time, the Raku potters began to compose a genealogy that would trace a clean and uncomplicated succession from fathers to sons over eight generations, culminating in the present. The resulting story of continuity is inspirational; it is also aspirational. The strain is apparent in two privately preserved documents full of errors and corrections and written in at least two hands, particularly in a 1695 text titled *Memorandum*, which resembles the Buddhist registers of deaths used to keep track of family memorial days when prayers were to be offered at a household altar or local temple.[21] The *Memorandum* lists dozens of relatives—mothers, brothers, sisters—who, though surely key contributors to the enterprise, disappear from the official version of the Raku history. Simple and streamlined genealogy, innocent of collaborators, was an indispensable art form.

To affirm the primacy and continuity of the headship, the Raku also introduced naming practices that identified the successors to the main lineage. Beginning in 1691, each Raku head took the name Kichizaemon during his incumbency (a practice that continues to this day). The name had appeared in an earlier generation, but its routine use commenced only after the completion of the genealogical documents. When they retired, moreover, former heads took Buddhist names ending with the character *nyū* to signal the transfer of authority. Thus, the (putative) fourth-generation head of the Raku house took the retirement name of Ichinyū in 1691, when his (adopted) son became Kichizaemon. That head took the retirement name of Sōnyū in 1708, when his son became Kichizaemon.[22]

These stories of family continuity were repeated in the production strategies of the Raku kiln, which summoned the fame and authority of the designated founder, the sixteenth-century potter Chōjirō. The workshop began to concentrate on styles that evoked his aesthetic: matte-black and matte-red glazes and simple, half-cylinder shapes. Going further, the workshop apparently sold ceramics named and modeled after Chōjirō's most famous tea bowls. When, for example, the influential tea master Sen Bunshuku wrote to Sōnyū with a commission, he requested two "Tōyōbō" tea bowls, two "Kimamori" tea bowls, and one "Kengyō" tea bowl—in each case using names made famous by Chōjirō and well known throughout the tea community.[23] The request was not for fakes but "respectful reproductions" (*utsushi*). And, indeed, a text attributed to Sōnyū's son implies that respectful reproduction became the primary business model for the kiln. "The Catalogue of Raku Vessels" ("Raku utsuwa mokuroku"), an inventory of the ceramics that could be ordered from the workshop, identifies current offerings by the names of Chōjirō's fabled tea bowls ("Ōguro," "Hayabune," "Kenkō," "Kimamori"). It also advertises incense containers, lid rests, and flower containers in Chōjirō's style. In effect, the legacy of the founder became the product line of the kiln.²⁴ Even the eleventh-generation head, who steered the family business through the difficult years of the Meiji Restoration, made reproductions of Chōjirō's work, including a complete series of his so-called "seven bowls" (*Chōjirō shichishu*).²⁵ Fidelity to the founder was the modus operandi of an immortality-seeking enterprise.

The Sen family of tea masters, which collaborated with the Raku kiln and other artisanal workshops enmeshed in the networks of tea practice, also capitalized on the reputation of its founder, Sen no Rikyū (1522–91), the most influential and innovative tea master of the sixteenth century. An important retainer of Toyotomi Hideyoshi as both a cultural advisor and sometime diplomat,²⁶ Rikyū died by suicide, at the command of Hideyoshi, for reasons still unclear. Although his own reputation only grew after death, it was left to his grandson Sōtan to establish the fortunes of the house in the expanding tea culture of the early seventeenth century. Success hinged in good part on constructing brilliant circuits of patronage, for Sōtan was able to place three of his sons as tea masters to exceptionally distinguished daimyo families. Kōshin Sōsa went to work for the powerful branch family of the Tokugawa at Wakayama castle in Kii.²⁷ Sensō Sōshitsu served the Maeda of Kanazawa, who controlled by far the largest daimyo domain in Japan. His brother Ichiō Sōshu served the Matsudaira of Takamatsu, collaterals of the Tokugawa. Each used his prestigious connections to found a school of tea practice based in Kyoto.

The essential connection was nonetheless to Rikyū, whom the extended Sen house began to put at the center of a mythohistory that it staged with particular pomp during the rituals commemorating his death.²⁸ Documented in detail are the services marking the 3rd, 20th, 50th, 100th, 150th, 200th, 300th, and 350th anniversaries. While the earlier services appear to have been simple mortuary rituals held by a family still recovering from Rikyū's suicide and the temporary confiscation of Sen holdings by the Toyotomi regime, the later anniversaries became occasions for lavish tea ceremonies incorporating objects tied to the founder.²⁹ Especially with the 100th anniversary in 1690, the family embarked on an essentially hagiographic celebration of an ancestor who, symbolic of tea's glorious past, was fully fused with its future.³⁰ So aggressively did the Sen imbue Rikyū (and the utensils, persons, and events associated with him) with a sacrosanct aura that scholars refer to his "sanctification" through a sedulous campaign of "revival."³¹

The campaign endured. The 150th anniversary in 1740 included Buddhist mortuary ceremonies at Kyoto's Daitokuji, as well as tea gatherings that reassembled the founder's programs of utensils. The abbot of Daitokuji appeared at the first, on 1740/9/4, when a portrait of Rikyū hung in the alcove.³² Most of the objects were treasures of the Omotesenke branch previously owned by Rikyū, such as a lacquer *natsume* tea container bearing his signature. The bamboo flower container was an heirloom carved by Sōtan. The second gathering, held on the following day, brought together elite Omotesenke disciples and more of Rikyū's utensils. And, day after day thereafter, the gatherings continued: eighty-six of them by 12/13 of the year. Each was an opportunity to perform the Sen history before followers of the various Sen schools, artisans who worked closely with them (such as the head of the Raku family), and other allies from the tea world.[33] Although records do not survive from the Urasenke and Mushanokōji branches of the Sen, it is likely that they hosted similar gatherings for this anniversary.

The 200th anniversary in 1790 was better organized, planned cooperatively by the three branch schools, and more fully documented—reflecting an awareness that records themselves are foundations of reputation. It occurred at a trying time of recovery, after the Great Fire of Kyoto, which raged throughout the city for two full days early in 1788,[34] had damaged or destroyed many of the objects and sites associated with Rikyū, thus assailing the core stock of Sen authority. The 1790 services required current house leaders to restage their story with a depleted treasure house. They spared neither expense nor imagination.

The first gathering of the series—hosted on 1790/9/14 by the head of the Omotesenke school and including as guests three leaders from Daitokuji—emphatically reaffirmed the continued presence of Rikyū's ghost, as if insisting that the legacy was indestructible. The hanging scroll reproduced Rikyū's death poem. The tea scoop, reputedly carved by his eminent early teacher, Takeno Jōō, had been authenticated by his grandson. The tea bowl, a black Raku piece by Chōjirō, bore a name Rikyū had selected, "Kamuro." Versions of the same gathering were restaged over three days for a variety of Daitokuji luminaries; additional gatherings were staged over the following month by all three Sen schools for relatives, tea masters, artisans, and the Kyoto elite. The utensils were all Rikyū all the time. Some were surviving tea scoops and bamboo flower containers made by him. Others were objects named or "owned" (*Rikyū shoji*) or "liked" by him (*Rikyū konomi*). Lest any guest miss the message of these resourceful attributions, carved statues and painted portraits of Rikyū oversaw all proceedings.

Notably, Edo joined in these celebrations. The Edo Senke school, a kind of branch division of Omotesenke, held commemorative tea gatherings that included both elite commoners and warrior leaders, from the daimyo Ikeda Masanao to Tokugawa bannermen and retainers.[35] The lord of Himeji castle, Sakai Tadazane, even organized his own Rikyū commemorations, witness to a Rikyū cult that had extended from the Sen schools to warrior circles.

The 250th commemoration of Rikyū's death, the last major commemoration in the Tokugawa period, occurred during 1839–40. Despite widespread social unrest and a general interdiction on ostentation, the Sen schools celebrated as lavishly as ever. Urasenke took the lead this round, opening with a tea gathering that, unusually, included a guest from the imperial court, Konoe Tadahiro (perhaps in acknowledgment of the contemporary nativist sentiments exalting the imperial tradition). There followed a series of gatherings for Daitokuji priests and no fewer than eighty other gatherings over the course of six months.[36] Until the end of the early modern regime, the Sen mounted the commemorative platform to perform a legitimacy rooted in the authority of the founder and his material legacy. And they did so for ever-expanding audiences of all statuses.

The structure that enabled this expansion, without compromising the authority of house heads, is the so-called family head (*iemoto*) system. It developed in the eighteenth century across a range of cultural disciplines in Japan, including tea, painting, performing arts such as *noh*, and certain styles of poetry, dance, the martial arts, and cookery. While the exaltation of founders and material legacies was common to great martial and commercial houses alike, the "family head system" belonged uniquely to arts practitioners in the marketplace who had to cope with competition not just from rivals but from insiders.

The system emerged when teachers of various cultural practices found their top disciples defecting from the main lineages to found schools of their own. To prevent such splintering, they elaborated schemes of "secret teachings" that could be passed only from a head to his designated heir. So, too, they increasingly regulated curricular and licensing structures to slow, and restrict, the ascent of students through the ranks. Successful disciples might eventually acquire and teach their own students, but only after rigorous training, the payment of fees, and the routine demonstration of obeisance to the school leader.[37] Over time, the privileges of these heads increased impressively: they assumed the rights to control the performance and practice of the art, to determine who could teach and transmit the tradition, to punish or expel members, to dispense names, to manage the material inheritance of the tradition, and to oversee all income from the practice.[38]

The commotion that led the Sen to adopt the "family head system" came from a number of tea masters who claimed to be true inheritors of the teachings of Rikyū and Sōtan. Sugiki Fusai (1628–1708), for example, a well-known disciple of Sōtan in Kyoto, broke with the Sen over accusations that Sōtan's sons had lost the art of tea and the spirit of Rikyū's practice. He identified himself as the orthodox heir in several tea texts that he circulated to his students.[39] Another Sōtan disciple, Yamada Sōhen (1627–1708), printed in woodblock one of the earliest commercial publications concerning Rikyū's practice, *Introductory Selections from the Way of Tea* (*Chadō benmō shō*). There, again denigrating Sōtan's sons, he claimed to possess the sole pure knowledge of Rikyū's tradition.[40] Additional authors, such as Tachibana Jitsuzan and Yabunouchi Chikushin, advanced similar arguments as tea schools multiplied in Kyoto, Edo, and other cities around Japan.

The Sen responded with much stricter control of the tea curriculum and a system of licenses to certify progress. The "Seven Exercises," created in the early eighteenth century, were primary gatekeepers for the growing population of students.[41] The heads of the schools also worked to standardize the aesthetic preferences of disciples through strategic commissions and gifts. In 1713, for example, the Omotesenke head commissioned two hundred black tea bowls from the Raku kiln to mark both the fiftieth birthday of the Raku head and the enduring alliance between the twined successors to Sen no Rikyū and Raku Chōjirō.[42] In 1738 the head of the Raku kiln made 150 red tea bowls, each boxed with an inscription from the Omotesenke head, to mark both the 150th anniversary of Chōjirō's death and the still-twined successors to the two houses. And in 1789 the Raku head made another 200 tea bowls, again boxed with Omotesenke inscriptions. All of these objects were dispersed among disciples, peers, and friends as tangible exemplars of a perduring aesthetic and relationship that was sustained by ever-renewed claims to authenticity.[43]

CONCLUSION

The elaboration among arts practitioners of the "family head system" draws attention, of course, to a defining difference between martial and commercial families. As Tokugawa rule gained traction, most martial families retained secure patrimonies that were concentrated in largely fixed titles and income rights, which they handed down in a normally orderly fashion through designated heirs. Commercial families had no secure patrimonies. Their income depended on the sale of goods and services to customers in a competitive marketplace that offered no insurance to any heir of survival, let alone prosperity. Contrast that with the case of *hinin*, or "beggar boss," families examined by Maren Ehlers in this volume, in which ultimogeniture was practiced, perhaps because of these houses' "relative lack of property." What links the martial and commercial families examined here is wealth.

Consequently striking in the histories I trace here is the congruence in family values and family practices. In both the martial and commercial examples we find a focus on venerated founders, genealogical prestige, clear linear succession of stem household heads, and material witness to the generational passage of authority. The "family head system" was unique to commercial families as a defense against an unruly market. Crucially, however, it was predicated on the very claim to legitimacy that already animated founders' cults and genealogical sleight of hand: the claim to authentic custody of exclusive traditions. If the business practices of the system had a new edginess (conveying "secrets" solely from head to head, structuring teaching in taxing modules, licensing progress in slow stages, releasing disciples on costly leashes), they remained the instruments of a household ascendancy lodged in ancestral reputation.

There is much, of course, that separates my examples. Beyond the status issues and the market exposure, neither the heads nor the genealogies were commensurate in historical significance. Indeed, the deified Ieyasu is a case apart from all of Japan's other leaders throughout time. So, too, the material legacies, though serving alike to transmit a virtuous authority across generations, were too various in volume, content, and deployment to stand close comparison. Above all, the actual experiences of the families over time—the vicissitudes of successive heads and the survival strategies they adopted—are particular and profoundly different.

Yet here, perhaps, we find the deepest similarity among them: their stories occlude the changes that enabled each house to survive for upwards of three centuries. In every case, their remote founders became brand names that concealed innovation under the cover of precedent. Reification was the message of family performances—in ancestor cults, genealogies, heirloom catalogues, death anniversaries, naming conventions, business practices—that so fused (putative) origins with continuing histories as to convert drama into banality.

Even today, the name of Tokugawa Iemitsu, one of the most influential of Tokugawa shoguns, barely survives outside specialist circles. Hosokawa Tsunetoshi (1634–1714), a major patron, poet, and scholar, is consigned to the far fringes of a tradition dominated by Yūsai and Sansai. The attention to Sen no Rikyū and Raku Chōjirō effaces the successors who responded creatively both to new trends in the world of tea and constant social pressure. And quite apart from writing out the dynamic futures of families, the ancestor fixation has distorted the ancestors themselves. So much of the record emerged late, and in ideological and promotional contexts, that the complex lives of founders are effectively hidden beneath their cults. Problems are no less persistent in the treatment of the material culture I have highlighted here. The heirlooms passed down in all four families tend to be addressed (in scholarship and museum exhibitions) solely in terms of their roles in the lives of the Great Men who collected them. Missed, as a result, are their at least equally interesting roles among the lively inheritors who created the cults, renewed and reinvented themselves through the circulation of the objects, and pressed ancestral "name and fame" into immediate service.

But the difficulty of pushing past the ancestors is no small testimony, in the end, to the success of the families that used them so resourcefully to ground their authority and conceal vigilant change. Continuity was a conceit of Tokugawa rule and, indeed, much Tokugawa enterprise. If it can sometimes blend in retrospect with stagnation, that illusion is only that, illusionary. Actors across the spectrum made lineage matter through routine affirmation. They hid themselves through routine disguise.

NOTES

1. Zoku 1995, 104, entry for Keichō 12/intercalary 4/26.

2. Entry for Keichō 14/12 in Shiseki 1986, 61–62; Zoku 1995, 159, entry for Keichō 14/12/11. See also separate registers of Tokugawa Yorinobu's and Yoshifusa's vassals and their invested properties in Tokugawa 1983, vol. 1, pp. 400–414.

3. Zoku 1995, 160, entry for Keichō 15/2. See also various letters to participants in the construction process, in Nakamura 1958, vol. 33, pp. 619–20, 629–34.

4. Totman 1967, 110.

5. Oyler 2006, 115–37.

6. Selinger 2013, 69–106.

7. Pitelka 2016.

8. Ōta 1991, 205, bk. 8, sec. 14; see also Ōta 2011, 246–47.

9. Takemoto 2006, 30.

10. Ōta 1991, 234–35, bk. 10, sec. 14; see also Ōta 2011, 277.

11. Lamers 2000, 216.

12. Schweizer forthcoming.

13. Pitelka 2016.

14. Totman 1967, 77.

15. Tokyo 1964, 12/24/756–865 and 12/24/652–739.

16. Wakayama 1989, 8–9.

17. *On'ie meibutsu no taigai*, part of the multivolume family record *Collection of Tangled Thoughts* (*Menkō shūroku*, also known as *Hosokawa-ki*; 1778). See the transcription of this document, as well as many extant objects named within, in Yamanashi 2001, 175.

18. Nihonshi Kenkyūkai 2001.

19. Noma 1967.

20. Mizubayashi 1987, 323–25.

21. For translations of these texts, see Pitelka 2001, appendix 6.

22. On the ceramics of each generation of the Raku family, see Hayashiya 1974. For an overview in English, see Hayashiya, Akanuma, and Raku 1997.

23. Sen and Kizu 1983, 86.

24. "Raku utsuwa mokuroku."

25. Hayashiya 1974, 165–68.

26. On Rikyū's place within late-sixteenth-century Japanese culture, see Pitelka 2005, 14–40.

27. Pitelka 2003.

28. Pitelka 2003.

29. Kumakura and Tsutsui 1989, 671–703.

30. Pitelka 2005, 83.

31. Murai 1985, 45.

32. Kumakura and Tsutsui 1989, 675.

33. Kumakura and Tsutsui 1989, 676.

34. For a discussion of how the same fire afforded "royal authorities" a new opportunity to rethink how they represented themselves, see Screech 2000, 148.

35. Kumakura 1989, 675–83.

36. Kumakura 1989, 683–92.

37. Pitelka 2005, 89–109. See also Morishita 2006, 283–302; Cang 2008, 71–81; Cross 2008, 131–53; and Surak 2012, 91–118.

38. Groemer 1997, 4–5.

39. Kumakura 1985, 128–29. See also Tanihata 1988, 163–70; and Tanihata 1999, 112–17.

40. Kumakura 1985, 127; Aikawa 1977, 199–252.

41. Pitelka 2005, 94–97.

42. Raku 1936, 80.

43. This is a small sampling of the many examples explored in Pitelka 2005, 97–102.

REFERENCES

Aikawa 1956
Aikawa Kōichi. "Chawa shigetsushū." In *Chadō koten zenshū,* edited by Sen Sōshitsu et al., vol. 10, pp. 199–252. Kyoto: Tankōsha, 1956.

Cang 2008
Cang, Voltaire Garces. "Preserving Intangible Heritage in Japan: The Role of the Iemoto System." *International Journal of Intangible Heritage* 3 (2008): 71–81.

Cross 2008
Cross, Tim. *The Ideologies of Japanese Tea: Subjectivity, Transience, and National Identity.* Folkestone, UK: Global Oriental, 2008.

Groemer 1997
Groemer, Gerald. "Translator's Introduction." In Nishiyama Matsunosuke. *Edo Culture: Daily Life and Diversions in Urban Japan, 1600–1868.* Translated by Gerald Groemer. Honolulu: University of Hawai'i Press, 1997.

Hayashiya 1974
Hayashiya Seizō. *Raku daidai, Tamamizuyaki, Ōhiyaki.* Tokyo: Chūō Kōronsha, 1974.

Hayashiya, Akanuma, and Raku 1997
Hayashiya Seizō, Akanuma Taka, and Raku Kichizaemon. *Raku: A Dynasty of Japanese Ceramists.* Paris: Maison de la Culture du Japon a Paris, 1997.

Kumakura 1985
Kumakura Isao. *Mukashi no chanoyu, ima no chanoyu.* Kyoto: Tankōsha, 1985.

Kumakura and Tsutsui 1989
Kumakura Isao and Tsutsui Hiro'ichi. "Rikyū no nenki." In *Rikyū daijiten,* 671–703. Kyoto: Tankōsha, 1989.

Lamers 2000
Lamers, Jeroen. *Japonius Tyrannus: The Japanese Warlord Oda Nobunaga Reconsidered.* Leiden, Netherlands: Hotei, 2000.

Mizubayashi 1987
Mizubayashi Takeshi. "Kojin no jidai kara ie no jidai." In *Hōkensei no saihen to Nihonteki shakai no kakuritsu,* edited by Mizubayashi Takeshi, 142. Tokyo: Yamakawa Shuppansha, 1987.

Morishita 2006
Morishita Masaaki. "The Iemoto System and the Avant-Gardes in the Japanese Artistic Field: Bourdieu's Field Theory in Comparative Perspective." *Sociological Review* (2006): 283–302.

Murai 1985
Murai Yasuhiko. *Chanoyu no tenkai.* Vol. 5 of *Chadō shūkin,* edited by Nakamura Masao et al. Tokyo: Shōgakukan, 1985.

Nakamura 1958
Nakamura Kōya. *Tokugawa Ieyasu monjo no kenkyū.* 4 volumes. Tokyo: Nippon Gakujutsu Shinkōkai, 1958–1962.

Nihonshi Kenkyūkai 2001
Nihonshi Kenkyūkai, ed. *Toyotomi Hideyoshi to Kyōto.* Kyoto: Nihonshi Kenkyūkai, 2001.

Noma 1967
Noma Kōshin, ed. *Shinshū Kyōto sōsho.* Vol. 1. Kyoto: Rinsen Shoten, 1967.
Ōta 1991
Ōta Gyūichi. *Shinchō kōki.* Edited by Okuno Takahiro and Iwasawa Yoshihiko. Tokyo: Kadokawa Shoten, 1991.
Ōta 2011
Ōta Gyūichi. *The Chronicle of Lord Nobunaga.* Translated by J. Elisonas and J. Lamers. Leiden, Netherlands: Brill, 2011.
Oyler 2006
Oyler, Elizabeth. *Swords, Oaths, and Prophetic Visions: Authoring Warrior Rule in Medieval Japan.* Honolulu: University of Hawai'i Press, 2006.
Pitelka 2001
Pitelka, Morgan. "Raku Ceramics: Tradition and Cultural Reproduction in Japanese Tea Practice, 1574–1942." Ph.D. dissertation, Princeton University, 2001.
Pitelka 2003
Pitelka, Morgan. "Sen Kōshin Sōsa." In *Japanese Tea Culture: Art, History, and Practice,* edited by Morgan Pitelka, 86–109. London: RoutledgeCurzon, 2003.
Pitelka 2005
Pitelka, Morgan. *Handmade Culture: Raku Potters, Patrons, and Tea Practitioners.* Honolulu: University of Hawai'i Press, 2005.
Pitelka 2016
Pitelka, Morgan. *Spectacular Accumulation: Material Culture, Tokugawa Ieyasu, and Samurai Sociability.* Honolulu: University of Hawai'i Press, 2016.
Raku 1936
Raku Kichizaemon (Seinyū). "Rakuyaki." In *Chadō zenshū,* edited by Iguchi Kaisen et al., vol. 14, pp. 51–108. Osaka: Sōgensha, 1936.
"Raku utsuwa mokuroku"
"Raku utsuwa mokuroku." Unpublished manuscript in collection of Tōkyō Geijutsu Daigaku.
Schweizer forthcoming
Schweizer, Anton. "Furnishing Dream Lands: Materiality and Spatial Performance in Toyotomi Hideyoshi's Osaka Castle." *Representing Things: Visuality and Materiality in East Asia,* edited by Lillian Tseng. Cambridge, MA: Harvard University Press, forthcoming.
Screech 2000
Screech, Timon. *The Shogun's Painted Culture: Fear and Creativity in the Japanese States, 1760–1829.* London: Reaktion Books, 2000.
Selinger 2013
Selinger, Vyjayanthi R. *Authorizing the Shogunate: Ritual and Material Symbolism in the Literary Construction of Warrior Order.* Leiden, Netherlands: Brill, 2013.
Sen and Kizu 1983
Sen Sōoku and Kizu Sōzen. "Mushanokōji Senke." In *Chadō no genryū,* edited by Sen Sōsa et al., vol. 6, pp. 69–100. Kyoto: Tankōsha, 1983.
Shiseki 1986
Shiseki Kenkyūkai, ed. *Keichō kenbunroku anshi, Keichō nikki, Keichō nenroku, Genna nenroku.* Tokyo: Kyūko Shoin, 1986.

Surak 2012
   Surak, Kristin. *Making Tea, Making Japan: Cultural Nationalism in Practice.* Stanford: CA: Stanford University Press, 2012.
Takemoto 2006
   Takemoto Chizu. *Shokuhōki no chakai to seiji.* Kyoto: Shibunkaku Shuppan, 2006.
Tanihata 1988
   Tanihata Akio. *Kinsei chadōshi.* Kyoto: Tankōsha, 1988.
Tanihata 1999
   Tanihata Akio. *Chanoyu no bunkashi.* Tokyo: Yoshikawa Kōbunkan, 1999.
Tokugawa 1983
   Tokugawa Yoshinobu. *Shinshū Tokugawa Ieyasu monjo no kenkyū.* 2 volumes. Tokyo: Yoshikawa Kōbunkan, 1983–2006.
Tokyo 1964
   Tōkyō Daigaku Shiryō Hensanjo, ed. *Dai Nihon shiryō.* Tokyo: Tōkyō Daigaku Shuppankai, 1964–.
Totman 1967
   Totman, Contrad. *Politics in the Tokugawa Bakufu, 1600–1843.* Cambridge, MA: Harvard University Press, 1967.
Wakayama 1989
   Wakayama Kenritsu Hakubutsukan. *Kishū Tōshōgū no meihō.* Wakayama: Wakayama Kenritsu Hakubutsukan, 1989.
Yamanashi 2001
   Yamanashi Kenritsu Bijutsukan. *Daimyō Hosokawa-ke no shihō: Bunbu no rekishi to miyabi no bunka.* Kōfu: Yamanashi Kenritsu Bijutsukan, 2001.
Zoku 1995
   Zoku Gunsho Ruijū Kanseikai, ed. *Tōdaiki, Sunpuki.* Tokyo: Heibonsha, 1995.

5

Outcastes and *Ie*

The Case of Two Beggar Boss Associations

Maren Ehlers

Tokugawa society included a wide variety of outcaste groups that were organized around an occupation such as leather manufacturing or begging and that claimed monopoly rights on certain resources, usually on turfs that allowed for the collection of animal carcasses or alms from peasants and townspeople. Although the members of such groups did not intermarry with commoners and experienced social exclusion in many areas of life, they adopted one of the most mainstream institutions of Tokugawa society: the hereditary household. This chapter focuses on one of the most widespread types of outcaste status group—the *hinin* (beggar bosses)—and explores what kinds of households emerged within these groups, and what roles these households played both in the groups and for the *hinin* families themselves.

Groups of outcastes (*senmin*, or "base people") had structurally much in common with other, more respected status groups. They used guild-like organizations to defend and manage the resources most central to their livelihood, and also relied on the framework of the guild to allocate the duties they were required to perform for the authorities in exchange for official protection of their privileges. In the case of the *hinin* guilds, the most important resource consisted of access to a begging turf, and the most common duties included beggar patrols, management of beggar hospices, and other services pertaining to the world of mendicants and outlaws. By the middle of the Tokugawa period, many *hinin* groups were dividing these rights and duties up among the households of full members. Because of the implications households held for the performance of public duties, they could become subject to intervention by the group's leadership or even the warrior authorities if they failed to operate in the expected manner. At the same time, households also allowed *hinin* families to accumulate property and transmit it to their descendants. Although property and begging privileges could turn the headship of a *hinin* household into a desirable asset, the position also came with significant obligations vis-à-vis the authorities and confined its holder to a life of both legal and customary discrimination. The tendency toward the formation of hereditary households among both commoners and outcastes alike made it difficult for base people to escape their lowly background and reinforced the idea of outcaste status as a hereditary condition. This chapter illustrates the difficulty of crossing the boundary to commoner status by introducing the case of a *hinin* family in the nineteenth century for whom the household became both a vehicle and an obstacle to its ambitions.

The historical literature on the institution of outcaste households is still miniscule, probably reflecting the sensitive nature of the subject. Even in the postwar era, the descendants of former outcastes could face discrimination from employers, neighbors, and potential marriage partners if their origins became known, and the Japanese government reacted in 1976 by restricting public access to the modern-era household registers.[1] Many public and private archives also removed relevant materials from the Tokugawa period such as population records (*ninbetsuchō*) and death registers of temples (*kakochō*) from circulation. In recent years, a wealth of new documents related to base people has become available because local historians and descendants have cleared them for publication, but very few of the studies drawing on these records have so far engaged in the reconstruction of *hinin* households and lineages.[2] The most significant contribution is Tsukada Takashi's work on the *hinin* associations of Osaka, Japan's second-largest city (after the mid-1700s). In this chapter, I pair Osaka's case with that of Ōno, a town of about six thousand residents in a mountainous part of central Honshu that served as the castle seat of a minor domain lord.[3] Ōno town was home to a small but relatively well-documented *hinin* association, known as the Koshirō, whose households performed duties similar to those of Osaka's *hinin*. Urban *hinin* communities constitute the logical starting point for an investigation into *hinin* households because the *hinin* living in the countryside as village watchmen did not usually form communities of their own but existed under the wing of town-based groups of beggar bosses.

Osaka's four *hinin* compounds date back to the earliest years of Osaka as a warrior-governed castle town. They emerged when the new warrior authorities in the decades around 1600 granted four plots of tax-exempt residential land to homeless people, many of them immigrants from other parts of western Japan.[4] The Tennōji compound (established in 1594), the Tobita compound (1609), and the Dōtonbori compound (1622) were located in villages along the southern border of Osaka's townspeople quarters, whereas the Tenma compound (1626) was situated on the northern periphery of the city. Each of the compounds constituted a self-governing guild of beggar bosses, but they also coordinated their mutual affairs through the so-called Takahara Office, originally a hospice for invalid prisoners that was jointly administered by the four groups.[5] By the end of the seventeenth century, the Tennōji compound had a population of six hundred, including apprentices, family members, and subordinate groups of newcomers.[6] Ōno's *hinin* community was much smaller, with between three and seven bosses (i.e., household heads) and a total population of forty or less including underlings and family members. Yet the *hinin* groups of Osaka and Ōno resembled each other in their independence from other local groups of base people, a feature that set them apart from beggar bosses in Edo and Wakayama, for example, who were both subordinate to groups of leatherworking outcastes.[7] The history of Osaka's beggar bosses, especially in the Tennōji compound, is relatively well documented, thanks in part to the archives of village and warrior officials who were in charge of transmitting and receiving *hinin*-related communications.[8] In Ōno, the two elders of the townspeople community frequently recorded their interactions with the Koshirō in their administrative journals. By their very nature, most of these records tend to focus on the beggar bosses' public duties rather than their family lives or group-internal affairs because town elders and commoner village headmen communicated with the *hinin* primarily on behalf of warrior governments or in the context of town or village rule.[9] Yet some of them do convey information on the public functions and private interests of *hinin* households.

HININ HOUSEHOLD FORMATION IN THE SEVENTEENTH CENTURY

The early history of Osaka's *hinin* households is much better documented than one might expect for a group of mostly illiterate beggars on the margins of society. Most of this paper trail resulted from the shogunate's harsh repression of Christianity. In the 1640s the Tokugawa regime, which governed the city of Osaka directly, required all residents of Osaka, including those in the beggar compounds, to register with a Buddhist temple as part of its bid to eradicate the Christian faith from Japanese society. All *hinin* had to report their religious affiliation by submitting registers of religious surveillance (so-called *shūmon ninbetsu aratamechō*) on a regular basis through the commoner village officials in charge of the tax-exempt land on which they lived. The oldest (and only) surviving register, created for the Tennōji beggar compound in 1698, lists 600 *hinin* in 189 households.[10] Each of these household units included a head and often a few family members and apprentices. The majority of the households on the register were small; fifty-seven of them had only one member.

At the time this register was created, the Tennōji beggar compound had already been in existence for nearly a century. Its earliest members, at least those we know of, seem to have included many single, uprooted drifters who had migrated to Osaka from various parts of western Japan. Over the course of the seventeenth century, the Tennōji compound continued to absorb homeless beggars from the streets of Osaka and its environs; but at the same time, a core group of *hinin* emerged that coalesced into a body of hereditary members.[11] Many of the adults who appear on the 1698 register were born inside the group to parents of *hinin* background, even though marriages between established members and newcomers were still fairly common at this point. For Ōno, no population registers exist that might shed light on the composition of local *hinin* households.[12] But the death register of a temple in the castle town notes "the mother of Koshirō Kahei" in 1668, and lists other deaths of Koshirō and their family members for the years 1674, 1685, 1692, and 1693. In 1850, a head priest marked one of these individuals as the ancestor of a Koshirō lineage still in existence.[13] This death register demonstrates that by the second half of the seventeenth century, Ōno's Koshirō, too, had established ties with a Buddhist temple and were receiving posthumous names for their deceased family members. Most likely, they had also begun to report their religious affiliation to the domain authorities. By this point, the beggar bosses clearly constituted a distinct social group within the castle town that was known under the name Koshirō. In fact, the death register represents the oldest piece of evidence we have for the existence of this group.

Reading Tennōji's population register of 1698 in combination with lineage registers yields interesting insights into the development of Osaka's *hinin* lineages over time. Lineage registers were another by-product of the shogunate's persecution of Christianity. In 1687 the shogunate required all status communities in the country to track the offspring of Christian apostates over five generations for men and three generations for women. The Tennōji beggar compound created one such register in 1689 to record the descendants of seventeen *hinin* (including five couples) who had renounced Christianity in 1631.[14] This register indicates that of the five guild leaders who signed off on Tennōji's population register of 1698, four—the compound chief, the deputy elder, and three subbosses—were descendants of former Christians.[15] Taken together, the two registers demonstrate that some of these leadership roles had turned into hereditary positions. Compound chief Tarōemon, for example, was the eldest son of the compound's first boss, Heiji, who had abrogated Christianity in 1631 while still a minor. Tarōemon was succeeded by his third and then his fourth son and eventually by his nephew, whom he had adopted as a son-in-law. The compound's sixth chief Kumanosuke, Tarōemon's grandchild, married the daughter of Tarōemon's nephew and was later succeeded by his own son, grandson, and grandson-in-law. This evidence suggests that the position of compound chief remained with Heiji's lineage until the early eighteenth century. The preferred succession seems to have been from father to son, but chiefs could compensate for a lack of male offspring of appropriate age by appointing their sons-in-law, who were often the children of close relatives. There was at least one other *hinin* group in Osaka—the Dōtonbori compound—that also chose some of its leaders by hereditary succession at that time,[16] and the same seems to have applied to the *hinin* community in the castle town of Wakayama south of Osaka.

In Wakayama, however, not all leadership positions were monopolized by a single family and rotated among a few distinguished lineages instead.[17]

With regard to leadership positions, at least, hereditary male succession was thus practiced from an early point within Osaka's *hinin* compounds. But if we widen the focus to the guilds as a whole, the *hinin* households in the seventeenth century still seem to have been fairly unstable. The larger *hinin* families in the Tennōji compound, which are the only ones for whom there are enough data, practiced a form of ultimogeniture, meaning that their older children all left the parental home upon reaching maturity and established their own family units, leaving only the last child behind to live with the elderly parents.[18] In Wakayama, ultimogeniture also extended to leadership roles as it was usually the youngest son who succeeded his father in the position of guild chief.[19] The reasons for this apparent preference for ultimogeniture are still unclear, but the beggar bosses' relative lack of property could have been a factor. The poorer the family, the less incentive children had to stay behind and claim an inheritance from their parents.[20] Another possible explanation is that the *hinin*'s begging turf was still expanding in the late seventeenth century in conjunction with Osaka's overall growth as a city. At that time, the children of established beggar bosses might still have encountered relatively favorable conditions for the establishment of new, self-supporting household units.

CRISIS AND INTERVENTION: *HININ* HOUSEHOLDS IN THE SECOND HALF OF THE TOKUGAWA PERIOD

By the late eighteenth century, the situation of *hinin* guilds in the two towns had changed considerably. In Osaka, the full guild members—the "young men" (*wakakimono*), as full members outside leadership positions were called irrespective of age—now maintained clearly identifiable households, which could be inherited and usually involved ownership of a physical building and the land on which it stood. The most important property of these *hinin* households, however, consisted of access rights to one or several town blocks (so-called *chō*, which were run by self-governing associations of house-owning townspeople) in the city of Osaka. In return for obtaining alms from the residents of these blocks, the "young men" dispatched their underlings to work there as watchmen—in other words, to patrol the neighborhood for unlicensed beggars and criminals.[21] Such access rights to one or several blocks effectively represented begging rights and were registered as "watchman shares" within the group. Although each household was ideally associated with only one share, it was possible for one household to own several shares at once. According to the final Christian lineage register from the Tennōji compound, which dates to 1775, the majority of descendants of former Christians who still fell under the reporting requirement at that time belonged to the class of "young men," and either dispatched underlings to blocks in the city of Osaka or worked as watchmen themselves for villages in Osaka's vicinity.[22]

The social structure of the *hinin* compounds thus coalesced over time into professional guilds of beggar bosses with a core of hereditary members. But by the late eighteenth century, that structure was already showing signs of erosion. According to a guild-internal document from around 1800, the number of young-man households in Osaka's four *hinin* compounds had been declining for the past couple of years. A similar problem surfaced among Ōno's Koshirō in 1845, and the *hinin* communities in the cities of Kyoto and Sakai (both in the Kinai region near Osaka) likewise experienced significant losses of members in the late Tokugawa period, not only among underlings but also among full hereditary beggar bosses.[23] What were the causes of this apparently widespread trend, and how did the *hinin* guilds and the authorities react to the loss of active, duty-performing *hinin* households?

The case of Ōno domain shows that the domain administration perceived the shrinking of the local *hinin* guild as an urgent problem with public ramifications. A conversation on this issue took place in 1845 among the domain's town governor, one of the town elders, and one of the village group headmen (the equivalent of the town elders in the countryside).[24] The town governor informed the two commoner officials that the number of "town watchmen" (i.e., the Koshirō) had gradually dropped to four because the amounts of alms these watchmen were able to collect in the countryside were no longer sufficient for them to make a living. With a total of four, the governor suggested, the watchmen would be unable to perform their most important duty for the domain—the patrolling of the castle town against disruptive begging and crime. The governor instructed the town elders and village group headmen to help "increase the number of *hinin*" by reminding villagers to provide them with sufficient amounts of alms. Although this conversation dealt only with the behavior of villagers, it is possible that the almsgiving customs of the townspeople also received scrutiny at this time.

The number four brought up in this context did not refer to the total number of people of Koshirō status but to the number of Koshirō households, which was equivalent to the number of duty-performing watchmen. These households constituted economic units that provided their members with sustenance through begging rights, and Ōno's domain government condoned and even protected these begging rights because it wanted to mobilize the Koshirō for patrol duty. While the Koshirō had always been few in number, the group's membership dropped indeed quite noticeably in the course of the 1830s. In 1837, there had still been seven beggar bosses instead of four, and the total population of the Koshirō's settlement also fell from forty-five in 1815 to thirty-three in 1834 and shrank further in the 1840s.[25] The Tenpō famine in the 1830s probably had something to do with this decline. Whether any Koshirō died during this famine is unknown, but the crisis probably diminished the Koshirō's income by impoverishing or even eradicating households in town and villages, leading to the drop in almsgiving described by the town governor. Some Koshirō could have reacted to this loss of income by leaving Ōno town and trying to make a living elsewhere.

In Osaka, the surviving documentation reveals the *hinin*'s own perspective on the problem. In 1804 the "young men" of the Tennōji beggar compound submitted a petition to the guild leadership in which they declared that the number of households had dropped to 70, from about 120 households at an unspecified point in the past.[26] Of these 70, only 50 were regularly performing duties for the shogunal city authorities and paying their guild-internal dues; the remaining 20 were headed by widows or retirees and lacked an adult male head who would have fulfilled the household's labor obligations. While the petition did not give concrete reasons for this decline, it implied that in the case of the 20 nonperforming households, the former family head had left the compound to live in a townspeople's block or another beggar compound and either continued to derive income from the household's begging share (here referred to as *katoku*—literally, "estate") or had entrusted it to someone else. The petitioners complained that this practice had increased the burden on the households that remained. This petition and other related documents demonstrate that in Osaka, as in Ōno, every *hinin* household represented one duty-performing beggar boss. To improve the guild's ability to fulfill its duties, the "young men" petitioned the leadership of their compound to force absentee household heads or whoever else had been entrusted with a begging share to perform the concomitant duties on the group's behalf. Osaka's documents thus shine a bit more light on the process of guild decline than Ōno's. They show that Osaka's *hinin* often left the guild of their own accord and moved into another beggar compound or even a town block. It remains a matter of speculation whether beggar bosses had to hide their origins to live among townspeople, but by the latter half of the Tokugawa period, many blocks in Osaka and Edo had high rates of impoverished back-alley tenants who frequently moved from place to place, and tenements were often run by caretakers on behalf of absentee landowners. This situation discouraged block officials from implementing the checks on residency that the warrior authorities expected them to perform.[27]

For the *hinin* in the Tennōji compound, one major motive for abandoning their households seems to have been a reluctance to perform the duties associated with the position of household head. There is some indication that the *hinin* might have perceived their duty burden as excessive. By the late eighteenth century, Osaka's town governors maintained the so-called Criminal Bureau (*tōzokukata*), which regularly called up the leaders of the city's *hinin* guilds for police work in Osaka and its surroundings. In addition, it also mobilized the guild's "young men" as supplementary staff for its town patrols.[28] The mobilization of the "young men" greatly increased the burden on the guilds because until the second half of the eighteenth century, Osaka's city authorities had mobilized only the *hinin*'s leaders for occasional detective work and arrests and left the bulk of guild members alone. It is possible that some of the "young men" felt compelled to escape this pressure by abandoning their shares and leaving the group. The growing duty burden must have felt particularly onerous to those "young men" whose turfs did not yield much in alms to begin with.

By the late eighteenth century, the income gap between members of Osaka's four *hinin* compounds was widening. Some of that development can be explained by the character and profitability of begging turfs, which ranged from prosperous commercial quarters to downtrodden neighborhoods. The *hinin* guilds thus reflected the increasing economic polarization of the city as a whole. According to petitions from the nineteenth century, so-called low-income turfs constituted a serious problem for certain "young man" households in the Tennōji beggar compound.[29] The commodification of begging shares further encouraged the concentration of wealth in the hands of relatively few *hinin* households. By the eighteenth century, as mentioned earlier, the relationship between a "young man" household and an almsgiving block association was being expressed through the notion of the share, and shares could be bought, sold, and pawned among *hinin*. Some *hinin* households accumulated considerable numbers of such shares, and there were even cases of shares ending up in the hands of people living outside the compounds who could or would not perform duties together with the other guild members. Even shareholders who had not moved out of their compound seem to have found ways to avoid duty, especially if they had accumulated more than one share. They still dispatched watchmen to the blocks associated with their shares to fulfill their bargain with the townspeople, but did not always participate in duties such as the daily town patrols that had been imposed on their guild by the shogunal city authorities.[30]

In Osaka, the decline in *hinin* households proved difficult to reverse. Although in 1790 the leadership of the Tennōji compound prohibited its "young men" from selling or pawning their begging rights, it continued to make exceptions for parties that notified the guild leaders of these transactions and were deemed particularly needy.[31] This halfhearted measure did little to halt the loss of duty labor, and in 1804 the "young men" felt compelled to submit the aforementioned petition. In 1845 the guild leaders of Tennōji finally implemented a reform that directly addressed the ability of *hinin* households to provide duty labor.[32] They allowed households whose head was minor, sick, retired, or missing to let an apprentice or other person temporarily perform duty in his place. They also put pressure on households without a duty-performing male head to acquire one through marriage or adoption. Although the initial response to the measure seems to have been favorable, the problem resurfaced only two or three years after its implementation.[33] Apparently, the households with low-income begging shares were simply too poor to retain the young men they had appointed or adopted. Of the households that had adopted young males from other *hinin* lineages in and around Osaka in response to the new policy, many never got their adoptees to perform any duty, because the men in question bailed out of the arrangement upon reaching maturity. As the failure of the reform became apparent, some poorer households with more than one low-income share asked the guild leadership for permission to "merge" these shares, thus reducing the number of duty performers even further, insofar as many shares were counted as the equivalent of one duty-performing household. While the situation in the other three compounds is unknown, the Tennōji compound never managed to reverse its loss of duty-performing households. Yet there continued to be a considerable number of households in that compound that did manage to perpetuate themselves through marriage or adoption, whether from one of Osaka's four compounds, *hinin* associations in other cities, or village guard households in the Kinai region around Osaka.[34]

In Ōno, the domain government imposed a more lasting solution for the problem of unprofitable begging turfs. From about the mid-eighteenth century onward, the domain had been mobilizing the Koshirō for criminal investigations under the supervision of the domain's Criminal Bureau, an office named like its functional equivalent in Osaka. In the 1740s, the time of the first surviving town elders' journals, the Koshirō's police work was still limited to town patrols and guard work in the countryside, but by the 1830s the Koshirō were frequently performing duty as a quasi-police force, apprehending criminals and tracking down contraband in Ōno and other domains in collaboration with nearby *hinin* associations on an almost daily basis.[35] Clearly, a membership of four would not have sufficed to allow the group to continue with this kind of workload.

Ōno's domain officials chose a top-down approach to the problem and implemented it in a bureaucratic fashion. First, they ordered the village group headmen to undertake a survey of almsgiving customs as practiced in the villages up to the present. The survey demonstrated that the overall amount of alms had indeed dropped over time and that, moreover, the burden was distributed unevenly among the villages.[36] To remedy this situation, the domain government then asked the village group headmen to calculate precisely how much each village would need to contribute to enable the *hinin* guild to grow by at least two households. To do so, the village group headmen decided to apply a formula similar to those used to assess corvée burdens and other obligations borne by tax-paying commoners in the domain. They based one half of the alms burden on the number of full peasant households in each community, and the other half on the amount of productive land. Villagers were required to precollect these alms biannually and hand them over to the *hinin* through their village headman, though they were free to divide the burden internally among households however they pleased. After the reform of 1845, almsgiving for *hinin* in Ōno thus began to resemble the process of paying the annual rice tax on land, which was also precollected and submitted by the village headman on behalf of the entire village. Internally, many villages in Ōno regulated almsgiving by assigning different burdens to different classes of households, such as ordinary full peasants or peasants with the right of audience with the domain lord.[37]

Unfortunately, no documentation survives to show how the order of 1845 was implemented, but the Koshirō do seem to have established new households in response. By 1847 the Koshirō's overall population including family members and underlings had already recovered to thirty from a low around twenty-three, and in 1852 there were at least five households instead of four.[38] By 1860, the guild had expanded to eight households with thirty-three residents and six village guards under their control.[39] The town elders' journals of 1860 offer some clues as to how the Koshirō might have gone about establishing new households. In that year, the Koshirō revived the household known as Shirōbei (probably the name of a former household head) that had been abandoned for some time. The Koshirō themselves proposed the revival of this household to the domain authorities because "duty had become heavier these days."[40] The description of Shirōbei's household in the town elders' journals tells us much about the character of Koshirō households in general. In an entry written in the third month of 1860, the town elder on duty referred to the household as both "a Koshirō called Shirōbei" and "Shirōbei's household," using the Chinese character for ie (household) that was also used to refer to commoner households.[41] In the same entry, he also used a term commonly associated with Buddhist temples without a priest, pointing out that "the Koshirō called Shirōbei has recently been without resident" (mujū).[42] According to the town elders, the Koshirō had made up for Shirōbei's loss by distributing his duty burden among the remaining guild members.[43] A few months later, the town elders noted that "Koshirō Shirōbei had been in a state of collapse for a long time, but was recently rebuilt."[44]

These entries show that in the context of the Koshirō guild, "Shirōbei" represented a duty-performing household rather than a particular lineage. The name continued to be used inside the beggar guild as a placeholder even after the original resident had disappeared and the building had collapsed. When Shirōbei's household was abandoned, the Koshirō "made up for it as a guild" and later chose to revive it rather than establish a new household from scratch. Perhaps they did so because the Shirōbei household was already associated with a specific piece of land and a carefully calibrated set of guild-based responsibilities and privileges. Its resurrection thus spared the Koshirō from making major changes to the structure of their group. It is also possible that the Koshirō had hoped from the outset that the loss of this household would be only temporary.

What steps did the Koshirō take to put the Shirōbei household back into operation? First, they "searched widely" for a successor and found one in the hinin watchman of Otomi, a village in Ōno domain, who had already been working under their control.[45] It was in fact quite rare for the Koshirō to integrate newcomers into their group, even though they regularly accepted begging paupers into the beggar hospice in the castle town, some of them long-term. Most occupants of the beggar hospice were probably not fit enough to undertake the job of underling or watchman, let alone beggar boss, which required a great deal of physical strength and resilience. Village watchmen, on the other hand, were experienced at performing police and patrol duty and were familiar with the customs of the guild. They often received visits from the town's beggar bosses and frequented the Koshirō's settlement in return, sometimes staying there for extended periods.[46] The position of village watchman seems to have been a typical entry point for unregistered drifters who sought integration into the guild. Two village guards who appear in sources from the 1780s, for example, had come to Ōno domain from outside, one of them as a masterless samurai from Kaga domain.[47] In 1837 an unregistered man from the town of Kanazawa became the underling of a Koshirō and was later sent as a watchman to a village in a nearby shogunal territory.[48] Because the headship of the Shirōbei household was directly associated with duty performance, physical fitness was a critical requirement for any candidate hoping to fill this position.

Once the Koshirō had finalized their arrangement with the watchman of Otomi, they rebuilt Shirōbei's "residence" (*sumika*) with money they had borrowed from the domain government specifically for that purpose.[49] In the fourth month of 1860, the new "Shirōbei" arrived in the castle town to "inherit the hut of the person named Shirōbei,"[50] and by the seventh month, he was already performing duty for the guild under his new name.[51] His example suggests that *hinin* households in Ōno came with a hereditary name as well as a homestead, and that the guild's need for a capable successor was at least as pressing as families' interests in passing the position from father to son. The town elders on one occasion referred to Shirōbei's home as a "hut" (*koya*). In eighteenth-century Osaka, the *hinin* described their houses as *ie yashiki,* the same term used for the houses of "respectable" townspeople. Although it is possible that the Koshirō's dwellings were indeed more humble than those of their Osaka counterparts, the Koshirō, too, might have spoken of their homes as *ie yashiki* in their group-internal documents and conversations, whereas the town elders might have expressed their disdain for people of beggar status by using the more disrespectful term "hut."

WEALTHY *HININ* HOUSEHOLDS AND THEIR ASPIRATIONS

Shirōbei's case underscores the close association between *hinin* households and duty performance that had been established by the second half of the Tokugawa period in Osaka, Ōno, and likely other towns and cities as well. It seems safe to assume that begging rights in Ōno were also distributed among households, though there is hardly any evidence for this other than the fact that one Koshirō was once described as visiting "his turf."[52] Unlike in Osaka, begging rights in Ōno do not seem to have been traded or pawned as shares. That is not to say, however, that Ōno's beggar guild did not develop a gap between rich and poor and that its members always subordinated their households' interests to those of the group. In the nineteenth century, one Koshirō household—represented by the Iemon-Isuke lineage—became notorious for its wealth and began to make occasional appearances in the town elders' journals. Its example illustrates both the ambitions of *hinin* in an age when social status was increasingly determined by financial success rather than birth, and the obstacles they continued to face because of their base background.

Iemon's name is first mentioned in the context of a criminal case in the town elders' journal of 1793.[53] When Iemon died around 1838, the headship passed to his son Isuke, who was succeeded by Isaburō, an adoptee from Kyoto, around the time of the Meiji Restoration.[54] The household seems to have been eager to shield its property from the other Koshirō. According to the first substantial entry on this lineage from 1837, the domain government ordered Iemon to provide hunger aid to the beggar bosses' "village," or "guild," in this year of acute famine.[55] When Iemon failed to obey that order, domain officials confiscated ten bales of rice from his storehouse and distributed them among the Koshirō, the beggars in the hospice, and even one of the leatherworking outcastes in Ōno town (here called eta, but popularly known as kawaya). All the beggar bosses except Iemon received the same amount of rice. In contrast to Iemon, who owned a plastered storehouse, all the remaining Koshirō households were suffering from the famine; one even tried to steal in order to survive.[56]

It made sense for the domain to force Iemon to share some of his reserves at that time, because famished commoners could hardly be expected to supply the Koshirō with more alms. Generally speaking, all status communities in Tokugawa Japan were responsible for sharing resources between their richer and poorer members, with community headmen playing a leading role. The samurai authorities did not usually grant petitions for seigneurial relief to the poor unless they were convinced that the status group as a whole was too impoverished to help itself. Yet Iemon's case is remarkable because Iemon was not the leader of his guild, let alone of the outcaste population of Ōno. The household does not even appear in any sources dating from before 1793, at least not under this or similar names. Had Iemon been a hereditary leader such as the eta boss Danzaemon in Edo or the four hinin bosses who operated under Danzaemon's control, it would have been a matter of course for him to relieve his underlings and subordinate groups in a time of need, but Iemon was clearly reluctant to take on that role.[57] The domain government seems to have known of Iemon's resources and decided to single him out for certain guild-related responsibilities on account of his wealth.

What could have been the source of Iemon's prosperity? In towns with larger beggar associations, the leadership always lived more comfortably than ordinary members because they received special allowances and begging rights from the authorities,[58] but as mentioned, Iemon was not the leader of the Koshirō guild. One possible clue comes from a land register of 1872 that lists Iemon's descendant as the only household in the village that owned agricultural land, but it remains unclear whether this property was a cause or rather an effect of Iemon's wealth.[59] One might speculate that the household held a particularly profitable begging turf with a large number of well-to-do village or town households. From an early point, Iemon's family received an annual payment of 40 monme of silver from the domain for unknown (probably land-related) reasons.[60] But the household's most profitable activity appears to have been moneylending. Iemon's successor Isuke made loans to townspeople, including those who engaged in shady business and would perhaps not have received credit elsewhere. In 1838, for example, he was placed under house arrest for transgressing status boundaries after doing business ("settling saké accounts") with two townspeople whom the domain accused of engaging in violence and hosting prostitutes.[61] In 1857 he was briefly jailed for taking profits from a gambling den and lending money to the players.[62] Isuke's behavior was probably the reason why the domain issued an order in 1843 against Koshirō moneylending to townspeople, but this ban was limited in scope and does not seem to have deterred the household from its financial dealings.[63] In 1853, for example, Isuke's "old mother" (presumably Iemon's widow) filed a petition with the town elders to enforce the repayment of a substantial loan she had made to a townsman, but instead of reporting her for punishment, the town elders simply asked both parties to resolve their conflict through mediation.[64]

Women seem to have been able to both own and inherit the property accumulated by this beggar family. The situation of women in *hinin* groups and households is still largely unknown and cannot be discussed yet in general terms, but when the "old mother" in Ōno died in 1864, her children fought over her estate, which amounted to 3,082.5 *monme* of silver plus a house and furniture, an impressive sum for an ostensibly penniless beggar family.[65] The "old mother" seems to have been the legal owner of the household's assets as long as she lived, while her son Isuke succeeded Iemon in the position of beggar boss. While it is possible that this arrangement was made specifically to guard the household against further orders from the domain to share its wealth with the other Koshirō, the family might indeed have considered the "old mother" as the legitimate heir of Iemon's estate. After some mediation by guild members, Iemon's younger son Bunkichi, who had returned from Edo to claim his inheritance, managed to secure one-third of the estate, leaving the remaining two-thirds to his brother Isuke and his two older sisters. In Osaka, too, the death of wealthier household heads could trigger conflict among family members. When, for example, the retired chief of the Tennōji compound died in 1768, a protracted conflict ensued among his relatives over his estate and the position of compound chief. Eventually, the chief's successor consolidated the entire inheritance in his hands, including the residence, a storehouse, movable property, a document box, and watchman shares for a number of profitable begging turfs that included the wealthy merchant house Kōnoike.[66] While these two cases hardly suffice to support any general conclusions about inheritance customs among *hinin*, they both suggest that the children and relatives of wealthy *hinin* did not necessarily take the inheritance rights of duty-performing household heads for granted, but believed that they, too, had a right to claim part of the household's assets.

In Ōno, the Iemon-Isuke lineage had found a way to make money without relying on the collective strength of the guild. It also tried to translate its money into social status by helping some of its children escape the stain of their base birth. In

1841, for example, Isuke's younger brother Bunkichi made a failed bid to establish himself as a townsman in Ōno by renting a flat in a temple precinct adjacent to one of the town blocks. When the people of that block association got wind of his origins, they protested his admission on the grounds that Bunkichi's presence would prevent them from interacting with the residents of the temple precinct at festivals and on other social occasions.[67] Bunkichi seems to have left Ōno shortly after this incident, but he returned in 1864 to claim a share of his mother's inheritance, this time as a townsman living in Edo. Apparently, he had succeeded in gaining admission to a town block in this large and anonymous metropolis.

Another Koshirō trying to pass as a commoner was Isuke's nephew Heikichi, the product of a liaison between Iemon's eldest daughter and a physician of commoner background living in Ōno town. In his youth, Heikichi was sent to the town of Fukui about thirty kilometers away to be raised in a town household, but in 1838 a townsman of Ōno attempted to adopt Heikichi as his son and heir. Unfortunately for Heikichi, the town elders hesitated to formally admit him to the town community after an anonymous informer approached them secretly to warn them about his outcaste background.[68] Although one of the two town elders initially argued in favor of overlooking the stain associated with Heikichi's maternal bloodline, he and his colleague, as well as the town governor, eventually decided to decline the petition because neither of them was ready to defend Heikichi's admission vis-à-vis the ordinary townspeople should the latter find out that the descendant of a Koshirō had been planted in their midst. Bunkichi's and Heikichi's experiences suggest that unlike their counterparts in Osaka, the members of Ōno's *hinin* community could not take up residence in a town block unless they obfuscated their origins or left their hometown for more anonymous places.

CONCLUSION

The *hinin* associations of Ōno and Osaka operated in towns of vastly different size but developed in remarkably similar ways. Both started out as groups of mendicants without any property to speak of, but gradually established themselves as an important presence in town life by providing services as beggar bosses. The performance of duties for the warrior authorities and commoners allowed the beggar bosses to consolidate their claim on begging turfs among townspeople and villagers, and enabled many of them to establish hereditary households that derived a regular income from one or more of these turfs. It seems that the development of stable households among *hinin* depended on the transformation of begging turfs into a form of property that could be passed down to the next generation. Eventually, the guilds of beggar bosses came to be structured around the institution of the household because each household head combined turf ownership and duty performance in his hands and was expected to do his part to help the guild fulfill its collective responsibilities vis-à-vis the authorities.

But the two cases also show that the guilds of beggar bosses came under strain in the second half of the Tokugawa period precisely because of their reliance on hereditary, property-owning households. One reason was that begging turfs proved a relatively unstable form of income as town society changed under the influence of commercialization. In Osaka, a gap was opening between richer and poorer *hinin* as a result of growing differences in the profitability of turfs in richer and poorer parts of the city. What is more, turf ownership itself became commodified among *hinin* and started to be pawned and traded as shares, resulting in the concentration of turf property in the hands of a few and the abandonment of low-income households. In Ōno, the Tenpō famine impoverished villagers and townspeople in the domain and indirectly affected the livelihoods of the beggar bosses who collected alms from these communities. In both towns, the overall result was a loss of duty-performing households, down to a point where the remaining members found it difficult to ensure the guild's collective obligations; in Ōno's case, the beggar guild's very survival seemed at stake. Ōno's Koshirō managed to reverse their temporary loss of households after the domain government intervened on its behalf and directly addressed the underlying cause of the problem, namely the profitability of the Koshirō's turfs. Osaka's *hinin* were less successful in that regard, perhaps because their decline was not extreme enough to spur the city authorities into action, or perhaps because their internal solution—the introduction of new options for households to provide duty-performing members—did not cut deeply enough to resolve the financial problems of poorer *hinin* households. In both towns, there was a growing disconnect between the resources of individual *hinin* households and the duties they were expected to perform. As the city and domain authorities increasingly relied on *hinin* for police work, it became less and less feasible to use household-based status groups of beggars for that purpose.

As base people, the members of *hinin* associations faced discrimination, and one might assume that some of them tried to escape their stigma by distancing themselves from their hereditary households. However, the sources on *hinin* groups in Osaka and Ōno hardly ever mention this problem, and we are left to believe that the loss of households among these guilds had ultimately more to do with financial pressures and the growing burden of duty than with the desire to escape discriminatory treatment. The case of the Iemon-Isuke household in Ōno does hint at the possibility that wealth might have helped some members of *hinin* households to gain a foothold in commoner society: commoners might have been more inclined to accept outcastes as adoptees, tenants, or employees if the latter were able to put money on the table. The bigger and more anonymous cities such as Edo and Osaka provided *hinin* with an outlet to overcome their origins and live as townspeople in commoner society. But as long as beggar boss households retained a claim on begging rights, they remained attractive enough for sufficient numbers of people to ensure the existence of *hinin* groups and the performance of *hinin* duty up until the Meiji Restoration.

NOTES

1. Ooms 1996, 307–8.
2. For a survey, see Yokoyama 2007.
3. See Ehlers 2018.
4. Tsukada 2001, 5–11.
5. Tsukada 2013, 25.
6. Tsukada 2013, 44–45.
7. See, for example, Fujimoto 2011; Tsukada 1987, 222–30.
8. Documents produced by the *hinin* of Tennōji have survived in the form of the so-called *Hiden'in monjo*. Village documents related to the Dōtonbori compound have been published in *Dōtonbori hinin kankei monjo*.
9. Some entries from these journals as well as from the journals of village headmen have been transcribed and published in *Ōno-shi shi yōdome-hen*. For unpublished entries, see the original manuscripts of the town elders' journals preserved in a number of private local archives, primarily Saitō Suzuko-ke monjo, Nunokawa Genbei-ke monjo, and Adachi Hiromichi-ke monjo. Photographic reproductions of these journals are available at the Office for the Compilation of Ōno City History (Ōno-shi Shi Hensanshitsu).
10. Tsukada 2013, 44–47.
11. This can be surmised from the lineage registers of Christian apostates (described below in more detail); see Tsukada 2007, 15; Tsukada 2001, 5–36; Tsukada 2013, 24–74; Tsukada 2014. In 1683 and 1691, the group incorporated particularly large waves of newcomers because the Osaka town governor had ordered the removal of all homeless beggars from the streets; see Tsukada 2013, 37.
12. The Koshirō needed to submit one register every four years; see, for example, "Tsutomekata oboegaki."
13. No death registers have survived from this temple (whose name shall not be disclosed here) for the time between 1775 and 1868.
14. Tsukada 2013, 26–32.
15. Tsukada 2013, 70–73, 117.
16. Osaka's Dōtonbori compound was led by members of one and the same lineage (also descended from former Christians) until the 1720s, when another line began to monopolize the position; Tsukada 2001, 7–14.
17. In Fukiage, the *hinin* community of Wakayama town, the position of chief was hereditary until the end of the eighteenth century, and Fukiage's chiefs strove to reserve the position for their direct male descendants; Fujimoto 2014, 355–64.
18. Tsukada 2013, 66–70.
19. Fujimoto 2014, 355–64.
20. According to Mita Satoko's reconstruction of households in Minami Ōji, a village of leather-working outcastes in the Osaka hinterland, many residents practiced ultimogeniture in the eighteenth century, frequently establishing branch households or merging existing ones. While the logic of household formation in Minami Ōji is not yet fully understood, many of these households owned very little agricultural land and lived for rent in extremely crammed quarters. See Mita 2018, 135–214.
21. Tsukada 2007, 154–59.
22. Tsukada 2013, 104–14.

23. Sugahara 1977, 96; Yamamoto 2002, 77–79.

24. *Ōno-shi shi yōdome-hen*, 1845.8.10, no. 893, pp. 659–60.

25. See, for example, the Koshirō numbers reported on the occasion of the annual rice gruel handouts in the town elders' journals.

26. Tsukada 2007, 66–74; Tsukada 2013, 147–50.

27. See, for example, Yokoyama 2005, 27–61.

28. Tsukada 2013, 140–47.

29. Tsukada 2013, 168–85.

30. Tsukada 2007, 70–73; Tsukada 2013, 124–34.

31. Tsukada 2013, 132.

32. Tsukada 2013, 160–73.

33. Tsukada 2013, 173–85.

34. Tsukada 2013, 185–86.

35. See, for example, MT goyōdome 1740, 1741, 1834, 1836, 1837, 1838, 1840, 1841.

36. *Ōno-shi shi yōdome-hen*, 1845.11.26, no. 898, p. 661; 1845.12.10, 14, 16, 20, no. 900, pp. 663–66.

37. *Ōno-shi shi yōdome-hen*, 1845.8.10, no. 893, pp. 659–60.

38. See the records of the annual rice gruel handouts, as well as MT goyōdome, 1852.

39. *Ōno-shi shi yōdome-hen*, 1860.10.21, no. 1208, p. 865.

40. Goyōki (Nunokawa Genbei-ke), 1860.3.12.

41. Goyōki (Nunokawa Genbei-ke), 1860.3.12.

42. Goyōki (Nunokawa Genbei-ke), 1860.3.12. Shirōbei last appears as a beggar boss in 1789, but might still have been active in 1834; *Ōno-shi shi yōdome-hen*, 1789.12.26, no. 377, pp. 276–77; MT goyōdome, 1834.4.22 (date difficult to decipher).

43. Goyōki (Nunokawa Genbei-ke), 1860.3.12.

44. MT goyōdome, 1860.7.11.

45. Goyōki (Nunokawa Genbei-ke), 1860.3.12.

46. *Ōno-shi shi yōdome-hen*, 1781.3.2, no. 157, pp. 125–26. On the practice of mutual visits, see MT goyōdome, 1834.4.22, 1834.8.16, 19, 20, 1834.10.6 (date difficult to decipher).

47. *Ōno-shi shi yōdome-hen*, 1781.3.2, no. 157, pp. 125–26.

48. MT goyōdome, 1837.7.24. Once, in 1786, the domain government forced the group to integrate a thief who had been punished with degradation to beggar status, but the Koshirō protested this move and called it unprecedented; *Ōno-shi shi yōdome-hen*, 1786.4.28, no. 273, pp. 200–201.

49. Two hundred *monme* of silver were granted; see the petition in Goyōki (Nunokawa Genbei-ke), 1860.3.12; the disbursal in MT goyōdome, 1860.7.11; and the repayment procedure for this apparently interest-free loan in Goyōki (Nunokawa Genbei-ke), 1860.12.3.

50. Goyōki (Nunokawa Genbei-ke), 1860.4.25.

51. MT goyōdome, 1860.7.21.

52. *Ōno-shi shi yōdome-hen*, 1783.11.4, no. 173, pp. 134–35; 1787.5.21, no. 306, p. 225.

53. MT goyōdome, 1793.5.29.

54. "Yokomachi shirabechō."

55. MT goyōdome, 1837.4.6, 1837.8.12.

56. Beggar boss Sōemon committed a burglary in 1834 and testified to having acted out of poverty; see MT goyōdome, 1834.4.22, 1834.8.16, 19, 20, 1834.10.6. The storehouse is mentioned in ibid., 1837.7.24.

57. Danzaemon, for example, provided aid to the monkey trainers under his control in order to rescue them from famine and destitution; see Tsukada 1997, 274. In Kanazawa in 1829, one of the bosses of the *tōnai* beggar boss association relieved the people inside his compound and was rewarded for his charity by the lord; see "Iburaku ikkan," 538.

58. Uchida 1987, 103; Asao 1995, 15–20, 29.

59. "Yokomachi shirabechō."

60. In some records, this payment is labeled "substitute for land tax rice" (*chishimai-dai*); MT goyōdome, 1834.12.26, 1835.12.23, 1855.12.16; "Ōno-han goyōki," 1865.1.11.

61. MT goyōdome 1838.6.1, 2, 3, 5, 6.

62. Goyōdome (Adachi Hiromichi-ke), 1857.11.21.

63. *Ōno-shi shi yōdome-hen*, 1843.7.12, no. 846, p. 627. This order threatened sanctions only in case the Koshirō were bold enough to have their debt quarrels adjudicated by the domain.

64. Goyōdome (Adachi Hiromichi-ke), 1853.5.2, 21.

65. MT goyōdome, 1864.5.16.

66. Tsukada 2013, 120–24.

67. *Ōno-shi shi yōdome-hen*, 1841.8.9, no. 818, pp. 593–94; MT goyōdome, 1864.5.16. It is not entirely clear whether Bunkichi was interested only in the money or was also in the position of beggar boss.

68. MT goyōdome, 1838.4.6.

REFERENCES

Copies of all unpublished manuscripts, if not otherwise noted, can be accessed at the Office for the Compilation of Ōno City History (Ōno-shi Shi Hensanshitsu), Ōno City. Some entries in the town elders' and other local journals have been transcribed and published in *Ōno-shi shi yōdome-hen*.

Asao 1995
    Asao Naohiro. "Hiden'in to Ōmi no hininban." In *Nihon kokka no shiteki tokushitsu: Kinsei/kindai*, edited by Asao Naohiro Kyōju Taikan Kinenkai, 3–36. Kyoto: Shibunkaku Shuppan, 1995.

Dōtonbori hinin kankei monjo
    Dōtonbori hinin kankei monjo. Edited by Okamoto Ryōichi and Uchida Kusuo. Osaka: Seibundō, 1976.

Ehlers 2018
    Ehlers, Maren. *Give and Take: Poverty and the Status Order in Early Modern Japan*. Cambridge, MA: Harvard University Asia Center, 2018.

Fujimoto 2011
    Fujimoto Seijirō. *Kinsei mibun shakai no nakama kōzō*. Kyoto: Buraku Mondai Kenkyūjo, 2011.

Fujimoto 2014
    Fujimoto Seijirō. *Jōkamachi sekai no seikatsushi—botsuraku to saisei no shiten kara*. Osaka: Seibundō, 2014.

Goyōdome (Adachi Hiromichi-ke)
    Goyōdome. Docs. 3373:4 (1853) and 3374:6 (1857) of Adachi Hiromichi-ke monjo.

Goyōki (Nunokawa Genbei-ke)
Goyōki (1860, months 1, 3, 4, 6, 8, 10, 12). Doc. 422:42 of Nunokawa Genbei-ke monjo.
Hiden'in monjo
Hiden'in monjo. Edited by Okamoto Ryōichi and Uchida Kusuo. Osaka: Seibundō, 1987.
"Iburaku ikkan"
"Iburaku ikkan." In Nihon shomin seikatsu shiryō shūsei, vol. 14: Buraku, edited by Tanikawa Ken'ichi, 527–61. Tokyo: San'ichi Shobō, 1971.
Mita 2018
Mita Satoko. Kinsei mibun shakai no sonraku kōzō—Senshū Minami Ōji-mura o chūshin ni. Kyoto: Buraku Mondai Kenkyūjo, 2018.
MT goyōdome
Machi toshiyori goyōdome. Docs. 2376:26 (1740), 2376:27 (1741), 2380:40 (1793), 2383:51 (1834), 2375:17–20 (1835), 2383:52 (1836), 2384:53 (1837), 2385:54 (1838), 2387:56 (1840), 2387:57 (1841), 2388:63 (1852), 2389:64 (1855), 2389:65 (1860, months 2, intercal. 3, 5, 7, 9, 11), and 2390:67 (1864) of Saitō Suzuko-ke monjo.
Ōno-shi shi yōdome-hen
Ōno-shi shi. Vol. 9: Yōdome-hen. Edited by Ōno Shishi Hensan Iinkai. Ōno: Ōno-shi, 1995.
"Ōno-han goyōki"
"Ōno-han jisha machikata goyōki" 1865. Echizen shiryō. Kokuritsu Shiryōkan.
Ooms 1996
Ooms, Herman. Tokugawa Village Practice: Class, Status, Power, Law. Berkeley: University of California Press, 1996.
Sugahara 1977
Sugahara Kenji. "Kinsei Kyōto no hinin—Yojirō o megutte." Nihonshi kenkyū 181 (1977): 69–104.
Tsukada 1987
Tsukada Takashi. Kinsei Nihon mibunsei no kenkyū. Kobe: Hyōgo Buraku Mondai Kenkyūjo, 1987.
Tsukada 1997
Tsukada Takashi. Kinsei mibunsei to shūen shakai. Tokyo: Tōkyō Daigaku Shuppankai, 1997.
Tsukada 2001
Tsukada Takashi. Toshi Ōsaka to hinin. Nihonshi riburetto. Tokyo: Yamakawa Shuppansha, 2001.
Tsukada 2007
Tsukada Takashi. Kinsei Ōsaka no hinin to mibunteki shūen. Kyoto: Buraku Mondai Kenkyūjo, 2007.
Tsukada 2013
Tsukada Takashi. Ōsaka no hinin—Kotsujiki/Shitennōji/korobi kirishitan. Tokyo: Chikuma Shobō, 2013.
Tsukada 2014
Tsukada Takashi. "Jūnanaseiki kōki/Ōsaka ni okeru hinin no 'ie.'" In Kinsei mibun shakai no hikakushi: Hō to shakai no shiten kara, edited by Tsukada Takashi, Saga Ashita, and Yagi Shigeru, 193–218. Osaka: Seibundō, 2014.

"Tsutomekata oboegaki"
  "Tsutomekata oboegaki Tamura-hikae" 1810. Doc. 4450:176 of Tamura Kōsaburō-ke monjo.
Uchida 1987
  Uchida Kusuo. "Ōsaka shikasho no soshiki to shūnyū." *Hisutoria* 115 (1987): 73–115.
Yamamoto 2002
  Yamamoto Kaoru. "Senshū no Sakai 'shikasho' chōri to gunchū hininban." *Buraku mondai kenkyū* 159 (2002): 69–95.
"Yokomachi shirabechō"
  "Yokomachi yashiki tanbetsu shirabechō," 1872. Doc. 88:5 of Yokomachi kuyū monjo.
Yokoyama 2005
  Yokoyama Yuriko. *Meiji ishin to kinsei mibunsei no kaitai.* Tokyo: Yamakawa Shuppansha, 2005.
Yokoyama 2007
  Yokoyama Yuriko. "Zen-kindai mibunsei kenkyū no dōkō—seika to kadai." *Buraku mondai kenkyū* 180 (2007): 2–24.

PART TWO

Case Studies

Stem Adaptations and Threats

6

Governing the Samurai Family in the Late Edo Period

Luke Roberts

On an early summer day in 1824, Fukuoka Shō (1792–1858), a samurai wife in the castle town of Kōchi in the southwestern domain of Tosa, submitted a report to the domain police. It read:

> The foot soldier Sukegorō had earlier been employed in my house. Later he was given leave but even recently would come to the house. However, yesterday on the 25th he came after noon and I met him in the kitchen. [Our] son and heir Shōroku was away from home and the retainers of the house were not present at our meeting. Sukegorō said something rude and I reproved him but he became increasingly rude and turned upon me. I could not bear this and my only recourse was to kill him using the short sword of my husband Fukuoka Yūji.

> The above statement is true.

> Fukuoka Yūji's wife, Shō

> *This person is Teshima Heijūrō's daughter. Her husband, Yūji, is the Edo ambassador at this time and is not present.*[1]

Four months later, after much deliberation, the domain handed down its decision on punishments in the case: Shō's husband, Fukuoka Yūji (1790–1845), had his 200 *koku* fief reduced to 130 *koku,* he was relieved of his important office as ambassador for the domain in Edo along with its 450 *koku* supplementary office fief, and he was ordered to return home to Kōchi.[2] The domain also removed other relatives of Shō and Yūji from their government posts and banished the male household servants. The judges remanded Shō to the custody of her husband, who was ordered to "keep his wife under his strict control." Two female servants of the household were explicitly absolved of responsibility.

What led to this series of punishments, and why did they take the form they did? After all, Shō had the right to dispatch Sukegorō under a law that allowed people of samurai status to kill those below them if they were deliberately rude. But the judges found other aspects of the case not to be right. The crux of the issue seems to have been the domain's finding that Shō was "living improperly." It is not clear what exactly this term meant, but it conveyed without doubt a negative judgment of Shō's behavior as well as the conduct of her entire family and household. Nevertheless, in the end, the domain's verdict restored peace. Shō and Yūji remained married, and after an interim of punishment the Fukuoka family prospered politically and economically well into the late nineteenth century. The neat ending provided by the official judgment and its outcome obscures, however, a set of complex private negotiations among family members themselves—notably Yūji, his mother, and his male kin—that, according to another source, preceded and followed the incident and its adjudication. These "inside" negotiations reflect a subculture of samurai family values and practices differing from official principles and laws; they show us that—much as with commoner families—samurai families perceived a clear distinction between government interests and their own, and they gave more authority to women than the government was willing to accord.[3] Here I explore this tension while analyzing the organization and decision-making processes of samurai households through the story of the case and its family and communal contexts.

THE SOURCES

Any discussion of Shō's case must begin with a discussion of the sources, because they are not transparent and they fundamentally shape what we know—indeed, what it is possible to know—about the events, their background, and their repercussions. Shō's own voice is scarcely heard; her statement to the domain police, quoted above, is the only record of the events in her own words. Almost everything we know about the case comes from domain records of punishment and a lengthy confessional memoir recounted after the fact by Fukuoka Yūji to his close friend, a writer named Yamauchi (Maeno) Akinari (1762–1847), a junior elder of Tosa domain.[4] In addition to his prestigious official position, Akinari was a local scholar and literatus who used the pen name Yōsha. His "Yōsha zuihitsu" (Yōsha's Miscellany), in which Yuji's story and punishment records appear, collects items of interest recorded over a period of about twenty years. Only one copy currently exists, and the absence of any reference to it in the writings of Akinari's contemporaries or late-nineteenth-century compilers of local historical documents suggests that it did not circulate.[5] Indeed, some of the contents were highly sensitive and potentially damaging to people in Akinari's own family and social world, and it is unclear whether the author intended his miscellany to be seen by anyone during his lifetime. But as is the case with diaries, he may well have had an imagined audience of close friends or even future descendants. Although the entries in "Yōsha zuihitsu" do not have dated headings, internal evidence suggests that they were written in diary form, ordered sequentially, and covered the years between 1813 and 1830. At some later point, sections became disordered or reordered during copying or rebinding. What survives is a neatly bound copy once consisting of seven volumes, of which five remain today.[6] Each volume, with between 80 and 210 entries, comprises extremely diverse texts and images, including humorous poems, news from Edo, petitions, accounts of strange events such as comets crossing the sky, historical documents, parodic literature, announcements of punishments of retainers, samurai lineages, and many other topics mostly pertaining to Tosa domain and the Yamauchi daimyo's household. Stories of commoners rarely appear in the text, unless they did something truly extraordinary such as catch mermaids, give birth to lizard-like children, or grow eight feet tall. The entertainment value of such fanciful stories notwithstanding, Akinari was most keenly interested in the affairs of the retainers of his own lord's household.

The activities of Akinari's peers were far from dull; life in Kōchi and the Edo mansions of the Yamauchi clan presented him with a surprising number of opportunities to record crimes and punishments. A domainal compilation of all punishments of ranking samurai of Tosa domain (fewer than eight hundred households) entitled "Gokachū hengi" (Disorders in the Household) shows that in the early nineteenth century an annual average of about five incidents of theft, murder, or fights required punishment.[7] Many men were punished because either they themselves or subordinate male or female members of their households were "living improperly." (This was, officially speaking, Shō's crime.) The legal documents excerpted in "Gokachū hengi" offer little explanation of "living improperly" or what behavior was being policed. By contrast, "Yōsha zuihitsu" is particularly useful as a source because Akinari not only transcribed the domain announcements of punishments of various samurai but occasionally followed up with examples of related town graffiti or the "inside stories" that came to him from gossip, from those directly involved in crimes (such as Yūji), and, in instances dealing with his own kin group, from Akinari himself and his family members.

Although such juxtaposed inside stories constitute only a small fraction of his miscellany, they are of great interest as entries into how Akinari and his peers interpreted events. Akinari himself knew that his "inside stories" were not purely factual. Noting that we cannot "know if this story is true or not," Akinari says he simply wrote down Yūji's narrative "just as it was told to a close friend." Likewise, historians know that no document, not even a hard gravestone, is an unmediated representation of the truth.[8] They must carefully assess the truth claims of each of their documents by understanding the context of its production in order to discern the inherent biases; then they must compare various sources to uncover disjunctures and untruths. Finally historians must assess and write a plausible narrative, fully knowing that a new document, or even a new line of reasoning, can overturn their carefully crafted stories. I have here compared Akinari's account of Yūji's narrative with the government documents of punishment, a brief mention in a bystander's diary, and various records such as lineages and gravestones to create a plausible narrative of the events and of the samurai family dynamics that gave rise to them, and to discover and query the places where the documents disagree so as to reveal the personal interests and larger ideologies that shaped their production.[9]

In Akinari's account, Yūji's telling of his wife's murderous attack on Sukegorō and events that came before and after it takes on a confessional tone. Yūji says he was relieved when he heard of the domain's judgment in the case; he had thought the incident would be the end of his household and was grateful for what he perceived as a lenient punishment. He also reported many other things, notably that, years before the murder, Shō had had an affair with Sukegorō when he was a servant in their household. A female servant discovered the affair and told Yūji's younger brother Sakonbei, who then disclosed it to their mother. Yūji himself was long away on official business. In his absence, Sakonbei and the mother conspired to cover up the affair, dismissing Sukegorō from the household and commanding Shō to act properly, under threat of divorce and public shame. Yūji claims not to have learned about the affair until several years later when, though unhappy, he forgave Shō at the urging of his mother and relatives. All was apparently well until, years later, Shō suddenly called Sukegorō back to her home and cut him down.

Although there is much about the incident that we cannot know with certainty, our access to Akinari's record and the official documents allows us to explore how samurai males viewed the inner workings of the household, how they narrated them for mutual consumption, and how they and their families responded as individuals to the public values that the samurai government enforced. For even though that government was made up of samurai, Tosa domain's institutional values and the family values of individual samurai diverged on many points, especially concerning the place and responsibilities of women in the home.

THE SETTING

The divide between the inner workings of households and their relation to the outer, public world is illustrated by the physical setting in which the events surrounding Shō's murder of Sukegorō played themselves out. The Teshima family house, Shō's natal home, survives in Kōchi to this day and helps us understand aspects of samurai life barely intimated in written documents.[10]

Immediately noticeable in the photo of the inside of the house (fig. 6.1) is the separation of the front or reception space (*omote*) from the private or family space (*oku*) by doorways with abnormally low lintels, which force one to bow deeply when passing between the two areas. Here is a clear sign that passage between the two spaces entailed a significant change of context. The rear of the house admitted

FIGURE 6.1. Interior of the Teshima house viewed from the front, showing two low doorways (right and left) separating the back from the front of the house. Photo by author.

only family members and, perhaps, very close friends. The separation between rear and front also was strongly gendered. The women of the house lived their lives primarily in the back portion, while the male head of the family would use the front of the house to receive guests. The wife of the household head (or his mother, if she still so wished) was normally in charge of managing the back of the house and the family economy.[11] The modern Japanese term for wife, *okusama* ("honored person of the interior"), derives from this gendering of space. In the Edo period, samurai wives were also called *naishosama* ("honored person of inside matters"), in reference to their responsibility for the internal aspects of the house. The spatial layout—and what acts took place where—is important because it influenced domain officials when they considered punishments for Shō and others involved in the murder case.

The main house was the residence for family, female servants, and, sometimes, dependent relatives; outbuildings were for other dependents and servants. Shō had a brother and a sister, and both her parents were alive when she married. Other relations may well have lived in the house, and perhaps male or female apprentices, as was common in many Kōchi samurai households.[12] A family of the Teshima's status and income was also likely to have had one to three female servants as well as two or three male servants. These servants, who filled many roles, added to the social complexity of the house. The longest-serving female servant would have been the wife of the chief manservant (the master's right-hand man), who held the only hereditary position among servants. Others, male and female alike, would normally have been hired on term contracts and been either unmarried or, if coupled, involved in discreet "commuter marriages."[13] A large number of servants in samurai households were children of lower-level retainers, such as foot soldiers, or moderately successful villagers and townspeople. For most, service in a warrior house was a stage in late childhood and early adulthood, used to gain the income, connections, and social training that might eventuate in superior circumstances.

Female servants lived in the main house, tending to the kitchen and garden, spinning, weaving, sewing, washing, and engaging in other tasks. They also performed personal services for the wife, the husband, and live-in relatives. Servants of the wife ran errands or accompanied her when out of the home. Female servants of the master assisted him only inside the home. Many also served as the master's sexual partners. A child by the master of the house belonged to him and would remain in the home when the servant left for other employment or marriage. The child's mother would be listed as "concubine" (*mekake*) in government records. Regardless of age, the children of concubines were listed as younger than any child born to the wife (in order to suppress inheritance struggles) even as they were retained in the home as potential heirs in the event of the absence or early death of an elder male child. Wives were encouraged to accept the presence of concubines, but not all complied. Conflicts between wives, husbands, and female servants over sexual relations, as well as the status and treatment of children, were common. At the same time, in the interest of maintaining the patriarchal *ie,* samurai wives were expected to be chaste.

Male servants lived in the front gatehouse or other outbuildings of the property to reduce opportunities for sexual liaisons with the women of the house. The Teshima residence had a gatehouse with four small rooms for such servants. One job of male servants was to act as gatemen who controlled access. They also ran errands. Their most socially privileged job, however, was to wear weapons and accompany the master as part of his retinue whenever he left on business or pleasure. They were, of course, expected to look after the master's interests, and because he was deemed responsible for their behavior, they could bring upon him shame and punishment.[14] Accordingly, the master had disciplinary authority and even the right (if rarely exercised) to execute a misbehaving servant. Firing a servant was the most common option in cases of serious dissatisfaction.

Yūji's natal home was a fifteen-minute walk from Shō's home. The family fief of 200 *koku* was greater than that of the Teshima, and Yūji's residential property was a bit larger. Still, the two families were of the same general status, and the basic architecture of their homes was likely similar as well.[15] The big distinction lay in the size of the kin group. The Teshima were head of a kin group with two minor branches. On Yūji's side there were thirteen Fukuoka households, all well connected; the most important served as domain elders of Tosa with a fief of about 2,800 *koku* at the time. Yūji's neighbor was his closest relative, Fukuoka Heima, who had a 500 *koku* fief. Heima and his ancestors regularly served in important posts in the domain and were allowed the privilege of maintaining those posts hereditarily. Yūji's line had been set up as a branch family of Heima's line two generations earlier and would customarily have deferred to Heima's advice and interests, just as both would have deferred to the Fukuoka lineage of domain elders. The heads of the various Fukuoka houses likely met regularly to discuss issues such as marriage and adoption plans and to protect their mutual interests.[16]

In sum, Shō and Yūji lived in a physical setting that mirrored a social world divided by crosscutting affiliations and divisions based on kinship, gender, seniority, status, and wealth. All of these factors came into play over the course of the several decades that preceded and followed the murder case, as individuals performed roles and duties appropriate to their status and gender but also improvised and sought advantage or alliance when they could to secure more desirable outcomes either for themselves or for their family.

THE FAMILIES

Shō was the eldest daughter of Teshima Heijūrō, a samurai with a fief of 100 *koku* and mounted-warrior status, which placed him in the broad middle level of ranking samurai. Heijūrō earned good positions in the personal service of various members of the lord's family. This meant he was often away in Edo on duty, but such posts increased his political connections and came with an additional 100 or 150 *koku* of office fief that more than doubled family income. The genealogy reveals that Shō's father initiated a period of successful appointments for the Teshima house lasting until the Meiji period. This success continued despite a number of domain punishments experienced by family members for misbehaviors.[17]

Yūji was the eldest son in his branch of the Fukuoka family. His younger brother Sakonbei (1796–1835) was also employed as a retainer and started his own branch family, something most noninheriting younger brothers could not achieve. Likely regarded as a man of talent, made more easily visible by the power of the Fukuoka clan, Sakonbei served as a page (*koshō*) of the daimyo, though with a stipend so small (15 *koku* and 4 rations [*fuchi*]) that he continued living in his natal home. Their father died in 1797 at the age of forty-five, when Yūji officially became household head, at age seven. His younger brother was one year old at the time. Because their mother had run the household for almost as long as either Yūji or his brother would have remembered, both sons likely felt particularly grateful and deferential to her.[18] Yūji was appointed page to Yamauchi Toyooki, the young lord-to-be, in 1806, at age sixteen, and probably began journeying with him to Edo on alternate attendance at that time. He thus began a career of personal service to the lord that kept him away from home for long stretches.

Exactly when Shō and Yūji married is unclear, but it was at least as early as 1815. Shō bore a son, Shōroku (1816–1841), in the summer of 1816, when she was about twenty-four years old and Yūji twenty-six.[19] They may also have had a daughter, mentioned in the official samurai lineages as wife of the samurai Murata Shōhachirō.[20] It is possible that Yūji's daughter was born to a concubine.[21] Unlike Shōroku, a daughter is not mentioned in narratives of the murder incident, which might mean she was born afterward or that she was considered irrelevant in documents imbued with patriarchal discourse. Since Yūji was known as a man of talent with a promising future, we can imagine that his marriage to Shō was regarded publicly as appropriate for both parties and even advantageous for Shō.[22] But that marriage was not happy, a factor in the violent incident of 1824.

THE AFFAIR

The inner workings of the families are intimated in "Yōsha zuihitsu," where Akinari records Yūji's description of the various debates among numerous interlocutors over what to do about Shō's purported affair with Sukegorō. According to this account, Yūji began his story not with the affair but a long discussion of what he saw as the problem of Shō's jealousy. He begins by saying, "My wife's character was filled deep with extreme jealousy, especially toward female servants of her husband [Yūji], such that they often asked for permission to leave employment because they could not stand the work. She was even so with my younger brother's female servants—wickedly jealous—and she generally abused young women so roughly that most requested to leave." Like most men of their status, Yūji and his brother quite likely had sexual relations with their female servants, and Yūji's emphasis on jealousy suggests that this disturbed Shō deeply. By beginning his story in this way, Yūji emphasizes Shō's role, not his own actions, as the source of marital unhappiness and discord in the household.

Women's morality primers of the day warned against jealousy toward concubines and mistresses, and against mixing with men who were not relatives, because both occasioned daily tensions between married couples in patriarchal households.[23] Female chastity was a virtue in samurai households, and female adultery a severely punished infraction in law codes. Male chastity was not an issue unless the man was an interloper or given to sexual excesses harmful to family finances or the performance of duty.[24] Yūji himself did not perceive any sort of double standard regarding marital fidelity and resented what he saw as his wife's unreasonable jealousy. In his account, he says that he frequently instructed her to control her behavior, but this was so unsuccessful that he often considered divorce.

Yūji's frequent absences from home may well have been another source of sadness and frustration for Shō. Yūji was likely away in Edo when Shōroku was born in 1816, leaving his mother, Shō, Sakonbei, and the servants to run the household.[25] In 1817 he was appointed to the demanding position of Edo representative of the domain, which would have kept him in Edo most of the time thereafter. In Yūji's narrative his mother expresses her frustration with his extended stays in Edo, and the same narrative has both Shō's affair and the murder happening during his extended absence.

According to Yūji, Shō entered into an affair with Sukegorō while he was away, and the affair came to light in 1817 when the female servant of Yūji's brother, Sakonbei, discovered love letters the couple had exchanged. She showed these to Sakonbei, who immediately showed them to his mother, saying that they would have to inform Yūji when he returned to Kōchi from Edo. His mother objected: "If we tell this to Yūji, then it is clear as day that he will divorce her directly. I am getting older and it is becoming much more difficult to take care of the children. Promise me you will not tell Yūji when he arrives from Edo!" Sakonbei felt uncomfortable, thinking that Shō should be punished, but he acquiesced to his mother's will. On the one hand, Sakonbei felt the need to restore proper order through punishment of the offending woman. On the other hand, he was the dutiful son wishing to obey his mother. In the end the latter won out, a testament to the mother's ultimate authority over the internal dynamics of the household.

The mother's comments indicate that she assumed Yūji's reaction would be to divorce Shō rather than punish her. Indeed this was a common response to infidelity.[26] But punishment appeared undesirable in this case as it would have provoked gossip and shame in the Fukuokas' social circle. It would also have made Yūji culpable of the crime of mismanagement of his household, for which he, in turn, would have been punished. Domain law, in effect, encouraged families to resolve things quietly.

The mother likely had all this in mind when, after conferring with Sakonbei, she summoned the servant Sukegorō to tell him that she had learned of the affair with Shō but wished to keep things quiet. Then she dismissed Sukegorō from the household with good references, telling him he should never return. Next she severely scolded Shō, who "took the matter to heart" and thereafter behaved with propriety. Two years passed with Yūji knowing nothing about the affair (even after his return home to Kōchi) until one day in 1820 when Sakonbei's female servant confided to Yūji's female servant: "The wife is always saying this and that about other people, but earlier she had this and that, you know, with a man called Sukegorō, and at the end of the day she can't go on being jealous about what other people do. Sakonbei knows all about this but the mother kept things quiet!" The servant then passed this information on to Yūji himself, who pressed his brother to learn the facts and subsequently sent Shō back to her natal home. In discussion, his mother confirmed what Yūji had learned but urged, using the logic she had employed with Sakonbei: "Since then she has reformed her ways and has not committed the slightest impropriety. I am getting older and if you divorce that person, there is no one else to take care of the children. Furthermore, you have jobs that always take you away to Edo. Please just treat this as an old wound. If you don't

agree, I think I will just die." She asked him to understand her request as performing his filial duty.

Yūji did not immediately acquiesce but discussed the situation with Sakonbei
and other relatives, who all agreed that he should forgive Shō. Then he said, "I was
very unhappy in the depths of my heart, but I called Shō back to my home." The
following aspect of this process deserve comment. Despite the fact that he was officially household head and living in a patriarchal political system that supported
his authority, Yūji did not get his own way through a quiet divorce. All of the male
relatives he consulted, well positioned to enforce patriarchy if they chose, apparently encouraged him to forgive Shō. They all appealed to the filial piety Yūji owed
his mother, a widely accepted reason for a younger male to accept the authority of
an older female in a samurai household.[27] In the end, the narrative portrays a Yūji
who put aside personal enmity and wounded pride to do as the family advised.

Upon hearing Yūji's version of the story, the writer, Akinari, made his own
opinions on the matter clear in his comments: "If one does not know about an
infidelity, then there is nothing to be done. But once one knows one's wife does
not hold to propriety, then even if one's mother says she might die because of it,
is it filial duty to not divorce the wife, or is it filial duty to have her leave? Well for
the benefit of the household, I humbly think that divorce is the way of filial duty."
Akinari veiled the conflict by defining filial duty as honoring the rectitude and
harmony of the ancestral (and paternally organized) *ie* rather than obeying one's
parents. In his view, divorcing a wayward wife was a better tactic for preserving the
household's long-term integrity. Half-hidden by this sleight of hand is Akinari's
anxiety concerning the disorder that might ensue if women actually controlled
men. He makes this anxiety clearer in another concluding comment: "There are
terrifying women in this world! Everyone must keep a wife, so they should defi-
nitely take [this event] to heart." For him, Yūji's forgiveness invited further disor-
derly conduct by wicked women down the line.

Comparison of this account of the actions and reactions of family members
and servants, and the views of interested observers such as Akinari, with the official accounts of supervising authorities found in other records suggests a fraught
interplay of gender and family dynamics in samurai families. As we shall see, the
picture emerging from this document is far more complicated than the domain's
official policy of maintaining male control of the household and its women. The
narrative represents, within an individual family, the strength of filial values
encouraging obedience to the mother. Even a wife's infidelity, moreover, could be
forgiven in the interest of smooth family management. Because the domain regularly punished household heads (and even collateral relatives) for the crimes of
servants and family members, it was effectively complicit in creating a culture in
which families had a vested interest in quietly hiding misbehavior.

This culture of secrecy played an important role in the collective decision to
forgive Shō. According to Yūji, many people expressed the desire to keep things

quiet so as not to shame the Fukuoka house. Indeed, managing secrecy was often at the heart of how Tokugawa governance operated.[28] As Amy Stanley has argued, many governments encouraged the private settlement of adultery disputes, and even more disputes were settled with the assistance only of village officials so as to avoid expense and the stricter punishments prescribed by law.[29] Samurai who wished to address adultery probably often decided among communities of relations to end things quietly with forgiveness or divorce. Such cases would normally not leave paper trails for modern historians. Yet, as Yūji's relatives found out to their detriment, when secrecy led to public incidents, many parties in the know could be subject to punishment.

Yūji attempted to maintain honor through forbearance, maintaining silence, showing obedience to his mother, and accepting the opinions of relatives rather than through engaging in violence or overtly seeking justice. So Yūji remained in the marriage, and Shō's affair was relegated to the past and to gossipy whispers among the many people consequently in the know. Thanks to this silence, Sukegorō suffered no punishment in the wake of the affair save for dismissal from his job in the Fukuoka household, and he eventually came in line to inherit the position of a domain foot soldier from a man named Reikichi, who had adopted him and planned to have him marry his daughter Moto.[30] Even after Yūji's mother died late in 1822, Yūji remained married to Shō. All would likely have ended quietly but for what Yūji called, in retrospect, his foolish decisions and Shō's fierce, passionate nature.

In 1824 Yūji was to go to Edo again to serve as the ambassador for his daimyo. This time, his mother was no longer present in the home and his wife, Shō, would be running the house in his absence. Before departing, Yūji says, he told Shō in no uncertain terms, "You have that history, so it is absolutely essential that you behave well and take care of the place and of your personal behavior in my absence with unwavering care and discretion. Sukegorō has not shown up here since that time, but all the more you must be aware of your status, maintain discretion, and be without any misconduct!" Shō replied: "Of course I have been well aware of what I should be doing ever since that time, but now with Mother gone, what should I do if that man comes around?" Yūji then said, "If that man comes by and says anything improper to you, then you should cut him down right then! I will leave you one of my short swords in my absence."

Yūji's decision to entrust Shō with a short sword reveals a fascinating contradiction between status and gender, trust and mistrust. Given Sukegorō's long absence, Shō's anxiety seems strange, though perhaps it was customary knowledge that men did prey on women when their husbands were away on Edo duty. This trope certainly underlies Chikamatsu Monzaemon's play *Yari no Gonza Kasane Katabira* (*Gonza the Spearman*).[31] Even so, it remains odd in terms of patriarchal values that, instead of ordering the chief manservant of the house to watch out for Sukegorō, Yūji entrusted his wife with his short sword and told her to use it. Few samurai women were trained in the use of a weapon and, if any were familiar with one at all, it would have been the quaintly antiquated halberd (*naginata*). Although some women were taught how to use a dagger if threatened with rape, even samurai women were not normally entrusted with swords, since they were thought to be "manly" weapons. Thus, the story depends on an intimate complicity arising from the ties of their marriage and their superior status to the servants in the house. In Yūji's story, Shō saw her salvation from shame in the trust shown her by Yūji, and he ended up regarding this grant of his trust to have been his mistake. Yūji told Akinari that after his words Shō "appeared obsessed with the idea that she could not uphold her chastity until she had killed Sukegorō with that sword."

Yūji's narrative suggests the servants later told him that, after he departed for Edo, Shō prayed daily at the shrine on the household grounds that she might cut down Sukegorō. If this is true, Shō's anger was extraordinarily deep. It may have originated in an earlier rape that was kept out of the record by a pervasive discursive bias that erased women's concerns, just as it did the concerns of servants. Or perhaps, as Yūji suggests, Shō's anger originated in her anxiety over her chastity. We cannot know. Despite being aware of what they perceived as her obsession, the servants were unable or unwilling to stop it. Indeed, the punishment records indicate that the servant Kichizō served as Shō's messenger to Sukegorō when she called him to the house. Sukegorō arrived and he went to the kitchen, in the back of the house, but the two remaining male servants stayed in the gatehouse at the front of the property, thus allowing a man from outside the family to enter the house's inner sanctum. No record indicates why they allowed this trespass. Certainly Shō's status as the wife of the house allowed her to give them orders concerning daily affairs. In this case the male servants paid dearly for Sukegorō's arrival in the private half of the house, because the judges held them responsible for protecting household honor, as if they were, as males, not subject to Shō's authority.

Few details of the immediate circumstances surrounding the murder exist. In her own statement to the domain police, Shō claimed that Sukegorō was "rude" to her, implying that he was being sexually forward and attempting rape. Legally, however, the matter was "rudeness." In cases of slaying a person of inferior status for rudeness, it was important to show that the miscreant was deliberately rude, usually by including a statement confirming that the samurai had first reprimanded a rude party who nevertheless persisted. This is what Shō claimed. While slaying an inferior for deliberate rudeness was within Shō's rights, the perpetrator had to behave properly and resort to violence only to defend the status order.[32]

The only words we have from Shō suggest that Sukegorō attempted to rape her. Might this have been the actual case, and Yūji's story an elaborate fabrication? This does not seem likely, because a wife's successful defense against rape would not have constituted a crime.[33] Also, Yūji's own honor would not have been at stake, because he was hundreds of miles away at the time. The only person to gain by covering up or distorting an assault story was the dead man, Sukegorō. The male servants would have been punished in any event, since it was their duty to control access to the property and their mistress. For anyone else involved, the story of an attempted rape would not have precipitated nearly the degree of household shame that derived from their actual punishments. So the punishment of many relatives for not managing things well, and of one of the servants for acting as a messenger, makes sense only if we accept the accuracy of the basic outline of Yūji's story. It is not likely that so many men would have accepted a great loss of income, status, and prestige just to cover up an attempted rape by Sukegorō.

Another difference between the accounts of Shō and Yūji is Shō's representation, in her official statement, that Sukegorō "even recently would come to the house," as if visits were a regular occurrence. House servants sometimes did socially visit their former places of employment.[34] By making such a statement, Shō was most likely trying to make the fact of his presence in the house seem natural and hide the fact that she had called him to the house. If she had not called him, it seems unlikely that the servant Kichizō would have been banished for taking Sukegorō a message from Shō. The spatial context of the killing also is consistent with Shō's mission to kill Sukegorō. Her possession of her husband's short sword in the kitchen rather than in her room would have been strange if Sukegorō had appeared suddenly.

At any rate, as far as the domain investigation was concerned, two legally damaging facts could not be avoided: the meeting and the murder took place in the back of the house, and no men of the household were present. These two facts, and the more general and vague accusation that "her daily manner of living was not good," became key elements in the judgments that were handed down four months later.

Public judgment also was not favorable. The day after the murder, and the same day as Shō's official statement, the low-status domain retainer Kusunose Ōe briefly mentioned the murder in his diary and then closed with: "The word in the streets about this is not very favorable."[35] This rapid response suggests either that gossip of an affair between Shō and Sukegorō had previously circulated about town, or that people just assumed infidelity was behind a woman killing a man. A few days later Ōe also recorded in his diary a related tragedy: Sukegorō's fiancée, Moto, the daughter of his adoptive parents, killed herself by *seppuku*, cutting open her belly, three days after the murder. Her father, mother, and adoptive mother had all died recently, and then her fiancé, Sukegorō, had been murdered in circumstances engendering gossip. Moto was certainly left in a desperate state with no one to depend on. But it is also possible that she killed herself out of intense shame. Ōe's description of her death as *seppuku* suggests that she made an attempt to regain honor rather than simply kill herself out of desperation.

In government discourse, however, *seppuku* was a masculine act, as was Shō's use of a short sword to kill Sukegorō.[36] Indeed, in the whole incident the only two people to use weapons—and apparently for the purpose of restoring violated honor—were women. The samurai men were inclined to passive acceptance and filial piety. However, purpose aside, neither woman could actually be accorded public honor through her act—one of them because of an official judgment of misdeed, the other because the legal system denied women the option of honorable suicide.

Officially, *seppuku* was permitted only at the lord's order and only to male samurai as a way of maintaining household honor following a serious wrongdoing. It was otherwise a crime, which often led to the face-saving locution "suddenly died of illness" in reports of unsanctioned *seppuku* by samurai.[37] Cutting open the belly by women and commoners was regarded as merely "suicide" (*jigai*), and, indeed, the domain court referred to Moto's death in this way. Whether the elision of *seppuku* derived from her gender or the crime is moot, since the former would have preempted consideration of the latter. The official description also explicitly exonerated Moto of any guilt in the affair but interpreted her motive for death as sadness: because so many relatives had recently died, she "had no one to rely on" after she lost Sukegorō. However true, the verdict narrates her femininity as passive and leaves unanswered the question of why she chose *seppuku*.

THE PUNISHMENTS

Yūji told Akinari that when he heard of the incident, he "became prepared for the destruction of his household and the end of its fortunes, but is now grateful for the merciful treatment which the lord handed out." As noted earlier, Yūji was relieved of his post as Edo ambassador and its allowance, had his own 200 *koku* fief reduced by 70 *koku*, and was ordered to be prudent in his behavior and strictly control his wife. How, in fact, were such cases normally handled in the domain? Tosa's law codes regarding marital infidelity were extremely vague on the point. Until a new, more detailed code was created in the 1850s, the law merely promised that "failure to show filial respect or other immoral behavior will be punished as a crime."[38] We must therefore rely on case judgments to infer standards of punishment. Records of early-nineteenth-century cases in which a samurai was punished for a wife or mother or daughter "living loosely" show that the samurai was convicted of the crime of poorly managing his household. The punishments generally entailed removal from government posts, denial of associated income, and reduction in the household hereditary income (usually around 10 percent, less than in Yūji's case). Banishment from the castle town and loss of status occurred in one case, but even there the house headship reverted to the eldest son. In no case was a woman issued any direct statement of punishment by the domain.[39] In all cases the man (or his son, if the principal was banished) was ordered to "strictly control" the woman. Thus, it seems that the punishments of both Yuji and Shō were within the norm for their peers.

Ordering a man to "strictly control" a household woman reinstated him as master of his household but rather shamefully instructed him that he needed to restore the order he had obviously failed to maintain. Although Shō herself was beneath direct address, her inappropriate meeting with Sukegorō and "outrageous behavior" were mentioned in every single indictment of the others. The judges described her crime thus: "Having the status of wife, it was inappropriate for her to have held that meeting at all, and we have heard of many aspects of her extremely outrageous behavior and improper lifestyle."[40] Clearly, the authorities presumed the responsibility of various males for preventing female misbehavior. After four months of investigation, judgments were issued to Yūji as well as many other parties. His cousin Fukuoka Heima, the head of a collateral house also of mounted-guard status, was relieved of his post because "as a relative he should have been thinking properly on this issue but did not." Probably implied is Heima's participation in Yūji's early consultations, although, it should be noted, Heima was not the family's head at the time. Heima or his father certainly encouraged Yūji to keep matters quiet, which is evidence of the latent tension between samurai family values and samurai government values. A month after the initial punishments, Shō's brother Teshima Kiroku (then head of her natal household) and Yūji's younger brother, Sakonbei, were both relieved of their appointments as pages and ordered to exercise prudence.[41] While we may infer that Yūji had consulted Shō's brother Yorimichi about the issue, his punishment may have resulted simply from his status as current head of Shō's natal home.

The three samurai household heads named above suffered loss of post and reduction in income, but the punishment for the male servants of the household was much more severe. The chief manservant, Wada Yusunojō, was deprived of family name and the right to bear a long sword and then banished to the domain's western reaches. Although not quite a full-fledged samurai position in itself, "chief manservant" conferred hereditary military status on its bearer. This severe punishment made Yusunojō a commoner and ended his line. The severity of his punishment resulted from his role as chief male in the household when the incident occurred "in the back of the house without a single retainer present." Yusunojō "was completely incompetent in this matter." Despite his role as a servant of the household, the judgment conveys a domainal expectation that he had the ability and authority to control his master's wife, something very unlikely in reality, which reveals yet another disjuncture between the internal ideologies of family and the formal expectations of government.

Two male servants of lesser status (komono) were both punished as well. With no hereditary status to lose, one, Ginbei, was banished to the western reaches for the same reason behind Yusunojō's sentence. Even Kichizō, who might have escaped punishment because he was not on the Fukuoka property at the time and was merely a child, was banished from the castle town and its four neighboring villages because he had served as Shō's messenger to Sukegorō. All males of the household, except the eight-year-old son, who was away at the time (perhaps sent away by Shō for his safety), were punished.

The domain also issued a judgment to one more male, formerly of the household. This was the murdered Sukegorō himself, who was treated as a criminal. The document explains: "If he were alive, we would certainly have punished him severely, but he was already cut down by Yūji's wife." The law codes of Tosa in the 1850s specify that a man who has an affair with his master's wife should be banished from the domain.[42] Whether this was the standard in the 1820s is unclear, although the domain may have seen his death at Shō's hands as proper punishment. The domain declared that while his body would not be subject to further punishment (such as public display), his adoptive house and lineage were to be abolished. In this way the murder itself was treated as the legitimate climax of an incident that revealed a degree of "loose living" and "household mismanagement" that the domain could not ignore.

In marked contrast to the treatment of the men, all of the women of the household were exonerated of responsibility, despite their certain knowledge of Shō's affairs. As was the case with Shō herself, we find here a sign of the lesser legal autonomy and lesser responsibility that derived from the status of woman. The domain expected the men to punish their women using their paternal authority, and the direct punishment of women in samurai households was not part of the theater of government. In contrast to the inner workings of families as presented in Yūji's account, the government acknowledged no women's authority and responsibility at all.

The rupture in paternalistic control reflected in the incident became, in the domain's hands, an opportunity for the parties to reaffirm their commitment to its ideals, evident in Akinari's concluding opinion that men should not obey their mothers and should strictly control their wives. Yūji himself told Akinari that he assumed personal responsibility: "In the end she took my words the wrong way. . . . I told her to cut that man down if he sneaked into the property, but he had not been there for years and I did not imagine him actually coming. She being a woman I did not even dream that she would kill him in that way. As I am the husband, these events cannot be said to be just my wife's fault." Thus taking responsibility, Yūji also deprived Shō of the autonomy she might have claimed in restoring her honor through violence, much as the domain deprived Moto of her honor in dying by *seppuku*.

We are denied the opportunity to read either Moto's or Shō's own reflections on the incident, which surely would have presented rather different stories. If they wrote anything, it has not survived. The judgments inform us of the paternalistic household organization that the Tosa domain government wished to see reaffirmed in the aftermath of the event. What mattered in the domain's narrative was the restoration of its order of things.

THE AFTERMATH

Although the immediate impact on the household and its relatives was significant, the incident did not have long-term consequences on Fukuoka fortunes in the public world of Tosa. Yūji's cousin Heima was restored to his position the very next year and, within a few more years, was appointed as Edo ambassador. Yūji recovered good graces by 1832, when he was appointed as aide to a Yamauchi prince and his income increased. Thereafter, he served in a number of well-remunerated positions as aide to the Yamauchi family. Nor were the fortunes of the children adversely affected by the parents' crimes. The daughter of the household married Murata Shōroku, head of a family of higher income and importance.[43] By 1836 Yūji's and Shō's son, Shōroku, married into and became heir of the main Fukuoka lineage in the domain (as one of twelve domain elder houses, with an income ten times that of Yūji).[44] Because Shōroku was the only son of Yūji and Shō, they, in turn, needed to adopt an heir. This child, in the household already, was Fukuoka Takachika (1835–1919), Yūji's nephew and the second of Sakonbei's two sons. When Yūji died in 1845, Takachika became family head, at age ten, and was subsequently raised by Shō. He later pursued an extraordinarily successful career, becoming one of the central officials and leaders in Tosa domain by the early 1860s and throughout the final tumultuous years of the Tokugawa period. In 1867 he was a coauthor of the Meiji emperor's "Charter Oath," and afterward gained the rank of viscount and served as a high public official in the new Meiji government.[45]

Patterns of documentation make it easy to say what happened to the important men in a woman's life. Of Shō herself we have only a few sparse facts. Yūji and Shō remained married and later shared the same gravestone, which states that Yūji died at age fifty-five in 1845 and Shō at age sixty-six in 1858 (fig. 6.2). By that time the family fortunes were far better than they had ever been. Shō's full posthumous name, Jihōin Seishitsu Meijū Daishi, translates as "Upholder of the Buddhist Law, True Wife of Bright Fortune who is as a Great Elder Sister." Each detail of the name seems to propose a resolution to the many problems tangled in the 1824 incident: her proper place in the household, her guilt or righteousness, and her moral authority. She likely began using the moniker Jihōin, "Upholder of the Buddha's Law," from the time of her husband's death in 1845; the remainder was added at the time of her own death. The end of the name, Great Elder Sister, reflects a posthumous ranking above the norm for samurai women (commonly "female believer" [shinjo]), suggesting that she had devoted herself to Buddhist faith and study during the remainder of her life. It might just as well reflect the greater wealth of a family able, at the time of her death, to pay the priests for a high-ranking name respectful of her position as the mother of a flourishing household. As with so many things, we cannot be sure.

FIGURE 6.2. The gravestone of Fukuoka Shō and Fukuoka Yūji, viewed from the side (a) and the front (b). Photos by author.

Perhaps the most surprising event of Shō's later life occurred in 1854. When she was sixty-two, the lord of Tosa granted her a pardon and she became free to live the normal life of a samurai widow and eldest woman of the house. No other case of female crime in the early-nineteenth-century record of domainal punishment occasioned such intercession.[46] The political power of the Fukuoka offspring was surely behind this absolution. Quite likely it was due to the efforts of the nameless daughter whose husband, Murata Shōsuke, had been appointed grand inspector (ōmetsuke) of the domain and was in a position to recommend who would be pardoned. Of course, the domain shaped the event to reinforce the patriarchy at the government's ideological core. The moment of pardon was the celebration of the sixtieth birthday of the retired lord of Tosa. Because age sixty marked a particularly felicitous "completion of the calendric cycle" and was a perfect occasion for the lord to reveal his munificent care for those beneath him, the pardon took the form of an order to Shō's son, Takachika, that he no longer had to "keep his mother under strict control." The person of Shō was obscured, identified not by name but as "mother" to the key male, her son. Takachika almost certainly found this an occasion to appreciate the generosity of his lord, as well as the erasure of a black mark from the household record. But the uncommon nature of this pardon also points to members of a samurai family working hard for its own particular interests and recognizing the important place of the mother as authority in the household and conduit of the lineage.

The sad tale revolving around the murder of Sukegorō provides a number of insights into samurai family values and government law concerning samurai households. The story of the incident and Shō's life reveals how the conflicts among family and household members were shaped in complex ways at the rifts and intersections between the values of samurai families and the values of samurai government. Samurai families were organizations in which women could actually hold much authority, most especially women in the position of mother of the household, and this seems to have been a generally respected value among male samurai. However, the government clearly desired—particularly in moments of crisis—to absolve women of most responsibility to the state and require patriarchs and other men of the household to be responsible for women's actions. This disjuncture between samurai government values and samurai family values led families to conceal their inner workings and present safe public images of patriarchal stability. Furthermore, government documents in general discursively erased the identities, desires, and activities of women. This documentary problem creates much difficulty for historians who desire to understand the actual workings of the samurai family and the place and experiences of women therein. Private and family documents are essential for historians interested in recovering some of the reality that was discursively whited out in government documents, and using both allows us to analyze the tension between the two fields of interest, government and family, that produced the narratives, silences, and secrets that sustained the gender and status hierarchies of the "Tokugawa Great Peace."

NOTES

1. "Yōsha zuihitsu." I am using a photocopy of a portion of the document that the owner, Kattō Isamu of Kōchi city, kindly allowed me to make in 1990. Mr. Kattō has since passed away, and the fate of his extensive document collection remains in flux. The entry for this incident includes official records of punishment and Fukuoka Yūji's narrative and is in vol. 5 on folios 24 and 49–51. Unless otherwise noted, all information comes from these four folios.

2. Shō's and Yūji's dates are based on gravestones in Kōchi on Hitsuzan hill behind Myōkokuji temple. Their location is noted in Yamamoto 1987, vol. 1, p. 65. No family documents are currently publicly known, as attested in Gakushūin Daigaku Shiryōkan 1993, vol. 4, pp. 110–11. The family lineage since Shō and Yūji's time can be found in Kasumikaikan 1996, vol. 2, pp. 434–35.

3. Walthall 1991, 50–51, 70; Stanley 2007, 321–23; Mega 1995, 15–48.

4. Yamauchi Kamon Akinari was head of the highest ranking of twelve junior elder (chūrō) lineages of the domain and had a fief of 1,100 koku. The family name is Maeno, but the head of the family used the bestowed name of the Yamauchi daimyo in documents used externally to his own house. Information about Akinari and this document comes from Kattō 1967. Kattō's article discusses a different 1821 incident, caused by Teshima Jungo, a distant cousin of Shō.

5. Such massive document collections as *Nanroshi yoku* (c. 1880), *Hakuwansō* (1881), *Tosa no kuni gunsho ruijū* (c. 1881), *Tosa no kuni gunsho ruijū shūi* (c. 1881), and *Kaizanshū* (c. 1900) contain no mention of "Yōsha zuihitsu."

6. Volumes 2 and 3 went missing in the late nineteenth century when they passed into the hands of Tosa samurai and scholar Tani Kanjo (1837–1911). Kattō 1967, 106. Based on my own photocopies (which cover only about a third of the pages of Mr. Kattō's volumes), there is no informative notation about the copy process, but the formal and consistent calligraphy and other stylistic evidence suggest it was made in the late Edo period by a professional scribe. Kattō regards the document as original, but the only two library seals inside are those of Tani Kanjo and Kattō Isamu, making it possible that the copy was commissioned by Tani.

7. "Gokachū hengi (1795–1852)"; "Gokachū hengi (1600–1803)."

8. Roberts 2012, 74–104.

9. This chapter approaches family dynamics by applying Edo period notions of spatial arrangements of authority, group autonomy, and performance of obedience to superiors, as explored in Roberts 2012.

10. Ōkawasuji Bukeyashiki Shiryōkan, http://www.city.kochi.kochi.jp/soshiki/39/buke-yashiki.html. The current house may have been rebuilt soon after the 1854 Ansei earthquake, and in the early postwar period it lost one to three original rooms on its west side, but it remains a good example of Kōchi samurai household architecture. The gatehouse, in which male servants lived, was built in 1855. Kōchi-ken Kenchikushikai 1995.

11. For useful explorations of the lives of samurai wives, see Suzuki 1993; Mega 2011.

12. The lineage of the Teshima family found in vol. 54 of the "Osamuraichū senzosho keizuchō" refers occasionally to both males and females as apprentices (*yōikunin*).

13. For an excellent discussion of the sexual and marital relations among servants, see Mega 1995, 15–48.

14. Kamata 1970. Many examples of Kōchi samurai being punished for servant crimes are found in "Gokachū hengi (1600–1803)" and "Gokachū hengi (1795–1852)."

15. Location of the residence is from an 1801 town map shown on pp. 32–33 of Tosa Shidankai 2001. The income figure is from the Fukuoka lineage in "Osamuraichū senzosho keizuchō," vol. 50.

16. No direct evidence of the Fukuoka kin group activities survives, but the diaries of similar mounted warrior–class samurai, Mori Hirosada and Mori Yoshiki, held in Kōchi Prefecture Library, reveal that the heads of the thirteen different Mori households met periodically to socialize, and consulted on marriages, adoption, and occasional crises. Akinari's "Yōsha zuihitsu" also frequently refers to consultations on issues affecting the Maeda kin group. Domain punishments of relatives also encouraged kin group self-policing. Kamata 1970, 63–78.

17. Punishments and subsequent forgiveness were common among samurai families in the early nineteenth century because overall stability seemed to be the main goal of domain government. The Teshima lineage is in vol. 54 of "Osamuraichū senzosho keizuchō." Shō's father, Teshima Heijūrō Magaki, died in 1818/7/14, and her mother lived until 1852/6/12 (notes of gravestone taken by Doi Toshimitsu). Her brother Kiroku Yorimichi was head of her natal family at the time of the incident. Shō's younger sister married Mutō Jinbei Yoshinao (vol. 39 of "Osamuraichū senzosho keizuchō").

18. Early mortality was common among samurai and meant that the domain frequently gave nominal headship of samurai houses to children such as Yūji, but the practical management of households required placing actual control in the hands of mothers. Yūji's mother's name is not mentioned in any documents that I have found. She may have acquired and used the retirement name Anshōin from the time of her husband's death. This name appears on her gravestone. My reading of a similar kin group's nine lineages, "Mori-shi keifu," shows that more than 30 percent of heirs were younger than sixteen when they inherited headship, suggesting that mothers were frequently in charge, not even including consideration of the stretches of time that a samurai served away in Edo.

19. Shōroku's gravestone records his birth date as Bunka 13 (1816/7/7). His gravestone is in the Nishikuma area of Kōchi, on the same site as that listed for Fukuoka Kunai Takamochi, described in Yamamoto 1987, vol. 1, p. 175.

20. Murata Shōhachirō Yoshitaka represents generation eight in the lineage entry under his name, in "Osamuraichū senzosho keizuchō," vol. 38. He had a large income of 450 *koku*, a very successful employment record, and the couple raised three sons.

21. Because paternity was the salient issue for Tosa domain records, only a child's father was listed in government-maintained lineages. If a son was adopted, his original father of record was also listed, but no mention of his mother was made. Women appear only in the position of "wife" and even then as the nameless daughter of a named father, because the domain's interest was in marriage alliance rather than maternity. Shō, for example, appears as "Teshima Heijūrō Magaki's daughter." Only those daughters who married can be located when they are mentioned as wives of other samurai in official genealogies. The card catalog index to the "Osamuraichū senzosho keizuchō" in Kōchi Prefecture Library lists every appearance of a man's name, and can be used to find when a man is listed as father of someone's wife. Daughters who died young or did not marry cannot be identified in this way.

22. Fukuoka Yūji Takaharu is the second-generation head in the lineage entry for Fukuoka Fujitsugu in the "Osamuraichū keizu chō," vol. 50.

23. Yonemoto 2016, 93–98.

24. Mega (1995, 125–53) shows that in Okayama domain the official punishment for a wife's infidelity was death and that this penalty was still invoked in the late Tokugawa period. Most domains used such penalties early on in the era but lightened punishments by the nineteenth century. Stanley 2007; Inoue 1965, vol. 2, pp. 65–67.

25. The familial problems caused by long absences of many samurai is discussed in Vaporis 2008, 192–96. Yūji was a page and likely accompanied the daimyo when he left for Edo in the spring of 1816. "Osamuraichū keizu chō," vol. 50. Alternate attendance dates are from Yamauchi-ke Shiryō Kankō Iinkai 1999, 143, 146.

26. Divorce was the result in a similar case involving another Tosa retainer, named Hattori Zenzaemon. According to Akinari's description in "Yōsha zuihitsu," one day Zenzaemon departed in the middle of the night to go hunting. Suddenly realizing he had forgotten something, he returned early, only to discover "four feet sticking out from under the covers of his wife's futon." Rather than killing them, as was his right by law, or taking them to officials for punishment, or even speaking to them, he quietly left unnoticed and, "wishing to resolve things quietly," the next morning sent his wife home with a divorce letter. Both he and she later separately remarried. "Yōsha zuihitsu," vol. 1, folios 20–23, in two sections titled "Sakamoto ke tōzoku hairi saijo e tekizu owase sōrō shidai todokekata nado" and

"Naijitsu no hanashi." The reason for the woman's divorce from Zenzaemon would not have been discussed but for the fact that in her second marriage she took on other lovers, and was stabbed by one of them in 1830. That incident and associated punishments are recorded in the "Gokachū hengi (1795–1852)," entry for 1830.

27. At this same time Akinari recorded his involvement in another dispute in which a mother played a similarly key role: a wife of one of his nephews wanted a divorce but he would not grant it. At first her family urged her to return to his house, but once her mother supported her, the men of the house and a half-dozen branch families mobilized on her behalf and the divorce was finally attained. "Yōsha zuihitsu," vol. 5.

28. The dynamics and discursive structure of this political culture are explored in Roberts 2012.

29. Stanley 2007, 325–26.

30. This information comes from the official punishment documents presented in "Yōsha zuihitsu," and also from the diary of a contemporary, Kusunose Ōe; Kusunose 1972–91, vol. 8, p. 44.

31. Vaporis 2008, 195–96.

32. For two other cases of slaying for rudeness in Tosa in which lack of propriety was the reason for punishment, see Roberts 2002, 30–35; and Kattō 1967.

33. Ōta 1994, 21–22, offers an example of a woman absolved of crime in a murder because it was an attempted rape.

34. The eighteenth-century Kōchi samurai Mori Hirosada notes many such instances in his diary, "Nikki."

35. Kusunose 1972–91, vol. 8, p. 44.

36. Ōe describes in detail and with admiration a samurai youth's *seppuku* that was treated by the domain as suicide to prevent it from being considered a crime. Kusunose 1972–91, vol. 2, pp. 96–97.

37. For example, it was widely known in Kōchi that the senior administrator, Gotō Kazoe, killed himself in 1797 to atone for a serious governmental mistake, though the government record says he retired and died of illness the next day, as in "Sendai gyōjo."

38. Shōno 1990, 298–99. A detailed code known as the *Kainan ritsuryō* was enacted in the 1850s. Compared to the codes of many other domains, it was lenient, stipulating light levels of local banishment for first offenses between most people, but banishment from the province for servants who had an affair with the wife of the house. Second offenses incurred one hundred lashes, and third offenses incurred the death penalty. Inoue 1965, vol. 2, p. 66. The phenomenon of authorities in Japan leaving the punishment of the wife up to the husband was common enough but not uniform. Stanley argues that following Tokugawa Yoshimune's legal reforms of 1742, the Tokugawa state punished women in adultery cases regardless of the husband's wishes, and punished with greater severity than before, but that many domain governments were moving toward less severe punishments. That seems to have been the case in Tosa. Stanley 2007, 314–20.

39. "Gokachū hengi (1795–1852)" cases for the following dates: 1817/9/18–12/18 (loss of post, fief reduction, the father strictly control his daughter); 1821/7/29 (fief reduction and brother should strictly control his elder sister); 1824/9/29 (fief loss, banishment from castle town but son inherits fully, son should strictly control his younger sister); 1829/3/7 (fief reduction, the husband should strictly control his wife); 1830/1/29 (fief reduction and brother

should strictly control his older sister); 1830/3/7 (fief reduction and husband should strictly control his wife); 1834/7/23 (fief reduction and husband should strictly control his wife); 1841/1/28 (accused is banished from the castle town and loses status, but son allowed to inherit and he should strictly control his mother).

40. As quoted in "Yōsha zuihitsu," and also found in "Gokachū hengi (1795–1852)" and in Kusunose 1972–91, vol. 8, p. 44.

41. These punishments are not listed in "Yōsha zuihitsu," which likely was recorded in the intercalary 8th month, but are listed in the Teshima's official lineage in "Osamurai chū keizu chō," vol. 54, for Teshima Kiroku, and vol. 50 for Sakonbei, and also in "Gokachū hengi (1795–1852)" for 1824/9/15.

42. Inoue 1965, vol. 2, pp. 65–67.

43. "Osamurai chū keizu chō," vol. 14.

44. "Osamurai chū keizu chō," vol. 50 (fact of adoption). The date of adoption is unknown, but the family grave shows that Shōroku's adoptive father, Takayasu, died in 1834.

45. Beasley 1972, 275, 277, 323; Jansen 1961, 75, 299, 317, 401.

46. "Osamurai chū keizu chō," vol. 50, noted in Takachika's career record for the first year of the Ansei era. The pardon is noted as an addendum in the "Gokachū hengi" entry for 1824/8/23. No such notation appears in any of the other female crimes in the volume.

REFERENCES

Beasley 1972
    Beasley, W. G. *The Meiji Restoration*. Stanford, CA: Stanford University Press, 1972.
Gakushūin Daigaku Shiryōkan 1993
    Gakushūin Daigaku Shiryōkan, ed. *Kyūkazoku-ke shiryō shozai chōsa hōkokusho, honpen 4*. Tokyo: Gakushūin Daigaku Shiryōkan 1993.
"Gokachū hengi (1795–1852)"
    "Gokachū hengi (1795–1852)." Vols. 22–26 in "Nanrōshi yoku." 50 vols., doc. 4141.84/5/51. In Tokyō Daigaku Shirōhensanjo.
"Gokachū hengi (1600–1803)"
    "Gokachū hengi." *Tosa shidan*, no. 54 (March 1936): 152–63; no. 55 (June 1936): 209–32; no. 57 (December 1936): 123–32; no. 59 (June 1937): 131–40; no. 62 (March 1938): 140–47.
Inoue 1965
    Inoue Kazuo. *Han hō, bakufu hō to ishin hō*. 3 vols. 1940. Reprinted, Tokyo: Gannandō, 1965.
Jansen 1961
    Jansen, Marius B. *Sakamoto Ryōma and the Meiji Restoration*. Princeton: Princeton University Press, 1961.
Kamata 1970
    Kamata Hiroshi. *Bakuhantaisei ni okeru bushi kazoku hō*. Tokyo: Seibundō, 1970.
Kasumikaikan 1996
    Kasumikaikan Kazoku Kakei Taisei Henshu Iinkai, ed. *Heisei shinshū kyūkazoku kakei taisei gekan*. Tokyo: Kasumikaikan, 1996.

Kattō 1967
Kattō Isamu. "'Yōsha zuihitsu' kara miru Teshima jiken no shinsō." *Tosa shidan* 118 (November 1967): 105–11.

Kōchi-ken Kenchikushikai 1995
Kōchi-ken Kenchikushikai Ōkawasuji Bukeyashiki Chōsa Tokubetsu Iinkai, ed. *Ōkawasuji bukeyashiki chōsa hōkokusho.* Kōchi: Kōchi-ken Kenchikushikai, 1995.

Kusunose 1972–91
Kusunose Ōe. *Hiuchibukuro: Kusunose Ōe nikki.* 17 vols. Kōchi: Kōchi Shimin Toshokan 1972–91.

Mega 1995
Mega Atsuko. *Hankachō no naka no onna tachi: Okayama-han no kiroku kara.* Tokyo: Heibonsha, 1995.

Mega 2011
Mega Atsuko. *Buke ni totsuida josei no tegami.* Tokyo: Yoshikawa Kōbunkan, 2011.

"Mori-shi keifu"
"Mori-shi keifu, 9 vols. Uncatalogued, Kōchi Prefecture Library.

"Nikki"
Mori Hirosada. "Nikki." Kōchi Prefecture Library (call no. K298 mori).

"Osamuraichū senzosho keizuchō"
"Osamuraichū senzosho keizuchō." Multivolume set of copies in Kōchi Prefecture Library (call no. K288 osa).

Ōta 1994
Ōta Motoko. *Edo no oyako: Chichioya ga kodomo wo sodateta jidai.* Tokyo: Chūō Kōronsha, 1994.

Roberts 2002
Roberts, Luke S. "Mori Yoshiki: Samurai Government Officer." In *The Human Tradition in Modern Japan,* edited by Anne Walthall, 25–44. Wilmington, DE: Scholarly Resources, 2002.

Roberts 2012
Roberts, Luke S. *Performing the Great Peace: Political Space and Open Secrets in Tokugawa Japan.* Honolulu: University of Hawai'i Press, 2013.

"Sendai gyōjo"
Mori Masana. "Sendai gyōjo." Kōchi Prefectural Museum of History.

Shōno 1990
Shōno Takashi. *Tosa-han Genroku ōjomoku no hōseishiteki kenkyū.* Tokyo: Tōyō Daigaku Shuppankai, 1990.

Stanley 2007
Stanley, Amy. "Adultery, Punishment, and Reconciliation in Tokugawa Japan." *Journal of Japanese Studies* 33:2 (2007): 309–35.

Suzuki 1993
Suzuki Yuriko. "Jukajosei no seikatsu: Rai Baishi no shigoto to shussan, ikuji." In *Josei no kinsei,* edited by Hayashi Reiko, 129–66. Tokyo: Chūō Kōronsha, 1993.

Tosa Shidankai 2001
Tosa Shidankai, ed. *Kōchi jōkamachi yomihon.* Kōchi: Kōchijō chikujō yonhyakunen kinen jigyō suishin kyōgikai, 2001.

Vaporis 2008
  Vaporis, Constantine. *Tour of Duty: Samurai, Military Service in Edo, and the Culture of Early Modern Japan*. Honolulu: University of Hawai'i Press, 2008.
Walthall 1991
  Walthall, Anne. "The Life Cycle of Farm Women in Tokugawa Japan." In *Recreating Japanese Women, 1600–1945*, edited by Gail Bernstein, 42–70. Berkeley: University of California Press, 1991.
Yamamoto 1987
  Yamamoto Taizō. *Tosa no haka*. 2 vols. Kōchi: Tosa Shidankai, 1987.
Yamauchi-ke Shiryō Kankō Iinkai 1999
  Yamauchi-ke Shiryō Kankō Iinkai, ed. *Rekidai kōki kōbunshū gekan*. Kōchi: Yamauchi-ke Hōmotsu Shiryōkan, 1999.
Yonemoto 2016
  Yonemoto, Marcia. *The Problem of Women in Early Modern Japan*. Berkeley: University of California Press, 2016.
"Yōsha zuihitsu"
  Yamauchi (Maeno) Akinari. "Yōsha zuihitsu." 7 vols. (vols. 2–3 missing). Private collection of Kattō family of Kōchi city. Photocopies of portions in possession of the author.

7

Fashioning the Family

A Temple, a Daughter, and a Wardrobe

Amy Stanley

How did early modern Japanese families apportion their property? Historians and social scientists do not agree on much about the Japanese "household system" (*ie seido*), and the issue of property is no exception. The sociologist Nakane Chie famously argued that impartible inheritance was a pillar of the stem family system, which envisioned the house as an unbroken line stretching from a distant past into an uncertain future.[1] Thus, to increase the likelihood of survival, a married couple would typically leave an inheritance to one (biological or adopted) son, leaving other children to fend for themselves. Supposedly, the pressure on the household head to preserve his descendants' patrimony was so intense that he could not claim the family fortune as his own: "Property belonged to the household and not to its head."[2] In response to Nakane's claims, the demographic historian Hayami Akira and others argued that impartible inheritance was a "myth."[3] Their critique was soon followed by scholarship that alternately challenged and defended the traditional interpretation of the Edo period household as patriarchal and patrilineal.[4]

The participants in this debate, which flourished in English-language scholarship during the 1980s and '90s, tended to rely on village and city block records that documented the inheritance of major assets, such as land and storefronts. But what about property held in other forms—in cloth, paper, and tortoiseshell, carved into hair ornaments and sewn into kimono? These mundane items were unlikely to appear in records submitted to the authorities, and they were not the types of "heirloom treasures" that Pitelka describes in this volume, things valued as symbols of an ancestor's political or aesthetic achievements. But as objects of both household consumption and production, they were important stores of value.[5] They made the work of the inside of the household—by women who drew up shopping lists and sewed hems and scrubbed out stains—visible in the outside world, where their proper display transformed labor into the intangible commodity of reputation. Yet even as they performed this service for the household, mundane items posed problems of meaning, boundaries, and ownership, in part because the household's collective claim on them was not a matter of public record. Moreover, while a farm or a storefront could be counted on to stay in place, clothing walked out into the world every day. Did all those kimono, overcoats, hairpins, and sandals belong to the individuals wearing them? Or were they household property?

The question matters because clothing had become an almost universal investment by the early nineteenth century, when even poor families possessed a few sets of clothes, and wealthy commoners could claim substantial and valuable wardrobes. This was a relatively late development. At the beginning of the Edo period, when everyday clothes were made of hemp, robes were durable enough to outlast their owners; it was said that poor mountain villagers spent their entire lives in a single robe. But by the mid-eighteenth century, when cotton textiles were widely available for purchase throughout most of the archipelago, ordinary people collected more garments in this less expensive, more fragile material and replaced them more frequently.[6] As the commercial economy spread to the countryside, wealthier families also acquired the means to purchase silk. Village headmen's wives and daughters even had nightclothes and waistcloths fashioned from luxurious silk crepe. Gifts for newborn babies included bolts of silk along with traditional foodstuffs, and newlyweds gave their parents crepe robes as thank-you gifts after their weddings.[7]

The shogunate, objecting to such excesses on principle, issued repeated edicts exhorting peasants to dress modestly in plain hemp and cotton. But for village elites, both male and female, dressing in the latest urban fashions had become a necessary component of sociability. Well-outfitted headmen, together with their wives and children, possessed several sets of "going-out clothes" to wear on social calls or at village meetings. These ensembles were typically the trendiest items in their wardrobes. According to Tamura Hitoshi's research on the clothing owned by peasants in Musashi Province in the second half of the Tokugawa period, rural elites became highly conscious of styles popular in Edo. If townspeople were wearing short jackets with silk panels, the village headman's son would promptly acquire a similar garment to flaunt at meetings; if finely patterned stripes were in vogue, the headman's daughter would acquire casual kimono of this design for her trousseau. Rural families found ways to incorporate even the expensive textiles popular among upper-class townspeople. When wealthy women in Edo wore entire kimono fashioned from imported chintz, village daughters might accessorize with chintz handkerchiefs.[8] This was a way to display a household's worldliness as well as its wealth. As knowledge of all kinds became valuable social currency in the late Tokugawa period, fashionable dress became an expression of a household's connection to the world outside the village. After all, a family that kept up with the fashion news from Edo was sure to command all kinds of useful information.

But the value of clothing was unstable and difficult to measure. Its social utility depended on context: a garment had to appear on the appropriate person in
the right place and at a suitable occasion. A long-sleeved robe that might define
a girl and her family as stylish and up-to-date in a northeastern village would not
impress anyone in Kyoto. That same robe, moreover, might be valued by different members of the family for different reasons. By the mid-nineteenth century,
audiences were familiar with the trope of the villainous husband who pawned his
wife's cherished kimono and turned a family heirloom into ready cash. In the most
famous example, from the play Yotsuya Ghost Tale (Tōkaidō Yotsuya kaidan, 1825),
an evil husband rips off his wife's hair comb and kimono so that he can pawn them
and finance a marriage to another woman. This violation is the beginning of a process of physical transformation that turns the virtuous wife, Oiwa, into a vengeful,
bloodthirsty ghost.[9]

In real-life families, too, where struggles over property came to less spectacular
ends, disputes over the ownership of clothing could be proxies for conflict over the
very meaning and boundaries of the household. Wardrobes linked the work of the
inside of the household to its public face, connected individual self-fashioning to
family reputation, and followed members of the family through the various social
and geographical contexts in which the household was embedded. They were also
easily liquidated and frequently accepted as surety for loans. Changing hands and
shifting shape, wardrobes slipped back and forth over the border between individual possession and household property, inside and outside, consumption and
production, use and exchange. They were caught up in the messiness of everyday
life, where presumptive rules about household formation, membership, succession, and conduct were continually tested—where, in the end, "the family" often
revealed itself as a set of incoherent and contradictory ideas. Here I follow one
such messy situation, in which members of a dysfunctional family assembled, dis-
assembled, and fought over one woman's wardrobe.

ASSEMBLING THE WARDROBE

In the summer of 1833, the family residing at Rinsenji temple in Ishigami village in
Echigo Province was large, fractious, and complicated. The head priest, Giyū, who
was also the head of household, had occupied his position for a decade. By 1833,
he had already married and divorced once.[10] At thirty-four, he had one child, a boy
named Kihaku; in time, he would have five.[11] They lived with his mother, who was
affectionately known as Rinsenji-no-haha (Mama Rinsenji), and his retired father.
A few of Giyū's siblings were still at home. His oldest sister, Kiyomi, had married
into a nearby temple several years earlier, and although she had a difficult marriage, it was surprisingly durable.[12] Two of his younger brothers, Girin and Giryū,
had been exiled after several instances of misconduct, including theft from the
family, adultery, and sexual assault.[13] But the youngest brother, Gisen, still lived at

the temple, and so did three younger sisters: a little girl named Ino, sixteen-year-old Toshino, and twenty-nine-year-old Tsuneno, who had already been divorced and returned home once.[14] Both Tsuneno and Toshino were preparing to be married in the coming months, perhaps to lessen the burden on their older brother.

Over the course of the hectic summer of 1833, Giyū drew up several documents as he tried to figure out what his sisters would need for their trousseaus. Some were shopping lists, complete with dates of purchases and prices paid; others were records of engagement gifts that had arrived in the form of cloth and clothing; still others appear to be brainstorming on paper, including hastily scrawled notes and price estimates that would eventually turn out to be wrong. In time, a few of these lists would be bound into booklets containing other information about the weddings, including guests invited and dishes served. The rest were folded accordion style and packed away. Nine records pertaining to the weddings, some consuming several long sheets of paper, survive in the Rinsenji document collection, now held in the Niigata Prefectural Archives.

As Giyū concerned himself with record keeping, the women of the household were hard at work behind the scenes. According to the inventories (all of them products of Giyū's brush or that of his secretary, Denpachi), many of the items purchased, such as individual cuffs and hem linings, had to be sewn into robes at home. This required substantial skill, which could be lucrative in other circumstances. Years later, when Tsuneno was leading a life very different from the one her parents had planned, she monetized the skills she had practiced on her own trousseau. From a rented room in Edo, she wrote home requesting that her mother send her a ruler and some scraps of cloth: "Most of what I do recently is sewing. . . . I'm making a striped crepe robe for my master."[15]

Because they sewed, women must have decided how to apportion the household budget between raw materials and finished pieces. They must also have solved the fashion quandaries that appear occasionally in the annotations to the inventories. One document, a list of things to be ordered, poses a question: "Should this unlined kimono be striped silk crepe or should it have a fine pattern?" It is followed by an answer: "The fine pattern is better."[16] Other lists include definitive judgments on issues no priest could be expected to know anything about, such as how many cotton collars would be sufficient for a young lady's wardrobe. (Apparently, two were not enough.)[17] As Yabuta Yutaka argues, this division of labor—between the men who recorded the details of domestic affairs and the (often highly literate) women who conducted them—was typical of properly functioning households.[18] The 1833 inventories reflect the collaborative domestic labor of people who agreed on the meaning and value of the items they were listing.

Of the two weddings, both in 1833, Tsuneno's seems to have occupied more of the family's attention. Before her marriage, to a wealthy peasant in the nearby village of Ōshima, Giyū drew up a list of the clothing she already possessed. It catalogs fifty-seven items, including five lined silk kimono; fifteen cotton-padded robes in pongee, silk crepe, and striped and patterned cotton; six obi sashes, some of expensive satin and damask; five unlined cotton robes for summer; various pieces of silk crepe underwear; and several kinds of outerwear (a rain jacket, a stylish sleeveless jacket, and two wrappers). Although nothing in this wardrobe was made of imported cloth, the list does mention styles that originated on the Asian continent and places of manufacture that spanned the Japanese archipelago.[19] Twenty-nine-year-old Tsuneno had "São Tome," "Nanking," and "Ōme" stripes; a "Tamagawa-dyed" silk crepe inner robe; a kimono lined in "Chichibu" (silk); and a "Mooka" cotton informal summer robe. Well before the family bought anything new for her trousseau, Tsuneno's clothing signaled her household's connections to a national, even global, economy, one in which girls across Eurasia wore the names of places they never expected to see.[20]

Although this was already a formidable collection, her mother and her older brother judged it insufficient. After collaborating on a draft list of things to be ordered,[21] they went shopping in the weeks before the wedding. They bought (or in one case, had remade) an additional fifty-three items, most of them purchased from a clothier in Takada. They bought raw materials (bolts of white cotton, raw cotton, glossy silk, and ramie); commercially fabricated cuffs, collars, and hems; accessories such as shoes, hairpins, and handkerchiefs; and a complete set of white clothing, possibly for the wedding ceremony. There was one major splurge: a formal kimono in black basket-weave silk with an obi. And since Tsuneno would need to store all these things, they also bought boxes for needles and hairpins, a chest, and a standing wardrobe.[22] By the time the shopping was finished, Tsuneno had accumulated over a hundred pieces for her trousseau. However impressive, the collection was by no means out of the ordinary for a young woman of her status. It resembled, for example, one assembled for the daughter of a village headman in Musashi Province nine years later. Tsuneno had many more padded robes (she lived in snow country, after all) and fewer trendy items such as short winter jackets and chintz handkerchiefs (perhaps because such styles had not penetrated Echigo as early as 1833). But both girls possessed the luxurious items that distinguished truly well-off village women from their social-climbing peers: satin obi sashes and silk underclothes.[23]

A collection of this caliber was extremely expensive. Giyū estimated that 14 *ryō* and 3 *bu* would be required to round out her wardrobe.[24] This turned out not to be enough. A bill from their favorite Takada clothier for one day of shopping alone came to over 12 *ryō*, which Rinsenji paid out in installments over the following two weeks.[25] The household certainly had access to multiple streams of income, including donations from parishioners and rent from temple lands, but outfitting two brides in three months strained its finances.[26] For Tsuneno, the second to be married, Rinsenji found it necessary to accept a gift from the prospective groom's family: they contributed 15 *ryō* in "preparation money" so that their new daughter-in-law could be properly outfitted.[27]

This gift, a substantial sum for even a prosperous rural family, was crucial because a trousseau conveyed social meanings that hard cash could not. If Tsuneno simply needed ordinary garments from time to time, her in-laws could have bought them as the occasion arose, making the initial gift unnecessary. But what Tsuneno really needed was a complete and prestigious wardrobe to bring into the marriage and, ideally, to display at the wedding.[28] A fully realized trousseau signified that her own household had invested in her future, and thus neither side of the newly created family had an interest in advertising the fact that the money for it had actually come from the groom's father.[29] The trousseau sent the message that Tsuneno's marriage was a union of two estimable households, roughly equal in status, that would endure throughout the seasons and ritual cycles requiring this elegant set of garments.

But even the most thoughtfully assembled trousseau could not ensure a happy marriage. Four years after an auspicious start, Tsuneno was abruptly divorced and sent home.[30] Her brother, Giyū, was concerned for Tsuneno's future, as this was her second divorce. He was also nervous that he might have to return the 15 *ryō* that the in-laws had contributed to her wardrobe. Ordinarily, a trousseau would be returned together with the divorced woman.[31] But the gift complicated matters, and Rinsenji was short of cash: Tsuneno's marriage had coincided with the Tenpō famine, which had made it difficult to collect rents, and the temple was having trouble paying some of its debts.[32] Even worse, Tsuneno's brothers Girin and Gisen had also divorced, and they were living at the temple. Giyū was at a loss. "This year Tsuneno, Girin, and Gisen all divorced," he complained. "The temple is struggling, and we will have to help our poor tenants make it through the winter."[33]

Happily, Tsuneno's former father-in-law assured her family that his initial gift did not need to be returned.[34] This was a magnanimous gesture, but it was also pragmatic. Outfitting a prospective daughter-in-law had been the price of arranging a socially appropriate marriage for their son. Once the marriage had failed, it was difficult to recover an investment that was now held in the form of kimono and accessories associated with a rejected bride. This was the problem with converting household assets into cotton and silk: the social value of stylish clothes could be realized only if the appropriate person wore them. Had Tsuneno's former in-laws demanded a return of the clothes, they could not have sold them without revealing their contribution to the original purchase. And if the same clothes appeared on display at the family's next wedding, the message would be contrary to what the family originally intended. It would signal that the household had brought in an unsophisticated woman who could not afford her own wardrobe.

Meanwhile, at Rinsenji, any questions about who paid for the clothes were concealed amid the cotton prints and glossy silk linings packed away in Tsuneno's chest. If they had once represented a joint investment between Rinsenji and her ex-husband's family, following the divorce they were effectively hers. So, when Tsuneno married for the third time in 1837, to a man living in the castle town of Takada, there was no need to itemize her belongings or buy new things. She already possessed a wardrobe befitting a prosperous wife, no matter who had provided the start-up funds.

Unfortunately, Tsuneno once again found that a fine trousseau could not guarantee a successful marriage. She was divorced for the third time after only a few months with her new husband. The reasons are not made clear in the documentary record. Perhaps Giyū did not wish to record them for posterity, or maybe he did not think they merited attention. Tsuneno's wardrobe was another matter. A marriage could end quietly, but the fate of the furniture and accessories was carefully documented. When Tsuneno returned to Rinsenji, he wrote, her furniture and possessions came with her.[35]

DISASSEMBLING THE WARDROBE

In 1839, a year and a half after her third divorce, Tsuneno ran away to Edo. According to a letter she wrote to her uncle (which was probably partly fabricated, as she changed the story later), she had been on her way to a hot spring resort to receive treatment for an eye disease when she met up with a group of thirteen young people heading for the capital. Among them was a male friend who invited her to join them. Tsuneno, who had been looking for an opportunity to see Edo, gratefully accepted. But she did not have cash on hand, so the friend had an associate take her things to a pawnshop in Takada, where he exchanged the clothes she was carrying for travel funds. The letter lists the pawned items as padded robes in striped silk crepe and cotton, lined underrobes in scarlet crepe and brown patchwork, a patchwork undergarment, a long winter coat in patchwork, a glossy silk unlined robe, a set of patterned handkerchiefs, a mirror, and a box of hairpins.[36] Apart from the hairpins, the mirror, and possibly the unlined robe, none of these items had previously appeared in a Rinsenji inventory. The clothing was casual but new, or at least remade. That is, it was precisely what a young woman would take with her if she intended to leave home and start over again in a more stylish place.[37]

Tsuneno had always thought of her clothes as valuable, not only because they could be worn and displayed to her advantage but also because she had put so much work into creating them. In 1829, during her first marriage, she quarreled with Giyū when he had tried to buy a robe she had made from her brother. It was my work, she insisted, and my skill; I'll decide what to do with it.[38] But when she decided to run away, her wardrobe took on a different meaning: the social messages and personal memories attached to her garments became less important. It did not matter that she had hoped these clothes, worn in the right way, would make a certain impression. What mattered was how much they were worth in cash.

Tsuneno did not admit it in her letter, but even before she arrived in Takada, she had already sold several items of clothing to a man in Iimuro village and deposited the proceeds, 3 ryō, with her uncle.[39] She had probably intended to use the money to finance her travels, but she had decided to leave suddenly and unexpectedly on a day when she did not have any cash with her. It was unfortunate that she had to pawn the clothes she had meant to wear in Edo, but she had already come to terms with her new economic circumstances. If she did not want to depend on her family for spending money, she would have to rely on the only source of credit she had at her disposal: her clothes.

This might have been a new idea for Tsuneno, but it was common knowledge to most of her neighbors. By the second half of the eighteenth century, a network of pawnshops had expanded from big cities to post stations and market towns, and to the villages of rural Echigo. Not far from Rinsenji, the writer Suzuki Bokushi managed a pawnshop that his grandmother had started by lending out her pocket money to peasants who needed cash.[40] Throughout Japan, poor families pawned their summer clothes to raise cash to get through the winter. Tamura cites the example of a Shinto priest's household in Musashi Province that fell on hard times in the early 1850s and pawned its striped cotton and tie-dyed robes when they were out of season.[41]

From her letters, it is clear that Tsuneno understood the logic of pawning: interest on her loan of 3 *ryō* would add up over time, making redemption of her clothes more and more expensive. But she thought she could get around this problem, because she had left her travel money with her uncle for safekeeping. She wrote him twice, once from Takada and, a few days later, from the road, asking him to redeem the items as soon as possible.[42] In case he refused to comply, she also asked her family at Rinsenji for help. Two days after she arrived in Edo, she instructed her brothers to pawn her standing wardrobe closet and her chest (two of the three most valuable things purchased for her trousseau), to add the income to the money she had left with her uncle, and to send her the redeemed clothes. She went on to request the futon and quilt she had left in her bamboo chest, as well as a cotton-padded robe, which she had left hanging. There were two aprons, mirrors, a pillow, and shoulder padding in her long chest. Giyū should send those, too. As for the rest of her things, he should take good care of them for her, and she would send word when she needed them. She wrote in a postscript that she intended to go into service for a daimyo. If she found a place, she would need her entire wardrobe sent as soon as possible.[43]

Giyū had no intention of redeeming Tsuneno's pawned clothes or sending anything else. The problem, in part, was that he disapproved of her running away in the first place. He wrote to Tsuneno: "You lied and told me that you were going to Takada to seek treatment for your eyes and, instead, went to Edo—extremely wicked behavior. . . . You have written requesting that we redeem the items you pawned, but we cannot do that."[44] There was more to the story, however. Giyū's relatives in Edo had already warned the family in Echigo not to send Tsuneno her clothes. After her traveling companion deserted her, Tsuneno had appealed to her aunt and uncle in Edo for help. As they explained to Giyū, they dutifully checked into the young man's background and found all his relatives to be "suspicious people." They warned Giyū to be on the lookout for a letter posted from Kanda asking him to redeem the clothes and forward them to Tsuneno's new address. Such a request, they wrote, would be part of her traveling companion's plot to steal from the family.[45]

Still, Tsuneno did need clothes to be presentable in Edo. Because she could not be sent home before the weather cleared and an appropriate escort was found, she had to find work—something impossible when, as her uncle put it, she was "completely naked, with no clothes."[46] This was an exaggeration, surely, but, since Tsuneno had only her traveling clothes to her name, it was close to the truth. For people who knew Tsuneno's family, her appearance was embarrassing; for those who did not, it was disqualifying. A family friend in Edo brought her to a local employment office, which found her work in a bannerman's household, but clothing was still a problem.[47] When this friend wrote announcing the news of her placement, he requested two or three sets of clothing on her behalf.[48]

Denpachi, the family's secretary, replied.[49] According to a draft scrawled on the back of some loose pages of an illustrated book, Giyū could not send clothes, because the household's relatives, furious that Tsuneno had run off to Edo with a complete stranger, had determined to cut her off. To Tsuneno, such a response was beside the point: she viewed the clothes as hers and often pointedly referred to the places where she had left things (in her luggage, a standing wardrobe, a friend's house) as if to emphasize that they had been, and should remain, under her control. In the head priest's view, however, the clothes belonged to the temple and constituted a form of economic support. As long as Tsuneno was officially cut off, Denpachi explained, the head priest could not send them.

But luckily for Tsuneno, her older brother Giyū did not actually manage the household's wardrobe. Her mother did. This created a useful loophole for everyone involved. Denpachi, feeling sorry for Tsuneno, persuaded Rinsenji-no-haha to give him two cotton-padded robes "for the cold." Old and not likely to be missed, they match the description of two kimono in the inventory compiled before the shopping trips for her first wedding. Perhaps the head priest was more involved in this deal than he appeared; he recorded the transaction in an inventory compiled a few months later, indicating, in any event, that he was not unaware of it for long.[50] Even so, by exploiting the gendered division of labor in the household, he maintained the fiction that the temple was not supporting Tsuneno. To save face with the extended family, Giyū could not send Tsuneno cash. But his mother could send clothing as long as it was portrayed as an expression of affection and concern for her daughter's well-being. Tsuneno caught on to the distinction immediately. A few months later, after she had left the bannerman's service, she addressed her requests directly to Rinsenji-no-haha. She complained of the cold and asked for two sashes, underrobes, hairpins, and cotton and pongee lined and padded robes. At the same time, she asked for and offered token gifts never mentioned in letters to her brothers. For example, she requested miso pickles and offered hair oil and a large silver coin as a souvenir.[51] According to Rinsenji's records, her mother responded immediately, sending every item of clothing on the list plus bedding.[52]

While Rinsenji-no-haha's gifts were billed as manifestations of care, they were certainly intended to assert the household's control. Denpachi forwarded the first batch of clothing not to Tsuneno herself but to a family friend charged with delivering them and, then, reporting back to Rinsenji about Tsuneno's behavior. The friend was also asked to make sure Tsuneno conducted herself appropriately.[53] As was the case when he assembled her trousseau, the head of household was still trying to use clothing to shape Tsuneno in the image of a well-bred daughter. But now he was employing a new, more nakedly transactional strategy.

For her part, a more temperate Tsuneno confined her requests to cotton and pongee, relatively inexpensive materials. In some ways, she was refashioning her identity, discarding the extensive collection of a provincial bride for the striped cotton uniform of workingwomen in Edo (and across the globe).[54] But cotton was also less valuable than silk, damask, or satin, which made it easier to request from a family that was already suspicious that she intended to sell clothes for cash. It was to Tsuneno's benefit to emphasize her intention to use the clothing, not exchange it. In a letter to her older brother Kōtoku, she wrote, "I don't need my good clothes. But please, please, I'm asking you to send my heavy coat and two bad cotton padded robes to keep out the cold."[55] In another letter, sent from a different place of employment, she described her embarrassment over encountering the lady of the house in the ragged robe she was wearing.[56] She appealed to the household, in effect, to maintain her wardrobe as a sign of affectionate concern over the winter chill and a precondition of sociable presentability. This was the same logic that had applied when she was a daughter and a bride in Echigo.

But Edo was different from Echigo in ways that Giyū, a country priest, could not be expected to understand. In the big city, it was difficult to resist the temptation to exchange clothing for cash. A few months after she received a package of robes, hairpins, and bedding from her mother, Tsuneno was forced to admit to Denpachi that she had sold much of her wardrobe. Her tone was defensive: "I did receive a letter in which you told me not to sell anything, but I had not heard from you at all for a long time. . . . I never wanted to sell even one old robe, but for goodness sake I didn't even have one *mon* and I was helpless!"[57] Tsuneno was "helpless" without money because, unlike her relatives in Echigo, she survived by constantly deploying small amounts of cash. She had become a resident of Edo's backstreet tenements, where people moved often, lacked space for storage, and could not afford to plan ahead. They purchased most things they needed from street vendors, including small scoops of charcoal and individual portions of rice. For this reason, they were chronically in need of spending money, but as people without stable reputations and dependable incomes, they found it difficult to access credit. As Tsuneno found, clothes were an important—perhaps the only—form of security in such circumstances.

But pawning clothes always posed a trade-off between survival and respect-ability.[58] The very absence of reputation that made it difficult for Edo's poor to access credit put all the more pressure on appearances that signified trustworthi-ness, honesty, and diligence. Precarious people faced a constant conflict between the need for cash and the need to look employable enough to earn it. As Tsuneno pointed out soon after she arrived, "There are many places to go into service here, but without clothes I can't serve."[59] Over a century before Tsuneno's time, Ihara Saikaku, with typical exaggeration, observed:

> Even if no one offers a girl a job and she becomes like a masterless samurai, she clings to her one fashionably printed kimono, her wide silk sash, her one pair of split-toed socks, and her silk floss veil and ornamental comb, for these things are as important to her as the long and short swords are to a samurai: she would rather go without food for three days and drop dead than part with a single one of these items.[60]

Edo pawnshops nevertheless overflowed with silk crepe and cotton prints (as well as, famously, arms and armor). During the Tenpō economic crisis in 1841–42, informants to the city magistrates' offices noted that this oversupply precluded getting good prices for clothes. In fact, pawnshops were overstocked enough to drive most used-clothing shops out of business.[61] In Echigo, it may still have been possible to build a large wardrobe and a good reputation in the same way: slowly, piece by piece, in installments and on credit, by trading on a stable identity and a history in one place. But in the backstreets of Edo, identities were fungible and clothing was hard to hold onto. Contrary to Saikaku's remarks about starving but well-dressed maidservants, Tsuneno, like many of her peers, was willing to sac-rifice respectability for the immediate reassurance of cash; she knew the former could be reestablished with a new set of clothes. Peter Stallybrass's observation of midcentury London is equally true of an Edo awash in reluctantly surrendered kimono: "'Respectability,' that central nineteenth-century virtue, was something to be bought and, in times of need, pawned."[62]

However, from Giyū's perspective, when Tsuneno pawned her clothes, she was exchanging the entire household's reputation for cash. This was a deal that the temple's head of household was not willing to make. Unlike an individual, an estab-lished household could not refashion its identity as easily as changing clothes; Rin-senji had built up social networks in Edo over generations, and it could not retreat into anonymity.[63] When Tsuneno appeared at the city's Shin temples dressed in rags, she communicated two messages: first, that Rinsenji's daughter had rejected the life her family had arranged for her; second, that the household refused to take care of its own. According to Tsuneno's brother Gisen, who was also in Edo, Tsuneno knew this and took advantage of the situation. She even complained to outsiders that the household did not adequately support her. "I asked Tokuhonji [another Shin temple] to secretly lend her a futon," he wrote, "so now she will not be able to say that 'back home' never does anything for her."[64]

The role of clothing as a display of familial affection (or at least a simulacrum of that affection) turned out to be more important to the household's reputation than the men at Rinsenji had anticipated. Rinsenji-no-haha had maintained Tsuneno figuratively (if not literally) off the books, even when she was behaving badly, making clear that gifts conveyed care rather than a public statement of economic support. After Rinsenji-no-haha died, this loophole closed, and the remaining male family members decided not to waste any more of the household's resources on Tsuneno. This made the temple vulnerable to charges of heartlessness. Writing to the family years later, when a disheveled Tsuneno arrived on his doorstep after divorcing yet another husband, a samurai acquaintance observed that Tsuneno had one tattered robe to her name. He was shocked that her younger brother in Edo, Gisen, seemed unmoved by her state and noted disapprovingly that the two "barely had a sibling relationship at all."[65] Rinsenji was then forced to call Tsuneno home before she could cause any more embarrassment; she, again unable to get work because she had no clothes, was forced to comply.

CONCLUSION

Translated and converted into typeface, Rinsenji's inventories of Tsuneno's clothing look repetitive: "Item: a silk crepe lining. Item: a São Tome striped robe." Yet lurking behind a seemingly compulsive need to list and relist similar items over and over again are signs of accelerating conflict and even disintegration. Rinsenji's handwriting is replaced by Tsuneno's, then Denpachi's, then Rinsenji-no-haha's, then Gisen's, as the labor of managing the wardrobe is transformed from a cooperative endeavor on behalf of the household to a site of conflict among its members.

Giyū's distress at what he called "extremely wicked behavior" arose from the way Tsuneno had subverted his authority as the family's patriarch. She asserted control over her body by running off with a strange man and then supported herself in a strange city using the tools and resources her family had provided: clothing, literacy, and the ability to perform domestic work. It was fitting that she had initiated her rebellion at a pawnshop, a place where the mundane stuff of domestic life—the products of women's judgment, expertise, and labor—could be transformed into cash and credit. The exchange made clear that housework was not inevitably tied to the domestic realm and performed on behalf of the family. It could be monetized, taken into an impersonal outside world, and used as an assertion of independence or a weapon of familial destruction. A cotton robe intended as a display of household wealth and knowledge could be used to finance an elopement. A hairpin purchased to display at a wedding could be turned into rent for a seedy tenement. And parents who carefully supervised their daughter's education might find that their investment yielded unexpected returns.

Even when clothing was not exchanged for cash, its display exposed the contradictions inherent in the idea of an "inside" world of female domestic labor.[66] First, unlike the management of cash, which could be conducted largely out of sight, the management of clothing was always subject to scrutiny. No one knew how much cash a household could access; everyone in the community, whether a village or an Edo neighborhood, saw what clothing it could afford. Through their work producing, consuming, and repairing clothing, women made the invisible labor of accumulating wealth, typically seen as men's work, intelligible to the outside world.

The same distinction between a feminine "inside" and a masculine "outside" collapses when clothing is considered as an expression of affection. Among the women of Rinsenji, clothes tended to be treated as form of currency in an emotional economy that depended on the exchange of notes, pickles, and hair oil. This projection of intimate attachment was useful when the temple needed to send Tsuneno clothes after officially cutting her off; the transfer from mother to daughter could pass unrecognized by a household head obliged to save face with other relatives. When necessary, the expression of womanly affection could be disregarded in the "outside" world of men, even when it was plain to see. On the other hand, a perceived lack of emotional connection, symbolized by the sorry state of Tsuneno's wardrobe after her mother's death, could not be ignored. It was perceived by outsiders as a failure of intimacy and a sign that the family did not function properly. Clothing either rendered the realm of affect visible or signaled its distressing absence.

If the display of clothing blurred the distinctions between a household's "inside" and "outside," it also mediated the household's relationships to the various communities within which it was embedded. The same striped cotton robe, worn in Echigo or Edo, had different messages; it either distinguished the household by communicating familiarity with city styles or enabled the individual to pass through the urban labor market without attracting attention. In the provinces, a proper wardrobe cemented the household's reputation, developed over time in a comparatively stable community. In the city, it communicated respectability, a virtue rendered necessary by transience and anonymity. As Tsuneno (and her clothes) moved from the countryside to the capital, these functions became intertwined: a well-dressed Tsuneno in Edo was respectable, and she did comparatively little damage to her family's reputation. But a "completely naked" Tsuneno was different: she was only temporarily disrespectable, but she caused lasting damage to her family's reputation. As stories of her appearance in Edo filtered back home, Giyū found that his assertions of authority over his sister, so convincing on paper, could not compete with the messages conveyed by her inadequately clothed body on the street. For her family's correspondents, her tattered robes invited speculation that her household itself had unraveled.

Both reputation and wardrobe were carefully assembled products of collaborative efforts between men and women working within domestic spaces across generations. But in an era when even provincial brides might own a dozen silk kimono and men from temple families in snow country might study in Edo, names and robes had little utility if they were held too closely. They were meant to be carried into the outside world, where they would be worn proudly and used to enhance the reputation of the household's members. But once there, they could be discarded or exchanged in the service of some personal agenda. No matter how carefully they were monitored, neither reputations nor wardrobes could be managed by the head of household alone. Nor could they be disentangled. Giyū feverishly attended to Tsuneno's clothing, but her clothing and the image it communicated about the family eluded his control.

For this reason, mundane possessions can tell stories about the "household system" that are very different from those conveyed by more substantial assets, such as land and shop fronts. Because small items moved along with people, because they followed tortured trajectories without being passed down in an orderly fashion, they show us how households stretched across space in addition to marching forward in time. They also reveal how social and spatial context mattered to the constitution of the family and to the norms that governed its members. In Echigo, where Rinsenji was a coherent and hierarchically organized institution, Tsuneno was the prodigal daughter who needed to be chastised; her younger brother Gisen was the dutiful son who tried to bring her under control. But in Edo, as at least one of Rinsenji's correspondents made clear, Gisen was the offender who shirked his responsibilities by turning his back on his sister; Tsuneno was the victim who struggled with an inadequate wardrobe because her family would not take care of her. To "Tsuneno in Edo" (as she signed some of her letters, incorporating her place of residence into her identity), the equation was slightly different. Gisen was, indeed, a delinquent brother. "He treats me like a stranger," she complained.[67] And her family in Echigo was at fault, too, not only because they showed a lack of affection but also because they refused to give her what she was owed as a daughter of the temple. In declining to send her clothes, they withheld property she claimed as her own.

The struggle over Tsuneno's clothes was a proxy for a more complicated conflict. In Edo as well as Echigo, the "early modern family" existed in the minds of its members and the opinions of neighbors, relations, and even casual acquaintances. But they did not necessarily agree on who should be included in the family or what its members owed to one another. Some were invested in a family that responsibly stewarded property, others in a family that manifested care. Some thought of the family as an orderly march through generations; others as a tangle of siblings, uncles, and in-laws. And depending on the situation and their physical location, their definitions could change.

In that sense, the wardrobe, with its shifting shapes and adaptations to individual needs, may be a more useful metaphor for the early modern family than the metonym *house,* with its connotations of stability, unity, and permanence. The family was both carefully and casually assembled. It adapted to changing seasons and landscapes and fashions. It moved through space. How it should be constituted and who controlled it remained unsolved problems. The family balanced, precariously, on the boundary between individual and collective claims. And sometimes, shaken by conflict, it scattered.

NOTES

1. For an English-language summary of this argument, see Nakane 1990, 216–22.
2. Nakane 1990, 221.
3. Hayami 1983, 3–29.
4. An insightful overview of the literature on female household heads (and whether there were more or fewer than one might expect) appears in Anderson 2010, 23–27. See also Uno 1996, 569–94.
5. On traditional Japanese clothing as an item of household consumption and production, see Gordon 2011; and Francks 2012, 151–75.
6. Asaoka 2005, 46–50. Peasants in Kinai and Kantō were already wearing cotton in the early Tokugawa period. Wealthier peasants bought cotton cloth for new clothes, but others wore homespun or bought old clothes from cities. Cotton clothing did not become common among peasants in non-cotton-producing areas until the middle of the period, as the used clothing business expanded from Osaka. Nagahara 2008, 498–500, 517.
7. Tamura 2004, 229, 254–56.
8. Tamura 2004, 224, 229. Indian chintz was imported by the Dutch East India Company through Nagasaki until the 1830s, and it was considered higher quality than domestically produced chintzes, which started out as copies of foreign products. Fujita 2009, 194–201.
9. Tsuruya Nanboku 2013, 168–82. See also the analysis of this play in Shimazaki 2016.
10. "Giyū tsugime"; "Nairan ichijō."
11. "Kihaku tanjō ubuyashinai mimaichō."
12. Letter, Saisonji to Rinsenji, undated.
13. "Nairan ichijō."
14. Letter, Rinsenji to Jōganji, [Tenpō 3].1.25. Also, on Tsuneno's age and her first marriage, see Gotō 2016, 397–98.
15. Letter, Tsuneno to Yamazaki Kyūhachirō, Denpachi, and mother, Tenpō 11.5.22.
16. "Tenpō yon idoshi shigatsu nijū-san nichi Tsuneno-gi Ōshima-mura Koide-shi e enzuke sōrō ikken." Tamura Hitomi's research suggests that in the Meiji era, grandmothers served as "fashion advisers" for well-bred young ladies who were about to be married. See Tamura 2004, 365.
17. "Tsuneno tadaima made shochi no mono aishirabe sōrō koto."
18. Yabuta 1995, 225–54. However, in a different context, Yabuta found that the letters in a household collection authored by and addressed to women were generally orders for or requests to borrow kimono. Yabuta 2014, 34.
19. Fujita 2009.
20. On textiles, particularly Indian printed cotton, as global trade goods in the early modern era, see Riello and Parthasarathi 2009.

21. "Tenpō yon idoshi shigatsu nijū-san nichi Tsuneno-gi Ōshima-mura Koide-shi e enzuke sōrō ikken."

22. "Tenpō yon idoshi shigatsu nijū-san nichi kichijitsu Tsuneno Ōshima Koide nyūka shitakuchō."

23. See Tamura 2004, 227–29.

24. "Tenpō yon idoshi shigatsu nijū-san nichi Tsuneno-gi Ōshima-mura Koide-shi e enzuke sōrō ikken."

25. "Tenpō yon idoshi shigatsu nijū-san nichi kichijitsu Tsuneno Ōshima Koide nyūka shitakuchō."

26. On Shin temple women and luxury, see Starling 2012, 53–54.

27. "Oboe," Tenpō 4.4.3.

28. Lindsey 2007, 80–81.

29. The trousseau's symbolic value required creative accounting in other arenas as well. For example, in later letters home, Tsuneno referred to aprons. These, along with other plain work clothes, were absent from the temple's inventory of her things, which focused on items that conferred status on the household.

30. Letter, Koide Yasōemon to Rinsenji, Tenpō 8.5.27.

31. Fuess 2001, 82–90.

32. The previous year, Giyū had written a letter to a temple in Musashi Province explaining that he could not pay back a 10 ryō loan. Letter, Rinsenji to Shōryūji, Tenpō 7.8.8.

33. Untitled, [record of father's funeral], Tenpō 8.8.

34. "Tenpō yon idoshi shigatsu nijū-san nichi kichijitsu Tsuneno Koide yomeiri shoshikidome."

35. "Tsuneno Inada-machi Katō-shi e engumi manki."

36. Letter, Tsuneno to Yamazaki Kyūhachirō, Tenpō 10.9.23.

37. And, in fact, her later letters suggest that Edo had been her intended destination all along. See, for example, letter, Tsuneno to Kōtoku, undated.

38. "Nairan ichijō."

39. "Tsuneno kanjō torishirabe"; letter, Kin to older brothers, [Tenpō 11].10.25.

40. Moriyama 2013, 74–79.

41. Tamura 2004, 312–13.

42. Letter, Tsuneno to Kyūhachirō, Tenpō 10.9.26.

43. Letter, Tsuneno to Rinsenji, Tenpō 10.10.10.

44. Letter, Rinsenji to Tsuneno, Tenpō 10.11.9.

45. Letter, Moritaya Bunshichi to Rinsenji, Tenpō 10.11.22. Bunshichi and his wife, Mitsu, are referred to in subsequent documents as Tsuneno's aunt and uncle, but it is not clear whether they were maternal or paternal relatives. In fact, Tsuneno later disavowed all the letters she wrote in her first week in Edo and insisted they were her traveling companion's idea. Letter, Tsuneno to Denpachi, Kyūhachirō, and mother, Tenpō 11.5.21.

46. Letter, Moritaya Bunshichi to Rinsenji, Tenpō 10.11.22.

47. Tsuneno mentions the employment office in a later letter, to Kōtoku, undated.

48. Letter, Yasugorō to Rinsenji, Tenpō 10.11.22.

49. Letter, Isogai Denpachi to Isogai Yasugorō and Tsuneno, Tenpō 10.12.11.

50. "Rinsenji-no-haha Tsuneno no kirui shimatsu kata hikae."

51. Letter, Tsuneno to mother, [Tenpō 11].2.23.

52. "Oboe," Tenpō 11.10.14.

53. Letter, Isogai Denpachi to Isogai Yasugorō and Tsuneno, Tenpō 10.12.11.

54. Ikegami 2005, 283.

55. Letter, Tsuneno to Kōtoku, undated. It was generally considered ridiculous to wear silk crepe for housework. For example, see Yamakawa 1992, 122.

56. Letter, Kin to mother, Tenpō 11.9.28. Tsuneno changed her name to Kin after she married for the fourth time in Edo. Tsuneno mentions that she is working in a warrior household, but it is not clear where. On Tsuneno's checkered employment history, see Stanley 2016.

57. Letter, Tsuneno to Kyūhachirō, Denpachi, and mother, Tenpō 11.5.22.

58. The English word *respectability* has no exact counterpart in Japanese. Nevertheless, following Woodruff D. Smith, I am using it here to refer to the outward manifestation, through grooming and behavior, of moral competence. See Smith 2002, 204–10.

59. Letter, Tsuneno to Izawa Kōtoku, undated. And, "I can't work if I'm wearing only one silk unlined robe as I am now." Letter, Tsuneno to Kyūhachirō, Denpachi, and mother, Tenpō 11.5.21.

60. Ihara Saikaku, "Spending a Day at the Employment Agency" (c. 1689), quoted in Chaiklin 2009, 45.

61. Tōkyō Daigaku Shiryō Hensanjo 1960, 306–7.

62. Stallybrass 1998, 192.

63. On the link between individual respectability, clothing, and family reputation in early modern Europe, see Smith 2002, 210–15.

64. Letter, Gisen to Rinsenji, Tenpō 14.9.29.

65. Letter, Fujiwara Yūzō to Rinsenji, Tenpō 15.11.13.

66. On the household's "inside" and "outside" spaces, see Roberts 2012, 36–37.

67. Letter, Tsuneno to Rinsenji, undated.

REFERENCES

Anderson 2010
    Anderson, Marnie. *A Place in Public: Women's Rights in Meiji Japan.* Cambridge, MA: Harvard Asia Center, 2010.
Asaoka 2005
    Asaoka Kōji. *Furugi.* Tokyo: Hōsei Daigaku Shuppankyoku, 2005.
Chaiklin 2009
    Chaiklin, Martha. "Up in the Hair: Strands of Meaning in Women's Ornamental Hair Accessories in Early Modern Japan." In *Asian Material Culture,* edited by Marianne Hulsbosch, Elizabeth Bedford, and Martha Chaiklin, 39–64. Amsterdam: Amsterdam University Press, 2009.
Francks 2012
    Francks, Penelope. "Kimono Fashion: The Consumer and the Growth of the Textile Industry in Pre-war Japan." In *The Historical Consumer: Consumption and Everyday Life in Japan, 1850–2000,* edited by Penelope Francks and Janet Hunter, 151–75. New York: Palgrave Macmillan, 2012.

Fuess 2001
    Fuess, Harald. *Divorce in Japan*. Stanford, CA: Stanford University Press, 2001.
Fujita 2009
    Fujita, Kayoko. "Japan Indianized: The Material Culture of Imported Textiles in Japan, 1550–1850." In *The Spinning World: A Global History of Cotton Textiles,* edited by Giorgio Riello and Prasannan Parthasarathi, 181–203. New York: Oxford University Press, 2009.
"Giyū tsugime"
    Bunsei 6.2. Rinsenji monjo 2852. Niigata Prefectural Archives.
Gordon 2011
    Gordon, Andrew. *Fabricating Consumers: The Sewing Machine in Modern Japan*. Berkeley: University of California Press, 2011.
Gotō 2016
    Gotō Kazuo. *Komonjo de yomu Essa josei no Edo jidai*. N.P.: Niigata, 2016.
Hayami 1983
    Hayami, Akira. "The Myth of Primogeniture and Impartible Inheritance in Tokugawa Japan." *Journal of Family History* 8:1 (1983): 3–29.
Ikegami 2005
    Ikegami, Eiko. *Bonds of Civility: Aesthetic Networks and the Political Origins of Japanese Culture*. Cambridge: Cambridge University Press, 2005.
"Kihaku tanjō ubuyashinai mimaichō"
    Tenpō 3.5.18. Rinsenji monjo 911. Niigata Prefectural Archives.
Letter, Fujiwara Yūzō to Rinsenji, Tenpō 15.11.13
    Rinsenji monjo 2005. Niigata Prefectural Archives.
Letter, Gisen to Rinsenji, Tenpō 14.9.29
    Rinsenji monjo 2014. Niigata Prefectural Archives.
Letter, Isogai Denpachi to Isogai Yasugorō and Tsuneno, Tenpō 10.12.11
    Rinsenji monjo 1698. Niigata Prefectural Archives.
Letter, Kin to mother, Tenpō 11.9.28
    Rinsenji monjo 1713. Niigata Prefectural Archives.
Letter, Kin to older brothers, [Tenpō 11].10.25
    Rinsenji monjo 2049.
Letter, Koide Yasoemon to Rinsenji, Tenpō 8.5.27
    Rinsenji monjo 1686. Niigata Prefectural Archives.
Letter, Moritaya Bunshichi to Rinsenji, Tenpō 10.11.22
    Rinsenji monjo 1698. Niigata Prefectural Archives.
Letter, Rinsenji to Jōganji, [Tenpō 3].1.25
    Rinsenji monjo 1777. Niigata Prefectural Archives.
Letter, Rinsenji to Tsuneno, Tenpō 10.11.9
    Rinsenji monjo 1726. Niigata Prefectural Archives.
Letter, Rinsenji to Shōryūji, Tenpō 7.8.8
    Rinsenji monjo 450. Niigata Prefectural Archives.
Letter, Saisonji to Rinsenji, undated
    Rinsenji monjo 1763. Niigata Prefectural Archives.

Letter, Tsuneno to Denpachi, Kyūhachirō, and mother, Tenpō 11.5.21
    Rinsenji monjo 1710. Niigata Prefectural Archives.
Letter, Tsuneno to Izawa Kōtoku, Tenpō 10.10.10
    Rinsenji monjo 1709. Niigata Prefectural Archives.
Letter, Tsuneno to Kōtoku, undated
    Rinsenji monjo 1716. Niigata Prefectural Archives.
Letter, Tsuneno to Kyūhachirō, Tenpō 10.9.26
    Rinsenji monjo 1711. Niigata Prefectural Archives.
Letter, Tsuneno to mother, [Tenpō 11].2.23
    Rinsenji monjo 1699. Niigata Prefectural Archives.
Letter, Tsuneno to Rinsenji, Tenpō 10.10.10
    Rinsenji monjo 1707–8. Niigata Prefectural Archives.
Letter, Tsuneno to Rinsenji, undated
    Rinsenji monjo 2035. Niigata Prefectural Archives.
Letter, Tsuneno to Yamazaki Kyūhachirō, Tenpō 10.9.23
    Rinsenji monjo 1700. Niigata Prefectural Archives.
Letter, Tsuneno to Yamazaki Kyūhachirō, Denpachi, and mother, Tenpō 11.5.22
    Rinsenji monjo 1710. Niigata Prefectural Archives.
Letter, Yasugorō to Rinsenji, Tenpō 10.11.22
    Rinsenji monjo 1698. Niigata Prefectural Archives.
Lindsey 2007
    Lindsey, William. *Fertility and Pleasure: Ritual and Sexual Values in Tokugawa Japan.*
    Honolulu: University of Hawai'i Press, 2007.
Moriyama 2013
    Moriyama, Takeshi. *Crossing Boundaries in Tokugawa Society: Suzuki Bokushi, a Rural
    Elite Commoner.* Leiden, Netherlands: Brill, 2013.
Nagahara 2008
    Nagahara Keiji. *Nihon keizaishi: Choma, kinu, momen no shakaishi.* Vol. 8 of *Nagahara
    Keiji chosaku senshū.* Tokyo: Yoshikawa Kōbunkan, 2008.
"Nairan ichijō"
    Bunsei 12. Rinsenji monjo 2758. Niigata Prefectural Archives.
Nakane 1990
    Nakane, Chie. "Tokugawa Society," translated by Susan Murata. In *Tokugawa Japan:
    The Social and Economic Antecedents of Modern Japan,* edited by Chie Nakane and
    Shinzaburō Ōishi, 218–231. Tokyo: University of Tokyo Press, 1990.
"Oboe," Tenpō 11.10.14
    Rinsenji monjo 2099. Niigata Prefectural Archives.
"Oboe," Tenpō 4.4.3
    Rinsenji monjo 1693. Niigata Prefectural Archives.
Riello and Parthasarathi 2009
    Riello, Giorgio, and Prasannan Parthasarathi, eds. *The Spinning World: A Global History
    of Cotton Textiles.* New York: Oxford University Press, 2009.
"Rinsenji-no-haha Tsuneno no kirui shimatsu kata hikae"
    Tenpō 11.10.14. Rinsenji monjo 2099. Niigata Prefectural Archives.

Shimazaki 2016
Shimazaki, Satoko. *Edo Kabuki in Transition: From the Worlds of the Samurai to the Vengeful Female Ghost.* New York: Columbia University Press, 2016.

Smith 2002
Smith, Woodruff D. *Consumption and the Making of Respectability, 1600–1800.* New York: Routledge, 2002.

Stallybrass 1998
Stallybrass, Peter. "Marx's Coat." In *Border Fetishisms: Material Objects in Unstable Spaces,* edited by Patricia Spyer, 183–207. New York: Routledge, 1998.

Stanley 2016
Stanley, Amy. "'Maidservants' Tales: Narrating Domestic and Global History, 1600–1900." *American Historical Review* 121:2 (2016): 437–60.

Starling 2012
Starling, Jessica. "A Family of Clerics: Temple Wives, Tradition, and Change in Contemporary Jōdō Shinshū Temples." Ph.D. dissertation, University of Virginia, 2012.

Tamura 2004
Tamura Hitoshi. *Fasshon no shakaikeizaishi: Zairai orimonogyō no gijutsu kakushin to ryūkō shijō.* Tokyo: Nihon Keizai Hyōronsha, 2004.

"Tenpō yon idoshi shigatsu nijū-san nichi Tsuneno-gi Ōshima-mura Koide-shi e enzuke sōrō ikken"
Tenpō 4.4.23. Rinsenji monjo 1694. Niigata Prefectural Archives.

"Tenpō yon idoshi shigatsu nijū-san nichi kichijitsu Tsuneno Koide yomeiri shoshiki-dome"
Tenpō 4–8. Rinsenji monjo 1674. Niigata Prefectural Archives.

"Tenpō yon idoshi shigatsu nijū-san nichi kichijitsu Tsuneno Ōshima Koide nyūka shitakuchō"
Tenpō 4.4.23. Rinsenji monjo 1678.

Tokyō Daigaku Shiryō Hensanjo 1960
Tōkyō Daigaku Shiryō Hensanjo, ed., *Dai Nihon kinsei shiryō,* series 6: *Shichū torishimari ruishū,* vol. 2 (*Shichū torishimari no bu 2*) Tokyo: Tōkyō Daigaku Shuppankai, 1960.

"Tsuneno Inada-machi Katō-shi e engumi manki"
Tenpō 8.12. Rinsenji monjo 1673. Niigata Prefectural Archives.

"Tsuneno tadaima made shochi no mono aishirabe sōrō koto"
Undated. Rinsenji monjo 1680. Niigata Prefectural Archives.

"Tsuneno kanjō torishirabe"
Tenpō 10–Kōka 3. Rinsenji monjo 2096. Niigata Prefectural Archives.

Tsuruya Nanboku 2013
Tsuruya Nanboku IV. "Epic Yotsuya Ghost Tale," translated by Faith Bach. In *An Edo Anthology: Literature from Japan's Megacity, 1750–1850,* edited by Sumie Jones and Kenji Watanabe, 168–82. Honolulu: University of Hawai'i Press, 2013.

Uno 1996
Uno, Kathleen. "Questioning Patrilineality: On Western Studies of the Japanese *Ie.*" *positions* 4:3 (1996): 569–94.

Untitled [record of father's funeral], Tenpō 8.8
    Rinsenji monjo 1876. Niigata Prefectural Archives.
Yabuta 1995
    Yabuta Yutaka. "Moji to josei." In *Iwanami kōza Nihon tsūshi,* vol. 15: *Kinsei* 5, edited by Asao Naohiro et al., 225–54. Tokyo: Iwanami Shoten, 1995.
Yabuta 2014
    Yabuta Yutaka. "The Network of Nishitani Saku and Family Seen through their Correspondence." Translated by Matt Mitchell. *Sophia International Review* 36 (2014): 32–37.
Yamakawa 1992
    Yamakawa Kikue. *Women of the Mito Domain.* Translated by Kate Wildman Nakai. Tokyo: University of Tokyo Press, 1992.

8

Social Norms versus Individual Desire

Conventions and Unconventionality in the History of Hirata Atsutane's Family

Anne Walthall

Sometime between 1863 and 1866, Hirata Nobutane wrote an apologetic letter to his father that blamed his failure to manage his household on a "a desire for children." He faced several problems—bad relations with a prospective adoptive son and estrangement from his wife. One of his servant-concubines, Fuji, was trying to mediate with the young man. Nobutane turned to his father for help with the wife, perhaps because his wife might have been using her filial duty to her in-laws as an excuse not to live with her husband. Accusing another servant-concubine, the tattletale Teru, for causing the trouble between them, he wanted his wife back: "First of all to take care of my health, also to practice discretion so that doubts [between us] will not arise." Since his wife refused to give him a straight answer, Nobutane asked his father to tell her to return.[1]

The letter speaks to three issues of family dynamics in early modern Japan that concern me here: the imperative to reproduce the house from one generation to the next; the inclusion of temporary residents who complicated its composition; and the emotional relations between members. Although social norms governed what can appear to be highly regulated corporate families, they tell us little about how people actually navigated these issues and made choices in a system flexible enough to accommodate self-interest. A rule-ridden institution, the family was also, in the end, a voluntary association in which some members, at least, could get kicked out or leave.

While Nobutane's letter does not disclose whether his "desire for children" concerns offspring or a child brought in from outside, he had the alternative of adoption. Indeed, anthropologists and historians have long remarked on its remarkable incidence in early modern Japan compared to other societies in East Asia and across the globe.[2] Both commoner and elite households routinely adopted male heirs (sometimes children, sometimes adult spouses for daughters) as well as females intended as brides for adoptive sons. And because a host of rules, formal and informal, came to govern the process—its timing, the qualifications of adoptees, and the relations between adoptee and adopter—the house as a corporate unit is often seen as taking precedence over the lives and desires of its members. As Jane Bachnik puts it, "That the organization could continue takes precedence over how it continues."[3] Whether the evidence invariably supports this conclusion bears testing.

For the same reason, we should examine the composition of the household. The stem family (*ie*)—including a retired head or his spouse, or both, the current head plus his wife, and their children—defined an ideal in early modern Japan. Yet Nobutane's letter mentions the temporary residents Fuji and Teru, who fall into an ambiguous category between family and servants. Within the constraints of social norms and cultural expectations, families sometimes incorporated extraneous members who do not fit the parameters of the stem family as we understand it. The disjunction owed in part to complicated entanglements, particularly involving women who fail to appear in official records. What are we to make of them and how are we to position them?

And how, further, were entanglements within the household handled? How did married people feel about each other and marriage itself? William Lindsay describes a normative separation, expressed ritually, between wives who were accorded respect for skill in household management and prostitutes who were regarded as objects of lust and even affection. The wifely virtues of modesty and decorum found their opposite, or complement, in the courtesan's attractions of gaiety and wit.[4] Concubines do not figure in this scheme, which, in any case, assumes a male (and highly generalized) vantage. Getting beyond such simplifications presents a twofold problem for a social historian: evidence concerning conjugal relations is scant and not easily quantified; connections between the quality of conjugal relations and larger social trends are difficult to trace. Microhistory, however, offers a passage for elucidating emotional dynamics. If necessarily narrow in reach, it offers the reward of human interest.

I explore the issues I raise here—the reproduction of the house, its inclusion of temporary residents, and the personal relations among members—through the voluminous archive created by Hirata Atsutane and his descendants, now housed at the National Museum of Japanese History. It contains the manuscripts for Atsutane's many works on Japan's history and religion, not to mention medicine, divination, and foreign affairs. It also contains a household diary charting the growth of his school and the milestones in the lives of individual family members. Most numerous are the thousands of letters they received and wrote. This archive effectively documents the path taken by a poor but ambitious scholar of marginal status to found a school of Japan studies and, in so doing, perpetuate his legacy by perpetuating his house. There we find Atsutane and his heirs pursuing a conventional goal—to maintain and transmit family assets—but the steps they took were often unconventional.

ADOPTION AND ITS DISCONTENTS

Adoption figured in the recruitment of heirs to the Hirata family of scholars for several generations. We begin with Atsutane, an adoptee himself who adopted his successor, Kanetane. Kanetane was able to transfer the Hirata headship to his own son, Nobutane, but Nobutane, too, had to look for an adopted heir—one he sought prodigiously but without success. The motivations, circumstances, and outcomes of the cases differed. And their conduct resembled only superficially the norms generally governing adoption practice.

Born the fourth son of a mid-ranking samurai serving the Satake rulers of the northern Akita domain, Atsutane could inherit neither the headship of his natal family nor its privileged position in the ruling class. The only way for him to gain official status as the member of a lord's retainer band was through adoption as heir into another samurai family. Status mattered to him. Although he would gain fame as an intellectual, ideologue, and religious figure, Atsutane wanted membership in the class into which he had been born.[5] Fortunately for him, adoption had become crucial to household survival in his day and commonplace among all classes. Historian Kamata Hiroshi estimates that by the nineteenth century, up to 40 percent of all successions to samurai houses involved adoption. He infers that, lacking this mechanism, the samurai class would have died out long before the Meiji Restoration.[6]

Arrangements for most adoptions took place between the adoptee's parents and the adopter, but such was not the case for Atsutane. He had absconded from Akita at age nineteen and spent several years doing odd jobs in Edo, where he came to the attention of Hirata Tōbei, an Itakura domain retainer, sixty-nine years of age and in need of a son. Tōbei first brought Atsutane into his house as a dependent, then, having decided that he would do, set about the process of making him the Hirata heir. Yet because Atsutane had cut his family ties in running away, another house had to be found from which he could be received. As historian Itō Hiroshi writes, "It would not do for him to be picked up like a stray kitten off the street."[7] One of Tōbei's students in military science agreed to stand in as Atsutane's "uncle" thus allowing the adoption to take place. Next, Tōbei had to present a formal petition to the domain requesting permission to adopt Atsutane. Following an audience with the domain lord to obtain the required permission, Atsutane was inducted a week later into a guard unit with a tiny two-person stipend—approximately 1.6 quarts of rice a day, barely enough to feed two people. Aside from the irregularity of a murky family background, the adoption followed conventional procedure.

The scholar Ōtake Hideo divides adoptions into two basic types: those necessary for succession (as in Atsutane's case) and those not. Adopted successors might include outsiders, either as sons or sons-in-law; they might also include younger brothers of incumbent heads or the sons of elder brothers. (Atsutane's grandson, Nobutane, would eventually consider adopting his brother, something Kamata calls a "relay transfer."[8]) Emergency adoptions, when heads were critically ill, occurred on occasion, as did the posthumous adoptions that were officially forbidden but widely practiced. (One occurred in the natal family of Atsutane's adopted son.) And then there was temporary adoption (kokoroate), undertaken, for example, when a warrior wanted to ensure the survival of his house were he to die on a journey. Arranged before he departed, it would be dissolved upon his return. Adoption could also be used to establish a branch family, although historians think the practice had disappeared among samurai by the early nineteenth century, if not before. Finally, the wife of a head might adopt the child of a concubine to confer legitimacy, whether the child was in line to succeed, to be married to a successor, or to be married out. (Nobutane's wife would adopt a concubine's child.)[9]

For Tōbei, the adoption of Atsutane assured a successor to the Hirata house; for Atsutane, the adoption accorded the status needed to marry and become a full-fledged adult. A year later, after his adoptive mother died, Atsutane did enter into a marriage, with a samurai woman who became Tōbei's adopted daughter-in-law. Although historians point out that most samurai adoptions took place within a single domainal community, the three principals here had different lords. What brought them together was residence in the city of Edo, but also the relatively small size of each adoption pool there. Akita domain, for example, had 5,761 samurai retainers but only 391 men permanently stationed in Edo with their families (6.8 percent of the total).[10] Assuming that the domains of Tōbei and Atsutane's wife stationed similarly small percentages of their retainer bands in the city, all the principals had lousy odds of adoption or marriage had they been unwilling to go outside their domainal circles.

If adoption allowed Atsutane to claim samurai status, it did not land him in a felicitous situation. According to one story, Tōbei was the eldest son of a family of doctors but so despised the medical profession that he had his younger brother take over the headship, thus freeing himself for adoption by the Hirata, specialists in military science. He appears not to have thrived. When he died in 1809, only six people other than Atsutane and his wife attended the funeral. He was buried in a cheap coffin after a service that cost a pittance. Atsutane, now the house head, would keep the Hirata name throughout his life, even as he later broke off relations with the Itakura domain to seek a more illustrious patron before landing a position with Akita domain at the end of his life.[11] Although he and Tōbei had ostensibly pursued the adoption to perpetuate the Hirata house, neither had much allegiance to a lineage each joined for ulterior, essentially selfish motives.

Suspect behavior occurred again when it came time for Atsutane to adopt a son to marry his daughter. Adopting a son-in-law fit samurai practice, of course, but Kanetane, who became Atsutane's heir and the second leader of his school, was an inappropriate choice: an eldest son, he was expected to maintain his own father's house. Kanetane had become Atsutane's disciple around the same time as his younger brother did so. Why was it the older brother who, abdicating his responsibilities to domain and natal family, married Atsutane's daughter, O-Chō?

There are at least two accounts of how the adoption came about. According to a letter written by Atsutane some years after the marriage, "Kanetane disliked [his low stipend of] 5 *to* of rice, so he turned his house over to his younger brother and, as a wandering samurai (*rōnin*), became our child."[12] A retainer of the Niiya domain in Iyo, worth a meager 10,000 *koku*, Kanetane was presumably seeking a bigger stage for his scholarly talents. But according to a manuscript draft of Kanetane's autobiography, it was Atsutane, bemoaning his lack of a successor, who took the lead: "I really must adopt a son, but I have a homely daughter." With the help of a go-between who was another Hirata disciple, Kanetane became Atsutane's adopted son in the first month of 1824, when he was still a Niiya retainer. Given his official duties to the domain, he was able to stay at the Hirata house only five to seven nights a month. Atsutane's daughter went into service during that time and received training in the inner quarters of another daimyo house. Then, after giving the adoption a trial run and leading a double life for almost a year, Kanetane appealed to the domain for permission to retire (with the typical excuse of illness) and surrendered the headship of his natal house to the younger brother. The appeal was approved almost immediately; Kanetane spent more time at the Hirata residence; he married O-Chō on 1825.4.7; and the family subsequently issued a formal announcement that he had moved.[13]

In these two accounts, Atsutane and Kanetane each credit the other for seeking the adoption. Technically, they had to overcome three obstacles: Kanetane was from a different domain, had already been designated heir to his natal house, and had official responsibilities as a Niiya domain retainer. (In fact, it is doubtful that Niiya knew of the adoption before the marriage.) But Atsutane's 1842 letter glosses over all the obstacles, suggesting, at least in this instance, that individual desire took precedence over obligation to family and domain. The suggestion is remarkable on its face. The matter-of-fact quality of the letter nonetheless intimates that acting on desire may not have been uncommon.

A third adoption in the Hirata house offers a striking contrast to the earlier examples, in part because the family was now well established and highly desirable as a marital partner. Kanetane's oldest son, Nobutane, was trained from his birth in 1828 to succeed his father as Hirata head and leader of the family school. But like his grandfather, Atsutane, Nobutane had to resort to adoption to find an heir for himself. Unlike Atsutane (and Tōbei), Nobutane made choosing his heir into a competition.

It is not clear how many men and boys Nobutane went through in his search. By 1870 he had buried one boy listed as his natural son, along with two others whose status is ambiguous. A young man known as Masaji may have been brought into the household early on for a trial, though he disappears from the record. Another, named Shin'ichirō, had entered the Hirata household by 1869. We know nothing of his family background. On 1870.1.13, one of Nobutane's associates, a national government official and Hirata disciple, sent his younger son, Aoyama Sukematsu, to Kanetane for training and possible consideration as heir. Also in the mix was Nobutane's youngest brother, then called Kumanosuke.[14] The three on record (Shin'ichirō, Sukematsu, and Kumanosuke) spent some time being educated by Nobutane's father, Kanetane, who had moved to Kyoto following the Meiji Restoration. Nobutane himself was fighting his way through the bureaucratic turmoil of early Meiji state-building in the former Edo, now renamed Tokyo. In a letter to his parents, he wrote:

> Although I would like to decide to adopt my brother Kumanosuke right now, there is the matter of Shin'ichirō and the other, so first of all I want to wait and see [who should become] the legitimate heir or a common law child. The reason is that if I decide such a matter now, as a matter of course they will neglect their studies. If I establish the strict rule that someone who cannot do scholarship cannot succeed to the house, this will lead to competition, or at least that is my humble opinion. There is no way that someone who cannot perform as an adult can maintain the house.[15]

This passage shows a complicated understanding of who might belong in his family, for some members clearly held no more than provisional positions. Only at a later date would Nobutane decide who was to become the permanent heir. In the meantime, the three boys had to please a man who turned out to be a strict judge indeed.

In each of his letters to his parents, Nobutane commented on the boys' progress, based on the letters they sent him and the work they completed under assignment from himself or Kanetane. On 1870.4.19, he wrote: "I have received the letters from Shōkichirō [Kanetane's third son] and Kumanosuke. Although Shōkichirō's shows that he put considerable thought into it, Kumanosuke's is so wretched that I don't know what to do. . . . Please order him to practice his penmanship and study grammar."[16] Nothing Kumanosuke did pleased Nobutane. In a letter from 1870.6.14, Nobutane wrote, "[I]f he is going to become an embarrassment to the house, wouldn't it be better for him to be shut up inside? I am really worried about this."[17] Although Nobutane had planned for Kumanosuke to come to Tokyo with his wife, Kumanosuke's ill health forced him to stay in Kyoto and took him out of the running for the family headship, at least during Nobutane's lifetime.

Nobutane tried harder to turn Shin'ichirō into a suitable successor. In letters to his parents, he stated repeatedly that because Shin'ichirō was to be his son, he wanted to be the one to raise him. He told his younger sister, "If I don't get him under my roof, I don't think I will be able to think of him as my son."[18] But if Shin'ichirō was intelligent and clever, he did not study as hard as Nobutane thought he should. On the road to Tokyo, he was "full of mischief."[19]

Once Shin'ichirō was established in Nobutane's house in Tokyo, he proved to be nothing but trouble. He bit one of the attendants and threw stones at another; one day he took money from the accounts box and went to buy sweets without wearing his sword. Nobutane tried turning the boy over to his attendants, but when their backs were turned, Shin'ichirō removed his *hakama* (the divided skirt indicative of samurai status) and sword and ran out to go shopping.[20] The attendants could do nothing: "He is really more than O-Chō can handle and I don't know what to do about the situation either," wrote Nobutane.[21] On the second day of 1871, Shin'ichirō sent a New Year's greeting to his honorable grandparents. Written in carefully drawn block characters, the letter indicates that he saw himself as Nobutane's adopted son.[22] Within the next five months, he was gone.

In the competition to become the heir to the Hirata house, one boy remained, the eleven-year-old Aoyama Sukematsu (1859–1917).[23] Judging from Nobutane's remarks, Kanetane must have sent glowing reports: "Nothing pleases me more than the news that Sukematsu-sama-ko is doing well" (1870.2.3; 1870.2.14).[24] He arrived in Tokyo on 1871.5.22, according to a statement to the police made by Nobutane, who called Sukematsu his son (*segare*).[25] On 1871.5.29, in a report on the residents in his house sent to the Imperial Household Ministry, Nobutane called Sukematsu his adopted son (*yōshi*).[26] In yet another report, describing his family's circumstances, submitted in 1871.10, Nobutane called Sukematsu his *shoshi*. In modern Japan, this term means an illegitimate child or a child born of a concubine and not adopted by the wife. According to the authoritative dictionary *The Great Dictionary of the Japanese Language,* or *Nihon kokugo daijiten,* however, it once had additional meanings, ranging from sons not yet heirs to young children or youths.[27] What did the semantic differences between the terms mean for Nobutane's relationship with Sukematsu? Sukematsu was indeed young, Nobutane did adopt him, and Nobutane tried to treat him as though he were his own son.

Alas, the relationship between Nobutane and Sukematsu did not last long. Nobutane fell so seriously ill in the tenth month of 1871 that O-Chō wrote an urgent letter summoning his parents to Tokyo. They arrived just a couple of months before he died, on 1872.1.24. Following the death, Sukematsu decided to break off the adoption, ostensibly because it had become a relationship in name only. But in fact, Sukematsu's older brothers had established branch houses, his father needed an heir,[28] and he wanted to pursue Western studies, not the Hirata house specialty of ancient studies.[29] Taneo (called Kumanosuke as a child) became the Hirata family's household head for official business; finding a new head who could carry on the family's legacy of scholarship had to wait until a son-in-law, Tozawa Morisada, was adopted in order to marry Nobutane's daughter, in 1886. Sukematsu took a new name, one that combined the characters of his adoptive father and his natal father, becoming Aoyama Tanemichi, later a famous professor and medical researcher whose bust still stands at the University of Tokyo.

Tanemichi's decision to leave the Hirata house and pursue a career more to his liking suggests a relaxation in the norms that had heretofore restricted the options available to young men. After all, many sons in early modern Japan were adopted by fathers they had never met, so a lack of emotional attachment to Nobutane cannot have been the reason for Tanemichi's refusal of heirship to the Hirata house.[30] Likely it was a combination of other factors, such as the transformation of samurai into *shizoku* (former samurai) in 1869, the abolition of domains and establishment of prefectures in 1871, and the creation of a new educational system in 1872, which eroded the foundations of the Hirata house in its samurai identity, the Akita domain retainer band, and the Hirata School.

The need for a male to head the household, and for a male to have a household to head, meant that families looked first to adopt males. While the procedures followed in the Hirata family may have nominally conformed to the rules governing adoption in samurai households, they concealed considerable divergence from the norm in terms of eligibility, as we have seen. Males came into the Hirata family for a variety of reasons that reflected both their preferences and those of the family. In all cases, both sides took the time to get to know one another before finalizing the relationship. In contrast to men, women usually moved from one household to another through marriage. For this reason, adoption meant something different for them.

A case in point is Atsutane's third wife. One of his rural patrons, Yamazaki Chōemon, a town official and oil seller, arranged this marriage for Atsutane. Sixteen years younger than her husband, the woman could read and write and was particularly good at keeping accounts, but she was the daughter of a mere tofu maker. To conceal this humble background, Chōemon adopted her himself. An account by a student who boarded with the Hirata family for a month reports that, once Atsutane married her, "the household expenses were covered by her family, and he no longer had to worry about where his next meal was coming from."[31]

For this marriage, Atsutane took advantage of a widely practiced procedure of doubtful legality. The Tokugawa regime frowned on the sort of temporary adoption that, as in the case of Atsutane's new wife, occurred solely to raise the status of the adoptee. Discouraged for men, the situation for women was more ambiguous. After all, Tenshōin, the wife of the thirteenth Tokugawa shogun, had her Satsuma background laundered through the Kyoto aristocracy in order to achieve a sufficiently exalted status. And, in fact, with few exceptions, this form of adoption (called *koshikake yōshi*—adoption for the purpose of being adopted again) came to be permitted for women only. Another means for achieving the same goal was to rely on a "temporary parent" (*kari oya*). According to the historian Kamata, low-ranking members of the warrior class were particularly prone to use such expedients to adjust differences in status.[32] Even a doctor attached to the shogunate concealed his second wife's rural origins by this means.[33]

As Luke Roberts points out, rules were made to be broken during the Tokugawa period, so long as all sides made a pretense of obeying them.[34] Like the deathbed adoptions that might take place months after the adopter's death, adoptions for the purpose of equalizing the status of adopter and adoptee or husband and wife were officially forbidden because they blurred status distinctions, but they nonetheless happened. Along the same lines, the history of the Hirata house suggests that the ostensible reason for adoption—maintaining household continuity—could mask other factors, including personal preference and personal ambition. Incorporating women into the study of adoption forces us to consider other factors. Because they, too, were necessary for the house to continue, their adoptions fit the conventions of household succession. Still, unlike the men adopted or considered for adoption into the Hirata family, Atsutane's third wife went through a temporary adoption and subsequent marriage without the option of a trial run before the arrangement was finalized.

TEMPORARY RESIDENTS

In most cases, adoption functioned to maintain the stem family from one generation to the next, but members of the Hirata house used this mechanism for other purposes as well. We have already seen how Nobutane bent the rules in considering three young men simultaneously as potential sons; his grandfather, too, used adoption in a fashion uncommon at the time. These instances speak more generally to the Hirata family's porous boundaries, for a great many people flowed in and out of the household, some as student-boarders or servant-students, some as wet nurses and maids. These individuals would not have been considered members of the family. Others, such as maid-concubines, had more ambiguous roles.

Just three years after Kanetane's adoption and shortly after Nobutane's birth, Atsutane adopted another man, one who came with a wife and son. This was Ikuta Yorozu, of impetuous personality and enormous talent. He joined the school in the same year that Atsutane adopted Kanetane, although he did not meet Atsutane in person until a short visit to Edo just a week before Kanetane's marriage. Thereafter, he corresponded regularly with Atsutane, borrowed his works, entertained Kanetane when the latter paid a visit to his domain, and wrote texts for which he solicited prefaces from Atsutane. When his criticisms of his domain's policy led to his exile, he arrived with his family on Atsutane's doorstep on 1828.10.7. A few days later Ikuta changed his name to Ōwada Tosho Taira no ason Atsumichi.[35] Atsutane then adopted Ikuta as Kanetane's younger brother, though without making the adoption public by reporting it to the authorities. Instead, Ikuta became chief of studies for the Hirata School.[36]

The co-residence lasted only five months. For much of that time, Ikuta was traveling while his wife and son stayed at the Hirata house. Early in 1829, Atsutane's granddaughter died two days after coming down with smallpox. Ikuta's son caught the same disease and he, too, died. In the third month, some sort of trouble seems to have arisen between the Ikuta and the Hirata, because he and his wife moved out. Yorozu continued to attend Atsutane's lectures; he sometimes stayed the night or several nights. He wrote texts on themes selected by Atsutane, lectured on divination at Atsutane's urging, and, when he traveled, corresponded with Atsutane and Kanetane. The Hirata family archive contains copies of his works both in manuscript and published versions, many made and distributed decades after his death.[37]

Atsutane's adoption of Yorozu inadvertently exposed the family to danger. In late 1836 Yorozu moved to Kashiwazaki in Echigo, where he established a school to propagate Atsutane's teachings. Like much of the country, Echigo was then suffering the effects of a famine exacerbated by hoarding on the part of merchants and a decision by domain officials to export rice out of the region. While Yorozu repeatedly appealed to domain authorities for relief, to no avail, reports of Ōshio Heihachirō's rebellion in Osaka in 1837.2 provided a model for direct action. Supported by some thirty followers, Yorozu attacked the local deputy's office on 6.1. Government troops quickly dispersed the rebels and shot Yorozu (some reports say he committed suicide). The Hirata family soon learned that Yorozu's wife and two children had hanged themselves in prison (other reports say that she strangled the children and then bit off her tongue). Three months later, the magistrate in charge of temples and shrines sent a summons to Kanetane telling him to appear at once. When he did, he was questioned as to whether Ikuta Yorozu was listed on the Hirata family registry or not. Two days later Kanetane returned to the magistrate's office with a written statement to the effect that Yorozu was not so listed.[38]

Because of Yorozu's connection with the Hirata School and the Hirata family, a number of disciples either visited the school to seek clarification of the relationship or made inquiries through the mail. Kanetane wrote to an important disciple in Mikawa:

> I'm sure you've heard about Yorozu's violent death. Some disciples have worried that this has caused trouble for my house owing to the preface Yorozu wrote for *Thoughts on the Great Land of the Gods* [*Daifusō kokukō*, a text by Atsutane published the previous year].[39] Since I have received letters from the most unexpected places asking about us, I thought I should tell you about it. Really this has not caused any trouble for me at all, so please don't worry. But this is truly regrettable, a development with which I cannot agree, and all I can do is sigh.[40]

Although Kanetane tried to make light of the incident, it had consequences for the Hirata School in Echigo, where the disciples he had so carefully recruited dropped away and no new ones joined until 1858. According to Yoshida Asako, this revolt by a close disciple might well have threatened the continued existence of the Hirata School, had the previous adoption come to light.[41]

My interest in Ikuta's adoption by Atsutane lies not in its political ramifications but in its meaning for the structure of the Hirata house. Having already adopted Kanetane as his heir, on what grounds and for what purpose did Atsutane adopt Yorozu, and how does this act fit within the parameters of adoption practice? Was it perhaps an honor adoption—a way to give Yorozu status, once he had been exiled from his domain and turned into a stateless person? Or, given Atsutane's respect for Yorozu's scholarship, was it more likely an adoption made in order to set up a branch house (even though Japanese historians believe this type of adoption had already died out in the warrior class)? We usually think of establishing a branch house as requiring a division of real property. In this case, however, what Yorozu acquired was part ownership in the school's intellectual capital, to which he had made and continued to make contributions. One further point: although the Hirata diary states the date when Atsutane and Yorozu signed the adoption contract, there is no indication of whether it was ever abrogated. After 1830.4.2, when Yorozu returned from a trip to Izu, the Hirata diary stops referring to him as Ōwada Tosho, suggesting that the adoption may in some informal way have been dissolved. Warriors were held to stricter standards of reporting changes in family composition than commoners, but, even so, given that families were still to a large extent responsible for defining their composition themselves, a degree of ambiguity might persist.

Ambiguity in defining the status of family members, their relationships to one another, and their functions appears with particular clarity in the documentation left by Nobutane. We have already seen how he complicated the usual procedures for procuring an adopted son. He also brought several women into the family in hopes of fathering an heir. He always called them servants, never concubines, although that is what they were.

Aside from his wife, the woman who remained longest in Nobutane's household was a servant named Fuji. Hired on 1863.11.1, more than nine years after his marriage, Fuji was nineteen by Japanese count, or between seventeen and eighteen years old.[42] Nobutane was thirty-five. Although both Kanetane and Nobutane were living in the Edo barracks for Akita retainers at the time, Nobutane, as a domain bureaucrat, may have received quarters separate from those of his parents. The letter quoted at the beginning of this essay suggests that his wife was then performing her filial duty to her in-laws, or perhaps that was the excuse she gave to live apart from her husband. In any case, she had not borne any children. Since Nobutane was still a relatively young man, he may have decided to try a different vessel for his sperm rather than adopt an heir.

Fuji was the only one of Nobutane's servant-concubines to bear him a child. The first time she is mentioned in the family diary is on 1866.7.28, when she put on a maternity belt: "We just celebrated among ourselves by setting out red bean rice."[43] When Nobutane's wife O-Chō did the same two weeks later, members of Nobutane's sisters' families came for the celebration. O-Chō must have suffered a miscarriage, whereas Fuji gave birth to a girl, named O-Ishi, on 1867.1.4. When O-Ishi went to a doctor in the sixth month, O-Chō took her, suggesting that, as Nobutane's wife, she was responsible for his offspring. Hirata genealogies either list Fuji as Nobutane's second wife or let her disappear; O-Ishi becomes O-Chō's daughter.[44]

Fuji continued to live with the Hirata family for five years after the birth of her daughter. Following the announcement of the restoration of imperial rule at the end of 1867, Nobutane quickly got Akita domain to dispatch him to Kyoto. Except for Kanetane, the rest of the family remained in Edo until Nobutane summoned them to join him. Arriving there on 3.29 were "O-Chō first of all, O-Naka [a daughter Nobutane had briefly adopted from his uncle's house], O-Ishi, and others." Six days later, Nobutane's mother arrived accompanied by one of his sisters. As an afterthought, he wrote, "Fuji comes as well."[45] When the emperor moved to Tokyo, Nobutane went with him, while Kanetane and the rest of the Hirata family remained in what they hoped would someday again be the imperial capital. Two years later, after Nobutane had found a place for his residence and the Hirata School in a former daimyo compound in Tokyo, he sent for his family. O-Chō was to ride in a palanquin with sliding doors (presumably with O-Ishi); two of the boys in the running to become his heir were to ride in palanquins with hanging flaps. Listed as an attendant, along with three men including a relative, Fuji was to ride in an open palanquin as yet another marker of her inferior status.[46]

In addition to Fuji, Nobutane employed two other maid-concubines. When, for a time, he left his family behind in Kyoto to take up a career in the new central government in Tokyo, his disciples, deciding that he needed a woman to warm his bed, found Hisae for him. She also ran his household, though not to his liking, because she lacked decorum and flirted with his students. He once thanked his sister for sending Hisae clothing and on another occasion informed his mother that Hisae was not yet pregnant, indications that the family accepted and understood Hisae's position. During discussions concerning when to bring O-Chō to Tokyo, the matter of what to do about Fuji and Hisae came up. Fuji proved the more amenable. As O-Chō set about regularizing the household following her arrival in Tokyo, Fuji stayed, but Hisae did not.[47] In addition, Nobutane hired wet nurses for O-Ishi and the sons who would later die young. The nurses stayed with the family for brief periods on the borderline between family and servants.[48]

Nobutane's letters suggest that, when it came to women, the line dividing family from servants was porous. Although never dignified with the honorific O, so long as Nobutane was alive, Fuji maintained her position as O-Ishi's birth mother and, possibly, Nobutane's preferred concubine. Hisae was marginal and easily jettisoned when her services were no longer needed. We know that daimyo and the Kyoto nobility incorporated concubines into their families as a matter of course; to the end of his life in 1913, the last shogun, Tokugawa Yoshinobu, preferred to sleep between his two favorite concubines even though he had a wife.[49] Regardless of Nobutane's sleeping arrangements, it is remarkable that in the close quarters of samurai barracks he managed to get both his wife and his concubine pregnant at almost the same time. In terms of family structure, they held different positions; in terms of emotional response, the family respected O-Chō and felt a certain measure of affection for Fuji.

Yorozu, Fuji, and Hisae had positions in recognizable if unusual household categories—one as an unofficially adopted son, the others as servant-concubines. In addition to them, the Hirata family at one time encompassed two other people who fit less comfortably into any recognizable categories. Like Yorozu, both lived with the Hirata when Atsutane resided in a house rented from a shogunal deputy (the family moved into Akita domain barracks only shortly before he died, after he received domainal affiliation). The relative lack of supervision may have eased the incorporation of anomalous members.

One of these temporary additions to Atsutane's household, even more poorly documented than the servant-concubines, was a woman known only as "O-Fukuro" (mom) when Atsutane wrote the Hirata family diary and "Obaasama" (grandmother) when it was kept by Kanetane. According to one family history, she was "the mother who had been living in Osaka-chō and moved into Atsutane's house in 1818," soon after his third and last marriage.[50] Whose mother she was is not clear. From the family diary it appears that she must have led a carefree existence, visiting relatives and making pilgrimages to temples.[51] She stayed with the family until news came of Atsutane's death in 1843. What little is known about her suggests that she had a fictive kin relationship to Atsutane, one sufficiently strong to merit her upkeep for twenty-five years.

Another temporary resident in Atsutane's household was Torakichi, famous for having traveled with the *sanjin*, or "men of the mountains," more than immortals but not quite deities.[52] Atsutane first heard about him in 1820, when Torakichi showed up at the house of an acquaintance. After an interview, Atsutane, his wife, and two disciples invited the boy to the Hirata home. Torakichi visited several times and eventually spent the night. To keep him amused, the family played hide-and-seek. The boy attracted crowds of visitors, so much so that Atsutane had to inform the authorities of his residence. Wanting protection against the Buddhist priests and mountain shaman experts who tried to interrogate him, Torakichi had his elder brother ask Atsutane to take Torakichi on as an apprentice disciple. The family agreed and dressed him as a little samurai, to his great delight. Although mention of Torakichi tapers off after the first flurry of appearances in the family diary, he appears to have continued to live in the household as an all-purpose attendant and marginal family member. In 1825, his name was changed to Katsuma Daidōji, an appellation chosen by Atsutane's wife. He ran off several times but Atsutane always forgave him. Finally, on 1828.7.16, Daidōji decided to shave his head and become a Buddhist priest. He last appears in the diary when he came to pay his respects a month later.[53]

Obaasama and Torakichi held the most anomalous positions in the Hirata household. They were more than servants and stayed longer than students, and their long-term functions remain obscure. Obaasama appears to have joined the household because she found it more congenial than her previous lodgings. Torakichi at first provided information on the unseen world that Atsutane incorporated into a major work, but he remained with the family for years after it was completed.[54] Why did these people continue to belong to the Hirata family? In the end, when structure cannot account for their presence, we are left with sentiment. They stayed because all parties wanted it.

CONJUGAL RELATIONS

Atsutane, Kanetane, and Nobutane married, but the way they acquired their brides and their subsequent relationships differed. These experiences offer a useful survey of how men and women formed the partnerships that kept families going while suggesting sufficient flexibility in marital practice to allow some individuals to bring norms and desires into accord. Comparing marital life in Hirata history also points to a change: from a relative lack of societal constraint during the time of Atsutane, whose women enjoyed a fair degree of agency, to greater adherence to confining convention in Nobutane's day. The change corresponds to the increasing elevation of the Hirata men in the status order, from impecunious scholar on the margins of society to officials residing in the Akita domain's barracks.

When Atsutane sought adoption for himself, he had motives beyond recognition as a samurai. Before coming to the attention of Hirata Tōbei, Atsutane worked for a shogunal retainer who also employed a samurai woman named Ishibashi Orise. She worked as a maid in the interior of the retainer's home, standard practice for a woman seeking to improve her social skills before marriage. Atsutane and Orise fell in love and, as Atsutane wrote, "without her parents' permission, she pledged herself to me."[55] As we know from kabuki dramas, men and women employed in military households were forbidden to develop relationships not condoned by their superiors. Atsutane apparently concealed his love affair when he first ingratiated himself with Tōbei. Once he had status as an adopted son, he had to convince Tōbei that Orise would make a suitable adopted daughter before applying to the Ishibashi house for permission to marry her. The fact that the couple had made a secret pledge to marry would not normally have pleased either of these honest and upright samurai houses. According to Atsutane, "we had passionate discussions with our parents and others before she became my bride."[56] As Miyachi Masako has pointed out, "It was rare for a woman of Orise's time to have the joy of choosing her mate as she did."[57]

Atsutane and Orise thus made a love match without benefit of go-betweens or parental supervision. They had three children, two boys and a girl, but only the girl survived to adulthood. Orise herself died at the age of thirty, after eleven years of marriage. For the first forty-nine days after her death, Atsutane fell into a deep depression and did nothing but cry. He was just finishing one of his most important works, *The Sacred Pillar of the Soul* (*Tama no mihashira*), and in one of his early drafts wrote about Orise: "She served me faithfully while taking delight in the progress I made in my studies. She helped me to achieve success by working herself to the bone." He also wrote a number of poems expressing his grief at losing this beloved wife, lamenting the fate of his motherless children, praying for Orise's happiness in the afterlife, and remembering the eleven years of their marriage: "I was really difficult in those days, perverse, and out of sorts. Even though I knew I should not get angry, I would rail at things that could not be helped and scold her. She never lost her composure, but remained faithful to me." Recalling how the words had poured out of him while he was writing *The Sacred Pillar of the Soul*, he wrote: "It seemed to me that I achieved such extraordinary results because the miraculous spirit of my lover was helping me out."[58]

If Atsutane had not cut himself off from family and domain by absconding to Edo to make a name for himself as a scholar, he would have been bound by the samurai code of conduct that required parental consent for marriage. This same code bound Orise. It is extraordinary that a woman schooled in the samurai feminine virtues of modesty and decorum would risk damaging her family's reputation by falling in love. But she did, suggesting that under the right circumstances it was possible for women to have a say in whom they would marry.

Atsutane's second wife also made up her own mind about marriage, though to a different end. In the fourth month of 1818, a go-between brought word of a woman, age thirty-four and named O-Iwa, who was working as the chief attendant in the Edo inner quarters of the lord of the tiny Hinode domain in Kyushu. According to the Hirata family diary, she first came to Atsutane for a trial visit. The real move came on the thirteenth day of the sixth month. Two months later, on the nineteenth day of the eighth month, a note in the diary states that the marriage connection with the new bride had been severed. No explanation is given for this divorce but, according to Watanabe Kinzō, who made a thorough study of Atsutane's papers before the war, O-Iwa probably did not want to put up with Atsutane's poverty.[59]

This marriage does not feature prominently in biographies of Atsutane. It lasted a bare two months, making O-Iwa at most a temporary resident in his household. Although Itō Hiroshi surmises that her personality did not suit Atsutane,[60] it is at least as plausible that she preferred her career as a chief attendant. Regardless of who made the decision that she leave, O-Iwa merely skirted the margins of family life, leaving before she became so deeply embedded that rejection or escape would have been impossible.

As mentioned, a rural patron chose Atsutane's third wife and adopted her before sending her to Atsutane. When she arrived, Atsutane decreed that henceforth her name, too, would be Orise (with different characters than those used in the name of his first wife). This second Orise went with Atsutane when the shogunate exiled him to Akita in 1841 for reasons unexplained, but probably having to do with something he had published. The letters that both wrote back to the family in Edo document Orise's depth of affection for her step-daughter, then called O-Chō, as well as Atsutane's grandchildren. She frequently discussed with Atsutane the possibility of bringing one of the grandchildren to relieve their loneliness. Atsutane wrote to Kanetane: "Mother keeps talking about the seven of you and crying, and she wrote the letter enclosed with this one while she was crying. It was really too pitiful to bear."[61]

The letters Orise wrote to the family back in Edo indicate a deep and abiding concern for Atsutane's welfare and respect for him as a scholar. While they do not address directly the issue of conjugal affection, they suggest that the couple cared for each other, an impression buttressed by Atsutane's reports of his wife's feelings. A common metaphor for conjugal harmony was "working together like the two wheels on a cart."[62] Husband and wife had been brought together for the purpose of promoting Atsutane's scholarly reputation, a goal hardly precluding lasting intimacy.

By the time Atsutane chose Kanetane to marry his daughter, he had written and disseminated some of his most important work and gained renown as a scholar. As far as the two men were concerned, that daughter, O-Chō, was merely a means to solidify their relationship. We have no indication that her feelings were consulted at all. Said to have been so intelligent that, had she been a boy, she would have made a fine heir to the Hirata house, O-Chō, like her husband, dedicated herself to the house and its reputation. She read and memorized her father's books and, as her father's secretary, learned to write poem cards in his hand.[63] She had seven children, only one of whom died. The last child and fourth son, Taneo, was born in 1843, when she was thirty-eight, an unusually late age for a woman of that time to get pregnant, and a hint, perhaps, that the couple enjoyed a robust sex life.

Atsutane died before Nobutane was old enough to marry, but the grandfather had already enabled the Hirata family to become full-fledged samurai as members of the Akita retainer band. At the same time as they held down official positions, Kanetane and Nobutane ran the Hirata school, publishing Atsutane's works, enrolling posthumous disciples, and propagating Atsutane's ideas through lectures and letters. In his study of the "structure of difference" within warrior society, Isoda Michifumi has posited that, in some regions and primarily for those of high status, early modern samurai retained some autonomy because, in addition to being bureaucrats subordinate to their lords, they were also lords (ryōshu) in their own right.[64] For Isoda, autonomy came from direct landholding. I think the principle can be extended to operating a school. In other words, following Atsutane's death in 1843, Kanetane and Nobutane were subordinate to the daimyo of Akita as salaried bureaucrats while they maintained a measure of autonomy rooted in their scholarly domain.

Given Nobutane's dual roles, each with a strongly public character, it was to be expected that the choice of a bride would not be his alone. The role carried responsibilities, and the qualifications were strict: in addition to getting along with Nobutane and his parents, the bride had to be competent at running a household and interacting with outsiders. She also had to be well educated. Nobutane married for the first time in 1853, following negotiations with the bride's family, an exchange of betrothal gifts, a petition to the domain for approval of the marriage, and the delivery of the bride's trousseau. This first bride departed the family with so little formality that the family diary does not record it. Negotiations for Nobutane's second marriage, to the sister of shogunal doctor and Japan studies scholar Kubo Sueshige, began in the seventh month of 1854 and followed the same set of procedures as the first had, concluding with a union in the ninth month of the same year. Since Nobutane's mother had already changed her name to Orise following the death of her stepmother, Nobutane's bride took the name O-Chō. Even though none of her pregnancies ended in a living child, she suited Nobutane and his parents in all other ways and retained the family name even after she returned to her brother's house following Nobutane's death.

Scholars have long argued that, in early modern Japan, a wife's competence in household management outweighed her ability to bear children. O-Chō exemplifies this principle. The letter quoted at the beginning of this essay provides the only evidence that she was ever anything but the perfect wife or that she had feelings of her own. She appears in the family diary as a dutiful daughter-in-law who took care of her in-laws while Nobutane traveled and came to her husband's side only when he summoned her. Her few remaining letters merely relate news of current events except for the one that announces Nobutane's imminent demise. Her position as wife was unassailable; no matter how fond Nobutane became of his concubines, in his correspondence with his parents, at least, he always spoke of her with respect, praised her managerial abilities, and made sure the status difference between her and the concubines was maintained.

CONCLUSION

John W. Hall once described early modern Japan as a container society, insofar as the status system specified a place for each male individual—whether the ward for urban commoners, the village for farmers, or the domain for samurai. The family might also be seen as container, at least for the household head and his wife plus the heir and his wife. This study of the Hirata family shows one way in which these containers were constructed piecemeal over time and remained porous. Women could move from one status container to another, as did the second Orise when she went from tofu maker's daughter to wife of a warrior intellectual. "Temporary" residents of houses, such as Obaasama and Torakichi, as well as servant-concubines, such as Fuji and Hisae, could also slide between containers. Compared to men, greater fluidity characterized possible life courses for women, as did the potential for greater marginality.

What we see in the Hirata family records is a house coming into being and what that process meant for its members, especially regarding the relationships forged between house heads and everyone else. Although Atsutane got himself adopted into an unremarkable samurai family, his intellectual ambitions propelled the family onto an unconventional path. As long as he lived, a household of still-nascent distinction remained more fluid in incorporating women and temporary members than better-established families. Under Kanetane's headship, the family strove toward conventional prestige. By Nobutane's time, marriage practice followed the standard procedure of bringing in a bride. Nobutane attained such an illustrious position, first as domain bureaucrat and later as a central-government official, that he could command the services of multiple women and even have his choice of heir.

This vexed business of adoption and succession continued to allow flexibility. Atsutane manipulated adoption strategies in order to marry the woman he wanted (although, unlike commoners, samurai like Tōbei did not normally adopt couples) and to make Ikuta Yorozu his son (despite prohibitions against establishing branch houses). Kanetane jettisoned his position as head of his natal house to become Atsutane's adopted son. Nobutane compelled candidates for adoption to compete against one other. Throughout these machinations, the Hirata house pushed the boundaries of accepted procedures for samurai.[65] Ray Moore, in assessing the extent to which adoption enabled social mobility in the warrior class, concluded that it had little effect in quantitative terms, a conclusion shared by Japanese historians.[66] The collective consequences of adoption nonetheless conceal individual aspirations and fates. If the Hirata family used adoption for often-conventional reasons—above all to preserve and continue the house—the actions of successive heads suggest that achieving their goals required taking advantage of catch-as-catch-can opportunities beyond the normative strategies open to public scrutiny and approbation. The Hirata family was surely not the only one of whom this can be said. Their records, however, provide a particularly intimate view of the process and demonstrate the role that microhistory can play in shedding light on how individuals and families employed everyday tactics in what Michel de Certeau has called "the ancient art of making do."[67]

NOTES

1. Shokan 13–1–5.
2. On the frequency of adoption among the ruling classes in Japan as compared to China and Korea, see Marcia Yonemoto's chapter in this volume.
3. Bachnik 1983, 167.
4. Lindsay 2007.

5. For accounts of Atsutane's intellectual career, see Harootunian 1988 and McNally 2005.

6. Kamata 1988, 63.

7. Itō 1973, 44.

8. Kamata 1988, 69.

9. Ōtake 1988, 100.

10. Handa 2006, 125.

11. In a letter to Ban Nobutomo, Atsutane complained that the Itakura domain had repeatedly reduced his stipend, yet it expected him to continue to work full-time. Itō 1973, 107.

12. Watanabe 1942, 27.

13. Itō 1973, 180–83; Shokan 21–2.

14. Kumanosuke had been adopted by the Matsui house to marry its daughter in 1855 when he was just twelve years old; when she died two years later, he returned to the Hirata family. His formal name was Taneo.

15. Miyachi 2006a, 424.

16. Miyachi 2006a, 428–29.

17. Miyachi 2006a, 445.

18. Shokan 15–38–12–1.

19. Miyachi 2006a, 483.

20. According to Isoda Michifumi, among the signs for making sure that samurai did not mistake the rank of a person they might have to greet were the wearing of *hakama* and the carrying of a sword; samurai of *kachi* rank and above were never supposed to leave their gates without them. Isoda (2003) 2013, 78–79.

21. Miyachi 2006a, 491.

22. Hako 1–10–11.

23. Sukematsu's father, Kagemichi, had taken the boy and his aunt with him to Kyoto in 1868, when he moved there to work in the Bureau of Divinity along with Nobutane.

24. Miyachi 2005, 96, 98.

25. Sasshi 54.

26. Sasshi 55.

27. These are meanings derived from the thirteenth-century *Goseibai shikimoku*.

28. Uzaki (1930) 1998, 23.

29. Watanabe, document 6798.

30. Miyachi 2006b, 65.

31. Watanabe 1942, 24.

32. Kamata 1988, 75, 79.

33. Walthall (1999) 2005.

34. Roberts 2012.

35. *Ōwada* was the name of Atsutane's natal house; *Tosho* was a title given to house elders in Tatebayashi, Ikuta's original domain; *Taira no ason* indicated that he claimed descent from the emperor Kanmu through the Taira line, as did Atsutane.

36. Miyachi 2005, 39–40; Watanabe 1942, 154–55.

37. Miyachi 2007, 342, 357, 362, 374, 378, 379, 411, 413, 426, 429 437, 446, 455, 510.

38. Miyachi 2006a, 110–21.

39. *Daifusō kokukō* states that ancient Chinese texts mention a land to the east across a great waste called Fusōkoku, a sacred and pure land of the gods, the origin of rulers and

teachers. The first rulers of China, the so-called three sages and five emperors, all came from Fusōkoku. Thus these earliest rulers come from where the Japanese imperial gods reside. *Fusō* means "the cherry tree," and when this cherry tree withered, it changed into Mt. Fuji. Itō 1973, 189.

40. Yoshida 2012, 102.

41. Yoshida 2012, 103.

42. Sasshi 54.

43. Miyachi 2006a, 348.

44. According to the family diary, Nobutane also had a son named Heitarō, born 1868.6.1, who died that same year on 9.4. No mention is made of the mother. Miyachi 2006a, 375.

45. Miyachi 2006a, 374.

46. Miyachi 2006a, 384, 469.

47. Miyachi 2006a, 403, 408–10, 489–90.

48. There are no records of what became of Hisae, or of Teru, the servant-concubine mentioned in this chapter's opening quotation.

49. Endō 1985.

50. Bessatsu *Taiyō* 2004.

51. Miyachi 2005.

52. For a meretricious account of Torakichi, see Hansen 2008.

53. Watanabe 1942, 180–99.

54. The major work was *Senkyō ibun*.

55. Itō 1973, 48.

56. Itō 1973, 53.

57. Miyachi 2006b, 56.

58. Itō 1973, 96–99.

59. Watanabe 1942, 24.

60. Itō 1973, 118.

61. Miyachi 2006b, 62.

62. Walthall 2009, 13.

63. Miyachi 2006b, 63.

64. Isoda (2003) 2013, 16–19.

65. For an overview of the norms and regulations governing warrior adoptions, see Kamata 1988, especially 75, 89.

66. Moore 1970, 617–32.

67. De Certeau 1984, 30.

REFERENCES

Bachnik 1983
    Bachnik, Jane M. "Recruitment Strategies for Household Succession: Rethinking Japanese Household Organization." *Man* 18 (1983): 160–82.
Bessatsu *Taiyō* 2004
    "Chi no nettowaaku no senkakusha: Hirata Atsutane." Bessatsu [special issue] *Taiyō* (2004).

De Certeau 1984
  De Certeau, Michel. *The Practice of Everyday Life*. Berkeley: University of California Press, 1984.
Endō 1985
  Endō Yukitaka. *Onna kikigaki Tokugawa Yoshinobu zanshō*. Tokyo: Asahi Shinbunsha, 1985.
Hako
  Boxes in "Hirata-ke shiryō." National Museum of Japanese History, Sakura.
Handa 2006
  Handa Kazuhiko. *Akita han no bushi shakai*. Akita: Mumei Shuppan, 2006.
Hansen 2008
  Hansen, Wilburn. *When Tengu Talk: Hirata Atsutane's Ethnography of the Other World*. Honolulu: University of Hawai'i Press, 2008.
Harootunian 1988
  Harootunian, H. D. *Things Seen and Unseen: Discourse and Ideology in Tokugawa Japan*. Chicago: University of Chicago Press, 1988.
Isoda (2003) 2013
  Isoda Michifumi. *Kinsei daimyo kashindan no shakai kōzō*. Tokyo: Tōkyō Daigaku Shuppankai, 2003. Reprinted, Tokyo: Bungei Shunjū, 2013.
Itō 1973
  Itō Hiroshi. *Taigaku Hirata Atsutane den*. Tokyo: Kinshōsha, 1973.
Kamata 1988
  Kamata Hiroshi. "Bushi shakai no yōshi: Bakuhan hikaku yōshi hō." In *Gisei sareta oyako: Yōshi,* edited by Ōtake Hideo and Takeda Akira, 61–90. Tokyo: Sanshōdō, 1988.
Lindsay 2007
  Lindsay, William. *Fertility and Pleasure: Ritual and Sexual Values in Tokugawa Japan*. Honolulu: University of Hawai'i Press, 2007.
McNally 2005
  McNally, Michael. *Proving the Way: Conflict and Practice in the History of Japanese Nativism*. Cambridge, MA: Harvard University Asia Center, 2005.
Miyachi 2005
  Miyachi Masato, ed. "Hirata kokugaku no saikentō (1)." Special issue, *Kokuritsu rekishi minzoku hakubutsukan kenkyū hōkoku,* no. 122 (2005).
Miyachi 2006a
  Miyachi Masato, ed. "Hirata kokugaku no saikentō (2)." Special issue, *Kokuritsu rekishi minzoku hakubutsukan kenkyū hōkoku,* no. 128 (2006).
Miyachi 2006b
  Miyachi Masato. "Sannin Orise." *Rekishi hyôron,* no. 672 (April 2006): 54–66.
Miyachi 2007
  Miyachi Masato. *Hirata-ke shiryō shōsai mokuroku*. Sakura: Kokuritsu Rekishi Minzoku Hakubutsukan, 2007.
Moore 1970
  Moore, Ray A. "Adoption and Samurai Mobility in Tokugawa Japan." *Journal of Asian Studies* 29:3 (May 1970): 617–32.

Ōtake 1988

Ōtake Hideo. "Hōkōnin yōshi ni okeru oyako gisei." In *Gisei sareta oyako: Yōshi,* edited by Ōtake Hideo and Takeda Dan, 99–131. Tokyo: Sanshōdō, 1988.

Roberts 2012

Roberts, Luke. *Performing the Great Peace: Political Space and Open Secrets in Tokugawa Japan.* Honolulu: University of Hawaiʻi Press, 2012.

Sasshi

Booklets in "Hirata-ke shiryō." National Museum of Japanese History, Sakura.

Shokan

Letters in "Hirata-ke shiryō." National Museum of Japanese History, Sakura.

Uzaki (1930) 1998

Uzaki Kumakichi. *Aoyama Tanemichi.* 1930. Reprinted, Tokyo: Ōzorasha, 1998.

Walthall (1999) 2005

Walthall, Anne. "Fille de Paysan, Epouse de Samouraï: Les lettres de Yoshino Michi." *Annales Histoire Sciences Sociales* 54:1 (January–February 1999): 55–86. Reprinted in English in "From Peasant Daughter to Samurai Wife: The Letters of Yoshino Michi." *Annual Report of the Institute for International Studies Meijigakuin University,* no. 8 (December 2005): 97–109.

Walthall 2009

Walthall, Anne. "Masturbation and Discourse on Female Sexual Practices in Early Modern Japan." *Gender and History* 21:1 (April 2009): 1–18.

Watanabe

Watanabe Kinzō archive. Tokyo Metropolitan Library, Tokyo.

Watanabe 1942

Watanabe Kinzō. *Hirata Atsutane kenkyū.* Tokyo: Rokkō Shobō, 1942.

Yoshida 2012

Yoshida Asako. *Chi no kyōmei: Hirata Atsutane wo meguru shobutsu no shakaishi.* Tokyo: Perikansha, 2012.

9

Family Trouble

Views from the Stage and a Merchant Archive

Mary Elizabeth Berry

The texts I explore here, ranging from a popular stage play to a variety of manuscripts from a megatrader's archive, concern merchant houses in the prosperous if volatile decades around 1700. Their subject is the multigenerational stem family, the *ie,* which they treat as so elemental a source of identity and value that it requires, without justification, the axiomatic devotion of all members. And their focus is the existential threat to the *ie* posed by bad leadership, expressed either by the weakness of an incumbent head or the failure to assure sound succession from one generation to the next. Although there are great differences between the texts in genre and audience, each takes the survival of the *ie* as the paramount good, the responsibilities of heads as unequivocal, and the abdication of responsibility as unbearable. The play ends in tragedy; the archive lays out ingenious safeguards to prevent it.

Despite the assumptions of the authors of these texts, the election of stem family succession by merchants is puzzling, since the economic incentives that abetted the choice among other constituencies in Tokugawa Japan are hardly transparent for them. The *ie* spread throughout the samurai community, clearly enough, because martial title and stipend could pass to a single male successor. In a similar fashion, stem transmission in the outcaste community protected a range of begging and other privileges that were not divisible among heirs. While farmers faced some official controls on inheritance, their turn to the *ie* model was arrestingly coincident with the slowing of land development around 1700, when opportunities for reclamation were narrowing and the concentration of resources through unigeniture improved the prospects of family survival. Historically, we might note, farming households have been the principal adopters of stem succession as a recourse against unsustainable partitions of property.[1]

But among professional urban households the stakes were different. Like a martial stipend or a begging turf or an agrarian landholding, their assets certainly took material form. The primary property of the urban commoners we have seen thus far, however, was the intangible resource of a brand. Both the Sen and the Raku families secured lucrative commercial niches through the reputations conveyed by their names. Whether by offering instruction in the increasingly canonical art of the tea ceremony or fabricating ceramics to practice it with orthodox savvy, these houses capitalized on an authenticity (and authority) embodied in heads who promised integrity in the transmission of their arts and guaranteed value through lineal continuity. For any number of other professionals, luminous and lesser alike, branding could also help capture market share. Teachers, manufacturers, specialists in métiers ranging from carpentry to medicine—all traded in goods and services linked to the unbroken household names attesting to the unbroken excellence of the enterprises.

Still, the protection of brands does not require the formation of stem families. In commercial societies from London and Venice to Delhi and Beijing, the intangible capital of reputation has always been vital and frequently linked to family names. Yet maintaining it has not mandated, past or present, any single family configuration. Why, then, did Tokugawa business houses elect a form of succession that, on the one hand, was not necessary to shield an impartible asset and, on the other hand, carried heavy costs: the disinheritance of the head's siblings and nonsucceeding offspring; the concentration in that head of encompassing responsibility for both domestic and commercial affairs; and the constraint on entrepreneurship that follows from the submission of person to lineage and hereditary calling. What gains surpassed these costs?

Economic interest alone, of course, cannot account for the election of the *ie* model in early modern Japan. As the essays in this volume demonstrate, multiple factors buttressed stem choices that, if generally grounded in economic motives, resonated in disparate domains. They include the growth of ancestral veneration, which depended on multigenerational fidelity to ritual prescriptions; the focus of local governance on persisting lineages, which had reliable roots in their communities; the lure of elite example, which melded reputation with unbroken headship; and the sheer momentum of conformity with an apparent social norm. Did these factors move urban traders toward the *ie*?

In this chapter I examine retail merchants, perhaps the Tokugawa constituency least obviously drawn to a stem model of unigeniture and preservation of the family venture. I am concerned with both their representation in selected texts and the logic of *ie* formation those texts intimate—but *only* intimate, since, again, the *ie* is taken for granted by the authors as a norm, not examined as a choice. To anticipate some of the disclosures of the texts, let me mention, first, that the merchant *ie* appears there as an enterprise fully fusing household and business. No private unit of kin seems imaginable to the authors as a definition of family. Let me mention, second, that this *ie* appears entirely self-reliant. No structures of state or law seem relevant to the authors as external protections of family interests. In each respect, the texts invite reflection on the role of the *ie* as a defense against commercial trouble.

And my sources do focus on trouble. Indeed, from the outset of the Tokugawa period, the ever-enlarging literature on the family made peril a core subject. If they routinely portrayed the family as a bastion of social order and personal felicity, neither fictional nor nonfictional texts treated it as safe. Much of the trouble was generic. Thus, for example, a best-selling perennial, *The Family's Book of Bewares*, typifies the advice literature with its tireless lists of the hazards—both external (from bad weather to bad neighbors) and internal (from bad health to bad budgeting)—menacing most households. (The remedy? Forfend! Through ever harder and smarter work, combined with iron thrift.)[2] But much of the trouble, specific to the *ie,* turned on the seminal challenges of leadership and succession. They dominate the texts I take up now.

One was written by Chikamatsu Monzaemon, the most celebrated playwright of the era; the others by Mitsui Takahira, a fabled retailer and financier. Both authors were born in 1653. Both had samurai ancestors. Both flourished in the commercial economy that boomed around 1700. And each put the *ie* squarely in front of his audience. Chikamatsu spoke to theatergoers enmeshed in family trials; Takahira spoke to household members dependent on his own family's fortunes. Thus linked in numerous ways, the authors diverged deeply in experience. Chikamatsu, the younger son of a declining house of scholar doctors, served for a time at courtly residences and then found success writing scripts for the fiercely competitive producers, actors, and chanters of Kyoto and Osaka. His line disappeared with his death.[3] Takahira inherited a far-flung empire of retail and banking enterprises that he left strong enough to thrive throughout the Tokugawa period (and, with mutations, to this day).[4] The two men also addressed the fragile family in different ways. A maverick who put the contemporary family on stage, Chikamatsu made pain his subject in tear-drenched tragedies about human weakness. An organization man who perfected the art of admonition and reform, Takahira took pain for granted as the price of folly and focused on prevention. The two nonetheless describe the same universe, the same sources of trouble, and the same system of value.

I begin with Chikamatsu's play, which orients us in the milieu of the contemporary urban marketplace and the values guiding its imagined players. Although the tragedy centers, for many modern interpreters, on the emotional turmoil of a protagonist torn between obligation to his family and attachment to his lover, my reading draws out a different story. The tragedy centers, I think, on the senseless destruction of a merchant house by a narcissistically flawed head. Audiences are meant to weep, but less for a barely sympathetic protagonist than for the havoc he brings down on his *ie,* which the play portrays as the heart of merchant life.

CHIKAMATSU MONZAEMON AND THE *LOVE SUICIDE AT AMIJIMA* (1720)

Chikamatsu wrote well more than a hundred scripts, most of them on historical themes featuring the (implausible) derring-do and (wrenching) sacrifice of warriors. His fame is inseparable, however, from a small body of domestic dramas that are set in his "today" and focused, in the main, on urban commoners. All are tragedies. The masterpiece is the *Love Suicide at Amijima,* inspired by a spate of attested incidents (condemned as criminal by the Tokugawa regime) in which desperate couples chose death over intolerable lives. The lovers in *Amijima* are Jihei, a paper merchant age twenty-eight, and Koharu, a prostitute age nineteen. In the final act, Jihei kills Koharu and then himself. How the two arrive at this climax is Chikamatsu's subject.[5]

Stripping his plot of the elements that made the real-life incidents so riveting to the public, Chikamatsu declines to tell a sensational story or even a romantic one. We hardly see the lovers together before the final act, and then as sharers of sorrow rather than passion. At the narrative forefront is Jihei's household, where much of the drama unfolds. And that drama is driven by a single source: Jihei's consuming weakness. No sublime failing or fatal obstacle converts the protagonist into a tragic hero. He is banal but able to do awful damage to all those around him. Their pain, a family story, remains Chikamatsu's concern.

The author draws the family to the fore of his play with three narrative choices. First, he multiplies the relations between members and, hence, the weight of their obligations to one another. From the outset, and no fewer than six times thereafter, the script informs us that Jihei is married to his cousin—the only child of his father's younger sister—in a union combining conjugal and blood ties. Because his widowed and dying father had entrusted Jihei to his sister's care, the intimacy is compounded: the aunt acquires a sort of maternal role, which Jihei acknowledges by calling her mother. At the time of the play, Jihei and his wife have a son age six and a daughter age four. They effectively belong, then, to a three-generation *ie* made up of a senior couple (simultaneously Jihei's surrogate parents, in-laws, and aunt and uncle); the ascendant couple of Jihei and his wife (also his cousin); and the heir-in-waiting. One more important relative is Jihei's older brother, also a cousin to Jihei's wife and nephew to his in-laws. He has struck out on his own to become a prosperous flour merchant but remains a kind of guardian to his younger sibling, who runs the family's retail paper business.[6]

Chikamatsu's focus on that business is a second key to his plot. Never separating his players from their callings, the playwright fixes audience attention on the *ie* by fusing family and enterprise, identity and resources, one generation and the next. Repeatedly named as Jihei the paper seller, the protagonist heads a substantial house. In a sequence of carefully deployed details, the script describes the large frontage of the paper shop (three times the norm), its fine location (on the avenue leading to Osaka's prime tourist destination, the Tenma Tenjin Shrine), and its fortunate circumstances: the shop is "long established" and reputedly "well managed," and it sells "fine paper" to "customers who practically rain down."[7] Accordingly, the family quarters at the rear of the shop are appointed with the comforts of prosperous, not quite affluent people. The household has quilts and screens, a sunken brazier, wardrobe cabinets, and the paraphernalia for hospitable offerings of tea and tobacco. It also has excellent clothing. Jihei dresses for a crucial errand in "an under-robe of Gunnai silk, a padded over-garment of sheer black silk, a striped coat, and a satin sash"; he carries a short sword "ornamented with gold." A partial inventory of his wife's dowry includes fifteen robes made from such luxurious fabrics as Hachijō silk and Kyoto crepe.[8]

This thick material allusion surely served, in part, to situate a knowing audience in Jihei's orbit. Chikamatsu's play about a contemporary merchant house in Osaka was staged, after all, for heavily merchant audiences in the nakedly commercial arena of an Osaka theater. Money and display were on their minds. At multiple price points, clients paid for both floor space (from private boxes to crowded parquet) and amenities (from saké to charcoal braziers, from any variety of culinary fare to any variety of companionship) that marked their means. Above all, perhaps, clients paid to see and be seen in what served as a showcase for finery.[9] So, in this site of conspicuous consumption, Chikamatsu made his characters socially legible through their assets.

Far more than background detail, however, those assets direct attention to the real scene of the drama. If it is physically set in a cityscape of brothels, shops, and landmarks, the action belongs to the overarching world of the marketplace. There, gold coins and "new silver" make the music, while business inflects a lexicon of interest rates and exchange rates, service contracts and sales contracts, seals and signatures, accounting ledgers and payment schedules for debts. There arithmetic rules, as the players calculate the days before wholesalers must be paid, the years left on indenture agreements, and the likely returns on hocking padded silk.[10] And there Chikamatsu locates his play, which lingers lightly over the love affair between Jihei and the courtesan Koharu—almost three years old when the stage action begins—to focus on the fate of a commercial house.

Money is at stake from the opening dialogue. We learn in quick succession that the manager of her brothel has forbidden Koharu to meet Jihei, whose avidity is discouraging other clients; that a wealthy rival is planning to buy out her costly contract and establish the girl as his mistress; and that the paper merchant, hard-pressed to meet his debts let alone redeem his lover, has so "squandered his prestige and his money that his fortune is paper filled with holes, wastepaper unfit even for blowing his nose."[11] These revelations come before the narrator catalogues most signs of the household's seeming prosperity—its prime location and standing, fine merchandise and popularity, good furnishings and wardrobes. In their dark light, those signs point away from enviable privilege toward alarming jeopardy. A besotted head of house is running to ground the assets that the players and their audience understand as a legacy held in trust and the basis of the *ie*'s social life.

And, thus, the third key to Chikamatsu's plot: the playwright strips his protagonist of sympathy, hence placing his injury to the *ie* beyond forgiveness. We first encounter Jihei in Act I, set in the licensed-prostitution quarter of Sonezaki, where his older brother visits Koharu to dissuade her from continuing the affair. Disguised as a samurai client who sympathizes with her anguish, the brother elicits a confession from the girl: although she has pledged, in their hopeless circumstances, to die with Jihei, she wants to escape that fate and begs the samurai's help in breaking off the relationship. The confession is overheard by Jihei, waiting at the lattice of the brothel to steal a glimpse of his lover. Wrath consumes him. Calling Koharu a "rotten-hearted fox" and a "thieving whore," he thrusts his short sword at her through the lattice but misses.[12] During the following confrontation among the three, the brother reveals his identity and reproves Jihei for failing his household, angering his uncle, driving his aunt to illness, and forcing the brother himself into a humiliating disguise. Jihei admits to having been "bewitched by this old badger" and "deceived by this house-breaker." To demonstrate his "ten million regrets" over a now-shattered affair, he flings at Koharu the vows of fidelity he had exchanged with her for each of the preceding twenty-nine months. She turns over to the brother a small bag with her own corresponding vows. There he finds a misplaced letter that Koharu pleads with him to keep secret. As the brothers depart the brothel, Jihei cries out: "As something to remember, I will trample once on this woman's face." Then, "bidding you farewell with just this one foot," he "kicks Koharu on the temple."[13]

If provoked by the disloyalty of his lover, which we later learn is feigned, the violence of Jihei's reaction is grotesque. And it recurs in Act II, set in the paper shop several days later, where a morose Jihei learns that Koharu is about to be redeemed. Weeping "tears of molten iron," he offers his wife a ranting admission of anger, which combines bitterness toward the rival with hatred of the faithless "beast-woman" who had promised a "magnificent suicide" were any man but Jihei to claim her.

> Before I've been out of the way ten days, she is to be redeemed by Tahei. For that rotten woman, that four-legged [beast], I have no love left at all. But that Tahei will be bragging. He will spread the word throughout Osaka that Jihei's business has reached an impasse and he is pinched for money. Those with whom I have dealings in all the wholesale houses will stare at my face, and I shall be disgraced.[14]

At this, the wife reveals an exchange of letters with Koharu. Fearing that the affair would lead to Jihei's death, she had written the note discovered among Koharu's vows in Act I: "Between women there is a mutual sympathy. Do what must seem the impossible and sever [your relationship with him]. I beg you for my husband's life." And Koharu had responded: "He is precious to me, worth more than life itself, but being caught in an inescapable obligation [to a fellow woman], I shall give him up." The wife now concludes that the "virtuous" Koharu, if outwardly renouncing Jihei, will surely honor her promise by dying alone: "All we women are constant and do not change our minds."[15] She resolves to prevent the death.

Here the playwright homes in on his message. While confirming the venality of Jihei, Chikamatsu highlights the valor of a wife who, twice, intercedes to protect her household: first to save her husband's life by convincing his lover to forsake him; and now to save both the lover and the family by supplanting Tahei and raising funds to redeem the girl. The wife calculates that she can make a sufficient advance on Koharu's contract if she combines the money put aside to pay the wholesalers (after hocking the bulk of her wardrobe) with the money to be had by hocking the last of the clothing (hers and her children's).[16] So she dispatches Jihei to the pawnshops, impervious to both the material loss and the threat to her own status. (If Koharu cannot be established in a separate residence as Jihei's concubine and must enter the main household, the wife declares her readiness to assume the role of wet nurse, cook, or lay nun in retirement.[17])

The climax is set in motion by the arrival of nemesis. The wife's wary father interrupts Jihei's departure, discovers the looting of his daughter's dowry, and demands from Jihei a "bill of divorce": "You would peel the skin off your wife and children to acquire the means to chase a harlot. You pickpocket! My wife is an aunt to you, but to me you are completely unrelated."[18] After the father removes his desperately resisting daughter from the house, Jihei returns in Act III to the Sonezaki quarter and reunites with Koharu. The two make their way in a long, late-night walk to the Osaka locale of Amijima. There Jihei stabs Koharu and hangs himself.

Chikamatsu brings deep pathos to this final act, for compassion toward frailty inflects his stagecraft.[19] Jihei's closing sweetness toward Koharu, his gestures of rectitude concerning how their bodies will be found, his consuming sorrow, his dying invocation of Amida Buddha[20]—all such grace notes discourage any naked moralizing. The feeling that has always dominated a script short on action and long on tears takes over, as the sheer pain imposed by a weak man brings down the curtain.

The murder-suicide appears less a catharsis, however, than an ultimate act of waste. Chikamatsu has structured his play too starkly to allow release. Although fortunate in his circumstances, Jihei has all but abandoned his business, wasted its resources, and left his wife to cover his debts to wholesalers with her trousseau. Although surrounded by blameless relations, Jihei has withheld physical intimacy from his wife ("for two years I have been left alone"), made the "entire family . . . intensely anxious and sick with worry," and cast his children on frightening shoals.[21] No external trouble—an enemy, an unjust world, a vengeful god—helps explain his descent. No alternative ethos—which elevates personal happiness, say, over the good of the *ie*—underlies his choices. Chikamatsu projects a penitent Jihei who shares the values if not the character of his relatives. And with those two loathsome scenes, he frustrates any temptation to view Jihei as a hero of love. When he feels betrayed by his lover, Jihei spews venom at the girl and kicks her on the temple. When he hears of her imminent redemption by a rival, Jihei laments only the damage to his reputation: word will spread of the failing business and "I shall be disgraced." Jihei is all id, all selfish impulse, particularly in contrast to the wife and the lover whom Chikamatsu assigns the selfless virtues of loyalty to each other and their households. If Koharu is a loving victim of Jihei's folly, she pays the price with her life while despairing over the consequences for her impoverished mother.[22]

The playwright thus lodges the tragedy in the destruction of a family—an *ie* that knots household with enterprise—through the conceit of a bad head. And the play presumes, for its power, a shared audience understanding of the *ie*'s centrality, the head's charge, and his singular weight in ensuring survival. I return to these points after turning to the complementary texts of a merchant financier.

MITSUI TAKAHIRA AND HIS *OBSERVATIONS* (1720s), *REGULATIONS* (1694), AND *WILL* (1722)

Around the time Chikamatsu wrote *Amijima,* Mitsui Takahira was assembling notes on recent business failures in the real world. The resulting text, *Some Observations on Merchants,* focuses on fifty-some traders in Kyoto who inherited fortunes from industrious founders but ruined their houses through indulgence and Jihei-like recklessness: "Having been brought up after the family had already become rich and knowing nothing of physical hardships or the value of money," they "leave the family business to others and pass their time in idleness."[23] Takahira's subjects—the majority brought down when large loans to daimyo went bad—played well above Jihei's league. They nonetheless shared with Chikamatsu's protagonist a familiar catalog of faults. Many surrendered to sex (with both male and female lovers), luxury consumption (especially of huge homes and precious tea wares), and the lure of art (poetry, the tea ceremony, gardening, theater chanting, *noh* drama, courtly kickball). Some squandered resources on Buddhist temples. Most were ensnared in foolish loans by hopes of vast profits.[24] In general, they forgot both the "merchant spirit" (of vigilant bookkeeping, cautious investment, ceaseless discipline) and their "proper station."[25] In essence, they sacrificed their *ie*—their families, their family enterprises, and their ancestral obligations—to their own vanity.

Mitsui Takahira had no sympathy for men whom he judged inhuman and made the object of uncompromisingly cautionary tales for his successors. Nor did he hesitate to hit close to home. His father's eldest brother, the text reports, presaged the decline of his once-prosperous house by cultivating an interest in *noh* drama, building a stage, inducing his heir to perform, and neglecting the boy's education in the family business. That heir, "thoroughly extravagant in his tastes," abandoned himself to distractions (tea, chess, designing buildings and gardens) and irresponsible loans. The subsequent heir, a "person of no talent," lived on credit. A fortuitous adoption stalled but did not prevent the slide of the house.[26]

Such a fate was what Takahira determined to prevent in his own lineage, which was established by his father, Takatoshi (1622–94), the youngest of four sons born to a modestly successful saké brewer in the town of Matsuzaka in Ise Province. (The brewer's father, a samurai in service to the Sasaki daimyo of Ōmi, had retired there following the wartime defeat of his lord.)[27] Outrageously gifted in business, Takatoshi built a constellation of (at least nine) retail and banking operations that stretched, by the time of his death, from the headquarters in Kyoto to Edo and Osaka.[28] He also won recognition from the Tokugawa shogunate with appointments as an official draper and a licensed exchange agent; in the latter position he managed fiscal transactions between Edo and the Osaka-Kyoto area on behalf of the regime.[29] Although the financial enterprise came to dominate Mitsui interests, the trade in silk textiles remained the business's public face and the source of its reputation for legendary innovation. Takatoshi sold cloth in his showrooms at fixed prices for cash payments, cut it to lengths requested by clients, and supplied provincial salesmen with wholesale fabrics from Kyoto. He was a wizard at advertising as well as customer service. He probably employed hundreds of clerks in his last years.[30]

This legacy was large, and Takahira's approach to protecting it complex. Two manuscript documents—one written before and one after the *Observations*—addressed first the managers and then the kindred leadership of the house in order to illuminate a strategy for survival that combined rigorous oversight of operations with visionary planning for succession. The perpetuation of the *ie*—which "we must honor without fail, eternally and throughout the generations of children and grandchildren"—was the imperative. Fidelity to the founder—whose "divine protection" continued to ensure the family's prosperity—was the corollary.[31] A pendant to these documents, *Some Observations on Merchants* supplied real-life warnings of the doom awaiting anyone heedless of their admonitions.

The *Collection of Family Regulations*, dated 1694, itemizes the rules for preventing "ruin" in ninety articles directed to, and witnessed by, the managers of the Mitsui textile headquarters in Kyoto.[32] Setting the tone, the lofty preamble effectively conflates the Mitsui lineage with the imperial house (both are committed to the "family business") and the central shop with a daimyo's donjon (both are "main castles"). It also foregrounds the founder as the model for performance. Because Takatoshi pursued his calling "single-mindedly," "diligently," and "day and night until past the age of seventy," he "attained virtue in accord with the way of heaven" and, consequently, "peerless success." Similarly, managers and clerks who strive in their work (ever "alertly," "honestly," "sincerely," "unselfishly") will "certainly succeed." The promise of gain remains nonetheless subordinate to the "primary principles of loyalty and filial piety," for the *Collection of Family Regulations* casts the Mitsui staff as members of the Mitsui *ie,* each of them entwined in the hierarchy of familial attachment and obliged to deliver unwavering deference.[33]

Mixed throughout the *Regulations* are two practical emphases. The first, on good behavior, emerges in multiple articles that enjoin managers to hold clerks and other underlings to stern standards: no indulgence (in colored hair ties or perfumed hair oils, new or fancy clothing, saké or fine foods); no discretion over any but the smallest amounts of pocket money; no freedom of movement (whether at work or play, day or night); no unsupervised guests or access to the kitchen larder. Supervision was to extend not only to routine confirmation of guarantors but unfailing maintenance of the separate ledgers for recording the personal expenditures of clerks, their daily comings and goings, and the meals supplied by the kitchen. Such monitoring of the self was to be matched by safeguarding of the shop (according to detailed guidelines for fire-fighting, locking up merchandise every evening, securing the shutters, and the like).[34]

Thus alert to good behavior as the foundation of the enterprise, the *Collection of Family Regulations* attends in greater part to good procedure. Many articles cover the mechanics of management: scheduling inventories (month by month, with annual reconciliations); stocking merchandise (from the initiation of orders to the inspection of deliveries and the determination of prices); keeping accounts of debits and credits (day by day, with monthly reconciliations of master ledgers and the settlement of debts); and handling the heavy traffic (in goods, correspondence, and people) between Kyoto and the branch shops in Edo and Osaka that the headquarters supplied. Many other articles engage personnel practice. Managers are to confer regularly and candidly on "all matters" in the presence of several senior advisors who, in turn, are to report concerns to the Mitsui head. The managers, the advisors, and the head are to meet on the fifth day of each month in preparation for an assembly of all shop staff on the sixth day. In addition to the seals required for all ledger entries, significant documents are to be jointly witnessed by three managers. And, lest discipline grow lax, the *Collection of House Regulations* is to be read aloud two times each month.[35]

Acknowledging the dependence of a large enterprise on a large staff, the *Regulations* tilt decisively toward personal discipline, methodical practice, and mutual surveillance as the instruments of stability. Even so, there are intimations of a collaborative role for managers in abetting the development (not simply the survival) of the business: they are challenged to excel in their work, to scout out promising suppliers, to keep their eyes on provincial markets and exchange rates, to identify and reward talent in their subordinates.[36] Suggestive here are sentiments attributed to the founder, which would become part of Mitsui lore: "One excellent clerk can do the work of a thousand; one bad clerk can make most of the others bad. Distinguish that excellent clerk from the others and reward him."[37] If loyalty and filial piety bound the Mitsui staff to the family leadership, a synergistic respect for quality appears to have bound the leadership to the staff.

The second major document that illuminates Mitsui Takahira's approach to protecting the legacy of the founder is a combined testament and house constitution signed in 1722 and titled the *Will of Sōchiku* (the Buddhist name Takahira took in retirement).[38] Addressed to contemporary kin as well as succeeding generations of children and grandchildren, it includes fifty-one articles, both sweeping in exhortation and relentless in detail, that are divided into a prologue, sixteen sections with individual headings, and a conclusion.[39] The provisions served as the fundamental law of the Mitsui house throughout the Tokugawa period.

We find in them, as in the 1694 *Collection of Family Regulations,* addressed to managers of the Kyoto headquarters, a recurrent attention to daily business operations. What is central and singular in the *Will,* however, is a multifaceted engagement with the headship and control of the *ie.* It was failure at the top, after all, that brought down the firms described in *Some Observations on Merchants* and, in a humbler register, the retail paper business of Chikamatsu's *Amijima.* A bad head was as dangerous as a break in the lineage. Managerial discipline was only as reliable as the conduct of the leadership.

A key aspect of Mitsui conduct originated with the founder, whose ghost suffuses the *Will* as the declared source not simply of the family's prosperity but of Takahira's injunctions for preserving it. While evidence for tight transmission from father to son remains elusive on many matters, there is little doubt that Takatoshi articulated the crucial tenet of "one seed, joint prosperity," or strength through solidarity.[40] Thus, on the one hand, the Mitsui house was to have a single and clear head—the successor in the main line (from Takatoshi to Takahira and beyond) who would inherit primary responsibility for the *ie.* On the other hand, the house was to incorporate as principals the heads of collateral lines established by Takatoshi's younger sons. The 1722 *Will* of Mitsui Takahira recognizes five fraternal lines as joint members of a consolidated *ie;* it also recognizes three lines established by in-laws as affiliates of the *ie.*[41]

This model of consolidation was exceptional to the prevailing pattern (in families with substantial means) of separating junior lineages from the senior house as largely autonomous enterprises.[42] And it probably reflected the exceptional experience—in the generations of both Takatoshi and Takahira—of fraternal cooperation in running a business with interlocking retail and financial operations, as well as expansive capital assets, in three major cities (and several provincial nodes). Disaggregation would have boggled the minds of even star accountants. It would also have posed external dangers. In one of his concluding articles, Takahira rationalizes the solidarity model by citing the legend of a foreign king who demonstrated to his ten sons that ten arrows could be broken one by one but not as a combined quiver.[43] If union brought collective exposure to the weakness of any particular member, it fortified each against easy fracture.

The Mitsui model involved a complex assignment of shares in house assets to each of the fraternal and affiliated lines. It also involved elaborate stipulations governing the annual disbursements to them from the central treasury; the annual returns expected from them on profits; the administration of a substantial reserve fund; and the provision of support for widows, retirees, daughters, and surplus sons.[44] But the scrupulosity in the *Will* to such elemental matters was only a beginning. Good structures, even those binding brothers in a quiver, do not supplant persons. Hence, the *Will* invokes early and often the need for talent in each lineage head and sound preparation for leadership. In one long section, Takahira outlines a curriculum for the sons of partners who, from age twelve to age thirty, are to rotate through all the main Mitsui shops and master there all essential skills— from the most modest services for clients to advanced proficiency in purchasing, accounting, financing, and coordinating staff—until they are ready to assist the incumbent heads with formal assignments.[45] And those incumbents are meant to relinquish authority in a timely fashion by retiring around the age of sixty, earlier if disability intrudes. Should a head lack an appropriate heir, he is advised to adopt one from a collateral lineage, either a boy or (yes) a girl.[46]

Nor did the *Will* stop here, since the threat of a bad head is hardly foreclosed by good training and prudent counsel. Removal of a thorn must be an option. So the *Will* authorizes the assembled heads of the main and fraternal lineages to compel the retirement or separation of any one of them who injures the business or violates the collectivity.[47] There is more still. Takahira's *Will* confirms two innovations, both dating from 1709 or 1710, that institutionalized the Mitsui *ie* as a corporate holding transcending kin.

The first, the establishment of the Managers' Council, effectively lodged responsibility for the administration of Mitsui enterprises in a group of six or seven senior staff representing shops in Edo, Kyoto, and Osaka. "Putting the security of the house first," the *Will* states, the councilors are to "focus with a single mind on the harmonious regulation of superiors and inferiors" and, thus, to reprove both "heads in error" and "underlings in the wrong." The lineage heads must respect their judgment, reward exemplary performance with bonuses and pensions, and select successors from the circle of promising juniors being prepared for leadership by current councilors. So indispensable are the best of the councilors that even as the *Will* recommends retirement by age fifty-five or fifty-six, it exempts still-robust incumbents and insists on "unending" consultation with the others on all vital matters.[48]

The second innovation, the creation of the Executive Board, remains the paramount development in Mitsui history during the early modern period. The board did not displace the successor in the main lineage as the head of the Mitsui house; nor did it compromise the collective claim on resources, influence, and prestige of the principal collateral heads. In both the rhetoric of the *Will* and the subsequent conduct of business, however, the board emerges as the ultimate source of decision making concerning all Mitsui operations. The *Will* instructs board members to visit each shop annually (spending up to two months in Edo), inspect all books biannually, focus meticulously on capital flows and the quality of goods, watch market conditions (particularly in Nagasaki), and ensure the diligence of staff. The *Will* also requires them to convene monthly, attend the meetings of the Managers' Council, and deliberate thoroughly on all aspects of the business. And what of the board's composition? According to the *Will*, members should include three able and mature heads of the principal family lineages. But from its inception, and throughout the Tokugawa period, the board also included members of the Managers' Council. Kin and staff jointly controlled the Mitsui *ie*.[49]

No family, and no family fortune, is ever safe. The second-generation successor to Mitsui Takatoshi's conglomerate nonetheless put in place cordon upon cordon of protection in the most versatile campaign for survival launched by a Tokugawa-period house. The essential defense was sound management practice at the shop level. Additional defenses circled the headship: the consolidation of main and fraternal lineages to concentrate strength; the protocols for methodical training and orderly succession of heirs to abet stability; the provision for removal of errant incumbents to afford fail-safe correction. The definitive defense, however, embedded heads in a sort of senatorial system that all but obviated individual leadership. Entrusting immediate administrative responsibility for the Mitsui concerns to the Managers' Council, Takahira vested ultimate oversight of the house in an Executive Board—where the combined representation of kin and staff asserted both the unitary identity of family and enterprise and a consequent commitment to corporate governance.

REFLECTIONS ON THE TEXTS

The scale of the Mitsui holdings and the complexity of the safeguards surrounding them would have been unimaginable to the paper merchant Jihei and most of his real-life counterparts. Still, Takahira's documents and Chikamatsu's play spring from a common worldview. At a basic level, the admonitions of the documents hew to the same popular morality—conveyed throughout school primers and family manuals, neighborhood and village regulations—that informs the play. Resist temptations to laziness and neglect of business by ceaseless striving in the "family calling." Elude the lure of luxury by recognizing that "limits" lead to prosperity. Suppress vanity in selfless service to the house. And, above all, preserve virtuous accord in that house with reverence toward ancestors, loyalty and filial piety toward superiors, benevolence toward inferiors, and harmonious domestic relations.[50] Jihei knew these rules as well as anybody. He just couldn't live by them.

Here is the reality that both playwright and financier reckon with: virtue fails, rules get broken. One explores the consequences with pain-drenched pathos, the other forfends with gimlet-eyed practicality. Each, however, is guided by a shared understanding of what matters. Their common worldview locates the *ie* at the center of value. The rules exist to protect it. Breaking them, and thereby ruining his house, was Jihei's tragedy. Buttressing them, and thereby shielding his house, was Takahira's mission.

Indeed, so raptly do Chikamatsu and Takahira make the *ie* the highest good that competing values fade from their texts. We may find in *Amijima* a saving regard for the humanity of feeling (of the wife for her husband, the father for his daughter, the prostitute for her lover). Even so, the script withholds any redeeming purpose from the protagonist himself. He sows loss in the service of nothing. In Takahira's documents, the emphasis on the survival of the house is unconditional. The founding genius, Mitsui Takatoshi, might have served as a muse for continuing invention. He emerges, instead, as the creator of a legacy that must be conserved with unwavering fidelity. Any diversification of the business is forbidden as a reckless departure from proven competence and a source of damaging turmoil.[51] No less clearly, any distraction from the business is reproached as vain. While Takahira took pride in official recognition from the Tokugawa regime and enjoined all members of the house to faultless compliance with its law, his *Will* warns against deepening political service, which diverts energy from the *ie* while providing no demonstrable advantage. So, too, religious fervor. Appropriate observance of Buddhist and Shinto rituals (with appropriate donations) must not escalate to avid piety, another injury to the "family business."[52] The possible pull of other distractions—scholarship, say, or social service—falls beyond Takahira's ken. In fact, his Mitsui successors would venture into pursuits variously aligned and not with family interests: they became major players in poor relief, arts patronage, real estate development, and leveraged lending. The foundational documents of the house, however, make insular caution the creed of the *ie*.

Here, then, we return to my opening question: why was the *ie*, and its perpetuation, so important to merchants? Mitsui Takahira does not tell us. Nor does Chikamatsu Monzaemon. Arresting in their texts is the apparently self-evident imperative of *ie* persistence, which, despite the sacrifices entailed, remains so essential a frame for interpreting the human condition that it requires no justification. Takahira treats the many business failures described in *Some Observations on Merchants* not as a welcome thinning of witless competitors but an occasion to preach the lesson of lineage-first-ism: close ranks behind the founder and never court risk! Chikamatsu makes Jihei's crises not a study in passion but a morality tale about family damage: tame the ego to save the house! Bad behavior for both authors is the path to *ie* destruction, something transparently terrible. Nothing could be worse. The point gives pause since, as I note earlier, stem family formation, episodic historically and concentrated in agrarian societies, was new to Tokugawa Japan as a common practice outside the martial elite and hardly obvious as a desirable norm.

One lead appears in the *Mitsui Family Regulations,* where several striking analogies speak to a conception of prestige derived from elite practice. When the preamble equates the Mitsui and imperial houses (each is committed to the "family business") and then the Mitsui and daimyo headquarters (each is a "main castle"), the leap is not toward a presumptuous social parity but the comparable social gravity that established names, professional identities, and landmark locations bestow. For traders as for their princely models, the preamble implies, presence over time builds weight in reputation. And clearly linked to reputation is the concern with genealogical honor. Both Takahira's *Will* and the family records that were completed during the same year serve as panegyrics to a founder of distinguished descent and public trust who invested unrivaled energy in an abiding achievement. More than beneficiaries of this legacy, however, successors are bearers of consequent obligations. If the *ie* transmits genealogical honor, it also sustains it through the ancestral devotions—the passage of names, the maintenance of graves and mortuary rituals, the daily performance of filial piety—that acknowledge the "divine protection" of ascendants. The *ie* plays an ethical role as an instrument of gratitude.

Its primary role is nonetheless the protection of resources. Mitsui Takahira's inescapable preoccupation, in scores of regulations ranging from the shareholding of heirs to the conduct of decision, remains conservation of a material endowment. Social gravity and genealogical honor surely provided practical insurance. And those values may have figured ever more profoundly over time as psychical inspirations for perseverance. But the initial (and continuing) shifts toward the *ie* turned on fortification. Mitsui Takahira, the second-generation heir to a fortune made of innovation, dug in with defense.

Defense presumes danger. It is recognition of this reality, I think, that leads us to the heart of merchant choices of the stem family: efforts to explain the decisions of Takahira and his kind must grapple, in the end, with the fears that animated them. The weak-heir syndrome—so colorfully on display in *Some Observations on Merchants* and so tragically on display in *Amijima*—was a critical part of the mix, since bad incumbents and failed successions posed the immediate threat to the *ie.* Alone, however, it fails to explain why *ie* survival mattered so deeply in the first place and, in the Mitsui case, inspired such serious institutionalization. Binding brothers in the equivalent of a corporation, assigning control to senatorial councils, exposing all operations to the light of ledgers, seals, and mutual surveillance—these were acts that established the lineage as a trust. On the one hand, they formalized and routinized the internal relations of parties who decided to work together. On the other hand, they projected the house externally as a formidable unit of stability and dependability: it adhered to protocols of verification and signature; it valued name; it was organized to survive for a long time. Implicit here is the fear of exposure to outside as well as inside dangers that *ie* formation might deflect.

Mitsui Takahira does not describe the nature of those dangers, or the specific utility of the stem household in defending against them, in either his *Regulations* or his *Will*. Perhaps he took them for granted. Perhaps he knew that *Some Observations on Merchants* provided description enough. The cautionary biographies there certainly warn against imprudence and vanity in house heads. Just as certainly, they warn against a fiscally fragile shogunate and the many daimyo houses whose predatory borrowing practices figured profoundly in the ruin of most of the subjects. Their failures did expose, flamboyantly, the movement of wealth from a martial elite increasingly dependent on large loans to the great commercial concerns able to provide them. But they revealed no less surely the vulnerability of merchant lenders who were defenseless against default, lacked protections for private property, enjoyed no certain access to legal appeal, and thus remained quarry for a troubled regime. The *Observations* served as a textbook on the exposure of merchant resources to a quixotic polity. A series of fiscal reforms from the late 1690s into the 1730s—including lurching manipulations of currency and stringent controls on consumption—only added to the insecurity of high-end urban traders.[53]

For all traders, however, the swift growth of the commercial economy in Tokugawa Japan brought a host of new business challenges—from recruiting suppliers and workers to managing financial transactions—that posed grim risks in the absence of legal protocols and protections for making contracts, securing credit, and indemnifying property. What emerged in this vacuum was a web of insurance, spun by commoners themselves, which entangled the players in Jihei's world no less than Mitsui Takahira's. Large and small alike, merchants came to live by the bonds of guarantors, witnesses, seals, and oaths that made fast their ever more richly documented agreements concerning sales, service, loans, and partnerships. (Recall the drone of marketplace music—its contracts, promissory notes, due dates for debts, oaths, and chops—accompanying Chikamatsu's play.) Such devices may have warned the regime against predation in an increasingly organized, and vigilant, mercantile society. Preeminently, though, they acknowledged that the arithmetic of capital required conditions of trust.

But trust without assured legal recourse for injury is tough. Lacking that recourse, the authority of a guarantor or a seal had to depend essentially on the integrity of the signatory. Similarly, the viability of the commercial sector had to depend broadly on the leadership of stable concerns able to enforce an ethos of integrity. In this context, the formation of merchant *ie* appears to me a means of backing the sincerity of words with the weight of time—not just the social gravity or genealogical honor that signified fame for the most ambitious houses but the promise in even humble houses that ascendants and descendants were implicated as witnesses to any transaction bearing the collective name. The *ie* put the standing of the lineage behind the seal of the incumbent head.[54]

Did this standing necessarily entail unigeniture (the indivisible transmission of what, after all, was the intangible asset of name and brand that might have been shared among heirs) as well as fidelity to a defining calling (rather than entrepre-neurial diversification)? The evidence outside and even inside Japan (where the *ie* was hardly the sole choice of merchant families) says no. Yet both the bunker men-tality apparent in the Mitsui archive and the obligation to honor a legacy assumed in Chikamatsu's play point to a logic of cautious defense among *ie* adopters. Fusing the family with its business, the *ie* identified successive generations of kin with one core enterprise that they could corporately authenticate. Conveying authority from a single hereditary head to the next, the *ie* concentrated the capital of name in a socially legible form that uncertain legal circumstances invited. Over time, association and interdependence surely accelerated *ie* formation as well. If the security of families like the Mitsui derived from lineage continuity, it could only be enhanced by dealing with suppliers and other partners (from transporters to paper sellers) who themselves practiced stem succession. As lead firms sought the insurance of stem family witness, replication down the chain appears predictable.

There was a price, of course. Mitsui Takahira's adamant conservatism—designed to fortify a fortune against both internal trouble and the external dangers a unified *ie* might resist—put the house as enterprise over the house as persons of individual vision. The consequence for the Mitsui, and for many great counterparts across the social spectrum, was the atrophy of an increasingly symbolic headship submissive to managers. The willingness to pay this price illumines, I think, an early modern consensus that the corporately structured *ie* provided the best available recourse for protecting economic capital. The affective and morally inflected language of the Mitsui documents, and of Chikamatsu's *Amijima,* insists, too, that the *ie* pro-vided the best available locus for defining social identity and responsibility. Feel-ing, and the requirement for filiality among kin and nonkin alike, came to buttress, suffuse, and blur the economic imperative.[55]

NOTES

I acknowledge with gratitude the support of the Founders Fellowship, which I held at the National Humanities Center in 2014–15 when I undertook the research for this essay.

1. This and the following paragraph draw on material explored in the introduction to this volume and in the essays by David Spafford, Maren Ehlers, Morgan Pitelka, and Anne Walthall.

2. For the *Kanai yōjin shū* (the title I translate as *The Family's Book of Bewares*), see Tomiya (1729) 2010. For additional texts concerning family perils, see Koizumi 2010 and Nagamoto 2005 (which introduces the texts published in Nagamoto 2004–9). For treat-ments in popular fiction, see almost anything written by Ihara Saikaku, for example, Befu 1976.

3. For summaries of the scant surviving information concerning Chikamatsu's back-ground and personal life, see Suwa, Shinoda, and Tsuji 1979, 128–36; and Shively 1953, 12–18. Gerstle 1999 describes the context in which Chikamatsu worked.

4. For biographical information, see Mitsui Bunko 1980 and Miyamoto 2003.

5. For an English translation, see Chikamatsu 1953, and for the Japanese text, Chikamatsu 1958. Shively (1953) provides a copious introduction to the play as well as extensive annotation of the translation. See pp. 48–51 for the play's textual history and the sources used for the translation.

6. We do not learn why the younger brother inherited the business. But by expanding the group of elders Jihei is obliged to honor, this plot choice amplifies his betrayals.

7. Kamiya, or "paper shop/seller," functions as a sort of surname for Jihei. Details about the enterprise—including a frontage of 6 ken (roughly 36 feet)—appear in Chikamatsu 1953, 74, 76; and Chikamatsu 1958, 366, 368–69. Here and below, I have made minor modifications to Shively's translations.

8. References to the furnishings pepper Act II. For Jihei's costume, see Chikamatsu 1953, 83; and Chikamatsu 1958, 376. For the wife's dowry, see Chikamatsu 1953, 82; and Chikamatsu 1958, 375.

9. For illustrations of the theater environment, see Suwa, Shinoda, and Tsuji 1979; for an extended analysis that, while focused on kabuki, addresses issues common to jōruri, or puppet performances, as well, see Shively 1978. Amijima was first staged by a jōruri troupe at the Takemoto-za in Osaka in 1720.

10. The suffusion of the script with contemporary commercial argot accounts in good measure for the striking volume of editorial annotation in both Chikamatsu 1953 and 1958.

11. Chikamatsu 1953, 64, 66–67; Chikamatsu 1958, 358–60. Puns on paper are rich in Act I.

12. Chikamatsu 1953, 71–72; Chikamatsu 1958, 364–65.

13. Chikamatsu 1953, 74–75; Chikamatsu 1958, 367–68. "House-breaker" is a translation of yajiri kiri, someone who cuts through walls or fences to rob a house.

14. Chikamatsu 1953, 80–81; Chikamatsu 1958, 373.

15. Chikamatsu 1953, 81; Chikamatsu 1958, 374.

16. Note that the wife's leverage derives from her control of clothing, as is the case of the protagonist of Amy Stanley's essay in this volume.

17. Chikamatsu 1953, 83; Chikamatsu 1958, 375.

18. Chikamatsu 1953, 85; Chikamatsu 1958, 377.

19. For Chikamatsu's system of value, see Gerstle 1996; and Shively 1953, 28–29, 41–42.

20. To honor Koharu's pledge to Jihei's wife that she would separate from him, the lovers symbolically renounce secular attachments by cutting their hair and then die by different means at a short distance from each other. Chikamatsu 1953, 94–96; Chikamatsu 1958, 384–87.

21. Chikamatsu 1953, 80, 89; Chikamatsu 1958, 372, 380.

22. We understand that Koharu was indentured to the brothel to support her widowed mother, who might become a beggar without her. Chikamatsu 1953, 71; Chikamatsu 1958, 364.

23. For the text (Japanese title, Chōnin kōkenroku), see Crawcour 1962, 31–123. The quotation appears on p. 31. The text includes, in addition to the Kyoto cases, several group portraits of privileged merchants and, in an epilogue, notes on a number of Edo and Osaka houses. It was completed in the late 1720s by Takahira's son, Mitsui Takafusa, who attributes almost all of the content to his father (see pp. 122–23). In footnote 9 (pp. 11–12) Crawcour discusses the manuscripts he used for the translation as well as modern published versions,

all based on later and corrupt copies. No authoritative version has been published by the Mitsui Archives (Mitsui Bunko).

24. For discussion and a numerical accounting of the chief causes of failure, see Kyōto-shi 1972, 137–39.

25. For a still-peerless inquiry into the merchant ethos exemplified by the Mitsui texts, see Miyamoto 1977.

26. Crawcour 1962, 69–72.

27. The major source of early Mitsui history is the *Record of Our Business* (*Shōbaiki*), completed by Takatoshi's third son in 1722, which is far fuller than the *Record of Our House* (*Kadenki*), completed anonymously the same year. See Mitsui Bunko 1971, 16–22 (*Kadenki*) and 23–46 (*Shōbaiki*).

28. Takahira's *Will*, discussed below, names fifteen of the shops established by his house (an incomplete figure), nine of them predating Takatoshi's death. For the names and founding dates, see Mitsui Bunko 1971, 765–68 (in the *kaidai*, or commentary, section of the volume).

29. The titles are *gofuku goyōtashi* (awarded in 1687) and *kingin on-kawase goyōtashi* (awarded in 1691.) For discussion, see Kyōto-shi 1972, 151–44.

30. For biographical overviews, see Mura 1992, 57–77; and Kyōto-shi 1973, 258–60. Although the number of Takatoshi's clerks is unclear, records indicate that just three of the Mitsui shops were employing nearly one thousand clerks around 1770. See Nishioka 1992, 179.

31. Articles 1 and 2 of Takahira's *Will*, in Mitsui Bunko 1971, 1. "Divine protection" is the translation of *myōga*.

32. The document is the *Kanai shikihō-chō*, in Mitsui Bunko 1971, 66–78. The unnumbered articles are sufficiently unsystematic in organization to suggest accrual and revision over time.

33. Mitsui Bunko 1971, 66–67. This long preamble appears to be the original and core statement of a text that, issued shortly after Takatoshi's death, may otherwise repeat accumulated shop rules. See Mitsui Bunko 1971, 774–75 (in the *kaidai* section).

34. Scarcely any page of the *Regulations* lacks counsel on good behavior. For a representative sample, as well as recurrent insistence on keeping up the ledgers for comings and goings (*deiri-chō, tashitsu-chō*), personal expenses (*kozukai-chō*), loans (*kari-chō*), shop accounts (*kingin deiri-chō*), meals (*daidokoro-chō*), purchases (*kaimono-chō*), and other activities, see Mitsui Bunko 1971, 68–70.

35. See, for example, Mitsui Bunko 1971, 69–70, 72–74. The article concerning monthly readings is on p. 83.

36. Mitsui Bunko 1971, 67, 70–72.

37. Mitsui Bunko 1971, 37 (in the *Shōbaiki*).

38. See Mitsui Bunko 1971, *Sōchiku yuisho*, 1–16. For a selective and problematic paraphrase prepared for Eleanor Hadley, see Roberts 1974, 499–503.

39. What I call the prologue consists of the first six articles; what I call the conclusion consists of the final four articles. The headings of many of the sections, which include the remaining forty-one articles, appear below. Because neither the articles nor the sections are numbered, occasional ambiguities in distinguishing one article or section from another may result in somewhat different counts by different readers.

40. In opening and closing, Takahira represents his *Will* as a reaffirmation of his father's will (which is not extant). Mitsui Bunko 1971, 1, 15. "One seed, joint prosperity" is a translation of *dōmyō kyōeki* (Mitsui Bunko 1971, 1), sometimes rendered as *dōmyō itchi*. For analysis of Takatoshi's origination of the principle, see Mitsui Bunko 1971, 762–63.

41. The *Will* identifies Takahira's successors in his own lineage as heads of the consolidated house (*sōryōke, sō-oyabun*). It names six houses collectively (his own and five fraternal houses) as main houses (*honke*) and three others as affiliates (*renke*). See Mitsui Bunko 1971, 2–4.

42. The senior or main house was typically called the *honke,* the junior or branch houses *bunke* or *bekke.*

43. Mitsui Bunko 1971, 15.

44. The first five sections cover the essential financial arrangements. See Mitsui Bunko 1971, "In the Matter of the Headship and Its Execution" (Oyabun no koto narabi ni shioki no jidai), nine foundational articles, pp. 2–6; "In the Matter of Retirees" (Inkyō-ryō no koto), eight articles, pp. 6–7; "In the Matter of Younger Sons" (Jinan narabi ni basshi), three articles, pp. 7–8; "In the Matter of Daughters" (Joshi no koto), four articles pp. 8–9; and "On the Need for Relief Funds" (Ryōken arubeku no koto), four articles, pp. 9–10. For discussion, see Kyōto-shi 1973, 270–74.

45. "In the Matter of Training Sons and Grandsons for Entry into the Household Business" (Shison kagyō-iri minarai no koto), one article, in Mitsui Bunko 1971, 11–12.

46. Mitsui Bunko 1971, 6 (opening of the Inkyō no ryō section), and 3 (fourth article of the Oyabun section). Should we assume that the girl's husband would then be adopted as the family head? Takahira does not say.

47. Mitsui Bunko 1971, 3 (second article of the Oyabun section).

48. "In the Matter of the Duties of the Councilors" (Motojime yaku no koto), one article, in Mitsui Bunko 1971, 14–15.

49. "In the Matter of the Managerial Duties of the Executive Board" (Ōmotokata tōryō yaku no koto), one article, Mitsui Bunko 1971, 10. For two documents (dating from 1709 and 1710) that put the formation of both the Councilors and the Executive Board well before the completion of the *Will* and that confirm the membership of several councilors on the Executive Board, see ibid., 199–213 and 259–62.

50. For revealing samples in English of popular moralizing, see Ramseyer 1979; and Ooms 1996, 363–73 ("Regulations for the Villages of All Provinces").

51. "On the Prohibition of New Ventures" (Shinpōshō no kinsei no koto), one article, in Mitsui Bunko 1971, 11.

52. "On How to Understand Service to the Regime" (Kōgi aitsutome sōrō no wa kokoroeru-beki koto), one article, in Mitsui Bunko 1971, 12; and "In the Matter of Devotion to the Buddhas and the Gods" (Busshin shinjin no koto), one article, in ibid., 13–14.

53. For an introduction to these complex matters, see Matsumoto 1967; Kyōto-shi 1973, 258–82; and Hiramatsu 1981.

54. For a powerful analysis of the role of merchant intellectuals during the eighteenth century in establishing ideological and practical grounds for the rightful role of merchant expertise in the polity, see Najita 1987. This development followed the formation of houses like the Mitsui, however, and never eventuated in robust legal protection of them.

55. There are many resonances here with the essay by David Spafford in this volume.

REFERENCES

Befu 1976

Befu, Ben. *Worldly Mental Calculations: An Annotated Translation of Ihara Saikaku's Seken munezan'yō.* Occasional Papers 5. Berkeley: University of California Press, 1976.

Chikamatsu 1953

Chikamatsu Monzaemon. *Shinjū ten no Amijima.* English translation in Shively 1953, 63–96.

Chikamatsu 1958

Chikamatsu Monzaemon. *Shinjū ten no Amijima.* Japanese text in Shigetomo Ki, ed. *Nihon koten bungaku taikei.* Vol. 49: *Chikamatsu jōruri-shū,* 355–87. Tokyo: Iwanami Shoten, 1958.

Crawcour 1962

Crawcour, E. S. "Some Observations on Merchants: A Translation of Mitsui Takafusa's *Chōnin Kōken Roku,* with an introduction and notes. In *Transactions of the Asiatic Society of Japan,* 3rd ser., 8 (1962): 1–139.

Gerstle 1996

Gerstle, C. Andrew. "The Hero as Murderer in the Plays of Chikamatsu." *Monumenta Nipponica* 51:3 (1996): 317–56.

Gerstle 1999

Gerstle, C. Andrew. "Takemoto Gidayū and the Individualistic Spirit of Osaka Theater." In *Osaka: The Merchants' Capital of Early Modern Japan,* edited by James L. McClain and Wakita Osamu, 104–24. Ithaca, NY: Cornell University Press, 1999.

Hiramatsu 1981

Hiramatsu Yoshirō. "Tokugawa Law." Translated by Dan Fenno Henderson. *Law in Japan* 14 (1981): 1–48.

Koizumi 2010

Koizumi Yoshinaga, ed. *Kinsei chōnin shisō shūsei,* 17 vols. Tokyo: Kuresu Shuppan, 2010.

Kyōto-shi 1972

Kyōto-shi, ed. *Kyōto no rekishi.* Vol. 5: *Kinsei no tenkai.* Tokyo: Gakugei Shorin, 1972.

Kyōto-shi 1973

Kyōto-shi, ed. *Kyōto no rekishi.* Vol. 6: *Dentō no teichaku.* Tokyo: Gakugei Shorin, 1973.

Matsumoto 1967

Matsumoto Shirō. "Kanbun, Genroku-ki ni okeru daimyo-gashi no tokushitsu." In *Mitsui bunko ronsō* 1 (1967): 33–112.

Mitsui Bunko 1971

Mitsui Bunko, ed. *Mitsui jigyō-shi: Shiryō-hen.* Vol. 1. Tokyo: Mitsui Bunko, 1973.

Mitsui Bunko 1980

Mitsui Bunko, ed. *Mitsui jigyō-shi: Honpen.* Vol. 1. Tokyo: Mitsui Bunko, 1980.

Miyamoto 1977

Miyamoto Mataji. *Kinsei shōnin ishiki no kenkyū.* Tokyo: Kōdansha, 1977.

Miyamoto 2003

Miyamoto Mataji. *Gōshō retsuden.* Tokyo: Kōdansha, 2003.

Mura 1992

Mura Reiko. "Shinkyū shōmin no kōtai." In *Nihon no kinsei.* Vol. 5: *Shōmin no katsudō,* edited by Mura Reiko, 43–88. Tokyo: Chūō Kōronsha, 1992.

Nagatomo 2005
    Nagatomo Chiyoji. *Chōhōki no chōhōki: Seikatsu-shi hyakka jiten hakkutsu*. Kyoto: Rinsen Shoten, 2005.
Nagatomo 2004–9
    Nagatomo Chiyoji, ed. *Chōhōki shiryō shūsei*, 45 vols. Kyoto: Rinsen Shoten, 2004–9.
Najita 1987
    Najita, Tetsuo. *Visions of Virtue in Tokugawa Japan: The Kaitokudō Merchant Academy of Osaka*. Chicago: University of Chicago Press, 1987.
Nishioka 1992
    Nishioka Sei. "Kinsei toshi to ōdana." In *Nihon no kinsei*. Vol. 9: *Toshi no jidai*, edited by Yoshida Nobuyuki, 173–220. Tokyo: Chūō Kōronsha, 1992.
Ooms 1996
    Ooms, Herman. *Tokugawa Village Practice: Class, Status, Power, Law*. Berkeley: University of California Press, 1996.
Roberts 1974
    Roberts, John G. *Mitsui: Three Generations of Japanese Business*. New York: Weatherhill, 1974.
Ramseyer 1979
    Ramseyer, J. Mark. "Thrift and Diligence: House Codes of Tokugawa Merchant Families." In *Monumenta Nipponica* 34:2 (1979): 209–30.
Shively 1953
    Shively, Donald H. *The Love Suicide at Amijima: A Study of a Japanese Domestic Tragedy by Chikamatsu Monzaemon*. Cambridge, MA: Harvard University Press. 1953.
Shively 1978
    Shively, Donald H. "The Social Environment of Tokugawa Kabuki." In *Studies in Kabuki: Its Acting, Music, and Historical Context,* edited by James R. Brandon, William P. Malm, and Donald H. Shively, 1–61. Honolulu: University Press of Hawai'i Press, 1978.
Suwa, Shinoda, and Tsuji 1979
    Suwa Haruo, Shinoda Jun'ichi, and Tsuji Tatsuya, eds. *Zusetsu Nihon no koten*. Vol. 16: *Chikamatsu Monzaemon*. Tokyo: Shūeisha, 1979.
Tomiya (1729) 2010
    Tomiya Shōgetsu. *Kanai yōjinshū* (*The Family's Book of Bewares*). 1729. In Koizumi 2010, vol. 5.

10

Ideal Families in Crisis

Official and Fictional Archetypes at the Turn of the Nineteenth Century

David Atherton

The vernacular literature of early modern Japan describes a dizzying constellation of families. They look very different in the adultery stories of Ihara Saikaku, for example, the love suicide plays of Chikamatsu Monzaemon, the ghostly tales of Ueda Akinari, the bathhouse conversations of Shikitei Sanba, and the historical fantasies of Kyokutei Bakin. Here I explore one version of the family that achieved prominence in commercial print around the turn of the nineteenth century. It is small, stripped to basic roles (father, mother, son, daughter-in-law, daughter) and beleaguered by hardship. It is also sustained by members, steadfastly devoted to one another, who sacrifice gladly, and largely without help, to stay together. For such exemplary behavior, they are ultimately rewarded and celebrated by figures in authority.

This family is not a stem household *ie*, though it does sometimes include three generations. Nor do its trials realistically reflect contemporary life, though some are grounded in fact. A product of ethical instruction on the one hand, and sensationalized fiction on the other, this family transcends the particularities of domestic experience to appeal, with presumptive universality, to the core values and visceral emotions that attend primal relationships. The works I examine deal with small casts of players in extremis whose suffering and survival speak to the fears of the time as well as the changing resolutions available to a changing society.

What is striking about this family is its appearance in both official and popular media. I begin with the *Official Records of Filial Piety* (*Kankoku kōgiroku*), a fifty-volume compendium produced by the Tokugawa shogunate over the course of the 1790s and published in the commercial print market in 1801. It includes 787 narrative depictions of morally edifying behavior assembled as part of the regime's reform efforts during the Kansei era (1789–1801). Not all entries focus on familial relationships, but the vast majority do. And the story they tell is of filial children, loyal wives and daughters-in-law, and steadfast brothers who strive heroically for their households. Ostensibly accounts of real people, the narratives project the idealized patterns of fables.

The family of the *Official Records*—stripped down, beset by troubles, and redeemed by valiant sacrifice—also appears in the revenge fiction that thrived in commercial print from the mid-1790s through the first decade of the nineteenth century. Although revenge was a compelling theme in popular tales from the seventeenth century (and long a staple of medieval literature), the rage for the subject at the turn of the nineteenth century was unparalleled. So great was the demand that the popular writer Shikitei Sanba complained, in a work from 1805, that a writer had to "split his brains and wrack his guts, getting not a wink of sleep, to think up new forms of vengeance, uncommon murders, stirring encounters, and dangerous escapes."[1] The violence frames tales, at heart, all about families. Their moral logic derives from the power of filial piety, as selfless children undergo all manner of hardship to avenge the murder of parents. Often aided by family members but rarely by outsiders, they struggle against poverty, the trials of the road, illness, and other afflictions to kill their antagonists and restore family cohesion. Only at the end do the authorities step in to reward their edifying accomplishments.

The narratives in the *Official Records* and the popular revenge fiction are not identical, since the latter leans on violent and fantastic elements hardly compatible with the former. Yet their conception of virtue and their emphasis on family cohesion through sacrifice are so strikingly similar that a common impetus derived from a shared social context appears at work. That context was turbulent. If the Tokugawa "age of peace" was never free of upheaval, the decades at the end of the eighteenth century saw exceptional crises, particularly of depopulation. A result of both periodic famine in earlier years and the widespread practice of infanticide and abortion, the demographic crisis was brought to a head by the catastrophic Tenmei famine of 1782–87, which hit the northeast and northern Kantō with terrible force.[2] Hundreds of thousands starved to death. Many more fled to seek better lives elsewhere, leaving fields untended, production slashed, and villages hauntingly empty.[3] As death and migration devastated families, shogun and daimyo focused on efforts to return labor to the countryside. In Edo, which had always absorbed migrants from surrounding provinces, the Tenmei years produced an unsettling flood of refugees who sometimes engaged in disturbing and destructive behavior.[4] Among the participants in the violent rice riots that broke out in 1787 were impoverished arrivals from afar.[5]

Disruption of the family thus became tied to larger concerns over social unrest. And recovery of the family increasingly became the target of official and popular action alike. Authorities adopted policies for returning migrants to the land, discouraging infanticide, and promoting marriage and childbirth. Popular initiatives included publishing admonitory pamphlets against infanticide and proposing monetary rewards to support the establishment of branch households.[6] One symptom of alarm was the appearance, in the pages of popular fiction, of grotesquely exaggerated illustrations of abortionists.[7]

It was in this context of trouble, I argue, that a highly idealized vision of the family became a compelling vehicle for projecting moral clarity and inspiring social regeneration. As an all but universal unit of community forged by both biological and emotional ties, the family could appeal imaginatively, as other units could not, to readers otherwise divided by status and geography.[8] Because it was so visibly under assault and so broadly indicative of societal well-being, moreover, the family was key to any turn toward recovery. And at a moment when official institutions were under suspicion for maladministration and incompetence, the family remained the most trusted organ of allegiance. Stripped down to basic relationships that evoked potent values (filial piety, marital harmony, brotherhood), it could project an appealing fantasy of virtue ascendant, even in a time of strife. Regeneration had to start at home. We shall see, however, that conceptions of home would prove dynamic. The idealized family of the *Official Records* and the revenge fiction boom would mutate into something startlingly fluid within a generation.

THE SHOGUNATE'S MODEL FAMILIES

Matsudaira Sadanobu, who came to power as the chief senior councilor (*rōjū*) of the shogunate in 1787, initiated wide-ranging reforms that would begin to arrest social and economic crisis. Making the family a foundational concern and popular pedagogy a core mission, he instructed members of the shogunal academy in 1789 to assemble the names and stories of moral exemplars throughout the realm.[9] They subsequently solicited from central and domainal administrators both lists and accounts of subjects who had been formally recognized for acts of filial piety and other "exemplary" (*kitoku*) behavior.[10] Because the practice of acknowledging such paragons had long been established in the domains, records were abundant.[11] The shogunal academy compiled and edited the information over the following decade, publishing it in 1801 as the *Official Records of Filial Piety* (one of the shogunate's very few ventures into the popular publishing market).

The *Official Records* names individuals involved in no fewer than 8,563 instances of virtuous behavior.[12] Most entries date from the 1780s and early 1790s, but many date from midcentury and some as early as 1602.[13] The information is carefully grouped, first by province, then by jurisdiction: areas under direct shogunal control come before daimyo domains and care is taken to list the larger domains before the smaller. Each entry includes the name of the domainal lord as well as the location, age, and social status of the exemplar. Men are characterized by status (townsman or peasant, for example); women are described in relation to men (daughter of the peasant Uheimon; widow of the peasant Katsuemon). Crucially, each exemplar is defined by the virtue being recognized. While more than 60 percent of the cases illustrate the filial piety invoked in the work's title, other familial virtues are also celebrated: female fidelity, brotherly harmony, and household harmony. The compound virtue of "loyal filiality" appears on occasion, as do virtues not explicitly concerned with family, such as loyalty and diligence in agriculture.[14] To read the lists is to take a panoramic tour of the moral geography of the realm (from major cities and castle towns to villages and small islands such as Oki and Tsushima) and to find everywhere a sample of edifying figures diverse in status and walks of life.

Systematically winnowed, the collection omits much of the information submitted for review to focus on commoners—farmers and townsmen—and low-ranking samurai.[15] Its intended audience, in effect, seems to be not an elite expected to perform exemplary service but a general populace most vulnerable to hardship. Singled out for narrative elaboration are 787 "exceptionally outstanding" cases.[16] To make the material accessible to common readers, the editors recruited Ōta Nanpo (1749–1823), a shogunal retainer deeply involved in the milieu of commercial fiction.[17] An exemplary stylist, Nanpo experimented with different idioms, seeking an approach that would combine the accessibility of popular fiction with a tone of authority befitting a shogunal production.[18] The resulting narratives, though individually succinct and written in a straightforward style, contribute to a massive publication of fifty volumes.

What did the shogunate hope to achieve through such an undertaking? One answer appears in the notes that open the first volume. "If the hearts of those who read this work are roused, it will serve as an aid to moral cultivation (fūka)."[19] Identifying just what type of "cultivation" is meant to be modeled by so many biographies might be daunting were there not such consistency in the narratives. We find the basic message in the story of the townsman Hikoshichi, a "filial exemplar" from Hōki Province, who was formally recognized and rewarded by his lord in 1792.[20]

From the time Hikoshichi was six, we are told, his father suffered from paralysis and was unable to walk. "The impoverished household became yet poorer," and "because of the afflictions of hunger and thirst, his mother likely thought it difficult to go on living there and left for parts unknown." Young Hikoshichi, left alone to care for his ailing father, makes the rounds of the town to beg for food and, on occasion, the saké his father craves. At fifteen, he begins working for hire, scraping together enough money to buy back the hocked family home from the sympathetic lender (who returns it at half price, so impressed is he by Hikoshichi's fortitude). Hikoshichi ministers faithfully to his father, personally feeding him every day, but is sometimes kept late by work. When his angrily impatient father hurls a tray of food at him, Hikoshichi "soothed and coaxed him and devoted himself all the more to filial care." Following the death of the father, Hikoshichi faithfully carries out the funerary rites and gathers nearby relatives for the major service marking the seventh anniversary. "Fond of saké, Hikoshichi reportedly grew drunk and began to cry out of yearning for his father, raising his voice and grieving." In 1792, at the age of thirty-three, he was formally recognized by the domainal lord for his filial behavior and rewarded with silver.

Like most households in the *Official Records,* Hikoshichi's is burdened, not least by the departure of the mother, who serves as a quiet foil in the narrative. When the going gets tough, she gets going—right out the door, abandoning her family, as did many others who struck out alone to seek their fortunes during the hard times of Tenmei. Hikoshichi, by contrast, is made all the more devoted by hardship. The news that extended relations live nearby comes as a surprise, since the text never hints that they ever provided or were entreated for help. Hikoshichi devises a means of survival on his own. And he does so, the text intimates, with love. He repeatedly brings suffering upon himself to accord delight to his father and sheds tears of grief years after losing him. Dry-eyed in the face of poverty and the occasional recriminations of his father, Hikoshichi sobs in bereavement.

Here the text suggests that physical hardship pales before the emotional pain of family dissolution. And with its invocations of tears and the sympathy inspired in onlookers by Hikoshichi's ardor, the text invites readers to feel that emotional pain. Without overt moralizing, the *Official Records* relies on readers' identification with prototypical characters (in this case, a son under stress) to convert a basic representation *of* the family into an appeal *for* the family. In the wake of the Tenmei crises, when cities lured mounting numbers of migrants from villages and towns, Hikoshichi's story makes an appeal for rootedness—for placing family first and finding contentment in the choice.

Variations on this story recur throughout the *Official Records.* Hardship strikes a family, sometimes from within (a ne'er-do-well, an alcoholic, a hurler of insults), but uncomplaining members stick things out willingly and together. Indeed, drawing on mutual affection, many seem to find happiness in hardship. The message is one of family cohesion first. The focus, moreover, is narrow. Extended families and distant relatives—let alone neighborhood associations and domainal officials—disappear from almost all narratives. In some instances, self-help becomes the very mark of exemplary virtue.

Such is the case of Sayo and her daughter, residents of the castle town of Wakamatsu in Michinoku.[21] Because the business of the blacksmith husband goes bad, the family must relinquish its home to become renters, then edges toward collapse when the husband falls ill. The family son goes into an apprenticeship, while Sayo and the twelve-year-old daughter take to weaving reed sieves—work barely sufficient to cover the cost of miso and firewood. A neighbor suggests to Sayo that "it must be trying [to get by] with just your strength as a lone woman. If you could receive some aid from the lord, surely that would be of at least some help."

But Sayo replies: "Taking care of one's husband in sickness is the proper work of a wife. I should not seek aid from outside. As long as I do not fall ill myself, I will find a way to care for him, and should simply look to the day of his recovery."[22] The daughter concurs: "It will be bad for my father's recovery if we accept aid from the lord without reason. As long as my mother lives, she and I will use our strength together and there should not be any problem." Observers are so moved that one of the town officials appeals on his own initiative to the domainal lord. The family is rewarded with rice and the daughter is praised by the magistrate.

Why does the *Official Records* make official intervention a last recourse (and one pursued by outsiders)? The point suggests the deep investment of the compilers in the family itself as the bulwark against social disorder. By effectively advocating that problems be solved within the household, they stressed resourcefulness and encouraged readers to feel empowered, not oppressed, by their family roles. Sayo's story holds out the promise that perseverance is strengthening—that performance of the role of "wife" has greater power than a daimyo's silver.

Implied within this promise, however, may be the straitened condition of daimyo coffers. The compilers likely grasped a popular skepticism about the possibility of official support; they doubtless grasped as well the limited means of the authorities to ameliorate most instances of suffering. Making self-sufficiency itself the sign of virtue, they achieved two aims at a single stroke: promoting family regeneration, and tempering expectations of external support.

Did they actually expect readers to embrace the message? Sugano Noriko describes the compilation as "an instrument of indoctrination under the rubric of popular enlightenment and renewal."[23] But because it was primarily meant to "create an impression of a unified political and moral realm," the goal was not so much promoting virtue as advertising an idealized vision of the Tokugawa order.[24] Niels van Steenpaal goes a step further, arguing that the *Official Records* is essentially a "performance" of the shogunate's benevolent governance, a demonstration of unity and propriety in the realm. Gestures toward educating commoners and inspiring virtue are no more than gestures. In fact, he suggests, the work may not have been intended for purchase at all. The mere appearance of the massive compendium in bookstores "performed" the purpose of witnessing good rule.[25]

Perhaps. But then why go to the trouble of crafting so many biographies and engaging Ōta Nanpo to make them readable? We have little evidence of how widely the work sold. Given its size, the cost would have been prohibitive for many.[26] It seems likely that Matsudaira Sadanobu, who resigned as senior councilor eight years before the project reached completion, had envisioned a more substantial print run than it finally received. Consider, though, that Sadanobu was a fervent believer in the moral and political power of books, as evidenced by his own voluminous reading and writing; his dabbling in the style of popular satirical fiction; and his concern with the ideological influence of commercial print on an expanding readership, which was keen enough to inspire new censorship protocols.[27]

He was also critically concerned with family regeneration. As lord of Shirakawa domain, he had not only sponsored financial incentives for marriage but, in an effort to combat abortion and infanticide, deployed performers: he enlisted Buddhist priests to explicate the dangers of hell with picture scrolls; he dispatched mediums to give voice to the spirits of dead children before village women.[28] As Satō Miyuki points out, these endeavors involved narrative persuasion aimed at the "ears and eyes" of audiences. This is the same confidence in story, and its appeal to feeling, that animates the *Official Records*.[29]

Only a sense of a real readership, I think, can account for the ingenious drama of narratives designed to be gripping. The tale of Kamematsu of Shinano is paradigmatic.[30] On an autumn evening in 1788, Kamematsu and his father are hunting in the mountains when a wolf attacks the father. The youth rushes to his aid, beats the animal with stones, and even tries to poke out its eyeballs with his thumbs. The wolf dies, the father survives, and Kamematsu is rewarded. The text summarizes his achievement: "Kamematsu was eleven this year and a delicate boy, but his ardor in aiding his father was enough to kill such a fierce beast. This was entirely a result of the depth of his filial heart."[31] The essence of the story is familiar: a protagonist discovers the inner reserves of strength that enable the survival of the family. And the story resonates with others to insist that honoring familial bonds—whether to a paralyzed father, an alcoholic brother, a sickly husband, or a vituperative mother-in-law—is a hard but salvific choice: one as grand as killing a wolf with one's bare hands. But the thrilling staging of the wolf fight itself seems baffling without an audience. The *Official Records* may surely have been a publishing performance designed to edify the browsers of bookshops. Readers, too, appear indispensable to an effort aimed at familial regeneration through artful instruction.

A CHANGING MARKET FOR FICTION

As the compilation of the *Official Records* was under way, changes were taking place in the world of popular fiction. Because of the heightened censorship protocols introduced by Matsudaira Sadanobu, writers and publishers grew cautious about material that might be thought to harbor politically satirical subtexts and, consequently, shifted away from the sophisticated humor ascendant in the 1780s to more accessible and moralistic plots that might prove popular among the increasingly literate consumers in the provinces. The question was, What material would sell best?[32]

Sales from the mid-1790s indicated that revenge plots might be key to larger markets. Nansenshō Somahito, for example, published in 1795 *The Blossoming of a Righteous Woman: A Revenge* (*Katakiuchi gijo no hanabusa*), an unexpected hit featuring a beautiful young woman who, unwittingly entangled in a vengeance between her fiancé and her father, sacrifices herself to save them both.[33] *Blossoming* is plot-driven, straightforward, derivative, and infused with a simple pathos rooted in family relationships. Its success helped push publishers and writers toward the formulas of revenge narratives. Featuring a murder in the first pages and a vengeance in the last, the plots appeared compelling even to inexperienced readers and—as studies in filial piety—were relatively safe from censorship. For all their violence and fantasy, moreover, they focused on affectively charged family dilemmas that readers from different walks of life could recognize at some level. Like the compilers of the *Official Records*, the producers of revenge fiction treated the drama of the family as a door to the heart of the common reader.

In the wake of *Blossoming of a Righteous Woman*, revenge works appeared with great frequency throughout the 1790s and, in the first years of the nineteenth century, flooded the fiction market.[34] Shikitei Sanba's complaints about the pressure to fabricate plots are illuminated by the career of Santō Kyōden, whose works I analyze below.[35] Kyōden was a best-selling author of (among other genres) illustrated fiction, a type of book in which narration and dialogue are written into the blank spaces of the illustrations that dominate each page.[36] He turned to the revenge theme in earnest in 1804, a year in which roughly half of the sixty works of illustrated fiction published in Edo were revenge tales.[37] By 1806, three of Kyōden's five illustrated works for the year were revenge tales, and the following year, it was five out of five. By 1809, however, he began relegating vengeance to a subplot and ceased putting "revenge" into his titles, and by 1810, the craze for vengeance had largely run its course—in Kyōden's fiction and in the publishing market in general.

Vengeance held a privileged place in Tokugawa law as one of the few acts of deadly violence permitted to nonofficials: an avenger could licitly redress the murder of a senior family member after applying for, and securing in advance, the approval of authorities. Instances of licit revenge were, in fact, rare under the Tokugawa regime (perhaps one hundred successful revenges over 270 years of rule).[38] But their spectacular quality captured the imagination of audiences on both the page and the stage throughout the Edo period. Authors and playwrights varied considerably in their treatment of revenge. If the conventions required murders at the beginning and the end of the action, the intervening plots unfolded with exceptional moral ambiguity in the work of Ihara Saikaku, for example, and kaleidoscopic emotional complexity in *The Treasury of Loyal Retainers* (*Kanadehon chūshingura*, 1748). My focus here, the illustrated revenge fiction from the turn of the nineteenth century, turned away from all such subtlety, however, to rely on formulas lacking in irony or equivocation. Writers eschewed realism, relied on ideological tropes and stereotypical characters, and delivered unadorned prose further distilled by illustration. Very few based their tales on historical episodes. The results became so clichéd, grumbled Shikitei Sanba that "this one or that one—they're all alike, all dancing to the same tune. Look at the illustrations alone, and you've already grasped the plot of the whole thing!"[39]

The same goes for the casts of characters. One good son resembles the next. Much like the protagonists in the *Official Records*, each lead figure is exemplary.

FIGURE 10.1. The poor but harmonious family at the outset of *The Women of Okazaki*.
From Santō Kyōden, *The Women of Okazaki: A Revenge* (*Katakiuchi Okazaki joroshu*, 1807). Courtesy of Waseda University Library.

Children are always filial, wives loyal, siblings committed to one another. And each, to signal lofty character, is attractive and intelligent. These characters make up typically small households enacting the core Confucian relations of husband and wife, parent and child, sibling and sibling.[40] They conventionally belong, moreover, to the samurai community, perhaps because revenge literature arose when vengeance was primarily a prerogative of warriors. Although commoners engaged in licit vengeance by the mid-Edo period, they seldom appear in the fiction.[41] Still, the samurai protagonists remain sufficiently accessible—they are variously low ranking, impoverished, or living in obscurity as *rōnin*—to appeal to a range of readers.

More important, the appeal of the stories turns not on any particular actor but the collectivity of the household as their true protagonist. The point is best conveyed by the illustrations, which are critical to each tale. For example, *The Women of Okazaki: A Revenge* (*Katakiuchi Okazaki joroshu*, 1807), by Santō Kyōden, opens with an image of a three-generational *ie* gathered about the hearth in a run-down dwelling (fig. 10.1). The aging head and his wife sit close to the fire; an unmarried daughter massages the father's shoulders; the heir and his wife work nearby, weaving sedge hats to provide some income; their four-year-old son lies asleep behind a screen. Everyone is smiling. The heir's

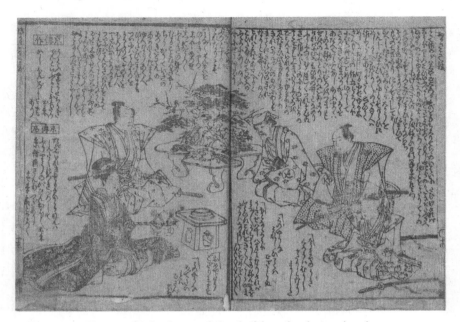

FIGURE 10.2. The avenging family rewarded and celebrated at the story's end.
From Santō Kyōden, *The Women of Okazaki: A Revenge* (*Katakiuchi Okazaki joroshu*, 1807). Collection of the author.

wife addresses her mother-in-law: "What do you think, mother? We may be poor, but with such filial children, could anything be more delightful?"[42] This family—content, hard-working, affectionate, and united—would not be out of place in the *Official Records*.

In the illustration that closes the story, the household is united again, but this time in fine clothing and arranged around an auspicious botanical display (fig. 10.2). The members have also changed. We see the aged mother, the heir (now the household head), and his young son. We also see the younger sister and her newly acquired husband. Absent are the aging father and the daughter-in-law. Even so, the members again express their contentment: "Nothing could be as happy as this!" "Our former sufferings now seem like an old tale."

Together, the images encapsulate a narrative focused more on the household unit than any individual player. As portrayed here and throughout these illustrated revenge works, the family is united (if impoverished) at the outset and then imperiled by an act of murderous violence. Subsequently cast out from home, the protagonists take to the road where, in disguise and frequently close to starvation, they endure punishing hardships before accomplishing their redeeming acts of revenge. The face of the household changes as some members die and others assume new roles. Yet through the act of revenge the family achieves recognition from authorities (typically with full reintegration into the social order) and recovers security.

In fundamental ways, the narrative mimics the accounts in the *Official Records*: an idealized family faces crisis but, through sacrifice, achieves recognition and security. Drama is paramount, however, as murder supplants more prosaic trouble and the road epitomizes vulnerability and isolation. Extremity is further heightened by the introduction of villains who personify affliction (they are calamity made flesh) and choices that put moral imperatives in collision and lives on the line. Still, the addition of villains and existential choices ultimately reinforces the worldview of the *Official Records*: the family, as the essential unit of identity and meaning, must somehow cohere if futures are possible.

The villain is typically a loner, unfettered by the bonds of affection or obligation, who is loyal to no one but himself. Authorities provide little protection against him. Thus, for example, the villain in *The Women of Okazaki* is Kanpeita, an unemployed samurai depicted as large, terrifying, clothed in black, and capped with wild hair. When his bribes and threats fail to persuade the virtuous father to permit a marriage with his younger daughter, Kanpeita murders the father, kidnaps the daughter, and bludgeons to death the daughter-in-law who intervenes. These acts set in motion the quest for vengeance. In killing the villain, the avengers will enact a fantasy of human control over the evil forces he represents and symbolically assert the power of a united family over avaricious self-interest.

Their corporate commitment is underscored by the chilling choices family members are willing to make on the way to executing justice. In *The Women of Okazaki*, the heir Sagorō (son of the murdered household head and husband of the murdered daughter-in-law) finds himself in a triple bind: he must avenge his dead father, care for his ailing mother, and serve as father and mother alike to his young son. As the family slides into poverty and starvation, Sagorō discovers that his mother has been feeding her own meager ration to his son. He prepares to make a horrible sacrifice:

> "In China there was a case of a filial son who buried his child under the earth [to save his parents]. If I can bring myself to kill my son, then I can tend to my mother." He quietly beckoned the child into the shadows. Because he was just four years old, he was completely innocent. Seeing his father beckoning him, he thought, "Maybe he will give me some rice." When Sagorō saw him looking so happy, he felt pierced to the heart and began to cry.[43]

His mother is making a similarly drastic decision:

> "Because Sagorō is a filial son, he treats me with care but gives my grandson just scraps, and he himself goes without eating for days at a time. Recently he looks so thin and weak, not at all the way he looked in the past. I've turned out to be an obstacle to the revenge, and my grandson is so pitiable as well. Since I'm just a useless old person, it's better that I end my life." Resolving to die, she began praying the

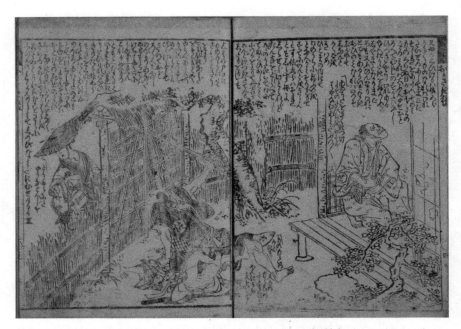

FIGURE 10.3. Virtuous violence brings the family to the verge of self-destruction.
From Santō Kyōden, *The Women of Okazaki: A Revenge* (*Katakiuchi Okazaki joroshu*, 1807). Courtesy of Waseda University Library.

nenbutsu, picked up a razor, and was ready to slit her throat. Sagorō knew nothing of this. Without telling his mother, and careful that she not suspect, he dragged his son outside, stuffed a handkerchief in his mouth, drew the dagger attached to his scabbard, and was just about to stab the child in the throat.[44]

The illustration depicts the household at this moment (fig. 10.3). Starkly unlike the harmonious family portrayed when the narrative opened, the members face away from one other as the mother touches a blade to her throat and Sagorō raises a dagger against a terrified child pinned to the ground.

The paradox here is inescapable: the very selflessness that demonstrates familial virtue puts the family at risk of extinction. Sagorō's house cannot survive suicide and infanticide. By posing choices that push virtue to violent limits, the revenge fiction assails the reader's emotions, and in so doing introduces questions about the viability of ethical imperatives for households in extremis.

Only to forestall those questions. For, just as the blades are raised, a voice calls out from the gate, "Wait!" And there appears the lost daughter-in-law—Sagorō's wife, the child's mother—who, bludgeoned earlier by the villain, has seemingly returned from the grave. (We will learn that the apparition is a magical bird who has assumed the wife's form to rescue the family.) With this supernatural intervention, the family recovers. Sagorō and his mother put away their blades and the child rushes to his mother's breast. The apparition addresses Sagorō:

> "I see that you are suffering from extreme poverty, but now that I am here we can work as husband and wife, take care of your mother, raise our son, and finally attain our goal. Until we achieve that long-cherished desire, it is important that you take good care of yourself, so do not suffer over things or let yourself get ill." Comforted in this way, Sagorō regained his strength and his mother was as happy as if she had been brought back to life.[45]

Thus restored, the family is able to undertake a successful vengeance.

The whiplash of the narrative, which transforms tragedy into recovery with the turn of a page, conveys competing lessons. On the one hand, it appears to insist that a family kept intact (in this instance by the return of the wife and mother) can withstand even poverty and violence to compose the lovely tableau that closes the story. Union overcomes adversity, devotion enables the mastery of circumstances, and suffering brings reward. And by spotlighting basic relationships and primal horrors (as a father raises a sword over his son), the narrative appeals emotionally to readers of all stations, inviting them to identify with the protagonists and take pleasure in the lesson of strength through cohesion. On the other hand, however, this story appears to insist that the family cannot save itself. The returned wife is no member of a resilient household but a miraculous apparition. What reader can count on supernatural intervention?

THE DEUS EX MACHINA

The self-help urged throughout the *Official Records,* wherein families face hardship largely alone, is not absolute, of course, since outsiders sometimes assist the virtuous protagonists and authorities ultimately reward them. The revenge fiction moves well beyond such friendly intervention, though, to stage rescues, in the face of disaster, by miracle. Deus ex machina plot twists become increasingly common in the later, longer works of illustrated revenge fiction, as plots become more convoluted and the casts of characters more thickly populated. Why should this be so? If the point really is that families cannot survive as autonomous units, no matter how ardent their members, why introduce fantastic salvation rather than conventional forms of support? If the point is that fanatical virtue is more dangerous than hardship, why save families in moments of peril rather than letting them destroy themselves? Is the point simply that the miraculous meets a need for more and more plot convolutions in ever-longer works dependent on cliffhangers to maintain excitement?

The identity of the deus ex machina, which is never random, helps point to an answer. In *The Women of Okazaki,* the savior is a female mandarin duck whose mate had been killed, over the protestations of the family father, by the villain. After the father, too, is slain by that villain, the bird remembers his generous intervention and comes, supernaturally, to the aid of his family (abetting, in the process, her own quest for vengeance). The rescue is portrayed, then, as the harvest of good deeds: reward awaits those who do right.

But it is also something more. Not simply an act of (fantastical) reciprocity, the rescue is an expression of affective bonds grounded in voluntary attachments and mutual relief rather than the obligations of status or local community. The very strangeness of the deus ex machina underscores the idiosyncrasy of relationships formed through feeling and shared goodwill. And it effectively opens up the insular family of revenge fiction to the possibility of new and surprising networks of support. Below the surface magic of the apparition is the deeper magic of expanding social connection.

The affective bonds signified by the deus ex machina remained crucial to revenge fiction even as the tight focus on the insular family faded. As the turmoil of the late eighteenth century receded under the impact of the Kansei reforms, writers remained fixed on the family, but in fresh formations. The small, inward-looking household—which represented the virtuous cohesion and self-reliance projected as an antidote to migration, economic unrest, and demographic crisis—never disappeared. Yet the opening up to less conventional relationships exemplified by the deus ex machina continued in the increasingly lengthy works of the Bunka era (1804–18). Writers began to look *through* the family to a social landscape beyond its bounds. Exploring how households and individuals could cohere in unconventional varieties of community, they also suggested new approaches to identity. I turn now to an example.

INTERLOCKING FAMILIES, NAMELESS COMMUNITIES, NEGOTIABLE IDENTITIES

Near the denouement of Kyōden's *Plovers of the Tamagawa: A Revenge* (*Katakiuchi chidori no Tamagawa*, 1807), the villain Unpachi comes across six statues of the Bodhisattva Jizō on a bleak moor. Floating above the heads of the statues are the heads of six people whom Unpachi has victimized: a samurai whom he murdered in cold blood; the samurai's wife, who rebuffed the villain's advances and later died of illness; an executed man, framed by the villain for a crime he did not commit; that man's wife, who, kidnapped before her marriage and sold into a brothel by the villain, ultimately died mad; and her sister, who committed suicide out of grief. The sixth head belongs to Unpachi's mother, who slit her throat because of her son's terrible deeds. The heads glare fiercely at Unpachi and cry out the crimes he has committed against them.

Aligned side by side in the illustration, they evoke a terrifying, otherworldly community—men and women, old and young, samurai and townsmen—called into existence by Unpachi's seemingly random violence and bound together by rancor (fig. 10.4). But they are also bound by multiple connections—of blood, marriage, obligation, and goodwill—that had united them in life. These surprising connections

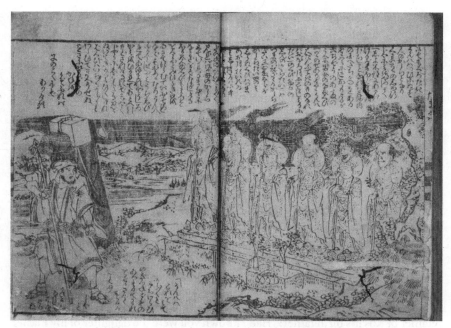

FIGURE 10.4. The deathly community of victims confronts Unpachi, in *Plovers of the Tamagawa*. From Santō Kyōden, *Plovers of the Tamagawa: A Revenge* (*Katakiuchi chidori no Tamagawa*, 1807). Courtesy of Waseda University Library.

are at the heart of a story that, in the end, is less about the disorder Unpachi wreaks on households than about the support the characters find in one another.

Thus, in an early episode of the story, we find the samurai and his wife helping the kidnapped courtesan to reunite with her family and, subsequently, to marry her lover. And before that lover is framed by Unpachi for a crime he did not commit, we find the same samurai couple helping him reconcile with his merchant father (who had disinherited him). These good turns are reciprocated. After the murder of the samurai, his widow and young daughter rely for support on both the natal and marital relatives of the courtesan. Unpachi sows misery; his victims give strength to one another.

Crucially, this strength derives from affective relations rather than social structures or conventional obligation. Rooted in chance encounters on the road that bind strangers across class and geography, the bonds are neither normative nor hierarchical, but horizontal and voluntary. And there is no suggestion that they are enabled by official activity and benevolent governance. If anything, the bonds provide a bulwark against disorder in the realm, even the failures of rulers themselves. The murdered samurai's wife and daughter turn to the former courtesan's family because they have been cast out by a cruel lord. When the courtesan's lover is wrongly executed, the culprit remains at large. The authorities guarantee neither protection nor justice.

If Unpachi brings the households together through his transgressions, the samurai's daughter, Kosan, brings them together through virtuous vengeance. Orphaned by the murder of her father and the death of her mother on the road, she remains committed to avenging her natal house even as she comes to play the role of "daughter" in a succession of other houses. Kosan acts as daughter to the ransomed courtesan and her merchant husband; then to their childless relatives; then to the courtesan's father-in-law, a wealthy bathhouse proprietor in Osaka. These families, like puzzle pieces, keep finding new ways to fit together in the face of disaster. When Kosan exacts revenge on Unpachi, she does so as the daughter of her slain father as well as of the households she enters subsequently. She is the lynchpin of a community without a name.

This vision of community—cross-class, translocal networks shifting in shape— is not without danger, since characters who assume multiple roles in multiple households in multiple locales forfeit clear family identities. Unexpected complications ensue. They arise for Kosan after she is adopted by the bathhouse proprietor and later meets, falls in love with, and marries the handsome young Kingorō. But once she discloses to him her true identity and requests aid in avenging her natal father, Kingorō blanches. He, too, had been orphaned when young and adopted into a childless household, Kingorō tells his wife. Fatefully, his birth father was a retainer of Kosan's birth father: "Had I known you were the daughter of my master, I never would have married you! Please, take this letter of separation and return to your home." Kosan sobs into her sleeve and replies: "How cruel of you. Please, think this over carefully!"[46]

In this tangle of identities, where do the obligations of the protagonists lie? Kosan and Kingorō married as members of unrelated adoptive households. Neither was born when their fathers were master and retainer. And they married for love. So, what now? The ethos of the *Official Records* would favor Kingorō: the prior and hierarchical relationship between the two families requires setting aside feeling to separate. Kosan thinks otherwise: "Even if long ago [our fathers] were bound as master and retainer, I have fallen in the world." She continues: "With my adoptive father as parent, I married you. Do not now think of me as the daughter of your master and create a barrier between our hearts!"[47] While Kingorō elevates a preordained obligation over feeling, Kosan imagines a variety of identities among which she can choose. In her quest for revenge, she affirms the bond to her natal house. In her defense of the marriage to Kingorō, she affirms the role of adopted daughter to a merchant. She crafts multiple selves without sacrificing virtue.

Kosan is the hero of the narrative; Kingorō is no match in intelligence and bravery. When the author puts the argument for self-fashioning in her mouth, he makes it the effective point of the story. Without intimating absolute self-determination or moral relativism, Kosan declares the freedom to align complex obligations at will and to navigate disparate identities through choice. Here we find a remarkable departure not only from the *Official Records* but from earlier revenge fiction as well. Remember that the heroine of *Blossoming of a Righteous Woman,* when caught between the obligations of wife and daughter, resolves the conflict through suicide.

Kingorō follows Kosan's lead and adjusts his interpretive frame: "For me, [the murderer of your father] is the enemy of my master! Whatever it takes, I will use all my strength to help you cut him down. Have no fear!"[48] The decision allows the two to stay together both as spouses and as partners in revenge. Kingorō's concerns about marriage to his "master's daughter" are quietly forgotten. But not quite, at least by the author if not by his characters. Once vengeance is achieved, the happy ending finds Kingorō rewarded with the very office and stipend previously held by his master, which, by erasing the status distinction between husband and wife, restores hierarchical propriety. This intervention suggests a need to right the status order for readers. Yet even more powerfully, I think, it affirms the boldness of the boundary-crossing at the heart of the story.

So, have we entered a moral landscape very different from the terrain of the *Official Records* and earlier revenge fiction? Yes and no. If the earlier texts indicate that hard sacrifices must be made among multiple roles and obligations, Kosan's story indicates that the multiplicity itself provides opportunities for self-definition that can be liberating. Still, the choices cannot be made with impunity or from selfish interest. The only character who switches identities heedlessly is the villain Unpachi. Nor does Kosan's story intimate that the household, with its hierarchical roles and ethical imperatives, is a source of oppression rather than stability and protection. Rather, Kosan's example suggests that in an unpredictable world, finding stability may require more than cleaving to conventional visions of the family. It may require an embrace of community and identity as dynamic, fluid, and elective.

CONCLUSION: FAMILY LEGACIES

The focus on Kosan's choices in *The Plovers of Tamagawa* points to subsequent directions in popular fiction. Decades of good harvests and population growth redirected writers from small households that must sacrifice to survive to widely connected households that embrace novel forms of community and supple visions of identity. While the families portrayed in the revenge boom had linked audiences throughout Japan as a reading public, the families of the next wave asked them to consider what held the social body together.

Thus, in *A Pure Tale of the Peak's First Flowers* (*Seidan mine no hatsu hana,* 1819), Jippensha Ikku tells the story of Sutegorō, the son of a poor *rōnin* who had been adopted into a merchant household when his parents died.[49] Disinherited through no fault of his own, Sutegorō wanders the realm, finds work in various corners of the merchant world, and—once reunited with a lost love—rediscovers his samurai lineage and achieves success. Again, self-fashioning is the theme. But the emotions that bind the hero to his merchant and samurai families come to the fore in what is regarded as the first "book of sentiment" (*ninjōbon*), a genre that would flourish through the end of the Edo period. The genre picks up, in a semi-realistic mode, the ideas explored in the story of Kosan, even as it insists with greater clarity that voluntary ties of affection are the source of union.

Fiction in a fantastic register likewise probed the changeable aspects of identity and the tensions between elective and normative communities. Kyokutei Bakin's *Eight Dog Chronicles* (*Nansō Satomi hakkenden*), arguably the most celebrated work of early modern fiction, focuses on eight mystically connected brothers who have been born from the wombs of different mothers, setting up a tangle of familial identities. This massive historical fantasy, published serially from 1814 to 1842, hinges on kaleidoscopic networks of social connection and deus ex machina plot twists that push the protagonists into situations where they must choose among family relationships of blood, affection, and supernatural affinity. And because the brothers must ultimately work together to restore a fallen lord's house and bring order to the domain, it links the consequences of those choices to the health of the polity. The work builds to a conclusion in which all relationships are at last clarified, fitting together like a magnificent puzzle. But the path to that idealized finale revels in explorations of the messiness of identity and the contingent aspects of familial and social bonds.

In retrospect, then, the decade of the *Official Records* and the revenge boom seems a unique (and peculiar) moment, both for its emphasis on an idealized, insular vision of the family and for the alignment of official and popular investment in that vision as a bulwark against social dissolution. The moment would not be repeated. The trajectories of the revenge theme and the *Official Records* project present a stark contrast after the 1820s, as stability once more ceded ground to famine and unrest. As Satoko Shimazaki has shown, revenge as a narrative of family restoration gave way on the kabuki stage to a fascination with the vengeance of female ghosts like Oiwa, who, murdered by her husband, returns to unleash her violent rancor upon the living in *Ghost Stories at Yotsuya* (*Yotsuya kaidan*, 1825). Oiwa points away from the supple identity choices of Kosan to a solipsistic obsession with personal grievance.[50] She inaugurates a popular celebration of protagonists who resemble the villains of earlier revenge fiction: shapeshifters beholden to no one but themselves who violently unravel the traditional stays of family and polity. By the chaotic last decade of Tokugawa rule, hoodlums, thieves, and murderers had become the great heroes of the stage.

By contrast, the shogunate responded to the turbulent circumstances of midcentury with a new raft of reforms and then, in 1848, attempted to launch a sequel to the *Official Records*. The authorities' return to an investment in the self-sacrificing family as a social bulwark seems quaint in comparison with the growing celebration of ghosts and gangsters. The project reached ninety volumes before unaccountably stalling.[51] Perhaps it was deemed too costly, or possibly the authorities feared it wouldn't sell. But I see the project's failure as emblematic of a simple resignation: this time the problems facing the realm were greater than even the most resolute family could solve.

NOTES

1. Shikitei Sanba 1805, 2-ura. The passage can also be found quoted in modern print in Honda 1973, 97.

2. Totman 1993, 249–59; Drixler 2013.

3. Drixler 2013, 130.

4. In 1786, for example, elderly beggars came flooding into the metropolis singing and performing an "eerie, trancelike" dance. Ooms 1975, 75.

5. Iwabuchi 2014, 202.

6. Drixler 2013, 130–35.

7. Satō 1996, in particular 71–74.

8. My articulation of this aspect of the argument is influenced by Sarah C. Maza's discussion of the role of literary depictions of the family in the imagination of social fusion in late-eighteenth-century France. Maza 2003, 61–68.

9. Sugano 1999, 494.

10. Sugano 1999, 494.

11. Domains in which similar compilations had already been produced included Tsu, Aizu, Chikuzen, Tosa, Obama, and Higo. Sugano 1999, 501.

12. The sole, unexplained exception is Hida Province.

13. Sugano Noriko provides a convenient table of the number of cases in a compendium broken down by "reign era and categories of virtue." Sugano 2003, 174–75.

14. The full list, included in the work's introductory explanatory notes, consists of filial piety (*kōgi*), loyalty (*chūgi*), loyal filiality (*chūkō*), female fidelity (*teisetsu*), brotherly harmony (*kyōdai mutsumaji*), familial harmony (*kanai mutsumaji*), harmony in lineage (*ichizoku mutsumaji*), appropriateness in manners and customs (*fūzoku yoroshi*), purity (*keppaku*), exemplarity (*kitoku*), and diligence in agriculture (*nōgyō shussei*). *Kankoku kōgiroku* 1999, vol. 1, p. 3. For the 60 percent figure, see Sugano 2003, 173.

15. These guidelines are expressed in the sixth entry of the explanatory notes at the start of the compendium. *Kankoku kōgiroku* 1999, vol. 1, p. 4.

16. *Kankoku kōgiroku* 1999, vol. 1, p. 3; Sugano 2003, 172.

17. Sugano 1999, 498. Sugano notes that, as Confucian scholars, the editors were more accustomed to writing in *kanbun* than in Japanese.

18. Kobayashi 2014, 46–47.

19. *Kankoku kōgiroku* 1999, vol. 1, p. 3.

20. *Kankoku kōgiroku* 1999, vol. 3, p. 5.

21. *Kankoku kōgiroku* 1999, vol. 2, pp. 252–53.

22. *Kankoku kōgiroku* 1999, vol. 2, pp. 252–53.

23. Sugano 2003, 178–79.

24. Sugano 2003, 173.

25. Van Steenpaal 2009, 47–50.

26. For the information we have concerning the work's publication, see Sugano 1999, 494–96. Unfortunately, we do not know how many copies were produced, though the

National Diet Library does possess a complete copy of the fifty-volume work. Sugano (2003) comments, "Anecdotal evidence suggests that a variety of people ended up acquiring it, including women," and also suggests the possibility that "instead of the entire text the *bakufu* sold or sent only the relevant chapters to each domain" (172).

27. On Sadanobu's extensive reading and writing, see Ooms 1975, 23–26. On his venture into satirical writing, which combined playful and morally suasive intent, see Iwasaki 1983, 1–19.

28. Ooms 1975, 57; Satō 1997, 35–36.

29. Satō 1997, 36.

30. *Kankoku kōgiroku* 1999, vol. 1, pp. 275–76.

31. *Kankoku kōgiroku* 1999, vol. 1, p. 276.

32. Tanahashi 2012, 28–31; Kimura 2009, 131–36.

33. Nansenshō Somahito 1983.

34. Tanahashi 2012, 30. The contemporary writer Kyokutei Bakin identified the height of the demand for revenge works as the end of the Kyōwa era (1801–4) and the beginning of the Bunka era (1804–18). Kyokutei Bakin 2014, 35, 294.

35. To limit my scope, I focus on revenge works by Santō Kyōden. Though not primarily remembered for his revenge fiction today, Kyōden was a pioneer of the theme in popular fiction. His works helped set the standard for the duration of the revenge boom, and many of the aspects I discuss about them extend to the body of illustrated revenge fiction as a whole.

36. I use "illustrated fiction" to translate the term *kusazōshi*. The revenge boom played out in the pages of its two subgenres *kibyōshi* and *gōkan*.

37. Hayashi 1987, 13.

38. This number is based on the table found in Hiraide (1909) 1990, 99–106. Some of the examples found in the table, however, are likely apocryphal, so the number is probably lower.

39. Shikitei Sanba 1805, 1-ura.

40. The one exception is the occasional inclusion of a loyal retainer, in narratives in which the family is of high enough samurai standing to employ a retainer. This retainer typically embodies the virtue of "loyalty."

41. Hiraide (1909) 1990, 99–106. According to Hiraide's table, after 1750 the rate of revenges carried out by nonsamurai begins to equal and at times exceed that of samurai revenges.

42. Santō Kyōden 1995b, 148.

43. Santō Kyōden 1995b, 170.

44. Santō Kyōden 1995b, 171.

45. Santō Kyōden 1995b, 174.

46. Santō Kyōden 1995a, 91.

47. Santō Kyōden 1995a, 90.

48. Santō Kyōden 1995a, 91.

49. Jippensha Ikku 1995.

50. Shimazaki 2016.

51. Sugano 1999, 496–97.

REFERENCES

Drixler 2013
Drixler, Fabian. *Mabiki: Infanticide and Population Growth in Eastern Japan, 1660–1950.* Berkeley: University of California Press, 2013.

Hayashi 1987
Hayashi Yoshikazu, ed. *Sakusha tainai totsuki no zu, Hara no uchi gesaku tanehon, Atari-yashita jihon toiya.* Tokyo: Kawade Shobō Shinsha, 1987.

Hiraide (1909) 1990
Hiraide Kōjirō. *Katakiuchi.* Tokyo: Bunshōkaku, 1909. Reprinted, Tokyo: Chūō Kōronsha, 1990.

Honda 1973
Honda Yasuo. *Shikitei Sanba no bungei.* Tokyo: Kasama Shoin, 1973.

Iwabuchi 2014
Iwabuchi Reiji. "Kinsei toshi shakai no hatten." In *Iwanami kōza Nihon rekishi,* edited by Ōtsu Tōru et al., vol. 11, pp. 177–212.. Tokyo: Iwanami Shoten, 2014.

Iwasaki 1983
Iwasaki, Haruko. "Portrait of a Daimyo: Comical Fiction by Matsudaira Sadanobu." *Monumenta Nipponica* 38:1 (1983): 1–19.

Jippensha Ikku 1995
Jippensha Ikku. *Seidan mine no hatsu hana.* In *Ninjōbon shū,* edited by Butō Motoaki, 3–93. Tokyo: Kokusho Kankōkai, 1995.

Kankoku kōgiroku 1999
Kankoku kōgiroku. Edited by Sugano Noriko. 3 vols. Tokyo: Tōkyōdō Shuppan, 1999.

Kimura 2009
Kimura Yaeko. *Kusazōshi no sekai: Edo no shuppan bunka.* Tokyo: Perikansha, 2009.

Kobayashi 2014
Kobayashi Fumiko. *Ōta Nanpo: Edo ni kyōka no hana sakasu.* Tokyo: Iwanami Shoten, 2014.

Kyokutei Bakin 2014
Kyokutei Bakin. *Kinsei mononohon Edo sakusha burui.* Edited by Tokuda Takeshi. Tokyo: Iwanami Shoten, 2014.

Maza 2003
Maza, Sarah C. *The Myth of the French Bourgeoisie: An Essay on the Social Imaginary, 1750–1850.* Cambridge, MA: Harvard University Press, 2003.

Nansenshō Somahito 1983
Nansenshō Somahito. *Katakiuchi gijo no hanabusa.* In *Makki kibyōshi shū.* Vol. 4 of *Edo no ehon,* edited by Koike Masatane et al., 87–120. Tokyo: Shakai Shisōsha, 1983.

Ooms 1975
Ooms, Herman. *Charismatic Bureaucrat: A Political Biography of Matsudaira Sadanobu, 1758–1829.* Chicago: University of Chicago Press, 1975.

Santō Kyōden 1995a
Santō Kyōden. *Katakiuchi chidori no Tamagawa.* In *Santō Kyōden zenshū,* vol. 6, pp. 59–102. Tokyo: Perikansha, 1995.

Santō Kyōden 1995b
Santō Kyōden. *Katakiuchi Okazaki joroshu.* In *Santō Kyōden zenshū,* vol. 6, pp. 145–87. Tokyo: Perikansha, 1995.

Satō 1996
Satō Miyuki. "Junan suru kodomotachi: Kansei kaikaku go no Santō Kyōden." In *Dokusho no shakaishi,* vol. 5 of *Edo no shisō,* edited by Edo no Shisō Henshū Iinkai, 68–82. Tokyo: Perikansha, 1996.

Satō 1997
Satō Miyuki. "Shoyūsareru kodomotachi: Matsudaira Sadanobu to Santō Kyōden." *Nihon bungaku* 46:10 (1997); 34–41.

Shikitei Sanba 1805
Shikitei Sanba. *Oya no kataki uchimata kōyaku.* Edo: Nishimiya Shinroku, Bunka 2 (1805).

Shimazaki 2016
Shimazaki, Satoko. *Edo Kabuki in Transition: From the Worlds of the Samurai to the Vengeful Female Ghost.* New York: Columbia University Press, 2016.

Sugano 1999
Sugano Noriko. *Kaidai.* In *Kankoku kōgiroku,* vol. 3, edited by Sugano Noriko. Tokyo: Tōkyōdō Shuppan, 1999.

Sugano 2003
Sugano Noriko. "State Indoctrination of Filial Piety in Tokugawa Japan: Sons and Daughters in the *Official Records of Filial Piety.*" In *Women and Confucian Cultures in Premodern China, Korea, and Japan,* edited by Dorothy Ko, JaHyun Haboush, and Joan R. Piggott, 170–89. Berkeley: University of California Press, 2003.

Tanahashi 2012
Tanahashi Masahiro. *Santō Kyōden no kibyōshi o yomu: Edo no keizai to shakai fūzoku.* Tokyo: Perikansha, 2012.

Totman 1993
Totman, Conrad. *Early Modern Japan.* Berkeley: University of California Press, 1993.

Van Steenpaal 2009
Van Steenpaal, Niels. "*Kankoku kōgiroku:* Bakufu jinsei no pafōmansu." In *Dai 32 kai kokusai Nihon bungaku kenkyū shūkai kaigiroku.* Tokyo: Kokubungaku Kenkyū Shiryōkan, 2009.

APPENDIX

SUGGESTIONS FOR FURTHER READING

The following bibliographic list contains suggestions for further reading on the history of the family in Japan, and in comparative perspective. The list is brief, and by no means comprehensive. It is divided into six sections: (1) review essays and general overviews of the history of the *ie* and family in Japan; (2) foundational studies of the *ie* and family; (3) comparative studies of the *ie* and the stem family; (4) the *ie* and family in historical demography and population studies; (5) studies on succession and perpetuation of the *ie*; (6) studies of marriage, childbirth, and fertility in the *ie* and family systems. The list is heavily weighted toward sources written in or translated into English, both because the scholarly literature in Japanese is far too vast to cite here and because the main audience for this appendix is the nonspecialist. Only selected major Japanese-language works directly pertaining to the six categories above, written by key scholars in each subfield, and not presently available in English are included. Readers seeking more guidance in Japanese-language sources are encouraged to mine the footnotes of the cited English-language sources, especially the review essays in category 1, and also to consult the reference lists for the individual articles in this volume.

REVIEW ESSAYS AND GENERAL OVERVIEWS OF THE HISTORY OF THE *IE* AND FAMILY IN JAPAN

Hayami 2016

Hayami Akira. "Historical Demography in Japan: Achievements and Problems." In *A Global History of Historical Demography: Half a Century of Interdisciplinarity*, edited by

Antoinette Fauve-Chamoux, Ioan Bolovan and Sølvi Sogner. Bern: Peter Lang, 2016.

Kurosu 2002

Kurosu, Satomi. "Studies on Historical Demography and Family in Early Modern Japan." *Early Modern Japan* 10:1 (2002): 3–71.

Wakita and Phillips 1993

Wakita Haruko and David P. Phillips. "Women and the Creation of the *Ie* in Japan: An Overview from the Medieval Period to the Present." *U.S.-Japan Women's Journal.* English supplement, no. 4 (1993): 83–105.

Uno 1996

Uno, Kathleen. "Questioning Patrilineality: On Western Studies of the Japanese *Ie.*" *positions* 4:3 (1996): 569–94.

FOUNDATIONAL STUDIES OF THE *IE* AND FAMILY

Ariga 1972

Ariga Kizaemon. *Ie (The Family/Household/Family System).* Tokyo: Shibundō, 1972.

Doi 1981

Doi, Takeo. *The Anatomy of Dependence.* Tokyo: Kōdansha, 1981.

Hirai 2008

Hirai Shoko. *Nihon no kazoku to raifu kōsu (The Japanese Family and Life Course).* Tokyo: Mineruboa Shobō, 2008.

Murakami, Kumon, and Satō 1979

Murakami Yasusuke, Kumon Shumpei, and Satō Seizaburō. *Bunmei to shite no ie shakai* (Ie *Society as Civilization*). Tokyo: Chūō Kōronsha, 1979. For an introduction to this work in English, see Yamamura and Murakami 1984, below.

Nakane 1967

Nakane, Chie. *Kinship and Economic Organization in Rural Japan.* London: Athlone Press, 1967.

Nakane 1972

Nakane, Chie. *Japanese Society.* Berkeley: University of California Press, 1972.

Ōtō 1996

Ōtō Osamu. *Kinsei nōmin to ie, mura, kokka—seikatsushi, shakaishi no shiza kara (The Early Modern Peasantry and Household, Village, and State from the Perspective of Life History and Social History).* Tokyo: Yoshikawa Kōbunkan, 1996.

Smith 1959

Smith, Thomas C. *The Agrarian Origins of Modern Japan.* Stanford, CA: Stanford University Press, 1959.

Smith 1977

Smith, Thomas C. *Nakahara: Family Farming and Population in a Japanese Village, 1717–1830.* Stanford, CA: Stanford University Press, 1977.

Yamamura and Murakami 1984

Yamamura, Kozo, and Murakami Yasusuke. "*Ie* Society as a Pattern of Civilization: Introduction." *Journal of Japanese Studies* 10:2 (1984): 279–363.

Yonemura and Nagata 2009

Yonemura, Chiyo, and Mary Louise Nagata. "Continuity, Solidarity, Family, and Enterprise: What Is an *Ie*?" In *The Stem Family in Eurasian Perspective: Revisiting House*

Societies, 17th–20th Centuries, edited by Antoinette Fauve-Chamoux and Emiko Ochiai, 273–86. Bern: Peter Lang, 2009.

COMPARATIVE STUDIES OF THE *IE* AND THE STEM FAMILY

Cornell 1987
    Cornell, Laurel L. "Hajnal and the Household in Asia: A Comparativist History of the Family in Preindustrial Japan, 1600–1870." *Journal of Family History* 12:1–3 (January–July 1987): 143–62.
Fauve-Chamoux and Ochiai 2009
    Fauve-Chamoux, Antoinette, and Emiko Ochiai, "Introduction." In *The Stem Family in Eurasian Perspective: Revisiting House Societies, 17th–20th Centuries,* edited by Fauve-Chamoux and Ochiai, 1–40. Bern: Peter Lang, 2009.
Hirai 2013
    Hirai Shoko. "Rethinking Theories and Realities of the 'Ie' in Japan." In *Finding 'Ie' in Western Society? Historical Empirical Study for the Paralleling and Contrasting between Japan and Europe,* edited by Takahashi Motoyasu, 29–61. Matsuyama: Department of Social Science Faculty of Law and Letters, Ehime University, 2013.
Laslett and Wall 1972
    Laslett, Peter, and Richard Wall. *Household and Family in Past Time: Comparative Studies in the Size and Structure of the Domestic Group over the Last Three Centuries in England, France, Serbia, Japan, and Colonial North America, with Further Materials from Western Europe.* Cambridge: Cambridge University Press, 1972.
Ochiai 2000
    Ochiai, Emiko. "Debates over the *Ie* and the Stem Family: Orientalism East and West." *Japan Review* 12 (2000): 105–28.
Ochiai 2009
    Ochiai, Emiko. "Two Types of Stem Household System in Japan: The *Ie* in Global Perspective." In *The Stem Family in Eurasian Perspective: Revisiting House Societies, 17th–20th Centuries,* edited by Fauve-Chamoux and Ochiai, 287–326. Bern: Peter Lang, 2009.
Saitō 1998
    Saitō, Osamu. "Two Kinds of Stem Family System? Traditional Japan and Europe Compared." *Continuity and Change* 13 (1998): 167–86.
Skinner 1997
    Skinner, G. William. "Family Systems and Demographic Processes." In *Anthropological Demography,* edited by David I. Kertzer and Thomas E. Fricke, 53–114. Chicago: University of Chicago Press, 1997.
Verdon 1979
    Verdon, Michel. "The Stem Family: Toward a General Theory." *Journal of Interdisciplinary History* 10:1 (1979): 87–105.
Wolf and Hanley 1985
    Wolf, Arthur P., and Susan B. Hanley. "Introduction." In *Family and Population in East Asian History,* edited by Hanley and Wolf. Stanford, CA: Stanford University Press, 1985.

IE AND FAMILY IN HISTORICAL DEMOGRAPHY AND POPULATION STUDIES

Drixler 2013

Drixler, Fabian. *Mabiki: Infanticide and Population Growth in Eastern Japan, 1660–1950.* Berkeley: University of California Press, 2013.

Hanley and Yamamura 1977

Hanley, Susan B., and Kozo Yamamura. *Economic and Demographic Change in Preindustrial Japan, 1600–1868.* Princeton: Princeton University Press, 1977.

Hayami 1979

Hayami Akira. "Thank You, Francisco Xavier: An Essay in the Use of Micro-data for Historical Demography of Tokugawa Japan. *Keio Economic Studies* 16:1–2 (1979): 65–81.

Hayami 2001

Hayami Akira. *The Historical Demography of Pre-modern Japan.* Tokyo: Tokyo University Press, 2001.

Hayami 2010

Hayami Akira. *Population, Family, and Society in Pre-modern Japan.* Leiden, Netherlands: Brill, 2010.

Kinoshita and Hamano 2003

Kinoshita Futoshi and Hamano Kiyoshi, eds. *Jinruigaku no naka no jinkō to kazoku* (*Population and Family in Anthropology*). Tokyo: Kōyō Shobō, 2003.

STUDIES ON SUCCESSION AND PERPETUATION OF THE *IE*

Bachnik 1983

Bachnik, Jane M. "Recruitment Strategies for Household Succession: Rethinking Japanese Household Organization." *Man* 18 (1983): 160–82.

Bernstein 2005

Bernstein, Gail Lee. *Isami's House: Three Centuries of a Japanese Family.* Berkeley: University of California Press, 2005.

Cornell 1983

Cornell, Laurel L. "Retirement, Inheritance, and Intergenerational Conflict in Preindustrial Japan." *Journal of Family History* 8 (1983): 55–69.

Hayami 1983

Hayami Akira. "The Myth of Primogeniture and Impartible Inheritance in Tokugawa Japan." *Journal of Family History* 8:1 (1983): 3–29.

Kurosu 1998

Kurosu, Satomi. "Long Way to Headship, Short Way to Retirement: Adopted Sons in a Northeastern Village in Pre-industrial Japan." *The History of the Family* 3:4 (1998): 393–410.

Kurosu and Ochiai 1995

Kurosu Satomi and Emiko Ochiai. "Adoption as an Heirship Strategy under Demographic Constraints: A Case from Nineteenth-Century Japan." *Journal of Family History* 20:3 (1995): 261–88.

Moore 1970
  Moore, Ray A. "Adoption and Samurai Mobility in Tokugawa Japan." *Journal of Asian Studies* 29:3 (1970): 617–32.

STUDIES OF MARRIAGE, CHILDBIRTH, AND FERTILITY IN THE *IE* AND FAMILY SYSTEMS

Lundh and Kurosu 2014
  Lundh, Christer, and Satomi Kurosu, eds. *Similarity in Difference: Marriage in Europe and Asia, 1700–1900.* Cambridge, MA: MIT Press, 2014.
Fuess 2004
  Fuess, Harald. *Divorce in Japan: Family, Gender, and the State, 1600–2000.* Stanford, CA: Stanford University Press, 2004.
Lindsey 2007
  Lindsey, William R. *Fertility and Pleasure: Ritual and Sexual Values in Tokugawa Japan.* Honolulu: University of Hawai'i Press, 2007.
Ochiai 1999
  Ochiai, Emiko. "The Reproductive Revolution in Tokugawa Japan." In *Women and Class in Japanese History,* edited by Hitomi Tonomura, Anne Walthall, and Joan R. Piggott, 187–215. Ann Arbor: Center for Japanese Studies, University of Michigan, 1999.
Ōta 2011
  Ōta Motoko. *Kinsei no 'ie' to kazoku: Kinsei noson no kazoku seikatsu to kosodate* ("*Ie" and Family in the Early Modern Period: Family Life and Child-rearing in Early Modern Villages*). Tokyo: Fujiwara Shoten, 2007.
Sawayama 2003
  Sawayama Mikako. "The 'Birthing Body' and the Regulation of Conception and Childbirth in the Edo Period." *U.S.-Japan Women's Journal* 24 (2003): 10–34.
Tsuya et al. 2010
  Tsuya, Noriko O., Feng Wang, George Alter, and James Z. Lee, eds. *Prudence and Pressure: Reproduction and Human Agency in Europe and Asia, 1700–1900.* Cambridge, MA: MIT Press, 2010.

CONTRIBUTORS

DAVID ATHERTON is Assistant Professor in the Department of East Asian Languages and Civilizations at Harvard University. He received his PhD in Japanese literature from Columbia University in 2013, where his dissertation focused on popular revenge fiction in early modern Japan. He has published on the poetry of Ihara Saikaku, early modern disaster literature, and classical Siamese poetry. He is currently completing a book manuscript on the representation of violence in early modern Japanese fiction and theater.

MARY ELIZABETH BERRY, Class of 1944 Professor of History Emerita at the University of California, Berkeley, is the author of *Hideyoshi* (Harvard, 1982), *The Culture of Civil War in Kyoto* (California, 1994), and *Japan in Print: Information and Nation in the Early Modern Period* (California, 2006). She is an elected Fellow of the American Academy of Arts and Sciences and a past president of the Association for Asian Studies.

FABIAN DRIXLER is Professor of History at Yale University. He is the author of *Mabiki: Infanticide and Population Growth in Eastern Japan, 1660–1950* (California, 2013).

MAREN EHLERS is Associate Professor of History at the University of North Carolina at Charlotte and the author of *Give and Take: Poverty and the Status Order in Early Modern Japan* (Harvard University Asia Center, 2018). Her research focuses on the social and local history of early modern Japan.

MORGAN PITELKA is Professor of History and Asian Studies at the University of North Carolina at Chapel Hill. His publications include *Spectacular Accumulation:*

Material Culture, Tokugawa Ieyasu, and Samurai Sociability (Hawai'i, 2016); *Handmade Culture: Raku Potters, Patrons, and Tea Practitioners in Japan* (Hawai'i, 2005); and the edited volumes *Kyoto Visual Culture in the Early Edo and Meiji Periods: The Arts of Reinvention* (coedited with Alice Tseng; Routledge, 2016); *What's the Use of Art? Asian Visual and Material Culture in Context* (coedited with Jan Mrazek; Hawai'i, 2007); and *Japanese Tea Culture: Art, History, and Practice* (Routledge, 2003).

LUKE ROBERTS is Professor of Japanese History at the University of California, Santa Barbara. He is the author of *Performing the Great Peace: Political Space and Open Secrets in Tokugawa Japan* (Hawai'i, 2012) and *Mercantilism in a Japanese Domain: The Merchant Origins of Economic Nationalism in 18th-Century Tosa* (Cambridge, 1998). He is coauthor, with Sharon Takeda, of *Japanese Fisherman's Coats from Awaji Island* (UCLA Fowler Museum of Cultural History, 2001).

DAVID SPAFFORD is Associate Professor of Premodern Japanese History at the University of Pennsylvania. He is the author of *A Sense of Place: The Political Landscape in Late Medieval Japan* (Harvard University Asia Center, 2013) and is currently at work on a second monograph, provisionally titled "The Corporate Warrior House in Japan, 1450–1650."

AMY STANLEY is Associate Professor in the History Department at Northwestern University, where she teaches Japanese and global history. She is the author of *Selling Women: Prostitution, Markets, and the Household in Early Modern Japan* (California, 2012). Her second book, *Stranger in the Shogun's City: A Japanese Woman and Her Worlds*, is forthcoming from Scribner in 2020.

ANNE WALTHALL is Professor Emerita at the University of California, Irvine. She has written a number of books, including *The Weak Body of a Useless Woman: Matsuo Taseko and the Meiji Restoration* (Chicago, 1998), which was translated into Japanese. She has also edited or coedited six volumes, most recently *Child's Play: Multi-sensory Histories of Children and Childhood in Japan* (coedited with Sabine Frühstück; California, 2017) and *Politics and Society in Japan's Meiji Restoration: A Brief History with Documents* (coedited with M. William Steele; Bedford/St. Martin's, 2017).

MARCIA YONEMOTO is Professor of History at the University of Colorado, Boulder. She is the author of *The Problem of Women in Early Modern Japan* (California, 2016) and *Mapping Early Modern Japan: Space, Place, and Culture in the Tokugawa Period, 1603–1868* (California, 2003). Her present research project focuses on the history of adult adoption in Japan from 1700 to 1925.

INDEX

Note: '*Fig*' following a page number indicates a figure; '*tab*' indicates a table.

Founded in 1893,
UNIVERSITY OF CALIFORNIA PRESS
publishes bold, progressive books and journals
on topics in the arts, humanities, social sciences,
and natural sciences—with a focus on social
justice issues—that inspire thought and action
among readers worldwide.

The UC PRESS FOUNDATION
raises funds to uphold the press's vital role
as an independent, nonprofit publisher, and
receives philanthropic support from a wide
range of individuals and institutions—and from
committed readers like you. To learn more, visit
ucpress.edu/supportus.